THE

FIRST

AMERICAN

WOMAN—

AND THE

YOUNGEST

PERSON

EVER—

TO

CIRCUMNAVIGATE

THE

GLOBE

ALONE

MAIDEN VOYAGE

Tania Aebi
with Bernadette Brennan

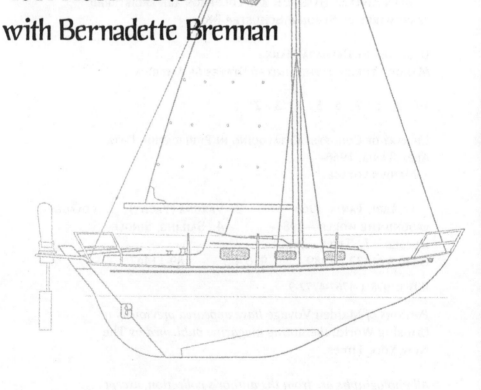

SIMON AND SCHUSTER
NEW YORK LONDON TORONTO SYDNEY TOKYO

Simon and Schuster
Simon & Schuster Building
Rockefeller Center
1230 Avenue of the Americas
New York, New York 10020

Copyright © 1989 by Tania Aebi

All rights reserved
including the right of reproduction
in whole or in part in any form.

SIMON AND SCHUSTER and colophon are registered
trademarks of Simon & Schuster Inc.

Designed by Barbara Marks
Manufactured in the United States of America

10 9 8 7 6 5 4 3 2

Library of Congress Cataloging in Publication Data
Aebi, Tania, 1966–
    Maiden voyage.

    1. Aebi, Tania, 1966–   . 2. Varuna (Yacht) 3. Voyages
around the world—1981–   . 4. Sailing, singlehanded.   I. Title.
G440.A24A32   1989   910.4'5   89-11467

ISBN: 978-1-4767-4772-9

Portions of Maiden Voyage *have appeared previously in* Cruising World, *the sailing magazine published by* The New York Times.

All photographs are from the author's collection, except the last two, which are copyright Susan Thorpe/Cruising World, *and appear by permission.*

FOR MY MOTHER

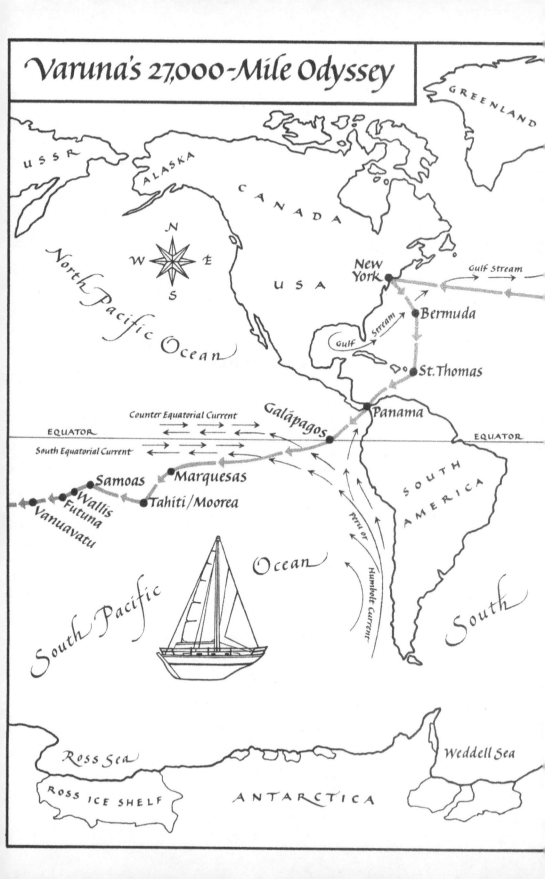

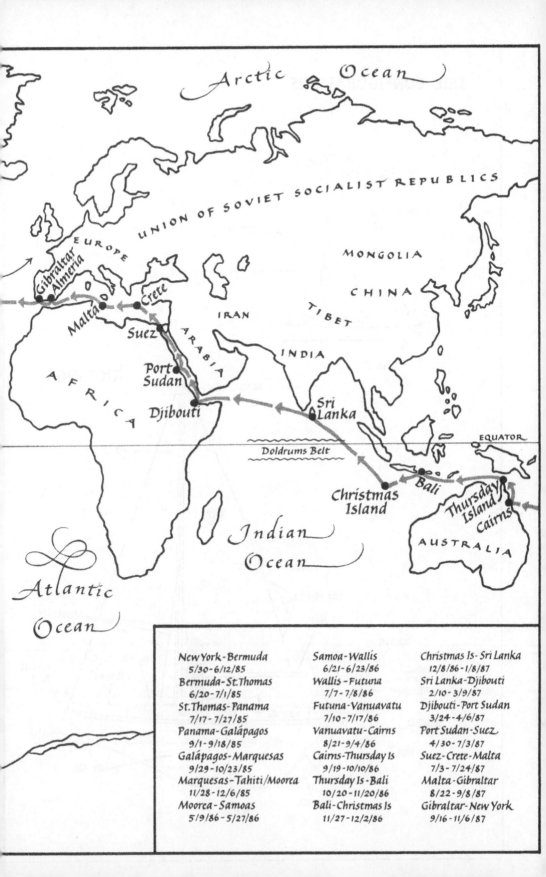

Arctic Ocean

UNION OF SOVIET SOCIALIST REPUBLICS

EUROPE

MONGOLIA

CHINA

Gibraltar
Almeria

Crete

IRAN

TIBET

Malta

Suez

ARABIA

INDIA

AFRICA

Port
Sudan

Djibouti

Sri
Lanka

EQUATOR

Doldrums Belt

Christmas
Island

Bali

Thursday
Island
Cairns

AUSTRALIA

Indian
Ocean

Atlantic

Ocean

New York–Bermuda 5/30–6/12/85	Samoa–Wallis 6/21–6/23/86	Christmas Is–Sri Lanka 12/8/86–1/8/87
Bermuda–St. Thomas 6/20–7/1/85	Wallis–Futuna 7/7–7/8/86	Sri Lanka–Djibouti 2/10–3/9/87
St. Thomas–Panama 7/17–7/27/85	Futuna–Vanuavatu 7/10–7/17/86	Djibouti–Port Sudan 3/24–4/6/87
Panama–Galápagos 9/1–9/18/85	Vanuavatu–Cairns 8/21–9/4/86	Port Sudan–Suez 4/30–7/3/87
Galápagos–Marquesas 9/29–10/23/85	Cairns–Thursday Is 9/19–10/10/86	Suez–Crete–Malta 7/3–7/24/87
Marquesas–Tahiti/Moorea 11/28–12/6/85	Thursday Is–Bali 10/20–11/20/86	Malta–Gibraltar 8/22–9/8/87
Moorea–Samoas 5/9/86–5/27/86	Bali–Christmas Is 11/27–12/2/86	Gibraltar–New York 9/16–11/6/87

SAIL CONFIGURATIONS

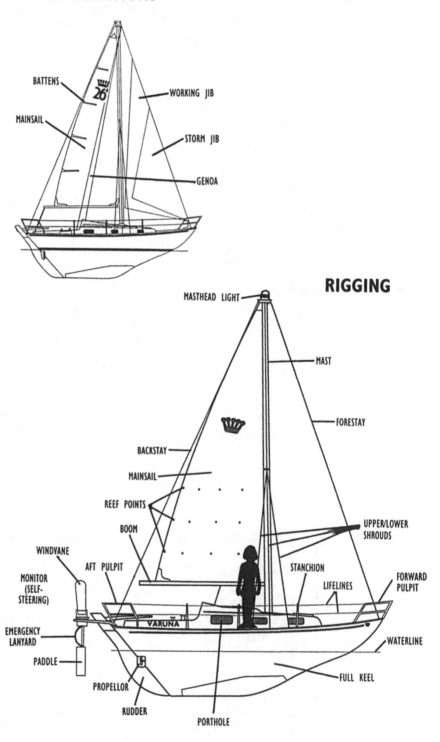

BATTENS

MAINSAIL

WORKING JIB

STORM JIB

GENOA

RIGGING

MASTHEAD LIGHT

MAST

FORESTAY

BACKSTAY

MAINSAIL

REEF POINTS

BOOM

UPPER/LOWER
SHROUDS

WINDVANE

AFT PULPIT

MONITOR
(SELF-
STEERING)

STANCHION

LIFELINES

FORWARD
PULPIT

EMERGENCY
LANYARD

WATERLINE

PADDLE

VARUNA

PROPELLOR

FULL KEEL

RUDDER

PORTHOLE

INTERIOR

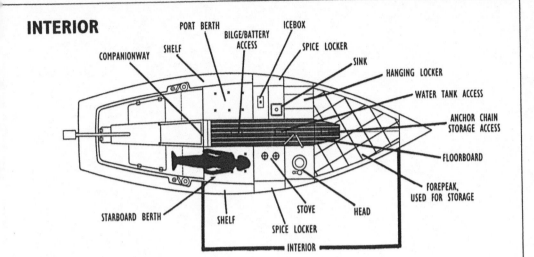

PORT BERTH

ICEBOX

BILGE/BATTERY ACCESS

SHELF

SPICE LOCKER

COMPANIONWAY

SINK

HANGING LOCKER

WATER TANK ACCESS

ANCHOR CHAIN STORAGE ACCESS

FLOORBOARD

FOREPEAK, USED FOR STORAGE

STARBOARD BERTH

SHELF

SPICE LOCKER

STOVE

HEAD

INTERIOR

DECK LAYOUT

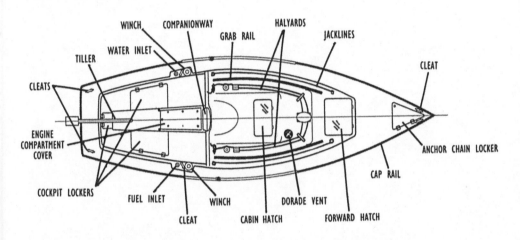

WINCH

COMPANIONWAY

HALYARDS

WATER INLET

GRAB RAIL

JACKLINES

TILLER

CLEAT

CLEATS

ENGINE COMPARTMENT COVER

COCKPIT LOCKERS

FUEL INLET

WINCH

ANCHOR CHAIN LOCKER

CAP RAIL

CLEAT

CABIN HATCH

DORADE VENT

FORWARD HATCH

CROSS SECTION

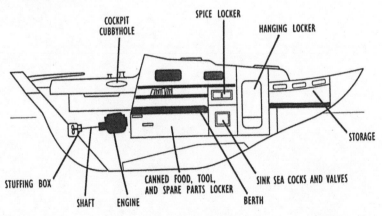

COCKPIT CUBBYHOLE

SPICE LOCKER

HANGING LOCKER

STORAGE

STUFFING BOX

CANNED FOOD, TOOL, AND SPARE PARTS LOCKER

SINK SEA COCKS AND VALVES

SHAFT

ENGINE

BERTH

ctober 23, 1987, another dawn—my thirty-seventh alone on the North Atlantic. Around me, the sea is a liquid mountain range of heaving swells, and I'm really scared. The winds and waves have been steadily increasing since yesterday, when they veered from southeast to northeast. Varuna has been knocked mast-down to the water countless times during the night and I haven't been able to relax, sleep, eat or think about anything other than staying alive. Following now are the biggest waves I've ever seen—probably 25 feet. It's almost winter and I've pushed my luck. The weather can only get worse.

"Four feet above, avalanches of white water crash across Varuna's back, swamping the cockpit. In the cabin, everything that hasn't been battened down has been thrown off the shelves. Pots, pans, cans and tools clatter together in the lockers. I'm wedged into my bunk, my foot stretched across to the sink to stop me from being thrown around the cabin. There are still 880 miles to go until home. I want to see the Statue of Liberty. I want to take a hot bath and eat something good. I want to see my family. . . ."

I stuffed my logbook onto the shelf behind my head, struggled out of limp long johns and stripped down before beginning the contortions of getting into foul-weather gear—first the overalls, then the jacket. It was useless wearing anything beneath the gear because it would have been stupid to jeopardize the precious dry clothes by wearing them outside, where they'd be soaked in seconds. I fastened the hood around my salty head, which was matted into itchy, sticky clumps of hair and crying out to be washed. Practically the only kind of shower I had been able to provide myself during the last month at sea was the occasional unexpected wave that crashed over me, increasing the sodium level on my skin. There was not a drop of fresh water on board to spare for the luxury of a wash. Even though I sprinkled myself liberally with talcum powder, my skin pinched up from the salt and my bottom was covered with sores from sitting on damp cushions for so many weeks. The cold, salt-encrusted lining of the foul-weather gear rubbed against my naked skin like broken glass, and I had to step into it at least ten times a day.

Crouched on all fours and peering out through the dark blue Plexiglas slats that sealed the companionway, I choreographed my next move and waited for the null moment between waves to lurch into action. OK . . . almost ready . . . ready . . . NOW! Quickly removing the slats, I clambered out to the cockpit and added one more bruise to the scars covering my legs.

"Come on, Tarzoon," I coaxed my feline buddy, "if you want to come out, now's your chance." He blinked up at me from the safety of his corner in the bunk, looking for assurance. *Varuna* leveled for a moment and Tarzoon leapt through the companionway, sniffing the air and sticking close. "It's kind of ugly out here," I confided, snapping the umbilical cord of my safety harness onto the lifelines of the boat and looking up the mast to the sky. No change from yesterday. If anything, it was worse. The wind velocity was gale force and holding between 40 to 50 knots. Rain pocked the water around *Varuna*, and low-hanging, dark masses canopied us. The last piece of land that these black clouds had shadowed was America, "maybe even New York," I said aloud, and the thought made the gloom seem almost friendly.

"We are so close, Tarzoon, and I have these feelings, New York feelings." If we continued on at this speed, we would have about eight more days left; if we dropped back to our average speed until now, it could take another fourteen.

Already I could feel the pulse of New York and could almost smell civilization in the air. I sensed the vibration of the subway and as the ocean mimicked the noise of rattling tracks, imagined being on the Lexington line #6 heading uptown. Soon, God willing, I'd be home.

Home, after two and a half years of seeing the four corners of the world from the deck of this little 26-foot sailboat. The gray horizon to the west was full of promise.

Landfalls were not alien to me. I had emerged from the ocean void to stand in awe of the jagged cliffs of the Galápagos, the verdant dream world of South Pacific islands, the cities carved from the rock of Malta. *Varuna* had shown me a world of physical challenge and jaw-dropping beauty; of ancient cultures; of generosity in the face of unspeakable poverty; a world where a smile is the greatest gift you can give or receive. Out of the past two and a half years, I had spent 360 days alone at sea, pressing ever westward, ever homeward. This final landfall would close the circle, end the dream and begin the most daunting unknown yet.

I squinted into the howling winds, hypnotized, watching every wall of water catch up, lift *Varuna*'s stern and take us surfing down its crest. With just enough time for me to crouch and hang on, the crest of another thousand-gallon mountain broke and engulfed us. Water rushed up my pants legs and leaked into my hood and down my neck, and slowly the cockpit began to drain as *Varuna* lurched drunkenly onward. Making the adjustments to the windvane, I took a 360-degree scan of the barren seascape. As far as the eye could see, there was nothing—nothing but angry graybeards marching toward an eternal horizon.

Tarzoon meowed by the companionway, wet and matted, desperate to get inside to safety before the next drenching. Following him below, I peeled off the wet rain gear and turned on the radio. The BBC announced that things were going better in New York since Black Monday, four days before. We had been at 50 degrees longitude then, in the midst of a flat calm, almost two-thirds of the way across the Atlantic. As the announcer described the Wall Street crash, I had been studying my chart, staring at the place where we were now, wondering how it would feel to be here. Now I knew.

Tuning in to Radio France and clutching onto handholds, I stumbled the two steps toward the toilet, which was out of commission. It was always closed up at sea, where I was surrounded by the biggest toilet on earth. I didn't need the little white pot and transformed its closet into a hanging locker with lines holding everything in. I wrapped the gear over one line as it dripped down on the floor, threw a dirty mop-up rag over the new puddles in the cabin and rearranged the kerosene heater and bottled water. The heater fell over again with the bucking motion, dribbling some fuel, stinking up the small confines and making me dizzy. "More than enough kerosene," I thought. "Wish it were water. I have only five bottles left. I hope it'll last."

Putting my thermal underwear back on, I saw Tarzoon chewing away at the coral fan Olivier had given me to bring home. "Stop it, you little monster!" I reprimanded, taking it away from him for the fiftieth time. It refused to stay in its lashings on the wall and kept tumbling down to my bunk and Tarzoon's teeth. Picking it up, once again I admired the intricacy of its lacy white fronds, thinking about Olivier and remembering how much he loved to dive in search of shells and underwater life. The fan had come from the San Blas Islands between Colombia and Panama and I remembered that it was one of the first things that I had remarked on in *Akka*, Olivier's boat. Here on *Varuna* with Tarzoon, after nearly circumnavigating the planet, it was disintegrating.

"I wonder what he is doing now," I said aloud. "If he was able to come to the United States, perhaps he's at the American consulate, applying for a visa. If he wasn't able to come . . ." My emotions and energy were already stretched to their limits and I knew better than to risk the torture of negative thoughts. But it was no use. Although I tucked the fan away in the toilet closet, safe from harm, everywhere I looked were reminders of Olivier, the quiet man who had become a part of my life in Vanuatu in the South Pacific. Without him, I knew, I would not be here today.

We were both crying when we kissed each other goodbye and I finally broke away from the little island of Malta, not knowing when or if we'd ever see each other again. Ahead of *Varuna* was the Mediterranean and then the North Atlantic. Olivier was headed back to his home in Switzerland. Our lives, which had been so closely aligned for so many months as we voyaged together around half the world—he aboard *Akka* and I aboard *Varuna*—now seemed filled with uncertainty. Only time would tell.

At sea, the crashing, banging and moaning sounds of a sailboat battling through a storm, however discordant, come together in a symphony of chaos. Any unusual sound or movement that disrupts it immediately stands out—like now. There was a slight knocking noise against *Varuna*'s hull at the bow and I turned toward the sound. The big jib, saved for lighter winds, was lashed down up forward and was working itself loose with the metal eye at the foot of the sail beginning to bang against the hull with each wave. It had to be retied before it was dragged overboard.

Pulling my gear back on, I crawled outside and clipped the harness onto a jack line as *Varuna* buried her bow in every wave. "I might as well get this over with right *now!*" I yelled and barreled forward, splashing through the water on deck, grabbing the rails and the lifelines along the way and viciously stubbing my foot against a chain plate.

"Oh, for Christ's sake!" I screamed, as another wall of water threw *Varuna* over on her side and drenched me. My hood blew off and my hair whipped about my face as I reached the pitching foredeck. I held on and began to work free the waterlogged knots in the line, gathered the sail, rolled it up into a wad and relashed it, quickly navigating my way back to the cockpit. At the spray hood, I took a quick check of the horizon, the deck, the rigging and the frothing ocean one last time before dashing inside. When I replaced the slats, the howling din diminished as the radio welcomed me back with Bob Marley's "Coming In from the Cold." I sat in a heap on my bunk and glanced at my watch. It was only 9:00 A.M.

The wind continued to cry through the rigging, the same sound as when it keened through the pine trees behind my family's house when we lived in Vernon. My thoughts drifted back to the days of my childhood, to my parents and to our lives of such confusion that the fury of today's ocean almost paled by comparison.

Looking at my hands, I smiled to see that they were now more callused than my father's had ever been during his years of eking out a living doing construction work. The day-to-day dampness at sea had soaked so deeply into the skin that the calluses now peeled off in shriveled white hunks. I thought of how proud my father was going to be; I had finally finished something other than a meal. My father, the collector of experiences, the gifted Swiss artist of boundless energies, had almost sent me to my doom. Although I might have set off on the voyage of his dreams, somewhere along the way, I had created my own.

For better or worse, my life was now woven from a different thread than that of the loved ones to whom I was returning. Very soon, I'd see the differences I had only read about in letters. I'd see my best friend from high school, Rebecca, whose first baby, my goddaughter Kendra, was one and a half years old already and whom I'd never seen. Many of my friends had gone away to college. Three had become heroes in the music world whom I had read and heard about in *Newsweek* and on the BBC.

Tony, my brother, wasn't in tenth grade anymore, but in college at Stonybrook. My sister Nina was in her third year at Cornell; and

Jade, the youngest, was in her senior year of high school. We had all done our best to correspond and keep in touch by means of tapes and phone calls over the past two and a half years, but as the months passed and as the landfalls became more distant from home, I sensed in the letters and in the rare static-free telephone calls that our lives had diverged more radically than I ever dreamed possible. Did they feel it, too? I wondered if I would ever fit in again.

My life had been a mixed package of wild circumstances until the day *Varuna* carried me out of New York Harbor at age eighteen. I thought back to that day and recalled the frightened girl I had been, filled with such unbridled visions of the future. Today, I found myself envying her innocence. Now that she had learned the perils of the game, I wondered if she would ever again be brave enough to pay the price for a dream of such dimensions.

My bony knees were outlined through the thin long-john fabric. Although I was not as skinny as I had been in the Red Sea, I still hadn't accumulated any insulation. The Red Sea, which separates like a forked serpent's tongue the continent of Africa from the countries of Asia, had almost finished me with its searing heat and relentless headwinds. Unable to sleep for more than thirty minutes at a time for twenty days as a result of the weather, the sea conditions and a continuously breaking engine, I was overcome with dizziness and fever spells, and my normally 120-pound frame had shrunken to a skeletal 105 by the time *Varuna* arrived in Egypt. I hadn't regained enough strength before setting out through the Mediterranean, and had paid the price by almost losing my boat and my life 200 miles off the coast of Spain, with only a brief respite in Gibraltar before heading across the Atlantic. I had no choice. The deadline was bearing down like a grizzly after a field mouse and I had to carry on.

The New York I was coming home to could never be the same as the one I had left at eighteen, but the names still felt as alive as nerve endings, and the sounds of them on my lips as we got closer were like a soothing mantra. Greenwich Village. TriBeCa. SoHo. Memories of home became clearer as the final miles ticked into *Varuna*'s trailing taffrail log. I envisioned the West Village, its cobblestone streets lined with little brownstones adorned with balustrades and gargoyles, surrounded by carriage houses, gardens, churches and parks. I remembered the artists popping out of the woodwork on Memorial Day and Labor Day weekends for the Village art show, and homosexuals with their erotic shops and bars, with names like The Pink Pussycat Boutique, the Ramrod or The Anvil.

My family lives in SoHo, three blocks down from Washington

Square Park and, to my adolescent mind, the center of what was important on the planet. I pictured the East Village, run down and abused by generations of social movements, drug addicts, gangs, bohemians and people outdoing each other in outrageousness. There were always freaks like the Sadomasochist with safety pins pinning his nipples and bottles through his ears and the Candyman, an eerie giant on roller skates with bushy carrot-red hair and a black top hat, always surrounded by young girls receiving his free hallucinogenic candies. There was the Purple Man riding around on his old rusty purple bicycle, making his own personal statement against capitalism by handing out newsletters with the telephone credit card numbers of major corporations. There were the Hare Krishnas, floating by in an orange cloud, crashing their cymbals, jingling and chanting. Young Puerto Rican gangs, dressed to kill, prowled the streets. Pimps slapped their whores around and drunks lay in heaps across the street, snoring and clutching onto their ever-present bottles of Thunderbird. There were musicians crooning on one corner and jugglers on the next. On the remaining corners were junkies, hippies and dreads whispering: "Smokes, 'ludes, trips, anything you need," and sometimes, "I'll take checks and credit cards."

The East Village was a tangled chain of tenements, squats, soup kitchens, correctional facilities and graffiti. Dark thrift shops, murky check-cashing joints, head shops, off-the-wall clothing shops, pawnshops and herb gates were monitored by the silent old people who had already lived through it all.

And, finally, haunting the bars and the clubs of the concrete jungle were the punks and street kids, the group to which I belonged as a teenager. In the East Village, everyone had a label; everyone fit in somewhere, no questions asked. I had a label then. What would it be now?

Tarzoon rubbed his nose against my face and I was brought quickly back to the present as *Varuna* canted downwind. "How's my little buddy?" I asked, taking him in my arms and scratching his belly. His purrs warmed my heart. I reached up to the swinging net over my head and pulled out the bags of pumpkin seeds and cat treats. The little hammock, a present given to me in Bermuda, my very first landfall, contained vegetables, snacks, odds and ends. When I first hung it across the cabin, it had been a brilliant white, but now it was gray, hanging by its last threads as if waiting for me to get home before retiring.

My mind was spinning, more from the pressure of homecoming

and new beginnings than from fear of the surrounding storm. For thirty months and 27,000 miles, there had been no uncertainty about the future. Every day, my objective had been clear—to head westward, to return home. For every storm, every calm, every emotional low and high, the one thing I could always count on was that eventually it would become a memory. Today, my mind was riveted on the future. The most daunting landfall of all lay ahead, on that horizon to the west. I was returning to a home that could never be the same as the one to which I said goodbye a lifetime ago.

There have always been people who called my father crazy. We never thought so. Why walk when you can run? he'd say. Why be inside when you could be out? Why stay home balancing your checkbook when you could be off riding a camel to Timbuktu, or climbing Mont Blanc, or driving a Land Rover across Africa? His dreams for himself and for us were all we wanted to hear when we were growing up. The world through his eyes was full of excitement and promise, of taking risks and landing on your feet, always with another great story to tell.

I remember one cold winter day, when I was eight, just before my mother entered the sanitarium in Switzerland, my father took us on one of his walks across the pastures near our house in Vernon, New Jersey. You need fresh air to *think*, he'd say with his Swiss-German accent, flinging wide the front door and barreling down the walkway. "I have to *breathe*."

Usually, we would have to run to keep up as he pondered and pontificated, waving his arms through the air like a mad conductor as he tried to sort out the chaos that was our lives in those days. With his blue eyes ablaze, his dark hair firing madly out of his head and the cold air turning his breath into clouds of steam as he plowed along, he was raw energy personified.

"Tania," he said, stopping to study a wire fence in our path, "come here, please, and grab this fence."

I obeyed and grabbed the fence, receiving a jolt to the chest that almost knocked me off my feet. My father laughed so hard that he had to sit down. It was an electric cow fence.

"Schnibel-puff," he said, calling me by his favorite nickname as I glared at him, "sometimes, you only learn things in this world the hard way."

Not long after that day, events took a turn and, it seemed, nothing was ever the same again. It would take ten years, until I was eighteen years old and about to set off alone around the world on *Varuna*, before I would begin to know just how right my father was.

The wind was blowing up a stink across the docks of the South Street Seaport beneath the towering glass monoliths of Wall Street in Manhattan. I tried to take a last glimpse of my family and etch their faces and this moment into my memory. It was four o'clock, May 28, 1985, and my adventure was about to begin.

"Are you ready?" my brother Tony and my father hollered in unison from the dock.

On *Varuna*, I hunched up in my foul-weather gear, squinting through the drizzle, and tried to hide my tears.

"Tania, *are you ready?*" my father called again. My head was spinning and words were lodged in my throat.

"Yeah. Yeah, I'm ready," I finally called back.

The dock lines thumped on deck as Tony pushed the boat clear and screamed, "Have fun, little sister! And be careful."

Varuna's engine putted away. I pushed the tiller and maneuvered, without mishap, out of the Seaport, where I had spent my last precious minutes at home. Peering through the mist, I looked for the boat that my father had chartered to lead me out of the Seaport to Sandy Hook, 20 miles away. Yes, I could see it ahead and altered to its course. Also, there was another boat following, *UBS*, a big Swiss racing sailboat, which had taken a bunch of people on board to wish me bon voyage. Waving from the deck were my mother; Tony; my sisters, Nina and Jade, and all my friends. They stayed close by for about a mile and then, for the last time, we called goodbyes and I Love You's back and forth, and *UBS* slowed and turned away. Trembling, I watched through streams of tears as the distance between us grew and they disappeared in the fog. Oh God. This is real. I began to shake violently. "What the hell am I doing?" I screamed at the water. "I don't want to go. I want to go back home. Oh my God!"

My father's voice crackled in over my little VHF hand-held

radio. "How are you doing?" he asked from the fishing boat just ahead.

"I'm wet and cold," I blubbered into the radio, unwilling to admit that I had never been so scared in my life.

"You're going to be fine," he said. "Hang in there."

That morning, I had awakened with Nina on *Varuna* to be picked up by a limousine and whisked off to the NBC studios to talk to Jane Pauley on the "Today" show, one of the five or six TV shows and newspapers that my father had called to tell of my departure. Between the bright lights in my eyes and the worry about my impending trip, I had been a nervous wreck.

JANE: Wow, this is incredible. How are you going to handle the big waves and the boat on the ocean all by yourself. You're only eighteen! What if you get into a storm? I'm going to do my best to convince you not to go.

ME: It's too late. I'm leaving this afternoon at four o'clock.

JANE: But aren't you scared?

ME: Well, yeah, I guess so.

JANE: What makes you think you can do this?

ME: I dunno. A whole lot of other ninnies have already done it. I guess I can do it.

Later that morning, I watched my television debut on a friend's VCR and cringed when I saw myself squinting into the lights; my gestures appeared epileptic. And those answers! I sounded like a stupid child parroting the reasoning of her father. It was no wonder Jane Pauley had tried to talk me out of going.

Everywhere I looked—the sky, the water, the air—was a sooty gray. The dampness was piercing and I pulled the sleeves of my jacket down over my hands as rain poured out of the sky in buckets. "Tania, look. Even New York is crying because you are leaving," a friend had said as I pulled away from the Seaport dock. I looked at the chart of the harbor inside the oversized Ziploc plastic bag in front of me, but had no idea of my position in relation to it. I concentrated on the vague form of the boat ahead. On both sides, *Varuna* was crossing paths with the immense rumbling hulks of all the liners, tugs and tankers traveling through and anchored in the harbor. As the fog thickened, every so often one of their horns would blast its

Morse signal to warn the passing boats. Suddenly, through the patter of the rain, I heard *Varuna*'s engine cough and falter. Put, put, put ... put ... put. ... Our speed decreased by half. I watched with a growing panic as the boat carrying my father was swallowed into the mist ahead.

My range of vision was a foggy perimeter of 100 feet. I grabbed the little hand-held VHF radio and steered *Varuna* on the same heading as when I lost sight of them. "Daddy, Daddy. This is *Varuna*," I called, over and over, beginning to cry again. "Can you hear me? Daddy, this is *Varuna*, come in *please*." Finally, they came back and I screamed, "The engine is broken again. What should I do?"

"You know the problem is in the fuel line," my father called, "and I showed you how to bleed the system. Come on now, you have a *sail*boat. You don't even *need* an engine. Put up those sails and let's go."

Gasping and hiccuping, I turned the boat into the wind, found the jib halyard, wrapped it around a winch, pulled it up and cleated it off as the sail flapped noisily. Heading *Varuna* downwind, I trimmed in the slatting sail until it filled with wind and we took off. This was the first time in my life that I had sailed a boat all by myself.

That morning, I had gone to say goodbye to Jeri, promising her I'd be back. I gazed around at the familiar space of her TriBeCa loft, which had been my home since my father had kicked me out of the house two years before. I climbed up to the cozy platform she had built for me over our walk-in closet, and hugged her cats, Bumblebee and Bula. Bumblebee put her nose up in the air, delicately licked my face and pranced off. Bula scratched and hissed at me for the last time. I took mental snapshots, trying to savor for the last time every essence that was New York.

When we arrived at the boat, journalists, TV cameras and microphones came swooping down on us. Once again, my responses to their questions were awkward monosyllables. I just didn't really want to go to college, I said. This seems like a great way to see the world and write about what I see. Yes, my father bought the boat in lieu of college tuition, but he's only letting me borrow it; I'm going to pay him back and support myself along the way by writing articles for *Cruising World*, a sailing magazine. No, I've never handled a boat by myself before, I stammered, but I have a lot of books and did take a course in celestial navigation. Why am I doing it?

"I dunno ... why not?" I said, with a nervous laugh. The journalists all looked at me as if I were nuts.

On board *Varuna* were last-minute presents and mementos tucked into every corner by well-wishers. There was an apple pie and a doll from my mother, homemade soups, chocolate chip cookies, green apples, sacks of books, a harmonica, *Fat Freddy's Cat* cartoons, a flute, letters and little packages marked to be opened at milestone points of the trip.

I shivered and sweated, looking for Jeri. She was standing inconspicuously behind the crowd. I ran to hug her and she held me close. I couldn't begin to express what I wanted to say to this generous lady who had helped me so much over the hurdles of the past two years. Crying uncontrollably, I kissed her goodbye. "Tania." she said, crying, "for me, you will always be my daughter. I love you. Be careful and always follow your heart."

I looked around. There was my mother, standing straight, trying to answer the reporters' questions, insisting to everybody how proud she was. I was in a daze. What do I do now? Is it time to go? There were Christian and Fritz, two of my family's closest friends, both artists—one a Yugoslavian and the other a Swiss—who, along with Jeri, had been surrogate parents to us for as long as I could remember. Christian put his hand on my shoulder. "Now be careful," he said, trying to be happy. "We want you to come back home." Fritz pounded me on the back, then hugged me, "See you in two years, little one," he said. "Take care of yourself."

I climbed over *Varuna*'s lifelines into the cockpit and through the companionway into my home—home for the next two years. Putting on my foul-weather gear, I took a deep breath, went back up into the cockpit and feebly waved for the last time to all those who couldn't come on the *UBS*.

Four hours of sailing later, with my hand numb on the tiller, *Varuna* was threading her way through a barrier of fish traps and rounding the bend into Horseshoe Cove at Sandy Hook where I was to spend the night, get organized and gather my thoughts before setting out to sea. My father coached me from the fishing boat in anchoring *Varuna* under sail, another first. The engine still had a little sputter left and therefore a small influence on headway. I dropped the jib, ran up forward, disengaged the brake on the anchor windlass and let the anchor and chain slide out. *Varuna* backed up sideways to the wind, just as she was supposed to, before reaching the end of the anchor rode. But then she kept on sliding back, headed for the beach, still with a broadside breeze.

"Daddy!" I shrieked. "Help me! The anchor isn't holding! I'm going aground!" The fishing boat quickly maneuvered itself into a position next to me. My father jumped onto *Varuna*, grabbed the chain and effortlessly pulled it back up.

"You didn't let out enough chain, Tania. My God, you let out only five feet when you can see that there is *fifteen* feet of water here. You know better than that." He was right. The chain hadn't even touched the ground.

"You're on your own now. Get some rest. Everything will seem fine after you sleep. Look how frazzled you are. I know that you are able to at least anchor a boat. Just get some sleep and call me on the radio before you leave. Goodbye, my daughter. Lots of strength and courage to you. I know you can do it. Now, show everybody else."

"No, Daddy, wait!" I cried. "Please stay with me a little while longer. I don't want to be alone yet."

"No," he replied, "the longer I stay, the harder it will get." He boarded the fishing boat, they pulled away and we waved until they were swallowed into the mist. Dazed and petrified, I was alone.

I climbed down in the cabin, found a pack of cigarettes and lit one with trembling hands. What was to become of me? Suddenly my future seemed as complicated as the pilot charts that were strewn about the cabin. My father and I had pored over them as he showed me how to decipher the curling lines, circles and symbols that covered the oceans of the world like hieroglyphics. Those symbols were a finger on the pulse of the sea. With them, I could second-guess her moods at certain times of the year, figure out the monthly averages of her currents, her prevailing winds, wave habits, probabilities of storms. From the pilot charts, I already knew more about the sea than I thought I would ever know about myself.

I tried to imagine all the exotic people I was going to meet and the wonderful things I would see in those places where *Varuna* was about to take me—Bermuda, the sun-drenched islands of the Caribbean, the Panama Canal, the prehistoric beauty of the Galápagos, Gauguin's paradisiacal South Pacific, my Shangri-la in Sri Lanka, the Seychelles, St. Helena and carnival in Brazil. Until today, those names had just been pushpins on the map of my brain. One by one, they were about to become my realities.

In 1983, two years before my departure day, I had never even set foot on a sailboat. We all liked to tease that it was my father's midlife crisis that set in motion the series of events that would change our family—and especially me—forever. After his forty-fifth birthday, his mind had started to work overtime and he began a period of constant worry. What had he done with his life? he asked himself. Was he enjoying it all? Was he missing out on something? He slowly lost interest in his artwork and seldom sat down at his drawing board anymore. When he did, it was to doodle wild-eyed monsters with exaggerated genitalia. His days were spent either worrying about the comings and goings of teenagers or maintaining his real estate. Rents from the buildings he owned had made him financially independent; he no longer had to sell his paintings to make a living and, in his eyes, there were no more emotional Everests to climb. He had time to think, to look at his life. He didn't like what he saw.

One day, while sitting on the toilet at Christian's house and flipping through a sailing magazine, he suddenly came upon the solution. Within a month, he had taken a mail-order course in celestial navigation, flown to Florida for a one-week learn-to-sail course and headed off to England to buy a 38-foot sailboat, *Pathfinder of Percuil.*

His plan was ambitious. With his children as crew, he would sail the boat from England to the Canary Islands by way of Spain, Portugal and Morocco. Then, with some friends, he would take her across the Atlantic to the Caribbean and then up the East Coast to New York. It was to be a real family adventure. At first, he was reluctant to have me along, fearing that the potential for arguments between us was too great within the confines of a 38-foot sailboat. But finally, his girlfriend, Jeri, convinced him that it was just the thing the two of us needed to repair our relationship, which had been severed when I was fifteen.

Sailing is an activity that can take years to master before heading off into the wild blue yonder. My father was itchy to get going, so instead, we had three days. He figured that whatever we didn't learn from *Pathfinder*'s previous owner, we'd learn as we went along. Those three days were a blur of sailing practice and man-overboard drills, where we learned the basic workings of the boat, how to raise and lower the sails with all the different spaghettis of lines, how the wheel or tiller is used to steer. The hardest concept to grasp was how the boat uses the wind to move forward. No matter how many times and ways it was explained to us, it wasn't until later on, as we crossed the Atlantic, that it all began to sink in. Only my little brother Tony, with his mathematician's mind, managed to grasp immediately the aerodynamic principles. With just a tiny glimmer of understanding, this lone hyperactive adult and three of his children sailed past the heads of Cornwall and out to sea.

The next month took us to Vigo and Bayona in Spain; Lisbon,

Portugal; Casablanca and finally to the Canary Islands. Seeing a new side of Europe was thrilling, but the real excitement for us was life at sea aboard *Pathfinder*. She was a kind and patient teacher, taking our clumsy handling in stride. We brutalized her every time we tacked; we manhandled the wheel, and sent the boom and sails flying across the cockpit to bash over to the other side, sending shudders through the rigging. We overtrimmed the sails and she'd heel so far onto her side that the roiling sea would come sloshing over the deck. We'd scream and uncleat all the sails in a panic, the sheets would whir through the mainsheet block and she'd round upright again, in irons, ready for the next exercise, while we tore around like the Keystone Cops trying to figure out what we were doing wrong. My father spent the lion's share of his time down below in the cabin, fiddling around with the navigation equipment, trying to figure out exactly where we were, while Tony, Jade and I rotated watches, trying to keep *Pathfinder* on course.

Aboard this forgiving boat, we became a closely knit team. Slowly and surely, we learned every nuance of her motions, separating her strong points from her weak ones. Aboard her, we all worked together with the sea and the wind to reach a goal and, for the first time in years, we took the time to get to know each other.

My father was right about one thing—sailing was special. Thoughts became clearer and simpler at sea, uncluttered by the pressures of responsibilities and familiar habits. It was easy to be happy. And during the night watch, my favorite time, the inky darkness of the sky would be lit by a twinkling mantle of stars; the boat would jog rhythmically through the sea swells, and sometimes, if I struck it lucky, pailfuls of phosphorescence sparked like fireflies in *Pathfinder*'s wake. It was during these times that my father and I slowly began to bandage the wounds of our past and know each other again.

We left *Pathfinder* in the Canary Islands for the winter and returned to New York—my father, Tony and Jade to their house and I, once again, home to Jeri. But this time, things were different. I had plans. I wanted to work for a few months in the city and make enough money to join Nina, Fritz, my father and *Pathfinder* for the 2,800-mile trip across the Atlantic.

I took a job in Manhattan as a bicycle messenger. Every day at eight in the morning, I jumped on my ten-speed and headed into the world of rush hours, elevators, crowded streets, traffic jams and outraged taxi drivers, delivering envelopes back and forth across the metropolis of New York City. Whatever the cons were in handling a bike through the mainstream of Manhattan's business day, the pros outweighed them. There were no fixed wages and no fixed hours. The faster I pedaled, the more money I made. It got so that I could get across the city in eleven and a half minutes flat and deliver an average of twenty messages a day.

Fritz had never been on a sailboat before, and both he and Nina were afraid of the water, so it was with a different sense of adventure that the four of us left the Canary Islands for the Caribbean two months later. On November 24, 1983, we bid farewell to the last piece of land for 2,776 miles and twenty-eight days.

Somewhere in the mid-Atlantic—I'm not sure where—a plan hatched in my father's head. He was apprehensive about our arrival home, fearing that I'd fall back in with old friends and bad habits. Aimlessness is a condition unthinkable to Ernst Aebi, a man true to his Swiss-German background who must either have a clear plan or be changing a plan at all times. For my father, living with someone without a plan is just about as bad as not having one himself. The closer we got to New York, the more it gnawed at him. Sitting back in the cockpit one evening, as he watched the sunset over a glass of brandy, he blurted it out.

"Tania, you know you must start to make some decisions about your future," he started. Oh, here we go, I thought. This was beginning to become a familiar conversation-opener. "OK, you don't want to go to college, but you still have to do something with your life." Although I sighed with exasperation, the trouble was that I knew he was right. I did have to do something, and, in truth, I had been giving it some thought. It was just that no great inspirations had come to mind.

"I'm going to go back to being a messenger for a while and then decide. Don't worry about it, Daddy."

"What do you mean? I am your *father* and I *have* been worrying about it. Anyway, I've come up with an idea."

"I really don't want to hear it," I said, in no mood for an argument.

"How about . . . if you sail around the world . . ." he was talking and conjuring at the same time, a dangerous thing. "How about if you sail around the world, and I'll buy the boat. I'll buy the boat and you can use it for the trip. I mean, I'd have to spend the money on tuition anyway if you went to college. You obviously have no intention of going to college, right?

"You mean to tell me you'd *give* me a boat?"

27

"Ernst, you mean you'd *give* her a boat?" echoed Fritz, looking up from his own brandy.

"Well, let's say I'd let you *borrow* a boat, but you'd have to be resourceful and support yourself along the way."

"You're kidding me," I said.

"Yah," said Fritz, "and then Nina could cross Siberia on crutches, right?"

"Don't be narrow-minded, Fritz," answered my father. "You're too much of a chicken to even jump in the water. Tania would even be able to write articles about the trip to support herself, especially since she has always liked writing. This way, she could begin some sort of career with a bang."

This didn't sound half bad to me. I had loved sailing on *Pathfinder* and thought how great it would be to sail to all kinds of exotic places, have my friends from New York join me along the way as crew and meet tons of interesting people.

"Not bad," I said.

My father took another sip from his brandy. "But, to make it really something, though, you'd have to do it alone. . . ."

"Whaddaya mean—alone?"

"I mean alone. Singlehanded. To make it *really* interesting you'd have to go around the world singlehanded. What do you think, that I'm going to buy you a boat for pleasure? No way. This would be a job."

"Alone? ME? That's nuts. Forget it." I stopped listening. The idea no longer held any appeal.

"Ernst Aebi," interrupted Fritz, "you are a crazy Schweizer. You know Tania. She could get herself killed." But my father was like a dog with a bone.

After a respite in the Caribbean, except for one knock-down, drag-out storm, our grand finale leg up the East Coast home to New York was an uneventful passage of a combined 1,700 miles in twenty-one days. There was plenty of time to reflect while still on the ocean. My plans for the future were modest. Whenever anyone had ever asked me what I wanted to do with my life, I had always said, "I want to travel around the world and see as much as I can." I had entertained visions of working as a messenger and saving up enough money to make that goal come true. My father's tales of his wanderings all over Europe and Asia when he was twenty years old had made me dream.

But going around the world on a sailboat alone, what kind of an idea was that? I was only seventeen. We had only sailed *Pathfinder* on three passages and I didn't even know how to sail a boat by myself. Anyway, how would I learn everything? Celestial navigation? Electronics? Coastal navigation? Heavy-weather sailing? Mechanical repairs? Meteorology? The list was endless. I didn't even know how to drive a car.

"You wouldn't have to learn it all at once," my father replied to these qualms. "Sailing is based on common sense and you'll learn very quickly once you start."

"But, Daddy, going out to sea all alone? How could I possibly handle everything on a boat all by myself?"

"It's easy, I'm telling you. You can read my books. Don't worry about the little things. They will take care of themselves. Think big! Think about the world that you will see. Think about sailing your own pretty little boat into an exotic foreign port and seeing it in a way that no Mickey Mouse tourist in a bubble-topped bus will ever see it. And this would be your job. That's the beauty of the plan. It would be your job to pay for the trip by being a writer. Writers need something to write about, right?"

"I guess so, but what if . . ."

"Yah. Yah. *If* my grandmother had wheels, she'd be a bus."

I let him talk. Crazy as it sounded, the more he talked and the closer we got to New York, the more the plan began to grow on me.

When we got back home, I went to visit my mother in Switzerland for two months and enrolled in a summer course at the University of Lausanne. People my age came from all over Europe to improve their French and make new friends. It seemed as if everyone I met had solid plans. They were continuing school or entering apprenticeships or going into family businesses or traveling for the summer before starting jobs. I felt like a tumbleweed. Except for this loco idea of sailing alone around the world, I had no ties to the future.

One evening, I put the idea forward to my mother and she surprised me with her support. By then, she knew that life wasn't blessing her with endless amounts of time and she philosophized, "Don't be scared of what may eventually happen. Live for the day, Tania, and always try to do great things."

The next time one of my classmates asked me what I was going to do once school was over, I hesitated, "I'm planning . . . to go around the world, alone, on a sailboat." I gave a nervous laugh. The push was on.

. . .

It was dark by the time I came out of my reverie and I began to feel a bit embarrassed over the earlier anchoring procedure. Hoping no one had been around to witness it, I peeked out the companionway. Another sailboat had come in and anchored next door, but I didn't feel like talking to anybody and ducked back below, staring through a porthole. Preparing my bed, a narrow bunk that stretched from the sink to a cubbyhole under the cockpit on the port side of the boat, I wiggled my way into my sleeping bag and after a few more tears for the loved ones and the life being left behind, fell into a deep sleep.

"Hello, are you awake in there?" The next morning I awoke to a man's voice and the sound of a dinghy circling *Varuna* and clambered outside.

"Hi. I'm awake."

"Could you use some breakfast?" asked the man in the dinghy. He didn't have to ask twice. I jumped in and we motored over to his boat to join his girlfriend for bran flakes, fresh strawberries, herbal tea and honey while they told me, "Hey, we saw you on TV last night. But, we figured you needed some sleep, so we didn't bother you." After an hour, I left my first friends of the trip and wached them sail out of the cove.

"Good luck, Tania! Good luck!" they called, sailing away.

"Thanks!" I called back. "I'm going to need it!" Good luck—that was practically all I had heard during the past few months.

I went back down below and reread all the letters of best wishes and examined presents that became *Varuna*'s first assortment of decorations. My mother had given me a Chinese doll she picked up in Chinatown on the way down to see me off. She had made my favorite apple pie and wrapped it in plastic wrap with a paper heart taped on top. I held the little doll in my hand, wondering if my mother would be there to welcome me home when I finished the voyage and thinking about her face as she said goodbye. We had said goodbye many times before, but this time we both knew it was different. I broke down again, but not for myself. My future was as limitless as this morning's horizon. The tears were for the cage of my mother's reality, for people born under the wrong star and for whom life can be so unfair. "I am doing this trip for you, too, Mommy," I said aloud. "I want to help you dream, and give you something to hope for."

Lost in thought, I organized all my belongings and cleaned up the boat, finding a bagful of wrapped gifts from Tony, Nina, Jade and my father, with tags telling me when to open them: "Congratulations on crossing the equator," said one. "Happy Birthday" said another. Others said, "Merry Christmas" and "To be opened 300 miles from Australia." I shook them and held them up to the light, finally stowing them in a safe, waterproof area. Then I found the sealed envelope from my mother. It was thick; there was something of a strange texture inside and, in large, gangly printing it said simply: "To be opened in the middle of the ocean." I quickly put the envelope away, deciding to save it for a special occasion.

Back to business, I tasted all the donated foods and threw out what wouldn't keep. Tiny though it might be, this was my first home. For the first time in my life, I was completely on my own. So many things were about to happen. I inhaled deeply, counted to ten, exhaled slowly to calm myself, and offered a silent prayer: "I'm scared, God. Be good to me, please. I'm off to see your beautiful world."

I bled the fuel system, listened to the engine purr for half an hour, finished cleaning up and slept one more night. In the morning, I called my father for the last time from America.

"Good luck, Tania," he said. "This morning I listened to the weather report and everything is A-one perfect."

On the first of June, under a clear sky, I turned on the engine and headed *Varuna*'s bow out into the blue unknown. A U.S. Coast Guard whirlybird hovered overhead, and a man leaned out to wave, screaming, "GOOD LUCK!" I squinted up into the sunshine and waved back. "Thanks," I called. "See you in a couple of years!" Behind me, the towers of the World Trade Center shrank in the distance and began to disappear beneath the horizon.

Two hours under way and about 10 miles into the shipping lanes, *Varuna*'s engine faltered again. "Oh well," I said to myself. "I have a sailboat. I'll sail." Finding the mainsail and jib halyards—one red-striped and the other black to avoid confusion—I pulled up the sails and felt them fill. *Varuna* gently heeled over, baring the starboard side of her maroon hull, and began to glide along in rhythm with the sea and wind. Perfect. We were on a beam reach, with the wind perpendicular to the boat, the point of sail at which any sailboat makes its best performance. The boom was sheeted in and she pranced along like a filly.

Varuna could be steered by an electric autopilot, adjustable to course changes. Without the engine, energy had to be conserved or the batteries would be drained within two days. Disengaging the power-hungry autopilot, I decided it would be better to figure out how to use my new Monitor wind-vane self-steering gear while the weather was still fine. Rather than running on electricity like the autopilot, the Monitor had a rudder attached to gears connected to the tiller by a block-and-tackle system. From the stern, it steered the boat with wind power. A wooden-paddle wind vane was set into a position determined by the relative direction of the wind and a compass course.

Although I knew the general concept, I had never used the piece of equipment before now, so I fiddled and adjusted the vane fractions of an inch in different directions. The fiddling made *Varuna* swing in wild deviations from the proper course until, finally, I began to figure it out. The Monitor was of the same system and similar design to the self-steering mechanism on *Pathfinder*. Already, it was clear how little attention I had paid aboard *Pathfinder*. It had been so easy to let my father do everything, to claim ignorance or to half-listen. From now on, there would be no such thing as excuses. The outcome of every situation would depend on my ability to cope.

With a gust of wind, *Varuna* suddenly tilted over at a 15-degree angle, sliding me to the other side of the cockpit, where my elbow banged against the winch. "Ouch!" I cried, rubbing the bruise. "*Varuna* is nothing like *Pathfinder*. She's so tiny." I couldn't remember ever having been this close to the water on a boat. Today was the first time that *Varuna* had ever been out of sight of land, and this little cockleshell was as untested as I.

Varuna was named for the Hindu goddess of the cosmos. She was a graceful 26-foot sloop and I was beginning to feel her spirit. Already thinking of *Varuna* and me as "us," I felt we were a couple and, as a couple, we'd have to forgive each other our shortcomings and help each other to learn. Continuing to fuss over the Monitor, I reflected on our search for the perfect boat for the trip.

My father and I had pored over the classified listings in sailing magazines for secondhand boats. The possibilities were narrowed down to anything between 20 and 30 feet that seemed seaworthy. I wasn't the world's most proficient mariner, and a smaller boat would help me learn more easily than a larger one. If problems arose on a small boat, we figured, they would be small problems. I would have to pull up small sails, and fix small leaks. My father even equipped *Varuna* with a mini tool kit with all sorts of miniature tools he had picked up at the bargain stands on Canal Street. Although they seemed perfectly adequate at the time, they were destined to corrode, disintegrate and be jettisoned one by one, within a month or two of my departure.

In October 1984, I had driven with my father and Christian down to the Annapolis Boat Show in Maryland. If we couldn't find a used boat, we'd have to try and find a good new boat. I had never been to a boat show and, although I eagerly explored every last display, nothing made my heart skip. I knew that I would instantly recognize the right boat when I saw her.

We had gone to the show not only to find a boat, but also with the hope of selling an article I had written about our voyage on *Pathfinder* to *Cruising World*, a reputable sailing magazine. They accepted it and, after some discussion, a verbal agreement was reached that they would publish the writings chronicling my voyage. But, in order to write those articles, I had to find a boat.

On the last day of the show, hidden among the hundreds of flashy boats on display, we found the Contessa 26 built by the Canadian company, J. J. Taylor. My father thumped around up on deck, checking to be sure the superstructure wouldn't flex under pressure. Christian knocked away on the hull, feeling the thickness of the fiberglass. I sat down below in the compact cocoon of the cabin, looked around and heard myself say, "I think this is the one."

She felt more right than any other boat had up until that point, and after several days of thinking it over, we went to Canada to visit the factory, a common thing to do before purchasing a boat. Satisfied with the diligence of the builders, at the end of the day my father and I sat with the president and a salesman who had sailed his own Contessa 32 around the world. They all looked at me. Say yes now and there would be no turning back. "Well, here goes," I thought, and sealed my fate.

I watched a tanker on my reciprocal course, probably heading toward New York Harbor. The sun was shining and the water was emerald green. Twenty miles down, 730 to go. I thought about how to read the barometer. "Does bad weather make a barometer go up or down," I wondered. "Up? Yes. No, down. I think." I glanced down through the companionway to the bulkhead over the sink where the barometer was mounted, and gasped. There was water sloshing all over the floor of the cabin!

"Oh my God," I screamed, "we're sinking!" I jumped below, trying to trace the leak and threw open the cabinet behind which were the sea cocks and valves for the sink. "Daddy always said to check the sea cocks *first*," I said aloud, remembering how he showed me where the cut-off valves were stationed, wherever intake and discharge holes passed through the hull of the boat—at the sink, at the toilet, in the engine compartment and in the bilge. A broken sea cock could sink *Varuna* in minutes.

His words rang in my ears as I located the two sea cocks under the sink. Miraculously, they seemed dry. Then I noticed a rivulet of water trickling from above, behind an upper locker, and pulled it open. Inside was one of the steel struts onto which were bolted the chain plates that passed through the deck. Chain plates were the hull attachment points for the rigging; they held up the mast and sustained a great deal of pressure. It was one of the six chain plates at deck level that was leaking; it was not an underwater problem and, therefore, not life-threatening.

"Elementary, my dear Watson," I pronounced with a sigh of relief.

In the last two weeks of preparations, my father had kept on bringing bags of different tools down to the boat—most of whose functions mystified me: caulkings, rivets, electrical tapes, glues and all sorts of synthetic troubleshooting materials. They always landed with a thump in the cockpit as he ran off to do more shopping. I was left to sort them out and, with a million and one other things to do, just dumped the bags into any free space available, figuring they would be pulled out and organized when I had some free time.

With feet up in the air, and one hand holding on to prevent me from falling headfirst into the locker, I dragged out the underwater epoxy and remembered my father tossing it to me saying, "Hey, Tania, here's something that I've never seen before—an epoxy that cures underwater. It might come in handy." I opened up the two components, mixed them together, ruining my first spoon of many, and went up on deck to slather it around the base of the chain plate. It molded like so much Silly Putty and hardened; finally the leak dribbled to a stop.

To celebrate my first evening at sea, dinner was spaghetti with pesto, one of the buckets of food donated by friends. I inaugurated my new pressure cooker, boiled up some water from *Varuna*'s tanks and threw in the pasta. The weather was calm; my first sunset was flashing brilliant, burnt-red shards of color across the sky and an occasional tanker meandered across the horizon. I shoveled a couple of forkfuls into my mouth, swallowed and immediately retched. What now? I thought, spitting out the last bits of pasta. Then it dawned on me. "Oh no. It can't be." I checked my water supply at the sink tap and moaned. It was true. The brand-new water tanks were contaminated with fiberglass from the factory and my entire water supply was useless. The only consolation was that I had brought aboard a supply of bottled mineral water, as well as sealed boxes of juice and soy milk. Making a mental tally of the potable liquid aboard, I figured that with rationing, it was possible to make do.

The following morning the barometer had fallen from 1020 millibars to 1005; a low-pressure system was approaching and I began to prepare myself for the first storm of the trip. It started quietly with puffs of wind coming from random directions. By 8:00 A.M., the sky had darkened and the wind piped up, bringing with it an icy chill. Putting on my foul-weather gear, I stuffed my hair into the hood, zipped up the jacket and went outside into the cockpit to wait. By 10:00 A.M., a full-fledged gale arrived, knocking *Varuna* all the way over on her side and keeping her there for the duration of the storm.

Squall line after squall line thundered over us, spitting out bolts of lightning. *Varuna* was lifted to the top of every boiling crest and then was sent careening down to the trough. I hunched in the cockpit, transfixed and petrified. As every dark cloud approached, the wind picked up and *Varuna* flew down the backs of the waves, heeling 35 degrees over on her port side. "We must have entered the Gulf Stream," I thought, with its warm water surging upward like a river in the sea from the Gulf of Mexico.

I checked my life harness, whose line attached me to a U-bolt mounting in the cockpit, and watched with awe the wrath of the ocean. White water roiled over the foredeck and back into the cockpit from both sides and my stomach leapt with every jolt to *Varuna*. Violently seasick, I just clung on and fervently prayed that my fate wasn't to go up in smoke from a bolt of lightning. I had grounding cables, but no idea how to use them.

After retching my guts up over the side, I crawled across the cockpit and headed below to find something to drink. I couldn't believe my eyes! *There was six inches of water above the floorboards!* Grabbing the bilge pump handle from the cockpit locker behind me, I shoved it into the pump sprocket near my feet and began pumping like crazy. After ten pumps, it seized up. God damn it! What happened? The emergency electric bilge pump came to mind. I jumped down into the sloshing cabin, pulled the switch, heard the pump churn to life, then flew up the two steps out to the cockpit to disengage the Monitor, grabbed the tiller and headed *Varuna* into the wind. She rounded up and her sails began to slap back and forth in the howling winds.

Stumbling up to the foredeck, I frantically began to pull down the storm jib. I had to right the boat to determine where the water was coming in. It was already higher than the sea cocks, so I couldn't tell whether or not it was coming in through a through-hull fitting. As *Varuna* straightened up, the washing-machine cycle began to calm belowdecks; above was the same blustery, squalling mess. "Dear God, help me!" I cried. Buckling my harness to a jack line running almost the entire length of the deck, I hurriedly began to search for the leak by scrutinizing the deck in minutest detail. What on earth could be responsible for this calamity?

Checking the anchor windlass at the bow, I couldn't believe my eyes. Beneath the windlass was a gaping hole for the anchor chain to pass through the deck and down a pipeline into the bilge. With every wave, water funneled down the hole, slowly drowning *Varuna!* I had been so damned ignorant that I had never even thought of blocking up this artery now pumping the sea into the bowels of my boat.

The wind continued to howl as the waves buried the bow where I crouched. Cold water streamed down my neck, drenching my clothes with salt water as I struggled to stuff the hole with the first thing I could get my hands on—Grand Union shopping bags covered with duct tape. I crammed in as many as possible, taped over the opening and pulled the jib back up. Running down below again, I stuck my head into the opening in the bilge where the chain was stored. The water influx had slowed to a trickle. I stopped to breathe. "Two emergencies down," I said, feeling the adrenaline still surging through my body. "How many more to go?" and turned around to survey my soaking-wet little home.

"Maybe Daddy was right," I thought. In two days, I had solved two major problems, and it really wasn't that hard. Maybe sailing doesn't require tons of deep dark secret knowledge. It was beginning to seem that everything could be handled with common sense.

"Hey," I realized with a sudden burst of euphoria, "I'm not seasick anymore!" My days of living under the influence of this horrible malaise were over. Through some miracle, I never got seasick again.

The storm eventually passed, and I fiddled with the boat, testing her in the changing winds. Although I was awed by the sea and fully aware of its threatening potential, surprisingly, it did not scare me. Before leaving New York, I had often slept on my comfortable futon at Jeri's, dreaming of being alone on the ocean, wondering if its depths and immensity would intimidate me once I was out in the middle of it. Now, I found myself relieved to be able to sit out in the cockpit, day or night, clear or overcast, and feel relatively at ease.

Around day six, there began a droning period of flat calm. The ocean was a perfect mirror, unruffled by even the slightest hint of breeze, reflecting *Varuna*'s shapely body and limp sails while Portuguese man-of-war jellyfish glided by. Dolphins came squealing out of nowhere, accompanied by flocks of squawking ocean terns overhead. They circled for a while, and then took off in search of a more responsive playmate. *Varuna* wallowed and rolled in a dreary rhythm, going nowhere for two days.

I had forgotten that there was always a swell on the ocean, and I began to experiment with ways to keep the boat from rolling so uncontrollably with it. First, I tried sheeting in the mainsail as tightly as possible. As *Varuna* began to roll in one direction, the sail slammed violently to the other side. Every time this happened— about once every fifteen seconds—she shuddered and her rigging emitted resonant twangs. I suffered, too, cringing with every slam until I couldn't take it anymore.

"There has to be a way to stop this boat from rolling without the slam," I thought, and went below, dug out my *Learn to Sail* book and flipped through it searching for inspiration. "Maybe if I take in a couple reefs," I said to myself, "it won't slam as hard." After shortening the mainsail by two reef points, I anxiously waited for the sharp retort and only heard a soft flapping every now and then. If there was a better way to do it, it was beyond me.

With the calm, I set about fixing the engine. In order to bleed the fuel system, it was necesary to unscrew two nuts before a little pump could milk the fuel out of the openings until there were no more air bubbles in the fuel line. But I couldn't get it to work. After a whole lot of pumping, there were still air bubbles in the line. Whenever my father did this, he always got rid of the air. What else did he do when the engine quit? Maybe he changed the filter? This was easier said than done. He had given me a special extractor that wound around the filter with a handle to give leverage. I slid it on and pushed and pulled. No response. I pushed a little harder. Still nothing. I positioned my foot on the handle and exerted all my force, twisting the filter canister out of shape, and then gave up. Two weeks later, in Bermuda, a mechanic who had to remove the filter with a vice grip told me I had been trying to unscrew it in the wrong direction.

During the evenings of the previous winter, after delivering messages on my bicycle, I had tried to study books on sailing and took night courses in coastal and celestial navigation. I passed the coastal course, having sailed aboard *Pathfinder*, but flunked the celestial navigation course, probably as a result of exhaustion after biking all day and not being able to keep my eyes open for the two hours of celestial triangle theory. Photocopying my father's mail-order course, I figured I'd learn the techniques along the way. It had been easy to procrastinate during the past few days because I had seen and talked to enough ships on the radio and they had given me my position with the aid of their sophisticated electronics. But now I needed to get cracking and teach myself celestial navigation.

I sat on deck with the sextant, pointing it into the sun, burning my pupils through the two mirrors, aligning the sun with the horizon to determine the exact angle between the two. The second they were lined up perfectly, I looked at my watch and recorded the precise time of the angle. With these two vital bits of information, taken twice a day with about a four-hour interval, one is theoretically supposed to be able to figure out a position, or "fix." I tried and retried it; the fixes just didn't seem right.

It was hard to imagine that these books, my calculations, the plotting sheets, the compass rose and the sliding rulers could ever possibly tell me where I was. It would have been a luxury to have a SatNav aboard *Varuna*—a machine where I could press a button and get my position from a satellite. Not only was a SatNav too expensive —probably over a thousand dollars—but my father and I had a mutual understanding that I would learn how to do everything on board without the aid of electronics. With electronics, there would always be the chance of failure or of power loss, just as I had now with no engine to recharge my batteries. Where would I be then, if I didn't know the age-old concepts of navigation? I sat for hours double-checking the instructions, taking sight after sight, trying to get two lines of position that agreed, until I got dizzy and the figures blurred.

On the evening of June 4, the barometer began to drop and I quickly set to battening things down aboard to prepare for some more nasty weather. Anything that could fly around in the cabin below was stowed: books, the pressure cooker, tools, food and clothes. Double-checking all the lines that were holding the deflated rubber dinghy securely in the cockpit, I took down the bigger genoa, replaced it with a smaller working jib, and took in a reef point on the mainsail, shortening its size by about four feet.

By the next morning, the swell had grown and strong gusts began to blow erratically from different directions. The sky transformed itself before my eyes into a dark ceiling of swirly gloom. I went below and bundled up into my warmest clothes and foul-weather gear. It was important to prepare myself and the boat before the worst of the storm hit because, after that, every trip up to the pitching foredeck would be extremely wet and risky.

I set and reset the Monitor, repositioning its vane into the wind, trying to find the point at which it would work best. I shortened the mainsail another reef point, but *Varuna* still pitched violently in the worsening conditions. There was still too much sail up. Finally, I took the working jib down altogether and shortened the main down to its last reef point until it was almost the size of a handkerchief.

With so little canvas up, *Varuna* rode the waves, pointing into the 40-knot winds. When the seas crashed over her bow, they were deflected by the spray hood shielding the cockpit, rather than hitting us broadside. All through the sleepless night and next day, I sat crouched in the cockpit, the life harness connecting me to the boat, and watched the sea change from a placid lake into this pot of boiling bouillon. *Varuna* pitched and yawed through waves that seemed as high as her mast. Jags of lightning spewed forth from the sky, one right after another, heralding thunderclaps that seemed loud enough to crack open the world. I counted the time between the lightning and the thunder trying to figure out the distance between *Varuna* and the bolts, "One alligator, two alli—" KABOOM! "Oh no, they're practically on top of us!"

For almost two days, we battled in the teeth of the storm, endlessly changing sails, changing tacks and changing direction. When it was possible to tear my eyes away from it all, I went below for refuge in *Varuna*'s wet, coffinlike little cabin. Although 26 feet long, she was only 7½ feet wide, with a living area below of about 15 feet, most of which was taken up with the bunk, sink, stove and head. There was no standing headroom, and even if there were, it would have been virtually impossible to remain standing anyway.

Heeled over on her side at 35 degrees, *Varuna* was like the house of no gravity at a carnival; to get around below I had to stretch from handhold to handhold like a chimp, or crawl along on the tilted sides of the boat. My bunk was soaked through from the leaking chain plate and from opening and closing the companionway slats, so I curled up in my rain gear on the lee side of the boat and tried to take my mind off the conditions with a book. Every hour, I went back out into the cockpit to check the horizon for ships, check our progress and adjust the sails. Lurching to the companionway, I removed the slats and timed my move to avoid the waves crashing over the deck, jumped outside and shoved them back into place before a wave could thunder down into the cabin. One second too early or too late and my bunk would be soaked anew.

I pulled out my meteorology books and charts, trying to understand those weather systems; the explanations seemed to be written in Chinese. Unbeknownst to me, the depressions were huge spirals—some 100 miles wide—rotating clockwise in the Northern Hemisphere and counterclockwise south of the equator, careening across the landmasses and the seas like whirling dervishes. As each depression approached, the barometer dropped; next, the wind gradually increased, eventually dying down, which indicated that we were in the center, and after a short while piping up like crazy from the opposite direction, meaning that we were sailing through the other side of the circle.

It would be two years before I would properly learn how to use a depression to advantage and have it actually help propel *Varuna* toward our destination. But right now I made the mistake of sailing directly into the depression. Not knowing any better, I wasted days of progress and completely jumbled my already shaky navigation. And, exhaustingly, *Varuna* had to be put through every point of sail: tacking into the wind, beam reaching perpendicular to the wind, quarter reaching ahead of the wind and finally sailing directly downwind with the sails boomed out on either side of the boat like butterfly wings. "Until I get the hang of reading the conditions," I reasoned, "I'll just have to muddle along and wait them out."

I was beginning to wonder exactly where we were. During the storm, it had been impossible to take a sight with the sextant. Not only was the sun blocked by clouds, but in order to take a sight, I had to retain a semblance of balance, and *Varuna* had been lurching through the waves like a bronco. June 8 was my first opportunity to pick up the sextant and, once again, aim it at the sun. With the mirrors, I lined up the sun and the horizon umpteen times saying, "Aha, I think I've got it." When I noted the time and angle and got to the paper with the myriad of calculations, my vision began to blur.

All over my chart I had plotted my DR or "dead reckoning" positions, the positions where I had thought we were during the storm, figured out by just advancing the last confirmed position with time and speed. Nothing added up. As a shot in the dark, I turned on the FM radio to see if I could hear anything from Bermuda. I heard a Canadian station and my mind went blank. Good grief! Did this mean we were up near Canada? It couldn't be. If that were true, we had been heading in the opposite direction from Bermuda for days. I worked and reworked the calculations until my eyes crossed. Even though they wouldn't come out the same way twice, I decided to trust my instincts, carry on and follow the original course.

As the saying goes, after every storm, there is a calm. The day of calm that followed the second weather system was a chance to dry out the boat and clean up. The shredded ice in the icebox had just about disappeared and I sat over my books slurping all the yogurts that would soon go bad. I began to distrust the calms, looking at them as great voids, just waiting to be filled by hellfire. I wasn't far wrong.

The next system that hit was different from the last two. It wasn't a spiraling depression. The sky remained wintery blue and clear instead of dark and stormy, but the winds were very strong at 35 knots. *Varuna* had her smallest sails up as we punched into the enormous waves kicked up by the Gulf Stream. It was my tenth day at sea, the batteries were dead and there was no more power to use the VHF radio. But, despite the deteriorating weather, there was the sense of a different energy in the air. On a hunch, I went below, grabbed the radio-direction-finder from its bracket and took it up to the cockpit. As I turned it on, to my amazement a faint signal came through the static in the headphones. Scanning the RDF slowly around the horizon, I heard the signal become stronger and louder until it homed in on the direction of St. David's Head RDF beacon in Bermuda. These beacons emit signals only out to a certain radius— St. David's Head was 150 miles—so at that moment we were somewhere within 150 miles of our landfall. The built-in compass on top of the RDF gave the exact heading. We were home free!

"All my navigation problems are over," I sang. "All we have to do is head east enough of the beacon to avoid the reefs." I double-checked the chart. The reefs surrounding Bermuda begin 30 miles offshore. If we made our approach to the east, we would be safe. This was no time for guesswork. I checked and rechecked my lines of position, hoping for the best.

During this clear-sky gale, I couldn't leave the cockpit and sat outside watching, wondering and worrying if I was doing the right thing. There was no one to help me figure anything out, no one to answer any of my thousands of questions, no one to tell me if I had too much sail up or if it was normal that *Varuna* was heeled over 35 degrees and if water should be pouring over the rail into the cockpit. I looked up at the mast and rigging and hoped that because they were new, they could handle the extra pressure of whatever I might be doing wrong. The Monitor steered merrily away, right on course, taking on all the waves intended for the helmsman. *Varuna* held up just as bravely.

A wave could come crashing over us; she'd delicately shudder, come out from under, shake it off and rise to the crest of the next. Buffeted from side to side, she always came back up again while I waited for her to break up into a million pieces. How much can a hunk of fiberglass take? I wondered. Slowly, I learned to trust her strength. Every time she rose to the top of a crest, I would hunch up in the cockpit under the scant protection of the sprayhood and hold on. She would pause, almost suspended in midair, before dropping down to the deep trough. My stomach was in my throat as we nose-dived and slammed into the sea, only to begin the ascent again. Rise . . . Pause . . . Drop . . . SLAM! Over and over and over.

On the chart, I had made a dot just north of Bermuda and marked it as the goal. For the past ten days, I had concentrated on that dot and scrutinized the inches between it and our position. On the eleventh of June, when the weather finally calmed, I took another sun sight, crossed it with the RDF bearing and found myself 40 miles north of Bermuda on the chart. I swallowed hard and stared at the dot. Even allowing for a large margin of error, I couldn't be too far off. The reality quickly sank in. At our present speed, the same time the next day, I could be on land! I gathered my senses and looked around. "The boat is a mess," I thought, "and I must stink like a goat. What will the customs man think if he sees this bedlam?"

I hurriedly began to organize the boat, arranged my papers and then stripped down and took a bucket shower, shivering with the shock of the water. As my body dried under the warm rays of the sun, I noticed I had shed several pounds since leaving New York almost two weeks before.

Next, I began to plan my approach. Memorizing the jagged out-line of Bermuda's reefy coast, I crossed and recrossed the bearings and took countless sun sights to determine the optimum angle for landfall. With one more night at sea before attempting it, I thought it would be good to get a bit of sleep and restore some strength for the morning approach. Every time my eyes closed, something jogged my memory and I'd jump up and pull out all the books and plotting sheets again to recheck the calculations. Many a sailor has tragically ended his journey atop the reefs of Bermuda and I had no intentions of joining the ranks of the unfortunate.

Up all night, I scanned the horizon ahead, peering through the blackness until I saw the objective. There ahead, like a pinprick star flashing its silent call, was the lighthouse marking the entrance to Bermuda. As we slowly closed the distance, I could see the sweeping beacon and, beyond it, the faint glow of lights from civilization. Nothing had ever looked so beautiful. "I'm coming!" I called out. "I'm coming as fast as I can!"

By dawn, the winds had eased mildly to the south. I tacked *Varuna* out to the east and aligned her, by compass and RDF bearings, to the entrance of St. George's Harbour. Approaching, it became possible to make out other sailboats slipping in and out of a narrow corridor of cliffs and, as we crossed the paths of those leaving, I waved to the crews. At the mouth of the harbor, a fishing boat bobbed up and down and I sailed up to it.

"Hello," I called to the elderly couple aboard. "Is there anybody around here that could help me out with a tow? And would you mind calling them on your radio? I have no more electricity and no engine." I was too unsure of my capabilities to risk navigating through the fringing reefs of the entrance or tacking back and forth past the walls of those looming sentinels of cliffs.

"Get some lines ready to throw to us. We'd be happy to tow you in," the skipper called back. They cheerfully pulled in their fishing lines and did the honors.

Fifteen minutes later, at 11:00 A.M., the twelfth of June, after 751 logged miles, I tied *Varuna* up to the dock and hopped ashore. After twelve days at sea, I weaved and wobbled with a severe case of rubber legs. Weathering two sizable storms and a possibly fatal leak, I had taught myself a mongrelized version of celestial navigation, the engine had conked out and we'd had no power. I had truly learned everything the hard way and headed straight for a telephone to call my father.

ollect call from Tania to Ernst," the New York opera-tor's nasal voice crackled over the phone lines. "Will you accept the charges?" A rush of excitement seemed to pour out of the earpiece of the public telephone on the quay.

"Yes! YES!" exploded the familiar voice. "What in the holy hell were you doing out there?" boomed my father, cleaning out my ears in the process. "I have been worried sick. We almost sent out a *search* party. *Hey, everybody! It's Tania!*" he screamed to the rest of the house. "Every skipper in Bermuda is on the lookout for you. Plus the Bermuda Coast Guard."

I smiled as he spoke, and leaned against the wall of the telephone cabin gazing out at the sailboats rafted up together in front of me. Flocks of seagulls squawked and soared across the clear June sky. The St. George's Harbour was a beehive of activity, full of sailboats stopping over on their ways to Europe and the East Coast of the United States. Mopeds zoomed back and forth on the narrow cobble-stoned streets lined with rhododendron. Suntanned crews scurried to and fro with armloads of provisions. Honeymooners sipped Mai Tais on the shady terraces with blooming bougainvillea overlooking the busy harbor. I stood drinking in the wonderful sounds, smells and visions of civilization.

"Tania, are you listening to me? There were other boats that left here the same time as you and arrived in Bermuda in five days! What happened? Oh, thank God you are safe."

"Well, I had a couple of storms and some dead calms and, with no engine, it just took a little longer than expected," I said. "But, Daddy, you know what? All things considered, it wasn't bad."

"Jesus Christ, Tania, I can't stand it. I have to come down and see you right away. Everyone here has been calling me a murderer. But I knew you could do it. I knew it! Do you need any help? I'll bring you whatever you need." The pride in his voice was something I had been waiting to hear since my turbulent early high school days.

"All I really need is something to eat," I said. "If you want, you can come and help me figure out what's wrong with the engine. Otherwise, everything's OK."

"Yah, that's just what I'll do. I'll be down there in two days." We said goodbye, and with my head straight up in the air, I wobbled away from the phone, breathing in the medley of scents associated with a land of sunshine and its inhabitants—grilled hamburgers, carbon monoxide, flowers, coconut suntan oil and warm garbage. I was most certainly the only girl on the small island to have sailed there by herself, and damn proud of it.

One year after being in Bermuda with my father aboard *Pathfinder*, here I was again, but now as the captain of my own vessel. For the first time, I felt initiated into the sailing fraternity as an equal, not just as the daughter of the skipper. Instead, my father arrived to face the new reality of being considered Tania Aebi's father. I found myself standing in pubs, sipping orange juice and comparing notes on navigation, the cantankerous weather and the "bloody Gulf Stream" with other sailors who actually listened to me.

Varuna's diminutive 26 feet was rafted up alongside a 60-foot blue schooner named *Lady Dorothy*, whose Israeli captain, Eli, was a large man of about thirty-five, and whose cook, a Canadian named Doug, was a little older than I. Immediately they took me under their wing and included me in every evening jaunt to the local restaurant, every game of Trivial Pursuit and every rambunctious after-dinner philosophy session under the stars. After my father arrived, they stayed up to all hours drinking Hennessy, preparing meals, comparing sailing routes and regaling each other with tall sailing tales.

My father stayed with me on *Varuna* for one week and paid a mechanic who got the engine purring again. I still hadn't made enough money from my articles to cover the expenses of leaving, plus the repairs, and promised to pay him back as soon as I could. He liberally smeared caulking around all the stanchions and possible leakage points on deck, while I cleaned up after him and raced around on a moped, buying charts, supplies, parts and provisions.

One night, when we sat down to work out the finer points in navigation, he was appalled to discover that I didn't know that two lines of position are needed for a fix. I had been navigating all the way from New York with only one.

He was incredulous. "How? How could you possibly locate this tiny island with your navigation completely screwed up?"

"I dunno," I answered. "I just homed my RDF in on Bermuda."

"You just homed your—ay-yi-yi. No, Tania, face it. You made it here by pure dumb luck." He closed his eyes and shook his head. "Tania, listen to me carefully. There are no RDF beacons that will help you find St. Thomas. You'll have to find it entirely on your own. Do you understand?"

"Yeah, sure. I know. But I had a lot of bad weather and hardly any time to work on my navigation. I'll get the hang of it on the way to St. Thomas."

He grimaced in pain. "You better get the hang of it. If you miss St. Thomas, you'll end up in Puerto Rico. If you miss Puerto Rico, God knows where you'll end up. You better be sure you understand everything before you leave. Ask Eli next door how to use the sextant properly. Bleed him dry of everything he knows."

"I will, I will, OK?" Truth be told, I was too embarrassed to let on that I was still having problems with this fine art. So far, there had been nothing that I couldn't figure out on my own by trial and error, or from books, and I was comfortable with the idea of keeping it that way.

Shortly after my father left, on my tenth day in Bermuda, I came face to face with another problem that was a little more pressing, a problem that would continue to haunt me for the entire voyage— leaving a safe haven behind and heading back out to sea alone. It took me two days of procrastination to cast off from Bermuda, from calling home for the last time until the fateful moment when I bid my last farewell to the crew of *Lady Dorothy*. Finally, I forced myself to stutter out the words.

"Well, guys," I said tentatively, "I guess I'm really off now." For me, no word will ever be more difficult to utter than "goodbye."

With my stomach in a constricted knot, on June 20, beneath another Bermuda-perfect sky, I waved to my friends and steered *Varuna* under power through the buoyed pass and reefs out of the harbor. The droning hum of helicopters, airplanes, cars and motorboats filled my ears when I turned off the engine, raised the mainsail and jib and set the Monitor self-steering on a compass course heading south to St. Thomas.

The rhythm of the gentle winds from the northwest helped push *Varuna* out of sight of land and calm my nerves, frayed from four days of preparations for departure. That evening, I pulled out the logbook and made the first entry.

"The weather today is warm and beautiful, we're jogging along at 5 knots, and already I miss Bermuda. The crew of Lady Dorothy *gave me a net vegetable hammock, which is now hanging above the starboard berth and filled with the bounty of Bermuda: onions, potatoes, green apples, limes and carrots. The cornucopia swinging above my head is a sweet reminder of* Varuna's *first landfall, now just a memory in our wake.*

"The past ten days have been a whirl of repairs to the boat, drying out her damp recesses, provisioning, studying my navigation, writing an article, trying to get some sleep, talking to tons of people and listening to Daddy. My whole visit to Bermuda flew by in a flurry of errands, shopping and mechanics. Now that we're finally underway, all I can think of is going back. I'll try to sleep now and forget about it all."

Psychologically, the first couple of days at sea were the most difficult to accept. After being abruptly cut off from civilization—the tearful frenzy of goodbyes, the tense conning of the boat out of a congested harbor and the dwindling proximity of land and its solidity—it took me a while to adjust to the radically altered life condition. It felt almost impossible to slow down and swallow the sudden peace and quiet, as my mind worked overtime conjuring up navigational nightmares and weather worries. Over it all, homesickness loomed like a dark cloud.

But, as the days went by, my inner clock gradually slowed down. It was as if my metabolism eventually calmed and my thoughts were able to attain a degree of clarity difficult to achieve on land, where everyday distractions buried the instinct for introspection. My senses were heightened by the simplest of tasks—trimming the sails, brushing my hair, studying the water or even slicing a carrot for a stew. They completely isolated themselves from one another and each became the most important thing at that moment.

But it would take several ocean passages before I could begin to understand how well—when there is no alternative—our bodies can adapt to a given environment. On this, only my second passage and the first day out of Bermuda, it was impossible for me to know that this contentment would always be mine. All I knew was that, for some reason, tomorrow would be better than today, and I went to sleep that night longing for the new dawn.

Our course for St. Thomas, a 900-mile passage that was expected to take about ten days, led directly into the Bermuda Triangle. The storied perils of that infamous area, whose boundaries comprised a vague triangle connecting Miami, Puerto Rico and Bermuda, had been built up from a century of fanciful stories about disappearances and extraterrestrials. Not being the overly superstitious sort, I pressed onward without much trepidation, half hoping to feel the legendary force field or sense the presence of a watching R2D2. But these idle musings were overshadowed by an eerier vision of a different sort as *Varuna* plowed into the Sargasso Sea, a free-floating swamp of seaweed in the middle of the Atlantic.

The clockwise spiraling of the North Atlantic ocean currents corrals the lumpy fields of Sargasso weed into an area of 100 square miles and up to 30 feet deep. Even Christopher Columbus on his journey to the New World wrote about being mired for days in the yellow-greenish hydro-mistletoe.

Varuna's experience may not have been quite as dramatic as Columbus's, but on day three out of Bermuda, the weed indeed came a-knocking, winding itself around *Varuna*'s rudder, the paddle of the self-steering gear and the propeller of the taffrail log, trailed to determine the speed and distance covered. Our speed decreased by two knots, and most of my time was spent hanging over the stern with the boat hook, trying to unseat the unworthy passengers.

As far as I could see, the berrylike bladders of the plants bubbled up through the warm water like an ugly alien bouillabaisse. Plodding slowly on, I had hideous nightmares of camouflaged creatures of the black lagoon, as big as the Empire State Building, just lurking in wait for me.

Varuna found it slow going through the Sargasso, with its squalls and dearth of wind, and after I had spent three days warring with the clinging weeds, the trade winds finally arrived. They introduced themselves slowly at first, with one gust—*poof!*—then another. I gleefully turned off the engine that had been vibrating my skull for seventy-two hours and prepared to acquaint myself and *Varuna* with the trades, the steady winds that dominate the tropics and subtropics around the world.

Southeasterly and moderate, they streamed overhead with uniform puffy white clouds dancing like Valkyries across the sky. In the freshening breeze, the last remnants of the Sargasso finally floated in our wake. The waves built up into an easterly swell and *Varuna*'s sails filled with the wind that for hundreds of years has propelled sailors across the trade routes of the world. We were on the road again.

This was the trade-wind belt, where we would remain for half our voyage around the globe. There was still some southing to do before we could run straight downwind with it, and *Varuna* leaned her shoulder to beat into the chop. Bracing myself against the spray hood, I watched the seawater run over the lee side of the deck, but unfortunately, not all of it drained through the scuppers to rejoin the ocean. Rather, some of it dripped below by way of those weepy chain plates and dribbled into the spice locker. If I procrastinated pumping out the locker for more than one hour, it overflowed onto my bed and proceeded to submerge all the food in the locker beneath the mattress. I hand-pumped the locker every hour thereafter—day and night—for four days. Finally, the wind eased to a more comfortable easterly direction, *Varuna* was able to straighten up a little and the leaks slowed.

My spare time between pumpings was spent trying to figure out where we were by dead reckoning and the occasional sun sights, which more often than not still weren't working out the way they should have. I kept changing sail and course according to my latest calculations until the estimated afternoon before landfall. Sitting in the cockpit, confident that I would be enjoying a cold Coca-Cola in St. Thomas the next day, I spied a ship on the horizon and hailed it on the VHF radio just to make sure. The radio operator's satellite fix notified me that, with our present course and position, *Varuna* would hit land somewhere in the middle of Puerto Rico. Shocked, not to mention a little worried about my dubious talents, I thanked him, signed off and quickly readjusted our course to the southeast.

Once her sails were trimmed, *Varuna* heeled over, washing her rail underwater, and headed as close into the wind as possible. Throughout the rest of the day and into the night, I fidgeted and scanned the horizon with nerve endings that were livewires of anticipation. The skyline was unchanged from earlier on in the passage, but soon, I hoped, land would begin to appear in the vast emptiness.

As the night progressed and the moon crossed the sky, I searched for that feeble little glow of life from the horizon that would become distinct separate lights by twilight, and by dawn would unfold the panorama of hills. I was anxious to get to land and very edgy. What if the island we were approaching wasn't St. Thomas? Ever so slowly the sun rose and, after having chewed my fingernails to the quick, I became more certain. Finally, the indistinguishable lump of land on the horizon separated into the fringing islets that were identifiable on the chart. The new agony of it all was that we were approaching nirvana at only three miles per hour! I could have walked faster than *Varuna* was sailing and I felt like jumping off the boat and running over the water to land.

It seemed to take forever before the pass between the Virgin Islands of St. John and St. Thomas became distinct. Finally, the verdant hills, littered with the satellite dishes, flashing radio towers and water cachements of St. Thomas towered behind the islets of Hans Lollik and Little Tobago ahead, and St. John glimmered in the rising sunlight to the east. *Varuna* seemed to sniff the land, too, and sped up as we threaded our way through the clear turquoise waters of the island chain.

The wind funneled around the south side of St. John and up through the passage, hitting us right on the nose. I turned on the engine for maneuverability through the choppy interisland currents and eddies and carried on, scrutinizing the shoaling waters. Just as we passed an exposed rock frothing with waves, put-put . . . put . . . pa . . . nothing.

"God *dammit!*" I screamed, throwing over the helm and turning *Varuna* on a tack toward St. John. "Why me? Of all the people on the planet that have engines, why does mine have to be such a bloody lemon?"

Still ranting, I scrambled down into the cabin and ferreted a screwdriver out of the toolbox. With a wild eye on land and boats, I dismantled the storage compartment in the middle of the cockpit, under which was the engine cover. As quickly as possible, I un-screwed the dozen stainless steel screws bolting down the cover to get to the engine under the floor of the cockpit. "Why? Why couldn't it break while I was at sea and not when I'm in the middle of a bunch of islands!" I continued my litany as jerry cans, sailbags, funnels, and coiled lines from the storage compartment fell on my head from the cockpit seat where I had thrown them. One screw refused to loosen, having oxidized itself to the aluminum thread. Just short of breaking the cover in frustration, I threw everything back into the cockpit and grabbed the harbor chart. The only way to get into the harbor and anchor was under sail. I pored over the channel and entrance markers and then headed *Varuna* back toward St. Thomas, tacking her gingerly back and forth through the eye of the wind, making slow progress into a channel congested with rocks and transparent shallows.

Inch by inch we rounded the south side of the island and sailed into Charlotte Amalie Harbor, which was bustling with at least a hundred boats at anchor and skirted with cruise ships, ferries and a busy-looking harbor front. Scouting out a clear spot with plenty of leeway at the back of the fleet to drop the anchor, I maneuvered *Varuna* over to it and, at the right second, headed her into the wind, rushed to the bow and dropped the hook. The chain paid out and hit the bottom; I waited to feel it dig in as we drifted back a bit, then let out about 75 feet of scope and cleated the whole thing off.

At 1:30 P.M. on July 1, I turned proudly and looked around the busy harbor; no one had noticed my spectacular entrance. I inflated the dinghy, rowed ashore to the Yacht Haven dock, bought that longed-for Coca-Cola and stood surveying my surroundings.

The urge to talk to somebody, anybody, after the ocean passage was more overwhelming than I ever could have predicted, and I looked hungrily around the docks for an unsuspecting victim. Grinning, I said Hi to everybody and had the feeling that if someone so much as uttered a "So, how was the trip?" floodgates of giddy description would burst open. Deciding to call home instead, I headed for a pay phone.

Soon after my arrival, my younger sister, Jade, joined me in St. Thomas, and brought with her my new crew member, Dinghy. One week before leaving New York, I had gone uptown to the ASPCA on 96th Street to adopt a cat. I was determined to sail with a friend, and if it had to be of the feline variety, that was all right with me. There, among the pathetic prisoners all desperately lashing out at the bars on their cages, I found the cat that was destined to sail with me halfway around the world. He was one year old, black, except for his white paws, face and belly. I had read that a black cat was good luck on a boat.

The last thing I needed was a frustrated tomcat, so Dinghy's departure for the wild blue yonder had been delayed to accommodate a neutering trip to the veterinarian. I had left New York with lots of cat food, cat litter and vitamins, but no cat. Once set free on board, Dinghy immediately curled up to sleep in the spot that was to become his favorite from then on—anywhere that was the most inconvenient for me. One night, he fell off the dock into the water, quickly learning that he loathed swimming, and from then on he seemed extra careful about his footing.

Jade stayed with me for two weeks and together we dinghied

around St. Thomas, went swimming, and took a ferry to St. John for carnival. Rio de Janeiro and Trinidad had fired our images of carnival and we pictured wild costumes, parties, singing, dancing and calypso. Sitting in a restaurant overlooking the streets, we were pretty disappointed to see drunken tourists and locals stumble along to the blaring rhythm of reggae and disco, pumped full volume from old trucks. No colorful costumes lent an air of gaiety to the spectacle and, stuck there until we could catch the morning ferry back to St. Thomas, we reminisced about other July Fourths in other places, found a couple of unoccupied benches away from the fanfare and fell asleep under the tropical night sky.

Back on *Varuna*, I vowed to solve the problem of the engine and leaky chain plates and found a local jack-of-all-trades, Mike, who had some experience with boats and offered to help. While Jade worked on a tan to impress her friends, Mike came aboard and immediately pointed to where I had put a hard epoxy over a flexible silicon, which my father had covered over again with more silicon. Mike shook his head. "There's your problem. The chain plates flex when they're under pressure," he explained, "and they need to have some give. The epoxy cracked and your father's silicon never stuck to it. He just went and made a bad leak worse."

Together, we scraped away all the compounds around the chain plates and started all over again with a super-strong flexible polyurethane bedding compound. The screw on the engine cover was removed with proper tools and lubricated. I still didn't know where the air leak in the engine came from, and Mike couldn't find it either, so after bleeding the fuel line, we decided that all systems were go. I saw a dark brown Jade off at the airport. The lockers were filled with fresh vegetables, long-life juices and more cat supplies and, on July 18, 1985, *Varuna*, Dinghy and I sailed out of the harbor.

Except for missing Jade, I shed no tears over leaving the busy port of Charlotte Amalie, with its five cruise ships a day of tourists swarming the streets in a mad rush of duty-free shopping, and its fast-food joints, Shop Rite and boutiques. Our next destination was Panama, the funnel into the Pacific, and except for the prospect of the lonely passage, I was eager to be under way and log some real miles between *Varuna* and the commercialism of home.

Upon leaving the Virgin Islands, we were once again in the trade winds, but this time running with them. This was *Varuna's* most glorious point of sail; with the wind at her back, her jib poled out on one side and her main let all the way out on the other, she went her fastest and the motion was the most comfortable. Because this was the beginning of hurricane season, I began to steer a course that skirted south of their stomping grounds toward the coasts of Venezuela and Colombia. The first night, I sat in the cockpit and watched the glimmer of Puerto Rico, St. John and St. Croix disappear under the inky horizon. With the sails and Monitor set, I stretched out under the stars and enjoyed our speed. We were making 6 knots, sometimes 10, as we surfed down the waves. In the first twenty-four hours, *Varuna* logged 129 miles into the 1,056 miles to go. "Wow," I thought, "at this speed, I'll be in Panama in no time flat."

The trip was promising so far except for one unfortunate situation: poor Dinghy was terrified and frantic, trying to figure out why our home was sloshing around like a washing machine. He hid inside the cabin meowing, his legs splayed out in all directions as he tried to minimize the motion. With eyes like saucers and ears straight up in a state of panic, he was probably wishing he were back in New York at the ASPCA. "It's OK, Mr. Dinghy," I consoled him, "this is how it's supposed to be." Hearing the sound of my voice, he would hesitantly venture out of the cabin and sniff the air. Every little wave would send him meowing back inside. Feeling responsible and guilty for his misery, I was reminded of myself on that first day out of New York, and I had to laugh.

"Don't worry, little buddy," I said, "you'll get used to it in a hurry. Just be glad you came aboard in the trades."

I was happy to have another living being on *Varuna* upon whom I could lavish attention. I felt ridiculous talking to myself, but now there was somebody who would at least perk up his ears at a noise. There was a warm body to cuddle up with at night and with whom to share a meal. After a while Dinghy began to acclimatize himself to his new lifestyle. On July 19, I wrote in my logbook, *"Dinghy finally ventured outside and even stayed a while. With his black and white coat, he looks like a dinner guest in tie and tails. I'm finding little fish stranded on deck and offer them to him, but he turns up his nose. I awoke this morning to find him in good spirits, mutilating all my rolls of toilet paper."*

With the trade winds, *Varuna*'s motion was steady and swift and she remained upright. I thanked God for small favors and enjoyed living aboard a level home, no longer having to sleep, eat, write or change sails in a vessel that was heeled over at a 30-degree angle. I no longer had to walk on the walls of a house that felt as if it had fallen over on its side. The sails didn't have to be changed once on this entire trip other than for little tweaks and adjustments to the course. The wind remained steady and true at about 25 knots from east. For a couple of days the waves swelled and broke over the Monitor into the cockpit. But no matter what happened, I just rejoiced as the taffrail log ticked away the miles. "No more of this nonsense about beating into the wind anymore," I thought. "Now, I'm just going to zoom my way around the world with the wind at my back."

For the first time, my days took on a shape and character. I awoke with the sun, around five-thirty or six. *Varuna* was heading west and the rising sun in the east shone in through the companionway and right onto my bed. The sun was my alarm clock, and if a pillow over my head permitted me a few extra minutes of sleep, Dinghy would prod me with his nose and begin walking all over me, anxious for breakfast. When the sun rose to about 15 degrees above the horizon, I would take the first sight with the sextant, then calculate and plot it on the chart. The next one was at noon and, in the meantime, I worked around the boat, making repairs, rearranging things, cleaning out the litter box, reading, munching away on crackers or fruit. At noon, after taking the second sight and crossing the lines of position with the earlier one, what I thought was an exact fix could be established. By then the sun was at its zenith and *Varuna* turned into an oven. During the afternoon, it was too hot to do anything too strenuous other than fitfully read, munch and drink, and throw buckets of water over my head. This simple way of life was broken up by the odd ship wandering over the horizon, or frighteningly nearby, with whose radio operator I would chat over the VHF.

I was becoming very much at home with myself and content with my monastic lifestyle, knitting or crocheting when the text of my books began to blur. Loneliness was never a problem, although whenever there was a particularly beautiful sight before my eyes, and there were many—a breathtaking sunset, a pod of pilot whales or a herd of cavorting, squealing dolphins playing in *Varuna*'s bow wave—I wished there were someone to share the moment or to share my enthusiasm when a sun sight worked out. Dinghy was there, but he didn't get too excited.

In the evenings, after the sun had made its full arc across the sky, the temperature cooled and I'd pull out my pressure cooker, chop up an onion, potato or cabbage, mix in a can of something and a cube of bouillon and make my meal for the day. This became standard fare and I never tired of it. I fed Dinghy, celebrated the sunset, then curled up in my bed again to read until the Sandman arrived.

I made my permanent bed on the port bunk with a lee cloth tied by two lines to the rail above on the ceiling stretching the length and forming a sort of cradle that stopped me from falling out as the boat tossed around. I arranged a sleeping bag inside the cradle for maximum comfort and I'd bundle up in this cocoon with Dinghy, as *Varuna* rocked us to sleep.

For my stimulation-starved unconscious, sleeping at sea was an adventure of its own. Every time I drifted off, my imagination created a dream world gone wild. Often, I'd awaken, calling out to somebody or reaching up to grab for a roast chicken, an ice cream cone or a fresh salad. After the food dreams, which were the worst, I could never go back to sleep and worked myself up into a state of salivation over the gastronomic mirage. Upon awakening, I would reach up onto the shelf above my head for the flashlight, pull myself out of bed and go outside to check the course and the horizon. Black shadows of clouds cloaked the constellations that were becoming as familiar and reassuring to me as old friends. There was Orion, the hunter, and the Dippers, twinkling signposts in the indigo sky. Occasionally on the horizon, the tiny green, red and white lights of a ship plowing to its unknown destination reminded me that I wasn't the only one left on the planet.

"The wind diminished a little today," I wrote on July 21, *"and, oddly enough, I don't miss land very much any more. On perfect days like today, I feel as though I could live autonomously on* Varuna *and happily sail the oceans of the world forever."*

Two days before our estimated arrival in Panama, the jutting curve of Colombia blocked the trades and wind dwindled to zero. Ships and tankers followed and passed us by, bound for the Canal and Costa Rican ports. *Varuna* chugged along under power after them, eager to join her big brothers at the Canal and, with them, leave the Atlantic behind. An electric excitement thickened the air that evening as we slowly inched toward our rendezvous with one of the greatest of manmade phenomena. But, as night fell, Mother Nature created excitement of another kind.

By nine-thirty, thunder booms and fiery lightning began to cut through the air. I quickly battened things down and closed all the hatches as rain began hammering the deck as if trying to pound *Varuna* to the depths. Relentless drumbeats of thunder deafened me, and the night sky was alight with the strobe of jagged-edged lightning bolts crackling down to the water. I huddled below for nine hours, holding a quivering Dinghy in my arms, sweating in terror of the heavenly Armageddon, crying, praying and waiting for the fateful moment that *Varuna*'s mast would be hit by a megavolt and we'd be burned to crisps. The thought of her little lightning-rod mast, the only object of height for miles around, petrified me into a motionless trance until the fury of each thunder squall finally wore itself out and died away. Two days later, on July 27, when I called my father from Panama, he informed me that my worries were for naught. *Varuna* had been fully grounded at the factory and, theoretically, we were safe from electrocution.

More than a country, the narrow Isthmus of Panama is an enigma that connects by a crooked finger the vast continents of North America and South America. But Panama—everybody's lover but nobody's child—wears a deep scar of progress across her slim wrist. That scar is called the Panama Canal. For me, the canal represented only a gateway to the Pacific. I didn't think too much about the living, breathing country outside the barbed-wire fences of the manicured, 10-mile-wide Canal Zone. But, by the time *Varuna* had traveled through the awesome lock system, I had not only seen another side of Panama, but I would begin to uncover another side of myself.

On the morning of July 27, after nine days' sailing from St. Thomas, *Varuna* closed the coast and joined the international parade of ships passing the immense jetty and entering the deep-water anchorage for vessels awaiting transit through the canal. A sailboat out on a jaunt turned around and sailed toward us. The lone sailor hollered over, the sound once again of a human voice unbroken by radio static.

"Hey, are you Tania?" he called, waving.

"Yes! Hello!" I called back, waving my hand out of whack.

"Welcome to Panama," he said. "We've been waiting for you."

After checking in with customs and immigration, I tied up in the marina near a sign that said Cristóbal Yacht Club and went ashore. The yacht club was bustling with people of many languages preparing their boats to transit the canal, as well as operators of local boats belonging to canal administrators and engineers. The focal spot was the twenty-four-hour bar filled with people lounging around, downing cheap drinks, looking for crew and line handlers, or kicking back after a day of hard work. Not quite the kooky bar out of *Star Wars*, the place had the interesting atmosphere of odd types, lounge lizards, wayfarers and action. Advice was cheap, and I was immediately and repeatedly warned about the danger of crossing alone over the railroad tracks that separated the club's premises from the surrounding town of Colón.

"There is danger," one canal operator warned me. "Every day, people are being mugged, raped and murdered in Colón."

"Please do not go there by yourself," stressed another.

"I'm from New York City," I said. "How violent could Colón possibly be compared to that?" The first operator answered with stories of people's fingers being cut off for rings, of men being forced to surrender their shorts, of individuals threatened with knives, and of chains being ripped from around necks. To make peace, I promised that I wouldn't press my luck and would only venture into town during daylight or with other people.

They were right. But, seeing it for myself, I couldn't help thinking that there was an exciting Latin air to the place, aside from the fact that crime really was rampant, every kind of drug was available and stolen goods were hawked left and right in the streets. The city was lined with dilapidated colonial housing around a teeming market, with double-decker tenements and projects surrounding the old French and Spanish quarters. The thumping bass beat of salsa and disco blared from every open window, laundry hung limply between the buildings and crooked TV antennas clung to the roofs. Old American bombers of cars sputtered up and down worn streets, while the reputed Latin temper flared on every corner.

The second day after my arrival, after traveling by bus to Panama City to get some traveler's checks and coming home late at night, I missed my stop, ending up in the middle of Colón. I had to walk alone through town back to the harbor, an action that flew in the face of every warning I had received since my arrival. On the doorsteps and stoops were shadows who cat-called without mercy. That night as I made my way through Colón, I didn't get mugged, but I did observe the pathetic look of a city with a depressing history and dashed hopes.

I didn't want to be one of those people who leaves Panama knowing only one facet of its personality. The more I learned about it, the more this hybrid of a country fascinated me, and I empathized with the Panamanians. Their laboring ancestors had slaved and died over a canal from which they never really profited. Today, the military and a handful of rich families hold the mace of power while the rest of the population is left to fend for itself in a system with different rules for different people.

In the early 1900s, the Americans were granted control within five miles on either side of the canal, establishing the Canal Zone that stretched the 60-mile width of the isthmus. It was cut off from Colón and the rest of the country by a barbed-wire fence and guards until the time the Zone was abolished in 1979, only six years before I arrived.

During my stay at Cristóbal Yacht Club, I met some people who took me to their homes inside the old Zone compound. I saw how the American employees had been provided with modern hospitals, supermarkets, movie theaters, good roads and the semblance of a utopian suburban life in the tropics. In the old days, on the other side of the fence, all the descendants of the people who had struggled to excavate the monstrous canal lived in utter squalor and poverty, probably watching through the barbed wire the everyday workings of the American dream.

If it hadn't been such a luxury for all shipping to be able to use a shortcut over the alternative of going around the dangerous Cape Horn at the southern tip of South America, Panama would still be rain forests belonging to neighboring Costa Rica and Colombia. It was sad to think that I was just another captain out of the thousands of ships using the canal for my convenience and, in a very removed way, contributing to the strife surrounding it.

To get through the canal, I had to spend a few days filling out reams of documents and tramping back and forth in the humid 100-degree weather to one office after another. *Varuna* had to be measured for tonnage to determine the cost of transit and I had to become savvy with the specific procedures of taking my boat through the locks. Every sailboat is required to have four 100-foot-long lines and an equal number of people to handle them, not including the captain of the vessel and a canal pilot. I began to worry about *Varuna* carrying six well-fed grownups.

To get a little experience and to see what was in store, one morning I took passage as a line handler on another sailboat, a common thing to do. While we were tied up to the dock waiting for a ship to pass, a pretty white French ketch motored up beside us. Its crew seemed to be in the midst of a party celebrating their boat's canal entry, and I noticed one of the men staring at me. He smiled and asked in French if I spoke the language. Thoroughly shy about my American accent, I answered, "*Oui*, a little bit."

"*Très bien*," he said, with a nice laugh. "I will speak English. I help this boat go through the canal today. Can you help bring my boat through tomorrow?" His accent was thick and his English halting.

"Well . . ." I hesitated. I really hadn't planned to do it twice in a row before taking *Varuna* through. That would seem to be a waste of time. "Well . . ." I looked at him awaiting my answer. He smiled. "Sure," I said. "I'll help you."

"My name is Luc. We rendezvous tonight at the yacht club in Colón? We will talk, *non?*" The boat he was on began to pull ahead. "What is your name?" he called as they entered the lock.

"Tania!" I called back.

That night, after taking the train back to the yacht club, I waited for Luc at the twenty-four-hour bar filled with "Zonies," those expatriate American Canal operators still living in Panama and helping the Panamanians learn the tricks of the trade. By nine-thirty, I'd had enough of the place and finally gave up on Luc. I went back to *Varuna*, penned a note and went out for ceviche with a kindly ship agent named Adrian who had adopted me soon after my arrival. Together, as we feasted on the spicy raw fish, Adrian shared with me his knowledge of the canal, and he gave me the book *The Path Between the Seas*, which recounted the story of the canal from beginning to end. As we ambled back to *Varuna*, I saw Luc waiting on the dock. "We must be ready at five in the morning," he said. "I come for you with my dinghy."

The next morning, with eyes still glued together, I was presented to his boat, *Thea*, and his crew member, Jean Marie. The couple whose boat Luc had helped bring through the canal, René and Catherine, were aboard also, returning the service, and Trudy, an American from California, was washing the dishes. We drank steaming bowls of strong coffee, European style, waited for the pilot to arrive and talked about who we were and where we were all going after transiting.

I found myself hanging on Luc's every word. He gave me a tour of his rugged 37-foot sailboat and captivated me with stories about his childhood in Africa. He was the son of a captain in the French army who kept moving back and forth across the continent to different stations. Luc had gone back to France to attend college and, since finishing ten years before, his wanderlust and career had taken him to live in New Caledonia in the South Pacific. He was a dreamer, a poet, a gardener of the imagination, with the capabilities and faith to make his dreams come true. A faraway light made his eyes gleam when he told me about the South Pacific.

"Oh, Tania, you are going there also?" he asked. "We must do it together. I will show you things that your cold American eyes would never see otherwise. I will show you places where the mango grows wild and untouched, where there are no footprints in the sand. I will show you waterfalls that will break your heart, and seals and fish that live in such peace that when we swim with them, they will take food from our hands and play with us like little children. I know the South Pacific and its gentle people. Don't hurry through this magnificent island paradise to Australia or you will regret it. Take my word for it, Tania. See the islands with me."

I was speechless. For me, everything that this man said was a paradigm. "I want to be free, Tania. For me, money is simply a way to pay for my freedom. I work only to have enough to sail to the places of beauty on the earth."

"That's *exactly* how I feel," I found myself saying, over and over again. As I told him what I was doing, he said how lucky I was to be able to do it so young. Luc was one of the first people I had met since leaving New York who didn't make me feel like a lunatic for being on a boat alone. He was one of the first people to recognize the beauty of the plan.

"I, too, want to see as much as I can," he said. "Before I die, I want to examine the farthest blossom on the farthest mountain peak." Everything Luc said struck the chords of my own dreams. Sentence by romantic sentence, his eloquent vision of the potential of life painted colors on the blank canvas of my future. I will always remember that day as one of magic energy, of floating on a cloud and of falling in love.

By the end of *Thea*'s canal transit in Panama City, Luc had agreed to help me take *Varuna* through the next day and I had finally pulled out of him that in the world of bills and deadlines and responsibilities, he actually worked as a designer of sewage-treatment plants. This struck me as particularly funny at the moment, although I couldn't find the words in French to explain why. At least I *thought* that's what he said he did for a living. The vagaries of our language barrier were to play several tricks on us in those early days.

That night, I took the train back to the yacht club, began to prepare *Varuna* and waited for Luc to arrive later on. When he came, he helped get all the lines together and we did some last-minute repairs to the engine. At bedtime, I arranged his bedding up in the forepeak, we awkwardly said goodnight and I curled up in my own bunk. After a couple of hours of mutual tossing and turning, I heard Luc get up and quietly come over to my bed. Soundlessly, he caressed my head. I froze and pretended I was asleep. He didn't try to awaken me, but just knelt there and then crept back to his bed.

I had met two young Danish teenagers in Colón who were visiting relatives and wanted to see the canal, as well as the daughter of a yacht club member. With Luc, plus the canal pilot and me, *Varuna* had the requisite four line handlers. They arrived at the dock the next morning and, at o'dark-thirty, we stuffed everyone aboard and headed for the first lock.

Our canal pilot was a serious young trainee named Alberto, who insisted on steering. The first set of massive steel doors opened before us pushing thousands of gallons of water in their path. In front of us, a large tanker motored into the cavernous pen 1,000 feet long and 110 feet wide, with another set of steel doors at the end. On the sides above the lock, little locomotives pulled the ship in and tightened the cables as it reached the proper position. We followed it into the lock, and four burly types launched messenger lines to us, thin ropes with loops and weights at the ends.

As we scrambled around on *Varuna*, our voices echoed off the tall Canal walls while we tied our own four 100-foot lines onto the messengers and the men pulled them up and tied the boat off on four quarters. The steel doors banged shut behind. Every aspect of our environment—the air, the water, the walls—reverberated with the groan and grind of tons of meeting steel, rushing water, machinery and turbines.

We were in the hands of this Cyclopean mechanical system from here until the top of the system at the level of Gatun Lake. We rose as the deluge of fresh water was pumped in from the lake, and *Varuna* strained to break free from her lashings, but the men on shore tightened the lines and took up the slack. I shared every captain's worst fear and imagined my boat breaking free and tossing around in this boiling vat like a rubber ducky.

When all was still, the far set of gates leading into the second lock opened and we waited while the massive propellers of the ship ahead churned into action and eased its bulk forward. We repeated this procedure twice, passed on through the third lock and motored out onto the peace of Gatun Lake, 85 feet above sea level. To the right rose the immense wall of the Gatun Dam, built from the excavation of Culebra Cut ahead, which blocked off the Chagres River and created Gatun Lake.

"The total amount of dirt dug from the entire canal prism," Alberto told us, "would be enough to build a Great Wall of China from San Francisco all the way to New York City." We were quiet as *Varuna* chugged from channel marker to channel marker, 23 miles across the serene beauty of Gatun Lake. The giant man-made pool was full of birds and trees that grew like castaways on little island tufts popping above the water. The boughs of other, less fortunate trees, submerged when the land was sacrificed to the lake, protruded above the surface and appeared to be struggling for a last breath of life.

The panorama that surrounded *Varuna* was an eerie one. On my third voyage through the canal in as many days, the submerged trees were becoming symbols, reminders of the land and the country that had existed there before the ambitious canal project. If only the trees could talk, I thought, what stories they could tell of toil and tribulation and time swept away.

Alberto told us of how the French were the first to attempt to create the path between the seas in 1879. To dig the canal, the French contractors imported black Caribbean islanders, Central and South Americans, Italians, Greeks and Chinese. In horrendous swampy working conditions, diseases like malaria, yellow fever, tuberculosis, typhus and cholera festered, with a toll of 25,000 dead. "People dropped like flies," said Alberto. The French desperately brought in new reinforcements, but despite ten years of trying, bankruptcy, loss of faith in the project and the complete depletion of their manpower resources forced them to give up, and the Americans had jumped in.

Luc and I sat together at *Varuna*'s bow and watched Alberto line up the channel alignment points that were set up on the hills in front and behind us. Two markers had to be lined up, one on top of the other, to let us know we were on course. When they separated, we knew that *Varuna* had drifted off the course, and therefore out of the channel, and we would hurriedly rearrange our position.

We approached Culebra Cut between Gatun Lake and the first descent in the Pedro Miguel Lock, while I went below and made sandwiches. I felt bad, knowing that everybody could have been on bigger and more comfortable boats, so I tried to make up for it with a feast. If nothing else, *Varuna*'s crew would be well fed.

"You see here?" said Alberto, with his mouth full of ham-and-cheese sandwich. "This channel dug through the cliffs was the worst stretch in the whole construction. Here, the workers had to dig through the Continental Divide, three hundred and ten feet high and nine miles wide. After completing one-third of the work, these mountains were what destroyed the French. When the Americans took over, they hired eighty six thousand people; seven thousand of those died."

We looked at the corridor of reddish-brown cliffs that lined the passage. As Alberto told of the hundreds of times the dynamite had exploded prematurely, killing many people, the immense scope of the statistics began to blur. But there was no denying the awesomeness of the Canal; the toll of its building was legendary. Even the great French painter Paul Gauguin survived his stint as a common laborer on the project. I remembered a West Indian poem from Adrian's book: "The flesh of man flew in the air like birds many days."

Varuna descended the Pedro Miguel lock to the Mira Flores Lake and then down the Mira Flores locks in much the same way she ascended. The only difference was that this time the water emptied instead of filling and the commotion was much less severe. After fifteen hours, we chugged out into the Pacific. As we motored alongside the jetty of Balboa Yacht Club, I bid Alberto farewell, as well as my other line handlers. They hopped ashore as Luc fended *Varuna* from the dock and we motored to pick up one of the moorings for the night.

"*Thea* is anchored in Taboga," said Luc, after everyone had departed. "It is not far from here. If you want, we can sail there, Tania, and be together."

He could do or say nothing wrong. We struggled to communicate, I with my rusty French and he with his broken English. But, somehow, we got our stories across. Or so I thought. Already I had visions of sailing to the ends of the earth with Luc. We untied *Varuna* from her mooring the next evening and began sailing the 5 miles to Taboga, my first Pacific island. In the pitch darkness, the glimmering lights on the horizon were like harbingers of my future and I sailed toward them in hopeful anticipation.

n the sixteenth century, on his voyage to the New World, Magellan entered the Pacific Ocean and, finding it as smooth as baby's skin, christened it El Pacifico, the peaceful one. As far as the Europeans were concerned, he had discovered this ocean, and at that time, he couldn't have known that the great body covered one-third of the earth's surface and gave rise to vicious storms. Over four hundred years later, as *Varuna* forged out of the Panama Canal and away from the only ocean she had ever known, neither did I. The next year would be spent discovering the islands of the Pacific. It was to be an ocean of revelations, farewells and new beginnings.

Taboga Island is to Panama City what the Hamptons on Long Island are to New York. During the week the pace was slow and workaday, but come Friday afternoon a daily ferry disgorged a crowd of families dressed in their Sunday best, who swamped the small hotel and the empty village cottages for the weekend. Arriving midweek, we had the place to ourselves.

Our first day in Taboga, we followed stone paths lined with flowery, sweet-scented bushes and hedges that threaded through the tiny community. Children played in the streets while mothers washed and hung laundry to dry on their terraces and backyards. We counted about five cars on the island, which made for an odd contrast with carriages drawn by donkeys, their heads bowed down in the searing heat as their tails swished away hordes of flies.

Varuna, *Thea* and a third boat, *Saskia*, rolled on their anchors off the beach with the incoming swell. That evening, we watched the sunset from the terrace of a small open-air restaurant overlooking the harbor containing ten little fishing boats, our three sailboats and, in the distance, as if put out to pasture, two ancient hulks of fishing seiners. Several knobby green islands protected the exposed harbor from the Pacific beyond.

"I will show you everything beautiful in the world, Tania," Luc said over dinner. Squirming, I looked down at my untouched plate of shrimp as the waitress came to clear it away. Life was getting complicated.

From the first day on, *Saskia*, *Thea* and *Varuna* formed a sailing community, with *Thea* as the nucleus. She was the biggest, most commodious boat, stocked with the best food, and compared to *Varuna*, whose living space was hard-pressed to accommodate one small person, the 37-foot *Thea* seemed palatial.

One of Luc's favorite pastimes was cooking. He loved to conjure up gastronomic feasts from his galley, perfectly situated so that the chef was never alienated from the table's festivities. I joined in the teasing and jokes when sharing breakfast, lunch and dinner with these French musketeers, and in return washed the dishes whenever Jean Marie got tired of his dishwasher status.

Jean Marie was a Parisian who had been in the air force since he was eighteen. When he finally got out, he was thirty-three and set off immediately to fulfill his lifelong ambition to see the world. He had taken an airplane to Martinique, made the acquaintance of Luc, who was preparing to bring *Thea* to Tahiti, and joined on as crew.

René was from Brittany, a fiercely autonomous region on the northwestern coast of France. His wife had taken a teaching position in Costa Rica and had flown back to her school duties after transiting the canal a week before, leaving him on his own to bring *Saskia* to Costa Rica. René was vehemently French, and in testament, before leaving home, he had visited all the best wine châteaux and had built up an impressive wine cellar in *Saskia*'s bilge and lockers, which were jam-packed with a thousand rag-swathed bottles of every bouquet. The three philosophers would sit around before dinner, sniffing, swirling and admiring as if they were important buyers in Alsace.

René was the character of the group, distinguishable from the other two in many subtle ways, and in one way not so subtle. The only thing René ever wore was his bushy black beard and a beret to cover his balding scalp. That's it. Save for the hat, he paraded around stark naked in all his skinny, suntanned glory. I was taken aback at first, not knowing where to look whenever René approached, until I realized that Luc and Jean Marie never gave him so much as a passing glance. I finally got used to René in the buff, but I always wore my bathing suit.

Luc was the glue that held the group together with the wild stories from his travels and adventures, and the first few nights I went to bed with a pounding head from trying to understand the bawdy French, full of clichés, innuendos and different dialects. Luc's passionate Gallic narrow-mindedness reminded me of my father, and Jean Marie and René reminded me of the rogues' gallery of my father's eccentric friends always huddled around our kitchen table back home—everybody laughing or arguing, full of great stories to tell about the exotic places they had lived and all the crazy things they had done.

During the ribald dinner conversations around *Thea*'s table, my thoughts went back to our loft in New York and the artists, yodeling and fun of those childhood days. Over the years, as my father's artwork finally started meeting with success, he had made a lot of the kind of off-the-wall friends that can only be found in the art world. Most came and went, but the two main fixtures were always Christian and Fritz. Christian, who had immigrated with my father to New York, and Fritz, who arrived soon after, were his oldest friends, and so close to us that they had become part of the family.

In my father's circle of friends, one hand always washed the other. Once, before Fritz met success with his own artwork, he found himself short of cash and my father tried to help him out.

"Fritz, my building needs a paint job," he had said. "If you're interested in doing the job, it's yours."

"Great," Fritz answered. "Ernst, I'll do it right away." My father came back from a trip to Switzerland three weeks later and found his five-story Soho apartment building painted baby blue and covered by a mural of gigantic flying milk cows wearing parachutes. Now, 2,400 miles away from my family and friends, sitting around *Thea*'s table of eccentrics, I was reminded of those days and friends and felt comfortably at home.

I lingered in Taboga for many reasons, not the least of which was Luc. But also, *Varuna*, as well as *Thea* and *Saskia*, needed repairs and some general maintenance to prepare for the next passage. Luc and

I helped each other, René spent his days methodically fixing things around *Saskia* and Jean Marie amused himself wandering around the island. On one of his excursions, Jean Marie met a striking elderly beauty who owned a Popsicle stand on the beach. He brought her out to *Thea* on our third evening at Taboga.

"This is Kerima de Lescure. She is very special," said Jean Marie, "I wanted you to meet her." Kerima spoke no French or English, so we had to get by with Jean Marie's broken Spanish, filled in by lots of sign language. But when she spied Luc's guitar, the communication problems were over. She picked it up and began to sing the songs of a dreaming, stargazing poet. Every evening at her Popsicle stand, she would read to us from one of her volumes of poetry, always referring to *el sol* and *las estrellas*, the sun and the stars. Easily enchanted, Kerima was fascinated by my voyage and Dinghy and often repeated with her tinkling laugh, *"Muchacha solita con su gatito,"* little girl alone with a cat.

One day, in a fit of back-to-business, the three guys put their brains and hands together to fix the starter of Luc's engine, a dirty job. The day was a scorcher, so for relief while they sweated, I jumped overboard to scrub *Varuna's* bottom. If left unattended for long, the hull began to attract all sorts of marine life and barnacles which would hamper speed when we were finally under way. Dinghy meowed down at me from the deck, while with a mask, snorkel and a coarse brush, I dived under the boat to scrub away the plants. *Varuna's* underbody looked as if it had five o'clock shadow, and as I scrubbed, tufts of the hairy green beard floated down and dropped away. Even though all the barnacles growing on her underbody had died and fallen off after passing through the fresh water of the Canal, it was quite a job scouring off what was left. The results were worth the effort. *Varuna's* speed, with a clean bottom, increased by at least half a knot, sometimes more.

All of a sudden, with one-quarter of the boat done, a burning sensation rushed over my body and, within seconds, I was in agony. Unable to scream, I also couldn't pinpoint exactly from where the pain was coming. It seemed to overwhelm me from everywhere—arms, shoulders, back, guts. Panicking, I surfaced, somehow managed to pull myself up on deck and began to go into shock.

Luc looked up from his starter toward *Varuna* and, seeing that something was wrong, threw down his tools, jumped into the dinghy and roared over, followed by Jean Marie and René. I had been caught in the tentacles of a giant man-of-war jellyfish, and the barbed threads of its venom were still stuck to my back, dribbling around my stomach and over my arms. Luc and Jean Marie tried to pull off the phlegmy filaments while René jumped back into his dinghy and headed to *Saskia* to concoct a Breton old wives' remedy of clay powder and water to paste on the welts appearing all over my body. As the initial shock began to subside, I started to tremble, imagining the size of the Medusa that had hugged me.

I felt lucky to have had friends around to come to my aid, and the numb jellyfish welts were merely a red badge of courage for two days before they slowly disappeared with the help of René's soothing potion. When all was well, we decided to reprovision the boats and prepare to head out to the Perlas Islands, 50 miles into the Bay of Panama. On one of our last nights with Kerima, she composed a poem and did a painting on a T-shirt of Dinghy and *Varuna* at anchor and presented it to me as a gift. With Kerima's fingers elegantly fluttering over the guitar strings, Luc by my side and *Varuna* shipshape enough to take on the world, life felt like a series of endless possibilities.

During our ten days on the Pacific side of Panama, the only wind we had encountered had been very light day breezes. Otherwise, conditions had been benign, so we didn't worry much that the anchorage area of the Club de Yates y Pescas off Panama City was unprotected. After all, we were only going there for two days.

I had been lulled into a sort of complacency by the relatively tideless Caribbean. The Pacific was a new ocean to me; I had yet to know her moods and learned quickly that one should assume nothing with the sea. Although the boats were anchored nearly 1,000 feet offshore, the depth sounder indicated that the bottom was still a shallow 20 feet. But that's good, we rationalized, it'll be easier to pull up the chain when we leave.

Jean Marie prepared a spaghetti dinner that evening aboard *Thea*, and René brought two bottles of bordeaux. As I hopped in the dinghy and rowed over to join them, Dinghy became agitated and meowed across the water, calling me back to *Varuna*. During dinner, the tide began to ebb and a swell built up over the sloping underwater shelf and shallow bottom. I felt the increased rolling of *Thea* and went out on deck to check on the other boats.

"Oh my God!" I screamed. "René, come here fast! The waves are breaking next to *Saskia!*" He scrambled up on deck and saw that the tide was on a roll, moving out from under our feet. As we watched helplessly, the breakers retreated farther and farther back until they started unfurling over *Varuna*, then *Thea*.

Just as the reality of the situation penetrated, a wave came up from behind and swamped over *Thea*'s high transom. There was no way for us to row to our boats without great risk. It was like watching a cascading surf line on a Hawaiian beach from behind. Each wave picked up *Saskia* and then *Varuna*, throwing them on their sides and burying our homes under avalanches of filthy water. Screaming reassurances over to Dinghy, who was crying, echoing my fear, I tried not to think about the sewers that emptied into the bay nearby. All *Varuna*'s portholes were open and I cringed to think of the stinking wet cabin that would await me when I was able to get back.

For six hours, through the tide cycle, we helplessly watched our boats pitch and roll, while the sea level dropped an astonishing 15 feet. One more foot and *Varuna*, with her 4-foot draft, would be aground. *Saskia* already was; every wave landed her with sickening thuds. Fortunately, the bottom was soft mud, which is good holding ground, and the anchors held fast. When the tide rose, René and I dinghied back over the calmed waters to survey the mess. Climbing on board and hugging Dinghy, I could have kicked myself for not having anticipated such a devastating tide and finding out about it before leaving the boat. I vowed that it would never happen again.

A day later, after moving to another anchorage, while provisioning in the crowded marketplace in Panama City, we heard a man scream. Police and a curious crowd surrounded him and we pressed closer to see what was the matter. Somebody had cut off his finger for a ring. It was time to leave.

On August 20, 1985, I pulled up the anchor, raised the sails, hooked up the autopilot to the tiller, and headed *Varuna* southwest for Contadora in the Archipelago de las Islas Perlas. Many Panamanians to whom we had talked in and around the Canal had told us not to bypass the Perlas. "They are very beautiful. Deer run free on the island of Contadora, and on San José, you will find not a soul. Go and see the real Panama." "Why not?" I thought. "These will be my first semi-isolated Pacific island landfalls."

René had departed earlier that morning and Jean Marie and Luc left at the same time as I. Watching them ahead on the horizon as Taboga shrank away in our wake and the sea began to flow past *Varuna*'s hull, I mused over the happenings of the past two weeks. Luc was at the center of my thoughts.

I had never craved solitude. If anything, completely isolating myself from civilization as I was doing in sailing singlehanded on *Varuna* felt more than a little unnatural. Before meeting Luc, I could remember moments of great despair, when I felt I should be surrounded by friends, or finally be having a meaningful relationship with somebody special. Until meeting Luc, I had been having trouble accepting the fact that finding that person would be practically out of the question for the two years it would take me to get home. That thought had made me feel more alone in St. Thomas, Bermuda and Panama than I ever had in the middle of the ocean.

But almost from the moment we met, Luc swept all those fears away. In a matter of days, we had opened up to one another as I had never done before with anybody. He was fifteen years older than I. His gentleness when we were alone belied the carefree attitude he displayed to others, and made me feel loved and secure. I had never before met anyone like him.

For a 33-year-old, he acted like a little boy, and that charmed me. He had a passion for good conversation and, even better, for a good argument. Slightly chubby, he was sensitive about his weight and was forever asking if he was fat. I would answer, "Yes, you are an obese fat pig." He would smile.

Readjusting the autopilot to stay on course, I stared at *Thea* in the distance. They had just caught a fish and were hauling it in, the victim of a school trying to escape the hungry dolphins that squealed around the boats. I leaned back in the shade of the spray hood. Aside from the heat—it was about 100 degrees, without the slightest breeze —life was great.

The only problem in my little universe was the time schedule. Back in New York, my father and I had pored over the pilot charts and calculated the amount of time each passage would take with how many days would be needed in port before recommencing. According to our planned itinerary, I was to leave straight from Panama for the Galápagos, nonstop, and from the Galápagos straight for Samoa. This tight schedule was to be continued from port to port all the way around the world. The circumnavigation, according to our program, was to last two years. Now, as I tried to live it out, it became clear to me that keeping up with the original plan was going to be impossible. Here I was, not even one-quarter of the way and theoretically two months behind schedule.

The plan for circumnavigation had grown mammoth in scope since its modest inception on *Pathfinder* one year before and now seemed to have taken on a life of its own. My father had done some digging and discovered that if the voyage were completed before

November 1987, I would break the world record to become the youngest person ever to circumnavigate the globe solo, and he fell completely in love with the idea.

Two years can feel like an eternity when you stand before them, but already I felt the pressure of a deadline. *Varuna* needed all kinds of work that hadn't been anticipated. Without a shakedown voyage to get the kinks out before leaving New York, she now needed caulking to repair the leaks; the engine cover, which formed the floor of the cockpit, was also leaking badly and needed to be rebuilt; and the bunk had to be enlarged so that I could sleep in some kind of relative comfort. It was so small that I spent one hour every night trying to remember the position in which I had fallen asleep the night before.

I made up my mind to spend the hurricane season in Tahiti after arriving in November. It would be the first substantial island with everything required to do the work. Halfway across the South Pacific, I could wait out the dangerous weather and continue on to Australia by the end of the Southern Hemisphere's autumn. This was slightly different from the original plan, according to which I should already have been 4,000 miles farther, in Australia, for hurricane season. I intended to write to my father about it that night after arriving in Contadora and didn't look forward to his reaction.

After an extremely hot ten-hour day, with the engine faithfully put-putting away, I saw the low brown hills finally emerge from the haze ahead. A welcome wagon of dolphins joined in *Varuna*'s wake as we motored to the anchorage where we had arranged to rendezvous with René. There he was, coiling his lines in minimum attire, waving and grinning. Anchoring about 50 feet from *Thea*, I shut off the engine and breathed a sigh of relief as the sounds of water lapping against *Varuna*'s hull calmed my frayed nerves. Silence can never be as sweet as the split second after a diesel engine has been squelched after a long day of motoring. Luc hollered, snorkel, mask and speargun already in tow, "Hey, everybody, I am going to catch a feast."

I sat down on deck with a carton of soy milk and leaned against the mast. It was that perfect time, neither day nor night, when the light is saturated with oranges and reds. Anchored close to the rocky shoreline, I could make out nooks and crannies where little crabs were running in and out of crevices foraging for food. Just above the rocks, stately palms, frangipani, and pandanus blocked any view of houses. A small dirt road disappeared into the vegetation and called out to be followed tomorrow into an island yet to be discovered.

Farther along the coast, an old fisherman prepared to cast his net. He methodically gathered it into his arms so that when he cast it over the water, it unfurled like a bedsheet, with hunks of lead weighing down the edges. As the net opened, the nylon glittered in the waning light before dropping into the water of El Pacifico.

The Pacific! I'm really in the Pacific! My thoughts tripped, slid to a grinding halt and came up with bloody knees. It already felt as if I had been away for years, yet I was only at the threshhold of my voyage, far from the Indian Ocean and seemingly light years away from the Atlantic. Going below, I found paper and a pen and went back out on deck.

"*Dear Daddy,*" I wrote and then stared at the paper.

The lone angler began to haul in his net. Glimmering shards of wiggling diamonds strained to be free as he pulled them clear of the water. I knew from fishing with Luc on Taboga that all the fishes' attempts at freedom would be for naught, only making trouble for the person who had to disentangle them from the net, often ripping them apart to do so. Luc had shown me how to catch small sardines for fritters. Casting the net, I discovered, was a practiced art and, thinking of my own nets landing in a ball, I admired this lone fisherman's style, as he eyed the water, spied the ruffle on the surface that indicated a passing school, cast perfectly over it and pulled it in.

I looked down at my paper, hopelessly lost for words, and tried to explain myself to my father. The sky began to darken when I headed over to *Saskia* for a dinner of langoustes, and the letter remained unwritten.

Contadora was an island of exquisite tableaux, and wherever we went the black eyes of little roe deer followed our every move like Munchkins. During explorations ashore, these delicate long-legged animals would sprint out of our way, their tan and speckled bottoms disappearing into the brush. The roes were a rather miniature race of deer, about the size of a foal—the males balancing dainty antlers on their heads—and the island was full of them. Every so often, walking into the bodega, the little grocery store that had a few cans, some powdered milk, Tang and Popsicles, we found their souvenirs on the bottom of our sandals.

The air of Contadora carried the rich smells of a lush, rampant vegetation, barely held at bay by local machetes. Birds squawked, whistled and flew in between the trees while a few Contadorans played soccer on the rare clearings. The Contadorans are a handsome race of black-skinned, Spanish-speaking people whose ancestry dates back to African tribes of the sixteenth century. Today, most of the islanders work as domestics and handymen for the mansions hidden in the far corners of the island.

One day our wanderings brought us to an overgrown golf course and a duo of elderly gentlemen playing Petanque. I remembered seeing men in Little Italy near our loft in New York playing the Mediterranean lawn game at the neighborhood playground. The French regard Petanque with reverence, so Jean Marie, René and Luc just had to meet these two kindred spirits. We plowed onto the golf course and introduced ourselves like long-lost friends to Roland de Montague, an executive with a passion for isolated country houses on remote islands, and Roberto Vergnes, an explorer and avowed eccentric.

Roland was a stately and distinguished patriarch of a man, his bushy gray hair combed perfectly into place, his serene grace lending normality to the conversations that were to follow. His antithesis, Roberto, was slightly fat, small and bald with a potato of a nose and ears that jutted out like a koala bear's. We played a game of Petanque together and invited them back to the boats.

At this point, I was in a position where I had to speak French all the time, and my language problem often gave me throbbing headaches. My previous hard-won comprehension level had been improving by leaps and bounds with the different colloquialisms of my three friends. However, with Roberto, it was like making a beeline back toward the dead zone. He came from southern France, where people have a penchant for adding extra syllables to the ends of words and I listened for a cadence to grab on to, without luck.

On *Saskia*, René parted with a couple of the best of his close family of wines and Luc opened up a new bottle of Calvados to lubricate the conversation. Roberto really was one of the last true adventurers, con artists and pirates. Preparing his speech as if he were onstage in Carnegie Hall, he began entertaining us with his escapades.

"I am here visiting with Rolando and shall return to France in a couple of weeks to find sponsors and funding to go out to Cocos Island in search of Captain Henry Morgan's treasure," he began broadly. "You see, I know where it is."

"You do?" said Luc. "Give us a hint. We've been thinking of going there."

In Colón, I had heard about Cocos, the tiny island belonging to

Costa Rica, 450 miles offshore, out of the Bay of Panama, and ideally situated for a sailor on the way south to Cape Horn or north on the way to California and Mexico. There, you could reprovision with water, coconuts and meat from the wild pigs and goats that overran the place. Hundreds of years ago, all the marauding European sea-faring bandits would ransack the Incas, Aztecs or whomever they felt like bothering and would unload in Cocos when they felt threatened. According to logbooks and historical records, sometimes they never returned. Roberto fired up our imaginations, telling of his previous trips and the wily ways he took in getting there.

"I find a sailboat with an unsuspecting crew," he chuckled, "and tell them I know exactly where the treasure is buried. A fire burns in their eyes and I am offered passage. Always on my previous trip there, I would bury an old frying pan and when my companions and I arrive, I tell them that was where the treasure is. Off they run with shovels and metal detectors. Ping, ping, ping. 'We've found it!' they scream, and proceed to dig away. Meanwhile, I am off on the other side of the island, conducting my own research." He gulped down some more Calvados and continued with other stories, one more outrageous than the next. Every once in a while, the conversation would halt for my sake while Luc patiently translated a French pun that had sonic-boomed over my head.

We never decided whether to believe a thing Roberto told us, and I never made it to Cocos, but none of that seemed too important at the time. After a week, we bid these two characters farewell. René's wife was waiting for him in Costa Rica, and it was time to head west. We sailed to San José, the last island of the Perlas, and there we said goodbye to René. It was sad to think that the first group of people with whom I had formed a bond was beginning to disperse and head its separate ways.

"*Adieu, mes amis,* we will meet again," said René on August 31, as *Saskia* pulled out. "Tania, *bon chance!*" he called before turning away. I waved, wished him well in his new life and watched as his brown bottom disappeared like a roe deer over the horizon.

The next day, *Varuna* and *Thea* prepared to follow. Ahead was about a four-day passage to Cocos. For an early brunch, Luc dived for our last Panamanian langoustes while I made a drawing of a rainbow for him and a cassette to open after 300 miles at sea. We lingered aboard *Thea*, savoring the moments before raising the anchors and heading out to sea. Finally, Luc and Jean Marie were ready. The boats were ready. I was ready.

"Tania," said Luc, "you have the charts in order, you have the detailed drawings for the anchorage in Cocos, right? You have everything you need. All you have to do is find it," he taunted, "and Jean Marie and I will be waiting with some smoked ham for you."

"Yeah, I'm all right," I said. "I'll be talking to you on the radio, right?"

"We'll be there," said Luc and kissed me goodbye. They watched me pull up the anchor in a very weepy frame of mind. Jean Marie hollered, "*Courage, petite* Tania!" and they pulled away.

Levering the windlass handle, gathering the chain foot by foot, I thought about the forthcoming trip. If everything went as it should, I would arrive in Cocos in a mere four days. That wasn't much of a trip. I'd spent a lot longer at sea over the past three months. So what was I so upset about? Maybe I sensed that I was pulling up the anchor and heading out, all alone again, into the biggest ocean on the planet and still wasn't all that sure about my navigation. It would be eighteen days, not four, before I stepped ashore again.

I had been so caught up with the vagaries of the Atlantic Ocean up until this point, that the Pacific was like a blind date. For the first time, I pulled out the pilot chart and examined it to see what was in store. The Humboldt Current swings up along the coast of South America from Chile until just north of the equator where it veers west, helping to form the counterequatorial currents. This meant we would have at least 1-, and sometimes up to 3-knot, currents against us. Not only that, but the prevailing winds in the area during September headed straight from the west and southwest, the direction in which we wanted to go, hitting us right on the nose. *Varuna*, Dinghy and I would have to beat into the wind the whole way to Cocos—a dreary prospect, especially because I had been so sure the rest of the world would be downwind.

As we motored out on the windless Bay of Panama, *Thea* came up alongside for a moment and Luc and I arranged to communicate on the top of every hour by VHF until the distance between the boats prevented it. We would be able to stay within VHF range, which was about 20 miles, for a day or two anyway. I watched *Thea* pull away and admired her strong lines. Nearly twice the size and volume of *Varuna*, she could be out of sight in no time as soon as we were both under sail, but Luc, sensing my sadness, slowed down his engine in order to prolong our time together. Wind meant separation and, for once, I was glad for the flat calm.

The sea was a mirror in the brilliant sunshine and *Varuna*'s hull sliced through it like a blade. Thunderclouds that had seemed threatening earlier in the morning veered off toward the continent, and our skies were of the clearest blue. Setting the autopilot, I went below to get some shade and tried to read.

During moments like this, I often lost myself in a daydream of what I might be doing if I had stayed in New York. Would I still be a bicycle messenger? Probably. Or would I be traveling? Maybe. One thing was certain, I'd be dreaming of alternative lifestyles to messengering. As many as the hardships were proving to be with this particular mode of travel, I liked knowing that I was doing something special, something off the beaten track.

Other people may dream all their lives of doing a trip like this, but for me it stemmed from something much less romantic. It was a dramatic plan of my father's to upheave me from the rut that I had fallen into as a teenager. Upheavals had been common in my family long before this one, and I thought about the particular set of circumstances that had landed me here alone in the Pacific on the way to a treasure island.

When I was twelve, after the troubles, Tony, Nina, Jade and I were uprooted from the rural New Jersey country and parochial schools we had always known and transplanted to Manhattan, a whole new world. The thousands of students at I.S. 70, the public school I attended in Chelsea, were divided up socially into so many gangs, cliques and ethnic groups that the school seemed, at first, like a vast city entirely made up of children. Kids seemed to be waiting for a reason to fight, and I had quite a mouth in defending myself against the more menacing characters, considering myself lucky to get off with some mild harassment, kissy noises, derrière squeezes and the occasional slap. Other kids asked for a lot more trouble and it was always worst when two girls fought. Once a girl actually bit a nipple off an opponent. At I.S. 70, you needed a tough skin to survive, and I had spent my life developing a very tough one.

By the time I was thirteen, I had made several friends, some of whom were a couple of years older than I and went out a lot at night. These excursions were innocent at first, until I started lying to my father about babysitting or sleeping over at someone's house. My band of friends and I roamed the streets or hung out at McDonald's. At concerts, sometimes we went up to people in line and asked, "Wanna hear a song for fifty cents?" Whenever anyone would flip us the two quarters, we'd burst into a medley of TV themes from "The Brady Bunch" to "Gilligan's Island." We were just having fun.

I was getting decent grades at the time, so my father didn't ask too many questions. But almost every time I asked for permission to go to a concert or to hang out, he refused. I began to use the babysitting alibi regularly. It was easier to lie than to hear a long-winded lecture, and I became indifferent, not caring very much about anything except my friends and my lifestyle. I liked being a street kid.

The first two years of high school are a bleary memory of lying, sneaking out of the house at night, hanging out on the streets, going to clubs and following bands with names like The Bad Brains, The Mad and The Stimulators. I bought all my clothes at the Salvation Army and thrift shops, arranging outfits to make them look as strange as possible. We all wore construction boots with skirts, lots of makeup and black eyeliner and teased our hair. We painted badges and pins with slogans and statements that we stuck all over our oversized men's vests. My favorite was "Who Killed Bambi?" It was easy to get into clubs; the doormen knew that once inside, we'd start dancing like crazy and the place would start to hop. We'd ask men to buy us rum and Cokes, say thanks and beat it. We were little creeps, but we were good for business.

My father was convinced that all my friends were drug addicts, duds and scum, so I brought them home as rarely as possible. Our relationship deteriorated to lectures and accusations that would end in my bursting into tears and running to my room. One day I got home and found he had made a collage devoted to me. Poring over *The Village Voice*, he had cut out pictures of the most grotesque and bizarre punks he could find, plus the names of punk bands, pasted them all together, thrust it at me and asked what was the point of all this. I couldn't answer.

Eventually, the only way I could communicate with my father was through letters. Only through letters could I organize my thoughts and attempt to tell him how I felt about anything. I wanted him to know that I wasn't doing anything wrong; I didn't do drugs. He didn't believe me. I tried to explain that these were my first real friends and the only people I had ever known who accepted me for who I was. He didn't understand.

Things went from bad to worse. After a while in Brooklyn Tech, a high school that I loathed, I started to take five-period-long lunch breaks and my grades nosedived. Because grades were the only ticket to freedom with my father, I found somebody who sold blank report cards, bought one for ten dollars and made an honor student out of myself.

One gloomy afternoon, when my mother had returned to the United States from Switzerland for an operation, she took it upon herself to visit all our teachers to see how we were doing in school. Afterward, she called my father and asked him to meet her at a café across the street. He had vowed never to allow her in the door of our house for fear that that she would cause some kind of troublesome scene, or worse, that she wouldn't leave. He met her and returned a few minutes later with a white face. When he asked me how I was really doing in school, it was clear he knew. He ranted and raved, screamed profanities and then he and Jeri ransacked my room for drugs, thinking that could be the only explanation for my devious behavior.

It wasn't drugs, I tried to tell him, I just hated the school that looked like a prison, where the six-thousand students were anonymous numbers and all I had ever accomplished was to make a wrench and two nuts and bolts. Time and time again, I had begged him to help me transfer, but he had been steadfast. "No. In life, one has to learn to cope with those things that one does not like. One has to learn self-discipline."

He and Jeri took me to a restaurant to try to talk things over in as civil a manner as possible, but my father kept yelling, "Why? Why?" and I kept staring straight ahead until he slapped me across the face and I stormed out.

After that, he started checking my every move and double checking the alibis. Before I realized what he was doing, he almost caught me sneaking out in the middle of the night to an all-night club; luckily, I saw him before he saw me and gave him the slip.

In January of 1982, my father took Jeri to Europe for a Christmas present and left Christian to take care of us. I started cutting entire days of school, giving Christian lame excuses. One night, I was sitting with two friends at the kitchen table smoking cigarettes. Christian stormed in and accused me of smoking marijuana. He threw my friends out and I followed. When my father got home a few days later, Christian spilled his version of the story to him. My father had no reason to doubt his account. It was the last straw. He yanked me around by the hair in a rage, tore the lock off my door and said that from then on he was going to set his alarm clock for every two hours to check to see if I was in bed all night.

"No more phone calls—*in* or *out!*" he screamed. "No more piano lessons! No more babysitting or going out of this house for *any* reason except school!" I grabbed my coat and fake I.D. and made for the front door.

"If you walk out now," he hollered, "I will have one daughter less. You will have no home to come back to!" he screamed down the stairwell. "I'll never speak to you again, and you are forbidden to speak to Nina, Tony and Jade. I don't want you to *rot* them too!" His voice echoed in my ears as I ran out into the street. I moved in with Jeri when I was fifteen. My father told everyone he had disowned me.

Jeri lived with her two cats in an airy loft in Soho filled with colorful carpets, couches, plants and books. A collector of the arcane, she had knickknacks and paraphernalia on every table and every inch of wall space. Her kitchen was filled with big jars of pasta and spices, and there was always something wonderful cooking on the stove. She went over to talk to my father and they decided that she would try her hand at raising me. He was at the end of his rope.

The first thing Jeri did when I moved in was set the ground rules. "You're not allowed to go out during the week, but you can do what you want on the weekends. I love you, Tania. But you have to be honest with me. Do you understand?" I nodded, promising to try my best.

Jeri took me out of Brooklyn Tech and enrolled me at City As School, an alternative high school with the motto "Learning as an adventure" and a philosophy of education based on self-motivation. In addition to a few orthodox in-classroom courses, I worked for a Brooklyn city councilman, answering his hotline and helping his constituents solve their problems. I was also a tutor at a day-care center, and at night took a couple of college-level courses at the New School. Within two months, I was studying again, life had taken a turnaround and I was happy. My rowdy lifestyle didn't interest me as much as it once had, and slowly, with my friend Rebecca, I drew away from it all.

Jeri was a wonderful person to come home to every day. She was warm to every one of my friends and loving to me. After a few months, she asked if I would like to go with her to my father's for dinner. Did he want me, I asked? Whose idea was it?

"He wants you to come, really," she said. "He talks about you all the time, and he's always asking me what you're doing."

It took some coaxing, but finally I took the big step and went back over to the house with Jeri. I still didn't have much to say and sat quietly at the dinner table. But even though my father and I avoided each other's eyes, and even though I knew that I would never be able to live there again, it felt good to be home. The next time we would both live under the same roof was one year later aboard *Pathfinder*. The sea would be the great equalizer.

• • •

I looked out at *Thea*, a mile ahead, and checked the time. There were still fifteen minutes to go before radio check-in. Scanning the horizon, I noticed that up ahead the still waters of the immense gulf appeared to turn into a rapids, and as we approached the area *Varuna* started bouncing around. Instinctively, I screamed "Reef!" but I was wrong. Was it an earthquake? It stopped after about 60 feet and calmed, then picked up again like turbulent little strips of river for two miles. Skipjack tuna leapt by the dozen, birds swarmed in, pilot whales and dolphins squealed around the phenomena, and I was spooked, not knowing whether to think they were escorting me out or visiting something I hadn't heard about. At six o'clock, I flipped on the radio.

"Luc, what were those ripples in the water we passed?" I asked. "I've never seen anything like that. It scared the hell out of me."

"It was just some kind of tidal rip or current," he said. "It was probably carrying many fish with it. Didn't you notice the fishing boats?"

"Fishing boats? Oh, sure," I answered, trying to sound nonchalant. "There is a little wind now. Do you guys want to try putting the sails up?"

"Yes, look outside of your shell once in a while," he answered. "We've had our mainsail up for half an hour already."

Signing off, I popped out on deck and Dinghy followed, meowing for his dinner. Jean Marie was on deck hoisting their jib and I hurried to do the same. The wind had developed into a gentle northeast breeze over the starboard beam, and both sailboats, out of practice, shook off the cobwebs and sped toward Cocos. After setting the Monitor on a new course, and with new optimism about the weather, I pulled out the chart and calculated that, at the current speed, our trip to Treasure Island would take about three days.

For a while, the boats managed to stay within radio contact, and this was both good and bad. It was great to have the company, but it changed the rhythm of my days. Instead of developing a natural routine, as on previous passages, my day began to revolve around the radio. I measured time not by the transit of the sun, but by the number of minutes left before I switched on the VHF to talk to Luc. I found myself jumpy and more moody than usual, but attributed that to the fact that I was out of whack with life at sea.

After our first beautiful evening, thunderstorms began to march like armies across the muddy-looking ocean. Apathetically, I read and dried up leaks, waiting for the radio calls. The sea was churned up as plastic flip-flops, tree trunks, barrels and floating garbage rode by on the swells. My hands had become rather soft during our stay in Panama, and now began to wear raw from the constant sail changes as squalls came and went.

After four days of our fighting the contrary winds, currents and calms after the squalls, and four nights of sleeping, eating, reading and writing while living on the walls, the inevitable conversation occurred between *Varuna* and *Thea*. We would have to skip Cocos and would have to forge onward without stopping to the Galápagos, 500 miles farther to the southwest. If all went well, it would take me a week.

I read and reread my reference books dealing with the chilling Humboldt Current. The water around *Varuna* was very cold, even though we were approaching the equator. During the nights, I illuminated a masthead light while Jean Marie and Luc kept watch to stay within sight. During the day, the sky remained furiously dark as the strong current kept *Varuna* in a clutch that seemed, at times, to be pulling her backward. One day my taffrail log said that we had covered 100 miles and Luc's SatNav registered 75. For every mile we plowed through the water, the current had carried us back a quarter of another. Much to my surprise, *Varuna* kept up with and even surpassed *Thea*'s speed. She was quick, which pleased me, and capable of heading several degrees farther into the wind. Luc was envious, forgetting that, for me, the performance really didn't seem worth the discomfort of being within the confines of such a small vessel beating into the wind.

Every day, I turned on the engine to recharge the batteries for night lights and radio power. On the sixth day, the monster didn't want to turn off. I discussed the problem with Luc over the radio, and he told me to put my hand over the air-intake filter and it would stop on its own. Not knowing the air filter from Adam, I put my finger over the air vent for the fuel tank, which was easily accessible in the cockpit. After a few minutes, the engine rumbled to a halt.

The next day, I turned on the ignition switch, and the oil, amp and temperature lights illuminated the dark recess of the starboard berth under the cockpit. Outside, I pressed the starter switch, heard the starter turn the flywheel, but there was no combustion. "Oh no, not again!" I cried into the wind, fearing the isolation confronting me if it wouldn't start. I fetched my tools, unscrewed the cover for the umpteenth time and tried the only troubleshooting technique I knew—bleeding the fuel line. Nothing. Staring down at the fat little red monster of an engine, I tried to curse it, kick it and, finally, shame it into working. It just stared back at me.

"Luc, my engine stopped and won't start again," I said when I talked to *Thea* that morning. "We have to separate. I don't have enough juice to talk on the radio or to leave the lights on at night." My voice cracked and his came back out of the receiver.

"Did you bleed it?"

"Yes." I answered. "But I don't know what else to do."

"Well, let me think about it. Don't use up all your electricity, and turn off the radio. I'll call back in exactly half an hour." For thirty minutes I prayed that he would offer to rendezvous and help me make repairs. As the seconds on my Cassio registered 60 in the twenty-ninth minute, I flicked the radio switch on.

"Tania, can you hear me? Answer, please."

"Yes! Yes, I'm right here. What do you think I should do?"

"Listen, sail downwind in our direction and when we get close, I'll throw you a line and swim over to see what I can do."

I was euphoric. We were going to have a mid-Pacific rendezvous. Disengaging the self-steering gear and unsheeting the mainsail and jib, I pushed *Varuna*'s tiller over. We rounded until the wind was at our back and she cantered down toward *Thea*.

No longer a toy sailboat somewhere on the horizon, *Thea* got larger and larger as the distance between us shrank and I welcomed the familiar sight of her gray aluminum hull. *Varuna* rapidly made it to the other boat, gliding about 20 feet by before I rounded up, tripped to the foredeck and pulled down the jib.

As Jean Marie steered, Luc launched a line into my arms. The waves reverberated in between the boats as I wound the line around a cleat, completing the incongruous scene of two sailboats tied together in the middle of the ocean. Luc took one look of distaste at the frigid water, screamed a warning to the sharks and jumped in. My guardian angel quickly pulled himself along the line and then heaved his soaking self over the gunwale, landing in a heap on deck.

"Hello, *ma petite* Tania," he smiled. "Long time no see, eh?"

Like a nurse, I handed him instruments while he fiddled around with the engine, tinkered, shook and rescrewed things, basically the same contortions I had performed, before saying, "Well, I think you are engineless."

"No. I can't be. We have to be able to fix it somehow."

He shook his head. "I'm sorry, Tania. I have no idea what is

wrong with the beast." There was nothing to do but accept the predicament. The batteries would be drained in a couple of days, there
would be no more power and therefore no navigation lights, reading
lights or radio. Once again, just as on the way to Bermuda, *Varuna*
would be totally powerless and isolated, but this time, the passage
was a more complicated one. Also, without the radio, there would be
no way to stay in touch with *Thea*.

"Tania, you are the bravest person I know," Luc said, as we sat
in the cockpit eating a cabbage-beetroot salad that I prepared in a
zombie trance to postpone his departure.

"Me? You've got to be kidding. I am the last of the cowardly
lions. Look at me. I'm a complete mess. I have no power. We have to
split up. Nothing's going right."

"Yes, you are brave," he said. "The mountain climber who
climbs the most dangerous peaks is not brave. He likes to climb
mountains. Bravery is doing something that you are afraid of and
confronting your fears. Now, stop crying. You can do anything you
want to do. We will separate now, but in four days we'll see each
other again." We kissed each other goodbye and he jumped into the
water, pulling himself along the line through the waves to *Thea*
where Jean Marie stood waving. I waved as we each pulled up our
sails and got underway again. At first light the next morning, Dinghy
and I rushed up on deck to check the endless horizon. We were alone.

I would think of Luc's words on bravery many times during the
next two years, whenever I thought I couldn't go on. I saw the truth
in them, and the knowledge that I might really be brave, no matter
how frightened I was at any moment, kept me going.

For the next three days, *Varuna* beat into the strong southwesterly winds and chop, as I read, did the chores around the boat,
played with Dinghy and daydreamed about the future. Once in a
while, when the sun peeped out of the cloud-fretted sky, I'd grab the
sextant, take a sight and try to plot it out properly. But the fixes still
weren't working out the way they should have.

My navigation was based on the occasional fix from the SatNav
of a passing ship. With that I could easily advance my own position
with some degree of accuracy by dead reckoning. But ship fixes were
rare and from my own sun sights I felt no security. There was something very wrong with what I was doing and I couldn't figure out
what. When I did get the occasional fix from a ship, it never agreed
with my own calculations. Worry began to infect my days.

On September 11, my navigation confirmed a monumental occasion; we had crossed the equator and entered the Southern Hemisphere. For the inaugural milestone of the trip, there were presents to open and I decided to cheer up, throw myself a party and do it right. First, I cleaned the boat and then, wedged into the cockpit, took a bucket bath. Drying out in the sun, I noticed that the boat immediately began to smell better.

Next, I arranged the packages from my family on the bunk, made a festive meal of macaroni and cheese and, after feeding Dinghy, sat down and feasted till I was satiated. The great moment arrived and I ripped open the packages that everyone had earmarked for the equator. Tony had secretly made a cassette of the family dinner-table squabbles that he titled "Family Bullshit Tape." Nina gave me a bag of camper's chicken stew. My father gave me an envelope full of pictures of the family, snowy mountains and glaciers, a hundred dollars, candy, balloons and a hat umbrella. Gathering the loot together, I hooked up the camera. When everything was arranged and the camera focused, I looked down and saw my naked body.

"Oh my, Dinghy, look how silly I am. This will never do. I can't send this kind of picture home." Hurriedly rearranging the gifts to cover myself, I propped the hat umbrella on my head and clicked the shutter. Dinghy chewed on the balloons while I devoured the candy and that evening we drifted off into a contented slumber, dreaming about home.

In the middle of the night I woke up, went on deck for a routine horizon check and saw a fishing boat in the distance. I had been trying to hail several boats and it had seemed that no one kept radio watches, so it was a great surprise to have this one answer my call. The world crashed around me when the fix they provided still pinpointed us north of the equator. My navigation was completely wrong and we wouldn't cross that line until tomorrow.

Anxiety-ridden for the next couple of days, I checked and rechecked the calculations but couldn't find the error. "Please, God," I prayed, "let me find land." I worried myself literally to tears and dreamed of arriving up a strange river on the wrong island in the Galápagos. On day 14, after many calculations and minus a couple of fingernails, I convinced myself that I would see land. I awoke hopeful and turned on the RDF. Theoretically, we should have been within range, but no signal verified my beliefs. I worried that San Cristóbal's beacon, which was listed in the *Admiralty List of Radio Beacons* as having a range of 200 miles, might be out of commission and that I'd have to find the island without its help. "My navigation better be good," I muttered to Dinghy, and spent the day hallucinating clouds into land until I thought I would become cross-eyed.

Tantalizing images of potential land flew in the form of birds. There were hundreds of them, all scouting for schools of fish, their squawks combining with sounds of wind and waves into a din of confusion. I looked at them for a sign, for one of them to point me in the right direction. "If there are birds, there's gotta be land around here someplace," I said, peering ahead. The dolphins came in all their squealing glory and surrounded my disoriented home. I tried to communicate with them, pleading for an answer. Clouds were everywhere, teasing me with broken promises and false identities. My eyes burned as I endlessly scouted the horizon for a fishing boat that knew its own position.

Finally, the tension was too much. I turned *Varuna* around and headed east, away from supposed land, to avoid passing it accidentally. Pulling out my Bible, I read a passage from the Psalms and prayed for inspiration. I was a quivering mess and for good reason. If we missed the islands of the Galápagos, turning back would be close to impossible. The currents and winds of the trade route would not allow for the magnitude of such an error. From there, it was almost 3,000 miles to next land.

In an attempt to calm down, I concentrated on appreciating the beauty that surrounded me. The Humboldt Current, thick with plankton and the siege of anchovies that feed on it, was like a rich corridor of marine life. Often, I found Dinghy dragging in scaly flying fish or squid that had become marooned on deck. Pleased that he had provided for one of his own meals and that I wouldn't have to open another can from the dwindling supply, I wasn't quite so happy with the mess that his snacks left behind. Flying fish hold such a gluey substance to their scales that it wouldn't be surprising if rubber cement was derived from it. The squid invariably would leave behind a smelly inkspot on the fiberglass deck or my bed and Dinghy never cleaned up after himself, no matter the meal.

Hoping and praying for salvation, I sat in the corner of the cockpit and watched the waves. *Varuna*'s wake was fiery in the moonless night as the phosphorescent plankton gave an eerie neon glow to the rooster tail of water behind us. Staring, I just refused to believe that we were very far off the mark and pulled out that lovable RDF one more time. Lo and behold, the signal came through loud and clear.

"Hallelujah!" I wrote in my logbook. *"Land, here I come!"* I adjusted my course to home in on the beacon and by the next afternoon, after tacking in through the eye of the signal, finally saw the very definite knobby shape of San Cristóbal's volcanic peak sticking above the water. I sat and cried in relief.

Now that I had found land, for some reason Neptune did not want me there right away. The wind that had harassed us for sixteen days decided to quit the game and left us wallowing. Shaking out one reef, then another, replacing the jib for the larger genoa, I tried to catch every last waft of breeze. *Varuna* tried to make headway but was beating into it and going nowhere. Sitting in the cockpit, I hand-steered, trying to make up for the Monitor's slightly unsteady course in these conditions, until my bottom became sore from the hard surface. The wind remained feeble through the day and night as we drifted with the tides in and out of sight of the jutting peak. Frustrated, I vainly tried the engine, and even took out the dinghy oars, trying to row *Varuna* in, but it was useless. We just had to wait it out.

It was the next afternoon before a faint breeze returned and *Varuna* could make headway. What had seemed at first like a thousand tiny islands, slowly merged into one as San Cristóbal rose up from the horizon. Mirages formed between the peaks, creating an illusion of water, and steering in closer as the afternoon progressed, I realized it would again be impossible to make it into the harbor by nightfall.

This was unbelievable. I had been within sight of the island for two days and just couldn't fight my way into its harbor. I turned *Varuna* around for the second time in as many days and pointed her bow east. When night falls, it is dangerous to be this close to land with weariness setting in and no engine. When we were safely offshore, I heaved to by backwinding the jib. This way the actions of the sails canceled themselves out, keeping *Varuna* under control in the same place, with her head to the seas. That accomplished, I tried to get a little sleep before attempting another approach the next day.

As the rosy colors of dawn began to bathe the morning sky, I was already at the tiller heading for the security of a safe harbor. The primordial scene that awaited as I drew closer was something for which no reference book or geography lesson could ever have prepared me. The jagged islands of the Galápagos rose like ebony pyramids from the sea ahead, each an ancient volcano that erupted 7,000 to 10,000 feet up from the sea floor to stand over 5,000 feet above sea level.

Charles Darwin had called these his enchanted islands, where he had found inspiration and the proof he needed for his theories of evolution and natural selection. As *Varuna* inched closer, I knew I was seeing the islands for the first time the way Darwin had seen them aboard the *Beagle* over one hundred years before, from the deck of a sailing vessel that had made the long voyage from the Americas.

The swell of the South Pacific, unbridled since Chile and the southern latitudes, thundered and crashed against the menacing walls of rock ahead. Approaching with trepidation, I began to fear for the safety of my boat as we were clutched by the strong currents that surrounded the islands. The breeze that morning was dwindling and, as it did, steerageway was lost, the current overpowered us and we began to drift helplessly close to the nastiest shoreline I had ever seen. Several hundred feet closer and *Varuna* would be picked up by the breakers and dashed against those cliffs.

I gripped the tiller and pumped frantically, never taking my eyes from the cliffs while the rudder swished back and forth under the boat, giving us a modicum of rowing power. There was no continental shelf below, just the sheer drop of the volcano, so there was nothing for an anchor to grip. Finally, miraculously, we found a breeze that shook us free of the currents that in Darwin's time had convinced mariners that the islands themselves were moving, a misconception I could now well appreciate.

Following the coastline, I saw *Thea*'s mast popping above a headland and at 8:30 A.M. on the eighteenth day of this not quite so uneventful trip, I sailed into Wreck Bay, San Cristóbal, dropped the hook and pulled down *Varuna*'s sails. This had been my longest passage, if not in mileage, definitely in time. Coiling *Varuna*'s lines and folding the sails, I sat on deck to view my first truly alien harbor.

In the Galápagos, time stands still. These are the islands of the giant sea tortoises, of the kooky blue-footed boobies, of the prehistoric marine iguanas that cover the coastal rocks by the hundreds. They are islands of contradiction, where creatures of the Antarctic— penguins and seals—live in harmony with the most ancient of tropical species. Isolated from man, animals live and play together and fear no predators, and I was looking forward to going ashore and seeing them for myself.

From the deck of *Varuna*, I could see a small fishing village of colorful cement houses dotting the arid landscape, dominated by boulders and scrubby, alien-looking plants. The long-unheard sounds of people doing everyday things reached my ears as my eyes followed the line of the volcano up to the calderas that disappeared into a permanent cloud. Several small fishing boats swung at anchor nearby and directly in front, a couple on their sailboat smiled and waved. I waved back, looked closer and saw their nationality. "Wow, nice going, guys," I thought, "you're even farther from home than I am." They were from Japan, the Rising Sun draped around their backstay.

A smell of fires burning and the sound of people murmuring induced in me a peaceful moment of contemplation. At sea, I was never relaxed. My ears and consciousness were always on the alert for any unusual sound or weather change. The second the anchor dug into the ground, that tension dissolved.

A jetty protruded from what seemed to be the center of town and I could see Luc's blue dinghy bumping gently against the concrete wall. Although, in one way, I was anxious to go ashore, in another, I relished this moment and leaned against the mast trying to imagine Jean Marie and Luc's faces when they arrived. Looking at my knees, I noticed for the first time how bony they had become. The pants that had once fit hung loosely around my thighs. I had lost at least ten pounds since Panama, when I first met Luc, and wondered if he would notice.

I was in desperate need of a hot shower. Even here on land there was a chill in the air, not at all the way I imagined the equator would be. The pictures of snow and ice my father had given me for crossing Latitude 0° had been meant to create envy while I stewed in the doldrums, but they had gone off duty while we passed through their neighborhood. Stories of hundreds of windless miles were other people's tales. Until I neared land, the only doldrum characteristics I had experienced were the thunderstorms. Idly musing over an accomplished voyage, one quickly forgets the hard times and begins glorifying the good. As I thought about the dolphins and the whales, the phosphorescence of the night and sailing next to *Thea*, a distant shout echoed forth from the jetty.

"Tania! *Tania!* We're here!" Eagerly, I jumped up and waved to Jean Marie and Luc who leapt into their dinghy and came speeding over. "Oh, Tania! We've been crazy. What happened to you? We've been waiting for five days and I was so worried. This place is so beautiful, so many things happened to us. Oh, I have so much to say." The words came tumbling out of Luc's mouth as we hugged each other. "Oh, *mon Dieu*. You are so skinny. We must feed you."

It felt wonderful to have Luc care about me so much and I gladly surrendered myself to his ministrations. Jean Marie went back to *Thea* and Luc and I went ashore. Wobbling on unused leg muscles accustomed to the sea's motion, I told him all about my trip and he told me of theirs. They had arrived five days earlier in the north of Santa Cruz, the next island. Since then, they had been biting their nails waiting for me. Tomorrow, Luc said, he wanted to take me to the mountaintop from where they had just come. Hand in hand, we walked to a little café where I devoured a steak, and then we strolled together back to *Thea*.

The next day, we took a bus to the caldera, the caved-in peak of the mountain. Disappearing over the rocky terrain into a rain cloud, the countryside altered itself dramatically from a desert to a damp and misty world. Under the clouds, gnarly trees and grass flourished, and when we got off the bus, our feet sank into moist, reddish soil.

Succulent fruit grew in abundance from orange trees. The Indians who lived up there welcomed us into their foggy midst with wide, smiling faces. Hiking through a countryside populated by more cows than people, I found myself pushing away mildewy fronds that hung heavy and wet from all the trees. Donkeys pulled the carts of the islanders that we passed, and a very occasional car rumbled by. All sounds at the caldera were muffled and absorbed by the mossy undergrowth and I wondered what it would be like to live in a place where the sun rarely showed its face.

In a small hut overrun by chickens, a wrinkled old lady sold us a burlap sack full of incredibly sweet oranges for five dollars before we went to the center of the village, where we waited for the bus to take us back down the mountain. Everywhere, smiling faces turned our way and shyly watched the strangers. A small white church was the center of the settlement with shrouded nuns herding flocks of children into groups. Hyper and unwilling to be locked away in a classroom when they could be watching us, they showed off by doing cartwheels and handsprings calling out the only English words they knew: "Hello, thank-you. How are you. One two three." Luc laughed and, in a fit of adolescent energy, sprinted to a pile of the red dirt and tried to do a backflip. He fell over, the soil burying his embarrassed grin, and the whole square erupted into hysterical peals of laughter, young and old alike, while Luc took a bow. It must have been the mountain air.

The Galápagos were a brief but beautiful respite from the days at sea. Cactus took the place of hedge, and the streets of the small town were made of dusty sand. Everything I saw made me think of what a colony on the moon would be like. But, in order to protect the ecology, the Galápagos have strict visa laws and we were allotted only five days. We had to get serious and find out what was wrong with my engine. Luc spend a good day huddled over the monster, trying to figure out the problem, and the sad result was that the fuel injection pump seemed to be shot and the starter had seized up.

"Tania," he informed me, "you're going to have to make it to Tahiti under sail alone." I acknowledged that there were no two ways about it and felt my heart sink.

Luc still wanted to show me Santa Cruz, 25 miles away, so we provisioned well with produce, mutant watermelon-sized cabbage and every kind of vegetable. The largest supermarket was smaller than the bodega on our block in New York and had a very limited supply, so all I could buy was some margarine and canned sardines for Dinghy. These people were not rich, and weren't confronted with material wealth and its accouterments, like the Panamanians. As a result, everyone was equal and all seemed happy with their lives and secure enough not to resent us. Rather, in every restaurant or store or market, they tried to make us feel at home.

I handed out my meager supply of magazines and some spare T-shirts to the village children. They were so spellbound by the glossy pictures that they didn't even realize they were looking at the pages upside down. The only thing the older men requested was snorkeling gear to dive on their reefs. They even offered to pay, but we had none with which to oblige. If ever I return, I will stock up in Panama and make the Galápagos fishermen very happy.

Water tanks topped off, we set sail for Santa Cruz accompanied by dolphins and barking seals. At first, I did a double take to see their happy, whiskered brown faces. These adorable animals stoutly swimming away between islands were the last thing I expected and I wondered how to ever describe to anyone the marvel of seeing them paddle through the water alongside *Varuna*.

On the north shore of Santa Cruz, there lies a small bay in the crater of a volcano almost entirely closed off by walls of rock. We entered through a small passage and were greeted by an explosion of sound. Hundreds of seal cows, bulls and pups were barking to one another, lining the perimeters of a zoo with no bars. Iguanas strolled through the colony highlighted by San Pedro's cactus plants and bright fuchsia-red prickly scrub. The seals leapt into the water and barked in welcome as we sailed to anchor. They were completely unafraid of *Varuna* and me and it seemed all they wanted to do was play. Birds abounded, swooping into the water and resurfacing with fish between their bills. Pelicans honked and came to beg for food with baby seals who abandoned their toy red crabs, squealing in joy over a new kind of animal come to visit.

We caught some fish and witnessed a dance of the macabre. When we threw the entrails into the air, frigate birds came swooping down from their lofty patrol and performed aerodynamic feats to be the first to get the treat. Whatever they missed was fought over by the honking childlike pelicans. A little bird who had lost a foot in one of her battles even came to eat out of my hand.

The last matter to straighten out before leaving Santa Cruz was the navigational problem. My celestial navigation had been off for some reason and I had found the Galápagos only with the help from the RDF signal. The next landfall, the Marquesas, 3,000 miles away, had no RDF and by now, I should have mastered the art anyway. Luc sat me down and pulled out all his reference books. I found some old calculations and plotting sheets from my last passage that I thought I had properly attacked. We went over them step by plodding step and it soon became evident that Luc was quite rusty on celestial navigation, and used to having his SatNav do the work instead. I had calculated and recalculated the figures so many times trying to get the proper results, that I could do it with my eyes closed. The final result was Luc's admission that I seemed to know what I was doing better than he.

What could be the problem? The sextant? We looked at each other and I leapt into the dinghy to go back to *Varuna* and fetch it. To every problem there is a solution. This time it *was* the sextant. I had been using the plastic one that had been aboard my father's boat, *Pathfinder*. Through the years the plastic must have warped because the angles I was getting between the sun and horizon were slightly off. An unaligned sextant will get you nowhere.

Luckily, in the bottom of one of my lockers lived an excellent aluminum Freiberger sextant. I hadn't wanted to use it because it was heavier and more complicated than the other. When I looked through the plastic model, the sun and horizon were both in the same frame and all I had to do was bring down the sun in the mirrors and line them up together. On the other hand, the Freiberger had a split image with the sun in half of the frame and the horizon in the other. With *Varuna* erratically bouncing around at sea, it was an acrobatic feat trying to keep the two visible while getting them to meet. From *Thea*'s deck, I practiced taking sun sights, did all the calculations, and hit our position spot every time.

We had no more reasons for delay and our visas had expired.

Three thousand miles of Pacific Ocean separated us from the Marquesas Islands to the west-southwest. This journey was four times longer than any I had undertaken so far and I knew that it could take as much as five weeks to make landfall. To say the least, I was apprehensive about leaving.

Sailors who had already made the voyage recounted tales where boats with malfunctions were at sea for eighty days and others about calms that had gripped vessels for weeks. The 3,000 miles were already intimidating enough without considering that any of these woeful occurrences would befall me. I hemmed and hawed, finding always another minor technicality on *Varuna* waiting to be fixed. Finally, Luc said, "We are going. If you want to come, let's go. If not, stay." With such an ordinance, I had no choice. Luc gave me a package to open on my nineteenth birthday, and we said goodbye.

I watched *Thea* sail out of our crater anchorage and wondered where on the ocean we would be when I opened his present on October 7. Slowly taking a last look at the magnificent lunarscape of strange animals, I raised the mainsail, pulled up *Varuna*'s anchor from the last piece of land I would see for at least three and a half weeks and got under way.

5

Once upon a time, in a wall-to-wall concrete mega-city, there was a teenage girl who wanted to sail around the world. People came from far and wide to meet this courageous child. She feared nothing and no one. The oceans parted before her and the sea life serenaded her passage. The wind gods smiled down and blessed her with the gentlest of breezes as she swiftly conquered the world. This girl's name was not Tania.

The Galápagos skies were heavy with cloud and fussy with irregular wind as *Varuna* moved skittishly away from the islands toward the open sea. Luc had proposed that we stay within sight of each other until leaving the currents behind and I was more than happy to comply. During the first couple of days, over the radio, I compared the results of my navigation with Luc's SatNav. *Varuna*'s batteries had been freshly charged at the local generating plant in San Cristóbal, so now there was plenty of energy for emergencies, but not enough to waste on lengthy radio chatter. As soon as I was satisfied with my navigational capabilities, I was to be on my own.

The first two days, I felt tired and dizzy as *Varuna* beat past the islands, first San Cristóbal, then Santa Fe and Santa Maria. As they disappeared behind, sheathed in their spooky mist, I began to cry, thinking of the daunting 3,000 miles between us and our next landfall. Nowhere but in my minuscule *Varuna*, in the middle of an ocean, could the enormity of planet Earth make me feel so privileged yet so completely like a speck of nothingness. Today, it was the latter that produced my tears. They cooked into my stew; they dampened Dinghy's fur; and they formed circular wet spots on my pillow and charts. The more the anxiety welled up, the more my attention and energies focused on *Varuna*, and as we crept farther into the blue void, we drew even closer together. When I steered, her tiller was an extension of my own hand. When I slept, *Varuna* held me in an isolated cradle of safety.

As stubborn squalls and gloomy skies darkened my mood, Luc and Jean Marie tried to cheer me up whenever we talked on the radio. "Somebody is smiling on you," said Luc, "otherwise you wouldn't have gotten this far. After you make enough southing, you'll be in the South Pacific trades and this voyage will be one to remember. Immerse yourself in the beauty, and think about how lucky you are, doing something that most people can only dream about."

On the morning of October 1, I woke up and turned on the radio for the morning reveille. "Luc? Jean Marie? Can you hear me? *Hallo?* Can anybody hear me?" There was only static. Now that the dreaded moment had arrived and we had finally parted ways, I felt relief, knowing what had to be done. I had to find those faraway isles by myself.

I had a pilot chart of the entire Pacific Ocean, all 64 million square miles of it. On the chart, the Marquesas were a blurry peppering of dots below the equator, almost exactly between South America and Australia. My dividers continuously worked their way across the distance and measured the miles down to the last millimeter. Dinghy attacked the end of my pencil while I designed another chart, where I drew columns and in them wrote out the names of the days of the week from September 29 through October 23, their numbered dates, and mileage by the hundreds up to 2,800. I knew myself well enough to think in terms of small daily increments, because looking at the trip in its entirety was too overwhelming. A hundred miles at a time, or one day at a time, was manageable.

I took out my guitar and a music book of Luc's, set a personal goal to learn "The House of the Rising Sun" inside and out, and started picking away. In the Marquesas, I would give a concert if it killed me.

Now, with the first wave of confidence returning, I set out to master navigation. It fascinated me that I could successfully use a sextant, tables and plotting sheets to figure out exactly where we were on this vast chart, and I developed a series of sun-sight times for maximum efficiency. I even took extras, just for good measure. The first I took upon awakening, about seven-thirty; the second came ten to fifteen minutes before midday and then again just when the sun reached the apex of its saunter across the sky—noon sight or meridian. Just to be sure, I took one more sight in the afternoon. Sometimes I did without this last one because once the sun began its descent, it disappeared behind my winged-out mainsail and jib, which both faced west, and it became too much trouble to be worth the effort.

Maybe it was the fresh air and lack of tension; maybe it was my mind's total resignation to the fact that it would only have the present ingredients for stimulation, but I began to have whoppers of dreams that were so vivid I had trouble differentiating them from reality. Often, they were set in places I had never been. New York suddenly became Italy; then Tampa Bay, Florida; then Greece. Friends turned up in the oddest places and we would have long conversations. I was always stopping the boat and having fantastic adventures at imaginary tropical pit stops on the way to the Marquesas.

I felt happiest during the nights, when I knew I would soon sink into the dreamworld of sleep. There, I would be with old friends, doing and eating all sorts of things and having lighthearted adventures. It was like going to the movies every night, except I didn't have to pay to get in. I sat back with my feet up on the imaginary chair in front of me and watched as the dreams overflowed into my days, triggering a vast variety of memories and solutions to problems worked out during the night.

Twice daily, I checked off days and miles, and centimeter by centimeter, my pencil extended *Varuna*'s position on the chart. On the first page of the logbook, I wrote the name "Baie Taaoa, Hiva Oa," as if I might forget my destination en route. No way. I mouthed the words in English, Spanish and French, awake and dreaming, while crossing out the milestones on the chart. Although buffeted with cold wind and shadowed by grim skies for many days, *Varuna* barreled along at quite a pace with the trailing log beating a rhythm into my world, a metronome ticking away the time and miles as I strummed and sang away the afternoons.

October 7 was my nineteenth birthday and I was as excited as if I had just put a quarter into a Vegas slot machine and the whole casino was emptying onto my lap. Around 10:00 A.M., the sun made a dramatic and permanent appearance through the clouds; the few that remained became little puffs of lamb's wool prancing across the sky in the warming wind. I wrote in my logbook, "Thank you, God. What a beautiful birthday present," and took a sight, marking 138 miles from noon the day before. We had made 936 miles in eight days and my dividers triumphantly flew across the chart calculating the leftover distance and time. Only 2,029 miles to go.

I read, worked around the boat, adjusted the sails and the course, played games with Dinghy and planned my birthday meal. Notes were attached to the packages that awaited: "Happy Birthday, Tania. Love, Jade." "To open on your birthday, from your Daddy" and *"Pour ma petite* Tania."

For the previous thirteen days, the ocean and air had been too frigid to inspire indulging in much more than a bird bath. But today, sunny and relatively warm, was the big day, and I lathered up in the cockpit with my first bucket bath in almost two weeks. As the salt water poured over my head, I washed down the cockpit with the soapy water, and poured more over my head, and it flushed the drains clean. Happy birthday, body and nose.

Delaying the present-opening time to when the day's position was worked out, I sat and waited for something special to happen. Already that morning, during my search for stranded flying fish for Dinghy's breakfast, I had found a genuine nickel lying on the foredeck. How it got there remained a mystery that I spent the next half hour pondering.

I opened a can of bamboo shoots and water chestnuts for the birthday feast, shredded some cabbage and threw the whole thing together in a frying pan with Uncle Ben's rice, soy sauce and sesame oil. When it was cooked, I sat down and slowly savored the taste of *Varuna's* Suzy Wan version of Chinese food as Dinghy dined on his Galápagos-brand can of sardines smothered in tomato sauce. Then I did the dishes and cleaned up.

Even though I knew that the presents and messages from my family had all been prepared before I left New York, I treasured the little time capsules about to be opened. Thoughts from the people I loved had been wrapped up and frozen in time for four and a half months, and finally the long-awaited moment had arrived.

First, to set the mood, I pulled out my cassette player and clicked in the family tape Tony had made without anyone suspecting, the night before I left New York. Everyone was at the dinner table and seemed even more hyper than usual. After dinner, he had confessed and they had all written little notes to me. From my father, *"Dans ce meilleur des mondes . . . tout est au mieux,"* in this best of worlds, all is for the best, a quote from *Candide.*

"Tania, with love from your brother. I hope you are enjoying yourself and if you feel homesick now, after you listen to this tape, you won't be anymore. Love, Tony, the maker and producer of this tape."

"Remember yourself now and then. Christian."

"Since everyone used up the space, I'll just say have fun and remember me. Love, Jade. PS. Notice I said love. It took a lot of effort."

And finally from Nina, "I hope you like my singing and piano version of Für Elise. *Adios.*"

The voices from our round table at home swarmed inside *Varuna*, rebounding from the walls, and I thought about Nina, Tony and Jade. What were they all doing now? Was my father with Fritz in Holland or was he eating dinner at Raoul's on Prince Street again? How was Nina faring in her first year of college? I opened her birthday present. This time, it was dehydrated scrambled eggs. She was so funny—my aide whenever I used to sneak out of the house at night. My girl-friends Rebecca and Jill used to sleep over, and we'd count the creak-ing floorboards down the staircase after Nina had given us the all-clear sign. I felt a pang of guilt, remembering my embarrassment when she asked once to tag along on one of our jaunts. We reluc-tantly brought her, ignored her all night and she was hurt. Burst-ing with self-importance, surrounded by friends, I hadn't cared, until now.

Jade's present had a suspiciously familiar shape. It was a bottle of Bailey's Irish Cream, and the letter said, "Daddy told me I should make it a 'Happy Crossing the Equator Line' present. But, knowing your navigational skills, you probably won't even find the equator." I would be sure to tell her in my next letter how right she was.

Pouring myself a plastic cup of the creamy liqueur, I opened the package from my father. "My dear Tania," his letter began, "A very happy birthday to you. Wherever you are now, the thermometer probably says something in the 80's. Here, it is 36 degrees and sunny. A Saturday morning and all is quiet. The kids are still sleeping. Nina has her friend Adrian with her. Last night I found in the street an almost dead bamboo plant. I took it home to try to revive it and messed up my jacket along the way. I just got it back from the cleaners yesterday! I am jealous of your trip. God, do I wish that I was taking off for a long time. Be proud, happy, excited about the fact that you are doing it. Oh, there is not a word that says it exactly —something like ecstatic would do, but, even that is too tame. . . .

"Last night Fritz was in a solemn mood. As we ate dinner, he called to say that he was going *alone* to Raoul's for a steak *au poivre*, an espresso and a cognac. Would I join him for the espresso and the cognac? Of course I would. Boy, the cognacs just kept coming to us two originally gloomy guys. Somewhere along the evening, two ladies wanted to take us home to teach them Swiss German, but we refused since we were too busy making plans.

"And what plans! I shall quickly arrange my affairs, go to Holland and order THE boat. Then, in the fall, we will go together to Holland, get the boat and sail down to Buenos Aires. There, Fritz gets off and buys a horse and mule to go across the Pampas and the Andes to Santiago de Chile. There I shall be waiting for him after sailing alone around Cape Horn and a little visit to Antarctica. Then we sail up to the Galápagos, Panama, New York. Then I shall have my boat for the trip to the Northwest Passage. That's why now I'm not really jealous of your trip anymore. The little present should have some nostalgic meaning. We listened to it when Bobby was whining and Hank's Adam's apple was dancing. Be happy on your birthday and all other days. Daddy."

The present was a cassette of Franz Liszt's Hungarian Rhapsodies. I remembered back to the storm we had encountered in the Gulf Stream on *Pathfinder* between Bermuda and New York. Never before had I seen a sea so boiling and malicious, as our sailboat wildly bucked for three days in the wrath of Neptune. During the whole ordeal, my father had wasted precious battery power to boost our morale with the intricacies of Liszt and, indeed, we prevailed finally to see a clear dawn a day and a half later. Through it all, my father had never doubted himself, or his young green crew.

It was always a mystery to me how my mother and father could ever have been attracted to each other—he so wild and hungry, she so rigid and dark. She was nineteen when she carried me, "the same age as I am now," I thought, reaching for the envelope from her that I had found aboard that first night in Sandy Hook.

"To be opened in the middle of the ocean," it said in that disquieting printing. I had saved it for this day; after all, how could I possibly be more in the middle of the ocean than now? My mother had been on my mind and I wondered how she was and what she might be thinking. Although she had made us suffer so much when we were younger, I could never resent her for it. She was a wounded bird and, if anything, I loved her all the more for her secret torments. Whatever it was that happened in her life before she met my father was something that she would probably take to her grave.

It was at a party in Paris, when he was twenty-eight and she was nineteen that my father met my mother, Sabina Borrelli, or so she called herself then. A student of French literature at the Sorbonne, she was a beautiful Italian, with perfect olive skin, wide green eyes and long dark hair. She was brilliant, seemingly wealthy and very mysterious. "All the right ingredients," my father used to like to say. "She came home with me that night, made eggplant parmesan and never left."

But there were peculiarities. She was vague about her past, often changing the details of her childhood to suit the occasion, and although she said she was born in Torino, Italy, she did not speak Italian with an Italian accent. Multilingual, she seemed to speak no language with a native accent. Her German had a French accent; her French had an Italian accent. Italians who knew my father in those days said she spoke the Italian of a Pole. "She was a very interesting woman," he told us later, when we plundered his memory for facts about our heritage. "But your mother had many secrets."

Soon after my father immigrated to the United States, a letter arrived from Paris to his Englewood, New Jersey, apartment. "Dear Ernst," it began, "I am pregnant. . . ."

The envelope from my mother was on the verge of complete disintegration from the humidity, so I opened it carefully, hoping this would be a special moment. I had placed reminders of her all around me on *Varuna:* drawings, a pot holder she crocheted, the Chinese doll she gave me, the Bible from Switzerland and volumes of literary masterpieces she had pressed on me before my departure.

"You must educate yourself," she had said a hundred times. "The most important thing in the world is an education. It will open your eyes and you will see all the hypocrisy. You make fun of Mommy, but one day, Tania, you will see." Guiltily, I stole a furtive look toward the shelf of books and promised myself I'd crack the spine of a classic the next day.

Inside the envelope was a lock of my mother's long brown hair, tied with a piece of yarn. On a note was written: "I am with you."

The two letters, one from my mother and one from my father, lying next to each other on the bunk each aptly summed up their authors more than they would ever dream. It had all started with a letter and, the way things were going, it would probably end that way.

Maybe it was the eloquence of a round-the-dinner-table argument on the family tape, or the grand words of my birthday letters, or the Bailey's Irish Cream, or simply a lock of hair connecting me with my home and a mother I still hadn't quite figured out, but the tears welled up. I looked for the package from Luc and, just then, heard the familiar songs of the dolphins. A herd was alongside, squeaking a birthday chorus, their whistles resonating through the hull so I could hear them without even going outside. I grabbed Luc's present, unwrapped it and found the cassette of the classical guitar concerto by Narcisso Yepes I had loved on *Thea*.

"*Ma jolie petite* Tania," began his letter. "Today is your birthday and I come with my friends, the wind, the skies and the sea. You are nineteen years old today and you are all alone on a little sailboat in the middle of the ocean. I tried to remember what I did for my nineteenth year. I was in France, anxious about my future and only dreaming about a departure, for where, I didn't know yet. You, at nineteen, are living a great adventure and you are very lucky. On your little boat, there is before you the immensity of life. You will meet with stumbling blocks, anguish and storms, but also the calm mornings, when everything is enveloped in soft gentleness, when you wake up in the arms of somebody you love. That person will always be your home port and you will always come back to him. I think that you feel very lonely with Dinghy, wherever you are. But, close your eyes and receive the vibrations from all the people who love you and are thinking about you. In the middle of the crowd, you will find me. Right now, there is no one that can be less lonely than you. Keep your course and your faith. Love, Luc."

Tears were streaming down my face by the time I finished the letter. As beautiful as his words were, and as much as I did not doubt the sincerity with which he wrote them, I knew that Luc and I would never share a future. He was already married and had a child. When he had first told me about Fabienne, in Taboga, I had thought that she was a girlfriend. But as my rusty French became lubricated, less conversation flew over my head and the fog began to clear, revealing the obvious facts.

Fabienne was his wife. They had eloped when they were eighteen, had lived together ever since, and brought new life onto the planet. The pictures on the bulletin board behind his chart table were not of different beautiful women, but of one woman taken over the span of fifteen years. They had fought; she had left the boat in Martinique and was now in France. He wanted a divorce, he said, but the only problem was his son. Tristan was the love of his life.

"He renews my youth, Tania. With him, I discover the wonders of the world as they unfold before his eyes. I was a cynic and Tristan is showing me the beauty of life all over again. I don't know what to do. All I know is that I could never give him up."

Hidden in between the words he had spoken was the reality of our situation. He could never leave his family. No matter how miserable it made me feel, here in the middle of the ocean, I couldn't help thinking about what fifteen years together with one person really meant. His whole life, once away from his parents, had been spent with Fabienne. All his adult memories were of her. Christmases, every ocean passage, motorcycle accidents—the stories of his adventures all had a female character with the same name. In the Galápagos, I had begun to realize that we would never have a future together. Now, hard as it was, I had to try and accept that. Things were going to be different in the Marquesas and once again, it would be just me and Dinghy. Pulling out my logbook, I tried to put my feelings into words.

"The most beautiful, yet sad birthday I've ever had. Listening to the tape, I am crying. I miss my home and family and wonder if they are thinking of me today. The wonderful letters from Daddy, Jade and of course Luc. The Bailey's Irish Cream and even Mommy's hair. I have definitely left something wonderful behind, and when I return it will all be so different. I love Luc, Daddy, Mommy, Jeri, Nina, Tony, Jade and my friends. My ship is so small and the ocean so immense. Never ending, always another horizon. But God has given me his own special present: a beautiful sunny day. I love my crazy family and wish I could hear them laughing, fighting, anything. I try to imagine the sounds of voices, cars and living. But I am content with the rush of water, the wind, the leaks. Thank you, God, for life."

Finally, weariness overcame my racing mind. Jade's liqueur had really jazzed up my afternoon and, tuckered out, I pulled myself up from the cramped position wedged behind the table, grazing my hip bone. Cursing at the table, I swore that it would be the first thing to go overboard in *Varuna*'s upcoming Tahitian overhaul. I picked up the port berth's cushion, dragged out the lee cloth and tied it up to the handrails. Laying out the sleeping bag, blanket and sheet, I popped out on deck for a last check before bedtime.

The waves had gotten smaller and were coming directly from astern. The sky was brilliantly aglow as the sun sank behind the horizon, preparing the Marquesas Islands to the west for another sunset. *Varuna* gently glided downwind, rocking slowly from side to side. Because I had grown accustomed to living on the walls, this was sheer ecstasy and I climbed back down below in a slightly cheered frame of mind. Curling up with Dinghy in the crook of my arm, I puffed up my pillow, tried to sort out the kaleidoscope of birthday memories and finally fell asleep.

For two days thereafter, the wind slowly began to decrease and I listened to the sails flap, undecided whether or not to put up the genoa, my biggest foresail. Just as I would make the decision and begin the maneuver, the wind would pick up, the log would tick faster, and I'd procrastinate.

"The House of the Rising Sun" began to get boring, so I set two more musical goals—Beethoven's "Für Elise" and one of Bach's bourrées. I practiced until my fingertips were sore, then popped up pressure cookers full of popcorn and read. For two lethargic days, I plucked, chomped, dutifully suffered through *Lady Chatterley's Lover*, and then livened things up by becoming a spy in *The Aquitaine Progression* while the taffrail log ticked erratically and we waited for more wind.

The third morning, in a decisive frame of mind, I pulled down the jib to replace it with the larger genoa, and noticed that the spinnaker pole was disintegrating where it attached onto a pad eye on the mast. As the jib ballooned in and out with the erratic course, shards of metal grated off the pole. I needed a new spinnaker-pole head, another repair that would have to wait until Tahiti.

Catching a much larger area of wind, the genoa pulled *Varuna* surfing down the playing waves. The surging power almost carried us airborne as we took off like a rocket from every wave, landing when the wave caught up. Every so often, whenever we were thrown off track, the Monitor would not have time to react and the mainsail would steal the genoa's wind. It emptied, then filled with a *whoosh* and a resounding slam, and the pole would jerk against the mast again and again. I cringed every time, envisioning the metal shaving off the pole's head, and prayed that it would last until the Marquesas.

Once the genny was up, I stared at the chart, muttering and chastising myself for having been too lazy to put it up earlier, "If I'd put it up two days ago, we'd be forty miles farther along." But I had to admit, I really didn't care that much about speed. *Varuna* was swinging along and life at that point couldn't have been more beautiful. I went outside to stand at the spray hood and Dinghy jumped up to lie down in front of me. My legs slightly apart, I played with *Varuna*'s seesawing motion, remaining motionless except for bending at the knees and feeling my thigh muscles stretch.

The South Pacific was a sapphire-blue seaway stretching far out of reach. When the sun shone directly into the water, rays of brilliantly transformed light created an inverted star reaching down to the depths. Under us, there was more than 5,000 feet of water—almost one mile straight down—and I was humbled by it. I had witnessed the emotions of this gargantuan ocean, and she was tolerating mine.

From the wind and current driving glowing, phosphorescent plankton through the waves at night, to the whales who migrated thousands of miles during their lifetimes, the sea was life, and out in her middle a rich drama unfolded before me every day. We passed birds who hunted flying fish until they tired and landed, bobbing up and down asleep on the waves. For a while, a huge tortoise entered our world, her horny head straining for air as her stubby legs paddled away, a thousand miles from land.

"What is she doing here?" I wondered. "How long will it take for her to get where she wants to go?" I marveled that she didn't need to carry around a sextant and chart. On her back would rest tired sea birds, hitchhikers on the seaway. Pilot fish and mahimahi followed in the shadow of *Varuna*, pulled along by her momentum, while flying fish soared in the air as we plowed through their midst. Dinghy sat at the edge of the cockpit, entranced, staring at the bubbles passing us by.

One day, just shortly after the noon sight, the dolphins came, but not in the small flocks to which I was accustomed. As far as I could see, there were dolphins—every sort of dolphin. Small blue-and-white striped, large black, small brown and medium-sized grays—an international reunion. Birds squawked and swooped down to the water, positive that with dolphins around, there had to be food. At 3:00 P.M. on October 10, I wrote in my logbook, *"The dolphins are still with me. It seems like there are hundreds of them and I am screaming hello with lots of joy. They are doing endless flips and acrobatics and trying to talk to me. I am so happy for their company that I cry. The birds are here also. We're having a party and everybody's invited. There is so much wildlife that I even wondered for a minute: Am I near land?"*

I stared and whooped along with the dolphins all afternoon, and around six o'clock fell asleep dreaming of them. At one o'clock in the morning, I awoke again; they were still with us, calling, trilling, cooing. That they stayed for ten entire hours was pretty incredible, but I prayed they would stay until the Marquesas. I drifted back to sleep and when I awoke again, there was only silence.

One morning, I made out a pinprick of a sail way off on the edge of the western horizon. We were still 1,229 miles from land. I grabbed my binoculars, ran to the foredeck and, leaning against the mast, strained my eyes trying to figure out the boat's details. Turning on the radio, I called and called, "Can anybody hear me? Can anybody hear me? This is the sailboat *Varuna*. Over." Nobody answered. For the better part of the day, the boat remained visible about 6 miles away, yet deaf to my calls. I wanted so badly to talk with them and verify my navigation. All my lines-of-position, LOPs, were working out, but there still was that little nagging self-doubt. To have had somebody back up my position would have boosted my confidence. But, there was no response. I felt a little pride in thinking I was keeping a better watch than the other boat but, mostly, I was disheartened; I had been looking forward to that human contact, knowing it was so close. The next time I checked the horizon, it was empty.

On the morning of the sixteenth, I roused myself and went out to check the horizon just in time to see a low-hanging black squall drawing up from astern. I watched as a straight curtain of rain on the calm waters shielded the patch of angry waves. The breeze suddenly quadrupled and gusts lifted *Varuna* out of the water and carried her reeling along as the wind-vane paddle and tiller slammed from side to side, trying to control a completely overcanvased boat.

Veering up into the wind, the mainsail backwinded and the boom strained against the preventer cord that held it from a slamming jibe to the opposite side of the boat. The preventer was vibratingly taut and I rushed to uncleat it. Let out slowly, the boom worked itself to the other side, making the boat heel over all the more, dragged down by yet another problem. The mast and rigging were shaking in the wind with the spinnaker pole and genny dragging in the water. The mainsail boom joined the gear party skinny-dipping over the lee side. I ran to the cockpit and freed the halyards to let the main and genny go, hastily pulling them down and securing them. The havoc finally subsided and I climbed back belowdecks to survey my wet bed and belongings strewn about the tiny cabin. It had hardly been a life-threatening situation, but now, with my curiosity satisfied, I decided that from now on it would be better for all concerned to just shorten sail immediately before a squall hit.

The wind continued to play hide and seek for several days. On and off, it would wane, then pick up to a moderate puff, push us along, and then wane again. Regardless of strength, it always blew from astern. Sometimes we would crawl forward with slamming sails shaking the rigging and jarring my nerves. Whenever the taffrail log's ticking slowed down, I would gloomily reassess my average speed for the day, fidgeting and poking holes through the chart, and wait for more speed.

In the logbook, routine entries on navigation and weather conditions were broken by idle musings on this and that, or the lyrics to songs that kept running through my head. During the long nights, the dolphins returned to visit, announcing themselves with their familiar playful whistles, their paths lit by moonbeams. I never tired of staring into the phosphorescence that lit my sometimes speedy, sometimes poky, nighttime wake as I dreamed about the Marquesas and the South Pacific landfalls that loomed ahead. We were almost there.

On Tuesday, October 22, at eight-thirty in the morning, I pulled out the chart and crossed out Monday the twenty-first, and mile 2,800. There were only 165 miles to go and I knew that every bird flying by had recently seen land. Outside, the increasing heat of the day slowed my actions in response. Even though *Varuna* was making an average of 4 knots, the rolling, slamming motion gave the impression that we weren't going anywhere. Every ten minutes or so I climbed outside to scan the horizon, but there was only water—calm water. Climbing back down below into the shade of the cabin, I prayed for enough wind to let us get in the next day. It had already been twenty-two days and I was desperately anxious to confirm my landfall.

"I'm going crazy!" I scratched across my logbook as the wind dwindled to nothing and the day began to drift ever so slowly into night. *"We won't get in tomorrow."* Pulling down the sails to stop the slapping noise, I brought my mattress up to sleep in the cockpit for relief from the heat.

In the morning, I awoke to a breath of breeze against my cheek and the wind greeting us from the north. Quickly raising the main and jib, I set the Monitor and once again pointed *Varuna*'s bow toward land. A last sun sight confirmed our position and, optimistically, I began to clean up the boat. All morning long, I looked for the telltale cloud bank that hangs over islands. Although the vision of it eluded me, I was undaunted, knowing that my calculations were correct; we had to be about 55 miles away. I left my perch, leaning against the spray hood, and went below to make a batch of popcorn to ease the tension.

This was the big test. If I found Hiva Oa, my navigation was spot on. I sat at the stove, jiggling the pressure cooker so the kernels of corn wouldn't stick to the bottom, and thought about *Thea.* Luc and Jean Marie had already eaten their steaks and salads days ago, I figured, and were waiting for me. Were they worried? I pulled out my logbook and mapped out my first minutes on shore.

"My plan is, as soon as I begin to make landfall, I'll cook up a flan. Then, when I anchor, I'll celebrate with Luc and Jean Marie and share the Bailey's with them. If they're not home, that's all right, I'll celebrate alone. Then I'll inflate the dinghy, go ashore, check for mail, make a phone call. . . ."

Simple plans for a landfall of such personal triumph, but I wasn't feeling as victorious as I had thought I would. If anything, I felt sad that a passage of such beauty was actually behind me. The past twenty-three days had been the best part of my trip since I had sailed out of New York, and I already felt a tinge of resentment at having to leave my ocean behind.

I headed out on deck with the popcorn to resume my vigil and, climbing through the companionway, thought I saw another sailboat. "Come here, Dinghy. Do you see what I see?" I grabbed my buddy and held him up toward the other boat. Totally uninterested, he pulled away and leapt below onto the bed to escape the piercing sunlight. In my haste to get to the VHF and call the boat, I spilled popcorn all over the cockpit.

"Westbound sailboat on the horizon, westbound sailboat on the horizon. This is the sailboat *Varuna.* Can you hear me?" I called.

"*Salut,* Tania. How are you?" said a familiar voice.

"Luc?" I was shocked beyond belief. "Luc! What are you doing here? What happened? Is everything all right?"

"Yes, yes. We're fine," he answered. "It has just been a horrible trip. There wasn't enough wind and we've been eating rice for four days. We have no more food. Do you have any fresh vegetables? We are desperate for some. How was your trip?"

"Well, my trip was good. Sometimes not enough wind, but it was nice," I answered. "I just cooked the last of my fresh vegetables yesterday, but I have some canned food. You're welcome to it. I don't think we'll make it in tonight. Do you?"

There was little chance of it, he said. We briefly summarized our voyages and Jean Marie grabbed the transmitter to say hello. We decided to keep on sailing through the night and when we arrived outside the entrance to the anchorage, the two boats could drift until daylight.

Now I was thoroughly excited, and everything I did for the rest of the day was with trembling hands and eager anticipation. Preparing the cockpit so I could take a bath, I put the slats in the companionway and moved the cat litter from the floor. Throwing buckets of water over my head, I scrubbed my hair, imagining what the Marquesas were like. I had found them! The longest projected passage of my circumnavigation was over.

During the night, I steered the boat by hand part time, cooked the flan and tossed a canned vegetable salad. In unison, the two friends, *Thea* and *Varuna*, sailed into the lee of the island. As previously planned, at 3:00 A.M., the twenty-fourth of October, we arrived in Baie de Traîtres, Traitor Bay, and tied a line between the two boats, waiting for daybreak.

The moon was beginning to wane, but it still illuminated the outlines of volcanic peaks towering above and lining the bay. Stars twinkling in a velvet sky were the backdrop to the black outline of Hiva Oa. The pungent smells of vegetation and smoke from native hearths wafted out to *Varuna*. The only thing left was to see what I could only feel and smell, and with bated breath, we awaited morning.

Luc came aboard *Varuna* and we talked for a couple of hours, ate the salad, passed some to Jean Marie, and toasted our landfall. Jokes and laughter shot through the night air between the two boats. I heard about how they had played Scrabble every day and how Jean Marie had won only once. On the last day, Luc finally admitted to cheating the whole time and laughed at how Jean Marie never noticed. With the reunion and the banter, I was catapulted out of my peaceful solitude and placed irrevocably back in touch with humanity.

A hush came over us as the breaking dawn colored in the blackness of a world without sun, and our two drifting sailboats stood in quiet awe of the scene. Slowly the lights of the day were turned on, unveiling lush vegetation cascading down the rugged mountains that pawed like giant bear claws into the bay.

A beach lined in a thicket of coconut palms lay directly before us. Off to the right of the bay, three sets of masts were visible behind what looked like a small jetty protruding from the outer finger of land. Luc jumped back to *Thea*, threw me a line and, steering with the tiller to remain directly behind my tug, *Varuna* and I were towed through a narrow passage, between the end of the jetty and land, into the protected little harbor of Baie Taaoa. The enclosure was surrounded by more wanton tropical plants fringing the tops of little cliffs. A slight swell rebounded off the rock walls into the harbor and we joined a lone sailboat at anchor, gently rocking in the early morning calm.

What a feeling it was to cast off from *Thea*, let loose the anchor and have it hit the ground after twenty-four days and 2,965 miles. Murky brown water flowed past *Varuna*'s hull, testament to the heavy rainfall and runoff from the lush Marquesas. I inhaled the perfumed air, musky with the underlying essence of smoke from the morning fires, and remembered that this was a place where only a few people had the luxury of a stove. Tied stern to the jetty were two other sailboats, brightly painted fishing boats and the local sailing pirogues. Double-checking to be sure everything was secure aboard *Varuna*, I dived into the water and swam to my friends.

My images of the South Seas had always been colored by childhood picture books—exotic beauties carrying trays of fruit and pirogues racing through turquoise lagoons as laughing girls looked on. Almost all the portrayals of the Polynesians were of a handsome, smiling people, always giving, welcoming and acting like eternal children. Now that I was really here, I would find each of these images to be the rule rather than the exception.

Since the first explorer disembarked from the blue void to feast his eyes on these pagan South Seas islands, the palettes of our imaginations have been changed forever. The painter Paul Gauguin reached his zenith here; the poet and singer Jacques Brel, when he learned he had cancer, came here to die; and explorer Thor Heyerdahl came to Fatu Hiva, an island just to the south, in search of an isolated place to create his own utopia. The Marquesas have the power to make men dream of paradise, and their dreams have shaped those of generations.

The first legal course of action upon arrival was the obligatory customs check-in with the local *gendarmerie* in the village of Atuona, about three miles around the harbor and up a hill. My legs wobbled and my balance was way off kilter after so long at sea. Trudging into town on a dirt road covered with snail shells made me remember how little exercise the lower part of my body received on the boat. Only certain muscles had developed, while others had turned to Jell-O.

The mountain road was lined by orange, mango and tamarind trees and spattered with the riotous blooms of hibiscus. As we walked, the tap, tap, tapping of little hammers could be heard everywhere as women crafted the beautiful tapas they stretched from the pulp of trees before decorating them with intricate geometrical designs. Closer to town, shy groups of ravishing *vahines*, the beautiful women of Polynesia, stood around giggling. *"Bonjour,"* they said as we passed. This was French territory, and the Gallic influence was evident in the language spoken all around and in the tricolor flag hanging in front of the post office and *gendarmerie.*

Phone calls were placed through the post office, and I went there first, anxious to talk to my family at home and tell them I had made it. Jeri was first. The eleven digits of her phone number code left our small building, crossed the Pacific to California, zipped through the Midwest and, when the man signaled to me, I picked up the receiver and heard a ringing sound all the way back on the East Coast of the United States.

Jeri's voice was music to my ears. I had missed her and told her all about Panama, my trip, my birthday at sea, the Galápagos, the weather during the passage, the animals. She caught me up on all the local news at home and I was pleased to hear that not much had changed. Fritz was still his kooky self. Christian was preparing to come into the city and live at the loft with Tony and Jade because my father was planning a trip. How was my father? The same, she sighed. Although their relationship had ended the year before, she was still very much a part of us. After six years of being there when we needed a mother figure, she considered us her children.

"So who's Luc?" asked Jeri.

"He's just a friend," I answered.

"Really?"

"Yeah, well . . . really."

Next I braced myself for the call to my father. According to the itinerary, I should have been in Fiji by this time and still hadn't talked with him about staying in Tahiti for hurricane season. The man at the post office put the call through and my father accepted it jubilantly.

"Hey, Ding-a-ling! Happy birthday! How was it?"

Answering him in a flurry, I tried to make him feel my excitement. "The trip was great, Daddy. And guess what . . . *Varuna* crossed the whole 3,000 miles in the same amount of time as Luc's boat, which is double her size. I even got here *before* them. They had to catch up to *me* in the end."

"Wow, pretty good. Now, what are your plans for leaving?"

"Hey, wait a minute," I stammered. "I just got here. Come on already."

"Yah, yah. I just want to know if you're planning to stay one week, three weeks, two months . . . what?"

"Well, I haven't figured that out yet . . . probably two or three weeks. Anyway, there's something I want to talk to you about. What do you think about my staying in Tahiti for the hurricane season? The engine is totally broken, there's a lot of things that need work on the boat and I have friends who'll help me do it all. And *plus*, I have to wait out hurricane season somewhere, right?"

"Achh. The chances that you get a hurricane are slight. And even if you get one, big deal. You'll have a great story to write about."

"Ha ha. Very funny. Seriously, I really have to stop somewhere and do all the work. Don't worry. I'll be home on time. I have two years, remember."

No matter how lighthearted, our conversations always ended up making me feel as if I were shirking my duties. I'd just spent the past five months learning how to survive on a sailboat at sea, making daily decisions that directly affected my fate, yet every time I talked to my father, he made me feel like a child, causing me to seriously question my decisions. Regardless of the value of a good hurricane story, I finished the call deciding that the refit time would be spent in Tahiti.

I wrote down the number of my mother's apartment in New York so the man at the post office could put through my last call. Judging by all past experiences, this call would be a long one. When my mother used to call us in New York from her home in Switzerland, she would have talked all day if my father hadn't just hung up the phone after an hour.

Wondering what she was doing, I gazed idly from the doorway at little children playing with sticks and running around in the back-yard. Their skin was a beautiful *café au lait*, their brown eyes stealing quick glimpses at me from under their mops of black hair. I waved and they ran away giggling. The man behind the counter finally signaled and I rushed to pick up the phone. It rang four times, then my mother's voice came over the line.

"Do you accept a collect call from Donia?" asked the operator.

"Donia? You must mean *Tania*." Her voice, feeble as it sounded, still held the imperious bearing toward people in her service that had always embarrassed me as a child.

"Donia, Tonia, whatever," the operator's voice crackled.

"Yes, she is my daughter. Of course I accept the charges. . . ."

"Hello, Mommy," I said slowly. "I'm here in Hiva Oa in the Marquesas. I made it."

"Oh, my dear Tania. I'm so happy to hear your voice. How are you? Do you wear the undershirts I sent you? Are you protecting yourself with sunblock? Are you eating all your vegetables?"

"I'm fine. I had a really incredible trip. I'll tell you all about it. But first, I want to know how you are."

"Oh, I am very weak, but Tony and Jade are being very nice with Mommy. Will you please tell Daddy not to disconnect my phone? He is throwing tantrums only because I am trying to tell him the truth. He is threatening to cut me off. Tania, Mommy loves you. Mommy knows what is best for you. Daddy doesn't want to know the truth. I am trying to tell him but he refuses to listen. . . ." And off she went on one of her nonstop litanies about my father. Often, she would go on for so long that I sometimes felt like leaving the phone dangling and coming back later to see if she would even notice.

"Wait a minute, Mommy," I interrupted. "Before we start talking about all that, will you just please tell me how you are. Do you feel better?"

"You know how I am," she answered.

As much as I tried not to dwell on the situation, I knew well how my mother was. She was slowly dying, not only from the cancer that was rampaging through her delicate frame, but from demons that seemed to have overcome her when I was still a child. I always thought it had started on the night before my eighth birthday, after the car accident that she claimed was my father's attempt to murder her. But years later, he told me there was much more I didn't know.

Shortly after that accident, she stopped caring for her appearance and began wearing the same clothes for days, and then weeks at a time. Her moods darkened and the change in personality frightened us. We would beg her to make herself beautiful again, take her hair out of the tight ponytail, put on a skirt instead of the plain dark pants, to put on pretty shoes instead of clogs, but she refused.

To my mother, everybody who came to our house in those days

was a liar, cheater, prostitute or homosexual, and whenever her jealousy overcame her she'd fly into a fit of name-calling, virtually driving people out. Her hostilities also began to encompass my father's artwork, and when two pieces disappeared—a sculpture he had done and a table made by Fritz—she denied having anything to do with it. One day months later, while we were driving to school, I saw the table in a backyard and told my father. It was the house of a junkman who said he had found it in the dump. The sculpture turned up ten years later, when we got a phone call from some people in New Jersey who had received it from my mother. She had made them promise never to tell, but they had finally been overcome with guilt.

My father filed for divorce and custody when I was nine. It only made my mother rage all the more as she watched him pack his clothes, paints, brushes, canvases and stretchers. He moved to Soho in Manhattan, where he bought a loft with Fritz, leaving Tony, Nina, Jade and me alone in the emptiness of the house. My mother was miserable and desperate until she met the Intaglias, a family of religious fanatics that lived nearby. With them, she sought consolation and found a religious belief that embraced her confused passions and, even more important, showed her a way to help win permanent custody of her children. With the help of the Intaglias, she set out to prove that my father was a child molester.

For my mother, marriage and family were the most important things in life and, looking back, it seems she was trying everything in her power to hold on to my father by hurting him. I remember he used to tell us, "I swear, if I so much as showed admiration for a tree, Mommy would have it chopped down."

But my mother's problems were not the problems of a normal woman; she was more deeply troubled than we ever really imagined. Young as I was, I couldn't begin to know how to help solve her problems. I only saw that my mother was totally different from the storybook mothers of my classmates. As good as her intentions may have been, I saw a mother who made us wear the same clothes every day to school, day in and day out until I was twelve—plaid skirt, blue sweater, wool socks and dowdy little leather shoes. She said she wanted us to be dressed the way she had when she went to boarding school in England.

Because I was the eldest, I was prepared to do anything in my juvenile power to help my father get a good story for the courts and win the custody battle. Whenever one of my mother's long-winded sermons began to deteriorate into persecution tirades about my father, New York and everyone else in the world who was against her, I tried to defend him, often losing my temper. I got hit with wooden clogs, locked in the cellar and pelted with flying corncobs. Every time she pulled me around by the hair, I would carefully brush out all the loose ones, put them into an envelope and save them for my father to use as evidence in court.

For two and a half years Nina, Tony, Jade and I lived through endless sessions with psychiatrists and social workers who tried to interpret what we told them and decide which parent would be better for us. My mother had preachers who had never met the family sign affidavits saying they had seen my father performing unnatural acts with us; one affidavit that I saw by accident said he had forced us to have sex with our dog.

One day, she picked us up from school and we didn't take the normal route home. The back of our old lime-green Volkswagen camper was loaded with luggage and she headed for New York City. I thought, "Yay, Daddy finally won us and she's taking us to him," hoping our days of psychiatrists and Rorschach tests were over.

In New York, we drove to a shipping terminal and stopped in front of the *Queen Elizabeth II*. In late May of 1976, after a transatlantic journey of eight days, we arrived in Southampton, England, and settled into a home for old people in London that rented out rooms. One month later, on our way back from Kensington Gardens, my father was standing on the steps of our hotel. In my eyes, the Second Coming had occurred.

My father had tracked down the only person he had ever heard of from my mother's past. During my parents' first few months together in Paris, my mother had flown to London every three or four weeks. She said she was visiting her uncle, Charles, and always arrived back in Paris with enough money to keep her in luxuries until the next visit and unwilling to talk much about where she had been. Uncle Charles, she said, was the custodian of her trust fund, her benefactor and the only family she ever had. Upon her marriage, the money had stopped without explanation.

Ten years later, when my father contacted Uncle Charles to find out if he had any idea where my mother might be hiding us, he said that, yes, he had heard from her recently. His suggestions about our whereabouts not only led my father to our lodgings, but also to a new revelation.

Charles was not my mother's real uncle, nor did he know her as well as she had claimed. The only fragment of truth that my father had held dear about my mother was shattered. Charles then said that he thought she was about to leave England that afternoon for the Continent. There was no time to waste. Questions about the friendship with my mother would have to wait for calmer moments, and my father rushed through London to head us off. When they met on the doorstep of that old hotel, he and my mother looked at each other for a long time without speaking. The next time my father tried to contact Charles, he received word that he was dead.

Because we were on the other side of the Atlantic, my father decided to take us to Switzerland to see his family. We spoke no German and played with our cousins who knew no English, while my mother fought with my grandparents, my father, and my aunt and uncle, lashing out at them like a wounded wolf. One day, we went for a ride to see a glacier on top of an alp. My father drove, Grossmutti sat in the passenger seat and my mother sat in the back seat with us. Continuous arguments shook the car until I finally began crying to my mother to please stop. She slapped me across the face and my nose began to bleed.

"*Listen!*" she shouted back. "For Christ's sake, I'm fighting for our future!"

Grossmutti, seeing the blood, started yelling at her and also got smacked in the face. Like something from The Three Stooges, she turned around and hit my father, who had started hollering just as we rounded the bend on a hairpin curve. He slammed on the brakes and screamed at the top of his lungs, "This is *it*, Sabina! *I've had it!*" and headed straight for a sanitarium.

"Tania, may I come and be with you on *Varuna?* You know that Mommy is sick and that she will not get better." Her pleading voice jarred me back to the present.

"Mommy, you can't. You know I'm doing this alone. And even if Daddy agreed to pay for you to come, you're too weak. You should stay where there is everything to keep you as healthy as possible. And if you talk this long with everybody, how do you expect me to convince him to let you keep the phone?" I immediately regretted saying that, as she burst into tears, and tried to console her, as I impatiently glanced toward the bistro where Luc and Jean Marie sat waiting.

"Mommy, now that I am on land, I promise I'll call you one week from today and we'll talk about it then, OK?" I could still hear her whimpering. Tears had become a regular ritual with her over the years and my patience had developed narrow limits. I could imagine my father's face when he got the phone bill for a forty-five-minute call to the Marquesas, and tried to bring the conversation to a close.

"Tania, it is time that you knew the truth," she continued, unfazed. "Time is growing short and there is much to do, much to say. Daddy denies me, Tania." She began to cry again.

"Mommy," I interrupted. "Mommy, I'm sorry, I really have to go now. I love you. OK? I have to hang up. Say goodbye. Please. I'll call you in seven days . . . I love you . . . Bye-bye, Mommy."

Just before the phone reached the receiver, I heard her frail voice calling, "Mommy loves you very much. Never say goodbye, Tania, always say *see you* . . ."

Walking back toward the bistro in a daze, I imagined what was going on at home, and saw my mother's little studio apartment, one block up the street from my father's in Soho. Nina was off at school and Tony and Jade were living with my father, probably spending a lot of time helping my mother, visiting her, eating meals with her now and again. Except for their company, she was completely alone in the loneliest place in the world—the crowded island of Manhattan. She had left any friends she had in Switzerland four months before my departure and no one in New York cared about her except for my brother, my sisters and me. But she came back to the United States anyway, because she only lived for her children, she said, and her children were in New York.

I remembered begging my father to let her come, after spending a month with her in Switzerland. It was the month of my decision to sail around the world, when she had given me her blessing. She had been ill and hadn't seen her four children all together for two years. I wasn't able to let her life drain away in another country with only the occasional visit from one of us at a time. I wanted to help grant her greatest wish and bring her back to us in New York.

She had caused the family so much suffering that for a very long time my father was reluctant to help her in any way. Finally, he softened and allowed her back into our lives. He went to Switzerland, obtained a new passport for her, packed her belongings and brought her back. After setting her up in a studio apartment, he tried to have as little to do with her as possible. She had been too proud to ask him to bring her to New York and never knew that it was I who had begged him to let her come.

When it came to arguments with my father about my mother's welfare, I didn't always know what drove me to defend her so vehemently. The devastation she had wreaked on him and on our childhoods certainly was not lost on me. Indeed, stealing us away to England had been child's play compared to what she did later that same year. I hadn't completely forgiven her for the things she had done, nor did I understand what motivated her. I only knew that she was my mother, and as I grew older, my instinct to protect her overshadowed any of the old instincts to escape from her.

Hearing her voice that morning made me feel low and helpless, and memories of the past continued to steal the thunder from the splendor of my landfall. I stopped walking and let my eye slowly trace the line of tall palms swaying in the warm breeze above the village. Hiva Oa was draped in the velvet greens of a rain forest and, underneath my feet, was the power of earth newly formed from South Seas volcanos.

A monthly freighter, the *Aranuui*, made the rounds of harbors in the Tuamotus and Marquesas, picking up the sacks of copra headed for factories in Tahiti, and carrying passengers along from island to island. When the *Aranuui* arrived in Hiva Oa, Jean Marie decided that it was time to leave *Thea* for new adventures and Luc and I were now alone.

While we lingered in Hiva Oa, Luc tried once again to fix my engine. He kicked me off *Varuna* while he wrestled with it, saying, "I have to be serious now. Go away and don't distract me with your chatter."

"All right," I answered. "Call if you need anything."

A week later, as we prepared to leave, I went to get money for provisioning in my decoy can of WD40 lubricant; the bottom unscrewed and my money was in the hidden compartment. I couldn't find it, and after desperately searching the boat, finally asked Luc about it.

"Hmmm, a can of WD40?" he answered. "Oh yes. Now I remember. When I was playing with your engine, I threw an empty can overboard."

"*What!* There was four hundred dollars in that can. That was all the money I had in the world. You threw *four hundred dollars overboard!*" We searched the shoreline in silence and came up empty-handed. I was flat broke and, as much as I hated to, had to borrow money from Luc to pay for provisioning.

Ever since we arrived, the atmosphere between us had been charged, and I missed the comfort of our old relationship. We now avoided the touchy subject that stood like a fortress between us, and let pettier issues become the battleground where we released the tensions of our situation. As tenuous as things had become during our stay in Hiva Oa, our shared goal of reaching Tahiti remained the bond. One day, Luc called Fabienne and then told me that she and Tristan were going to meet him in Tahiti. I felt exhausted relief. The dread that something like this would be the final severing blow was behind me.

On November 18, I walked into town to place the weekly call to my mother. The phone rang twice and I was surprised to hear a West Indian voice accept the charges.

"Hello?" I said.

"I am Mrs. Aebi's nurse," she answered, "may I help you?" A lump formed in my throat.

"Oh my God. This is Tania, her daughter. Is she OK?" I shouted through the static.

"Your mother needs a twenty-four-hour nurse. But you can still talk to her. She just needs help now."

"OK, thank you." I waited, imagining a faceless person carrying the phone across the gray carpet over to my mother. The slurred sounds that came over the phone frightened me.

"Mommy, it's Tania. I can't understand anything you are saying, but I'll come home as soon as I can." I barely understood a feeble "I love you."

"I love you, too, Mommy. Hang in there. . . ." I hung up the phone and called to arrange a flight from Tahiti to the States, making a reservation for December 6, in two and a half weeks. It would take about ten days, depending on the vagaries of the weather, to sail *Varuna* 750 miles through the coral heads of the Tuamotus to Tahiti and secure the boat before flying home. Although I had thought I would be prepared for this moment, my head was spinning. I wanted to get home before it was too late, and ran to tell Luc we had to leave as soon as possible.

This was the beginning of a Christmas season of goodbyes. Goodbye to Luc, a friend with whom I had shared some of the most memorable moments of my life. And, hardest of all, one month later in Manhattan, a final goodbye to my mother.

t was four days after Christmas, at one in the morning, in Tahiti's Faaa Airport, that I stepped off the UTA flight from San Francisco, feeling blue and disoriented. In twenty-four hours, my airplane had just covered the same distance that had taken *Varuna* six months, and I was not yet able to put the events of the previous two weeks at home into any kind of perspective. My only clearly identifiable emotion was an almost desperate longing to get back to *Varuna*.

As I stepped out of the recycled air of the plane, the familiar fragrance of the island embraced me as a group of young, flower-adorned Tahitians stood singing near the customs line. One girl, wearing a wraparound *pareu*, presented as a gesture of welcome to each of the tired tourists a lei of Tahiti tiare, the delicate white flower that drowns Tahiti in its sweet perfume. As she put one around my neck, I remembered the ones that I had brought home for my mother and had hung above her bed. Fighting back the tears that had been welling up out of control since the call from Hiva Oa, I stepped forward at my turn and handed my passport and papers to a man behind the desk. Everything was in order; he stamped the passport and smiled. "Welcome to Tahiti."

Walking to the luggage carousel, I looked for my duffel bags and the box with a new jib, engine parts, spinnaker pole head, and self-steering gear pieces that Jeri had helped me pack. Passing through customs, I looked around for Luc, who had agreed to come and take me back to Papeete, where *Varuna* was anchored. I thought how nice it would be to see his familiar face.

"Taxi, *mademoiselle?*" asked a porter.

"No, thank you. I have a ride," I answered, and walked toward an empty bench. Luc hadn't arrived yet, so I sat down to wait.

It had been almost exactly one and a half months since the dreaded phone call home to my mother, when I realized that fate was dealing out her final cards. Thinking about the beauty of the Marquesas, the pressure of the trip through the islands to Tahiti, and the overwhelming sadness of being with my mother, it was hard to believe I had already been to and returned from New York.

After the Marquesas, I remember anticipating equally beautiful places with every landfall, but always experienced a slight disappointment. Never again did *Varuna* sail into such a magnificent display of nature's handiwork. On November 21, Luc and I had left Hiva Oa and sailed to the two southernmost islands in the Marquesas group, Tahuata and Fatu Hiva, planning to spend a couple of days between the two.

Fatu Hiva rose into the clouds like a wide-shouldered behemoth cloaked in green, and its beauty could haunt the soul of the most avowed cynic. Everywhere could be traced the life of the volcanos that had created these islands. The paths of ancient lava flows were visible from the sea by the different colors of plants that had followed them. Everywhere was a chaos of excess. Superabundant jungle vegetation, freshwater pools and paths smothered in decaying mangos, the stone-walled remnants of the terrace homes of an ancient civilization, colossal coconut palms and jagged boulders strewn willy-nilly. There was no sense of order, no consistency. When God designed the Marquesas, I thought, he must have been high.

Snorkeling in Tahuata and paddling around an outcropping of rocks to look for shells, I remember becoming mesmerized by the majestic underwater flutterings of a sea eagle—*fafahua* in Marquesan. The animal was gorgeous, with its great flowing pair of flipper wings and smooth gray body almost resembling that of a mini-dolphin. Remaining suspended, I watched as two manta rays in a mating dance soared by, their enormous wingspans ruffling the water in a captivating demonstration of synchronized swimming. I wondered what these graceful creatures made of me with my gangly limbs and a tube of bubbles coming from my mouth.

In Hanavavé we made friends with some natives and found something of value we could share with them. Preferring the modern methods of hunting over spearing and wrestling the wild boar and goats to the ground, they said they needed gun ammunition. Luc had some cartridges and gladly gave them away and, in return, both our boats were loaded to the bulwarks with papayas, limes, mangoes, oranges, enormous bunches of bananas, tomatos and sweet grapefruit the size of footballs.

But all of the joys had been overshadowed by a sense of urgency. Ahead were still 750 miles through the mine field of coral atolls separating us from Luc's waiting job and family in Tahiti and my flight home. With a last regretful glance back, *Varuna*, Dinghy and I sailed out of Hanavavé, the Bay of Virgins, alone again.

The Marquesas, Tuamotus and Societies, all archipelagoes of French Polynesia, tell the stories of time. As *Varuna* wove her way through, past and around them, their differing features revealed the geographical evolution of most of the islands in the South Pacific. As the volcanos erupted from the ocean floor and surged their way upward, the more aggressive peaks emerged above the ocean surface. The youngest of these volcanic islands are the Marquesas, which appeared most recently in evolutionary time. The Society Islands to the southwest are older, slightly eroded versions of the Marquesas, but there is a difference. Over millions of years, the sediment and coral reefs accumulated and formed shelves and barrier reefs around them.

The atolls of the Tuamotus are thickly clustered together and stood directly in my path between the Marquesas, and Tahiti in the Society Islands. They are the oldest of the three different clans and the erosion process is even more advanced. The peaks of the islands have been swallowed completely back below the sea from whence they came, leaving behind only the fringing reef. Where there once was a volcano there is now a deep lagoon with a ring of coral reefs around it. This last stage is called an atoll and it is the most dangerous for a sailboat. On an atoll, the only things of any significant height above sea level are the coconut palms. Assuming that a palm would be a hundred feet tall, on the best of days, with the clearest of views, from the deck of *Varuna* an atoll could only be seen from about 12 miles. This range of visibility decreased with any bad weather, and at night was nonexistent.

If I had had to sail through the archipelago by myself, relying on dead reckoning and celestial navigation, plus no engine, prudence would have dictated skirting the entire group. I didn't have a thirst for thrills and by no means any desire to pass through 5- to 11-mile-wide channels between the atolls, seeing nothing and knowing that humongous waves were crashing against the reefs on both sides of me. If my navigation faltered one step, I could end up in the same position as many other sailors had already found themselves: ship-less, homeless and wet. The problem with skirting the obstacle course was that it added 200 miles onto the trip and there was a plane to catch. I decided to sail the shortest route, directly through the Tuamotus Archipelago to Tahiti, behind *Thea* and her SatNav.

Luc lent me an extra battery that we had charged along with my two so there would be enough electricity for the radio. The trip was timed perfectly with the advance of the full moon, and the lunar light helped keep our boats within sight of each other during the nights. We set up a radio schedule for every three hours to compare notes and course changes. The conditions were mild and the boats moved at about the same speed. There wasn't enough wind to move *Thea*'s heavy bulk too fast, but just enough to make *Varuna* skip along, which balanced everything perfectly.

The eight days were spent eking out as much speed as possible from *Varuna*, altering and trimming the sails, reading, and eating the provisions of fruit, trying to keep a step ahead of the rotting ones. We threaded our way around the atolls, following each other through the fluky wind and squalls.

Day by day, more often than not we stormed our way like two angry children over the calm waters between the atolls of Manihi and Takaroa, then a day later, between Rangiroa and Arutua. As we crawled closer to Tahiti, the walls of depression around Luc and me built and steepened, and we finally began to take it out on each other. I couldn't know exactly how he felt about resuming his role as a family man; all I knew was that I was heartbroken about the way things had turned out, and as we got closer to Tahiti most of our radio contact ended up being aggressive and antagonistic. Even though he was dealing with his own confusion, I was still angry at Luc, who seemed angry at life. On December 2, I wrote in my log, "It's finally beginning to sink in. A whole long leg of my trip and a crucial chapter in my life is ending. Like Luc once quoted, 'To leave is to die a little.' It is difficult to accept it all. I feel out of control."

When I had told my father, from the telecabine in Hiva Oa, that I wanted to come home to New York to see my mother, he only added to my inner turmoil by urging against it. "Listen, Tania," he said. "When you left New York, you knew it would be over. We talked about it. You knew that this door would be closed behind you. If I were you, I wouldn't come back now. You'll just make it harder on yourself."

But I was incapable of coming around to his way of thinking, and he found himself incapable of dealing with it at all. My father's way of confronting the death of my mother was by leaving the country altogether. His letters and our phone conversations over the past couple of months had conspicuously avoided the touchy subject of her deteriorating health. Instead they had been full of his plans to enter the Paris-Dakar, a grueling car race from France crossing the Sahara through Algeria, Niger, Mali, then through Guinea and Senegal in northwestern Africa. The race, plus the preparations, would take him away from New York for several months. I felt a certain relief that he would be out of the country and occupied with his own adventures when I returned, and probably so did Tony and Jade, who would be left with Christian, Jeri and my mother.

Technically, ever since Panama I had been making Pacific passages in the wrong season and was never able to take full advantage of the strong southeast trades. With the dying winds, it was an excruciatingly slow passage to Tahiti, where after each day of disappointing progress I had to refigure and push back my ETA, which threatened to overlap with the day of my flight. For eight days, our sails flapped in the meager baby breath as we inched along, and as the time dragged by, I never stopped thinking about my mother, praying that I would arrive before it was too late. The sands of the hourglass were draining fast.

At 8:00 P.M. on the fifth of December, the horizon ahead was aglow with lights but we were still 40 miles from Papeete, Tahiti, our destination. My airplane was due to leave midday on the sixth and, helplessly, I watched the already feeble wind die again. The lighthouse of Point Venus flashed its beacon over the oily waters, lighting the dark every few seconds, increasing my agitation. Fishing boats zoomed across all four points of the compass as the gloomy night painfully shuffled through and morning dawned ugly and gray.

Squabbling over the radio and fighting our way toward the harbor, with the only wind coming from pesky squalls, Luc and I took in and then shook out reefs as they came and went. Ten miles from Papeete, the wind finally gave out altogether. I peeled a grapefruit, threw the peels overboard, and one hour later, they were still there. Overhead, my airplane thundered through the sky.

Now, feeling as if another lifetime had gone by since then, I sat in the airport listening to the rain pummeling the thin tropical roof, rushing through the gutters and coursing in waterfalls to the street. For the hundredth time, I looked up to see if Luc was heading my way. Except for a small group of rowdy taxi drivers and the echoing footsteps of the occasional lost soul, the airport was empty. If Luc had received my message and planned to pick me up, this discounted even a broken alarm clock. I had been waiting for two hours. Walking over to the taxi drivers, I asked one of the more talkative men for a ride into town, warning him, "But we may have to turn around and come right back."

"Pas de problème," he said, "get in." We loaded my two duffel bags, boxes and plastic bags into the car, and set off on the French-built highway toward town. In the tropics, in every language, it seemed that the answer to everything was just that. No problem.

In New York, everybody had looked pallid compared to the beautiful and suntanned Tahitians I had left behind. The population of this island is spread out along the shoreline, while the savage interior of mountains, gorges, cliffs and ravines remains largely devoid of people, except for the occasional hermit. The cosmopolitan Tahitian capital of Papeete is the center of French Polynesian government and industry, and it was as flashy as rumored on the sailor's grapevine, a sort of mini-Paris with a tropical overlay. Before going home, I had left *Varuna* tied up to *Thea* on Papeete's quay.

The city's expensive jewelry and clothing shops, terrace restaurants, galleries, supermarkets, churches and post office, separated from the quayside by a tree-lined highway, were quiet and dark at this hour, almost 4:00 A.M., but before long, the streets would be hives of action. Women at their stands, surrounded by friends and family, would be selling shell ornaments, ashtrays and jewelry to tourists debarking from cruise ships. The crowds of people would mill in the marketplace near their favorite vendors, choosing the luscious vegetables sold on one side; on the other, flies would chime in with the activity of weighing, cleaning and distribution of the vast variety of seafood. Chinese fabric shops, hardware stores, appliance centers and eateries framed the bustling market. To add to the confusion, the Tahitian buses, called *le truck*, would blast out Polynesian ditties pumped up to full volume.

When I first arrived from the more quiet ways of life in the Marquesas, it was all quite confusing, but as with any unfamiliar town, one finds the main squares, then works out from the nucleus; in Papeete, it was the market. Above the city, the peak of Mont Orohena towered, with a small ridge below forming a queen's tiara. It was only four hours into the stillness of a new morning, the time when even the late-nighters have finally succumbed to sleep. All the bustle of the city and the beauty of Mont Orohena were still slumbering in the last stolen moments of night.

My taxi and I arrived on the waterfront in the rainy darkness. I wanted badly to get into my little home, see Dinghy, be surrounded by my belongings and disappear from the world. I looked for *Thea*'s familiar hull. During the week before I left for New York, Luc and I had tied our boats together in front of a white church, our backs to the harbor's entry pass through the reefs. He had promised to watch over *Varuna* and take care of Dinghy while I was gone.

The taxi driver pulled over and waited while I walked to the embankment to see *Varuna* in between two unfamiliar boats. She was anchored from astern, tied bow to the shore with long lines about 20 feet away over the water, and there was no *Thea*. Someone had flipped over my inflatable dinghy to prevent the rain from filling it like a bathtub. I had to wait until a civil hour in the morning before asking one of the neighbors to give me a lift. That was nearly three hours away and I couldn't wait in the pouring rain for someone to wake up.

Wearily, I turned around and shrugged at my driver. "I'm sorry. There's nobody around. I guess I have to go back to the airport and wait until morning."

"Pas de problème," he said and we sped back out, doubling his fare. Lugging my things to a bench, I arranged my duffels to make a lumpy bed and fell to thinking about my mother and the home I'd left behind again.

The closed window smell of sickness that had overpowered me when Christian opened the door to my mother's apartment two weeks before had been a jolt, but nothing compared to the sight of her physical deterioration over the previous six and a half months. Shocked beyond belief, I immediately hoped that she hadn't noticed my look of horror. Half seated on her bed, she was skeletal and jaundiced.

She opened her sunken eyes and smiled slowly in recognition. "Tania, you have come." I rushed to her and held her close, worrying that I would break her fragile ribs, and tried to hide my tears in her flannel nightgown. It was one I remembered giving her in Switzerland two years before. She was the size of a child. She had been smaller than I ever since I had started sprouting out in all directions, but now the contrast between us was almost grotesque.

Over the next few days, she wanted to hear all about my trip and I told her stories about the animals of the sea, about the magical phosphorescence, about how pretty *Varuna* was as she flew downwind in the trade winds. I told her about the flight from Tahiti to Los Angeles that flew directly above the Tuamotus and how, from my seat, you could see the perfectly rounded shapes of the atolls. They had looked like a bunch of doughnuts, I told her, thrown onto a seablue baking sheet. She listened to my stories and smiled and then asked me to do some Christmas shopping for Nina, Tony and Jade. Nina came down from college, we bought a Christmas tree and decorated it in the living area of the studio. Every day, her nurse did her hair, and she insisted on sitting up for every guest, always intent on being a lady.

The walls of my mother's apartment were covered with pictures of the family, the same pictures that had followed her from apartment to apartment ever since the divorce. They were happy pictures of her with my father in their early days, and countless others of Nina, Tony, Jade and me when we were children. She had enlarged the photos to poster size, mounted and framed them and, as a result, the place looked like a shrine. Everywhere were larger-than-life reminders of captured moments, treasured memories of my mother's days in the sun. I sat with her for a large part of every day, listening to her labored breathing and letting the smiling faces in all the photographs take me on a voyage of memories. It seemed hard to believe that the beautiful woman in those photographs had been bearing such a heavy burden.

I knew that everything she had done during our childhood was an attempt to force a reconciliation with my father, the only man she ever loved. From the day of the car accident until the day we began to live with him in New York, she had lashed out at everything that stood between her and her husband and, after it was too late for any reconciliation, at anything that stood between her and her children. I made sure to tell her that I knew she had never tried to do anything to intentionally hurt us as, over and over again, she repeated to me the stories of her struggle.

After my mother had spent a month in the sanitarium in Switzerland, we went back home to New Jersey with my father and, for a while, she became the kind of mother we had only dared dream about. But slowly, the effects of her treatment began to wear off and her eyes began to get that troubled look that usually signaled a volcano of problems about to erupt. Sometimes, out of nowhere during tense moments, she would fling wide the front door and scream at the top of her lungs, *"Help! HELP me!"* Just as suddenly, she would calm down and close the door. This might have been understandable if she were trying to make it look to the neighbors that my father was abusing her, but our house in New Jersey was completely isolated. We didn't have any neighbors.

Her time of peace had been too brief an oasis for there to even have been much of a discussion about suspending the divorce proceedings and, as things deteriorated, my father reluctantly moved out again and went back to New York. The sessions with the psychiatrists recommenced, while the divorce continued to wallow through the courts.

One afternoon, when I was in the seventh grade, my mother came to pick us up after school, with another carful of luggage. She headed, just like the last time, for New York, this time ending up at Kennedy Airport. I should have called my father, but we wanted to believe that we were only going to California for two weeks, as she said. IcelandAir carried us and all our belongings to Luxembourg. My mother rented a car, we drove to Switzerland and ended up in the village of Huemoz where there was an American religious group, L'Abri.

How long we would be there and why were just two of the many things my mother chose never to divulge. For her, all truths were layered in fantasies, as if she lived in another dimension. Something could happen to all of us together and later on, when we talked about it, it was as if something altogether different had happened to her. Different story, different time, different place.

One day at L'Abri, I found her sewing name tags onto towels and clothes. "What are you doing?" I asked. She didn't answer. "Mommy, please tell me. What are you doing with these things?"

"I am preparing your clothes for boarding school," she answered matter-of-factly. "You will all go to a boarding school until I can find a house and a job and we can live as a family again."

The boarding school, the Château de Montcherand, was set in an old lord's castle overlooking what once were his lands and vineyards in the French-speaking part of Switzerland. Now it was owned by a religious charity group that took in about forty children whose parents couldn't afford to care for them properly. The day my mother dropped us off at the Château, we cried, begging her not to leave us, and she drove away, promising to return when she could.

As desolating as the experience was when it began, it actually turned out to be a period of calm in the turmoil that surrounded us. Suddenly, there was rhyme and reason to our days, from waking up to lights out. We were around other children and formed friendships. Being in an environment where French was the official language, we had to do some cramming with the help of the *tantes* who ran the school. Before long, we were back to our boisterous selves and all our new French-speaking friends knew at least two words in the English language: "Shut up!"

There was no word from my father during these months. He must have been crazy with worry, once again desperately trying to figure out where we were. I wrote letters to him, hoping to sneak them out to a mailbox, but they were always intercepted en route by one of the *tantes* and sent to my mother instead.

My mother had no friends other than the Intaglias, who refused to be of any help to my father, and she had precious few acquaintances, so he was left to unravel the mystery of our whereabouts by himself. It wasn't until she filed for a divorce in Switzerland and he was served the papers in New York that he was able to find us. One day, he arrived on our doorstep.

The *tantes* listened to my father's side of the story, they let him see us and, when we went out of our minds with joy at the sight of him, they were moved by the sincerity of the reunion. How could this be the same monster described by my mother? Over the months, they admitted later, they had come to doubt her stories, having witnessed firsthand her erratic behavior. Before now, they had been in no position to do anything about it.

According to American law, my mother had kidnapped us and my father automatically had a legal right to our custody. But we were in Switzerland and out of American jurisdiction; my father's hands were tied and there was nothing he could do about it. She had applied for a divorce under our Swiss citizenship. This was her last chance and she was going to make the most of it.

In Switzerland, unless it can be proven that a mother is completely unfit to care for her children, or that she is a raving maniac, she will always get custody. My mother had assembled a group of highly respected lawyers and religious people for her defense. Although none had met us or my father, a perverted enough picture of him had been painted to make any normal person shudder. The courts made the Château our legal guardians until the case was settled.

On the day of the trial, the last person my mother expected to see was my father, and he walked into the courtroom, prepared with all the evidence needed to prove that his wife was mentally incompetent. After the accusations and evidence were all out on the table, the judge decided in his favor. Confident that he would win on the point of doubtful mental fitness, my father had also foreseen that my mother would immediately appeal the judge's decision, which would cement the whole case back into the Swiss legal system for God only knew how long. He was ready. He knew that it would take about forty-five minutes to file the appeal. For forty-five minutes, he would have legal custody and the right to take us out of the school.

That morning, there was an air of suspense around the Château. We knew that exciting things were happening, and before he left for the courthouse, my father had sworn us to secrecy about how the day would unfold. The *tantes* helped pack our belongings, our Uncle Peter arrived from Appenzell to help, and at the appointed hour we sped to a rendezvous in the forest and jumped into my father's car. The two brothers hugged each other goodbye, and we zoomed off across the border, through France and on to Luxembourg to catch an IcelandAir flight bound for New York and a new life. It would be two years before we would see or hear from my mother again. She never even had a chance to say goodbye.

Seven years later, as I sat on my mother's deathbed, goodbye was a sentiment with which I had become very familiar. For two weeks, I tried to devote myself to her needs and pack as much kindness as possible into the short time we had left. Mostly, she just wanted me to listen. I was with her every day, visiting, helping her to eat, bringing her little goodies. The pictures and maps of *Varuna*'s progress seemed to capture her imagination more than anything else, and she made me put them up on the walls around her bed. She never complained and rarely cried out, unless it was in between the torpors induced by the painkillers administered by her nurse.

The one thing I hoped for during every visit over that Christmas holiday was that she would finally reveal to us the secrets of her past. I listened carefully as her stories rambled; I tried to read between the lines as she talked in confused riddles, but still the solution to the puzzle remained incomplete and, it seemed now, was about to die with her.

Christmas day was a bittersweet affair that came and went, signaling that the time to go back to Tahiti had arrived. I thought of my father with his Land-Rover, off somewhere in Africa, trying in his own way to avoid the painful realities of home, and felt bad for Tony

A champagne celebration heralds Varuna's launching

On the last few days before departure my father was omnipresent; my mother spent one night with me aboard my new home

Trying to organize Varuna's cramped forepeak

On the way to Bermuda, Varuna and I plow into our first major ocean swell

René's remedy for my man-of-war rendezvous

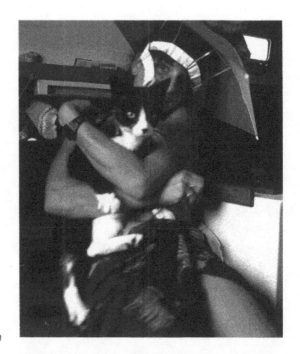

A premature "crossing the equator" celebration

Ashore with some bewhiskered inhabitants on Santa Cruz Island in the Galápagos

Varuna *and* Thea *anchored in the Bay of Virgins, Fatu Hiva—a spectacular landfall after an idyllic passage*

Repaired and ready to leave Tahiti—I trim in Varuna's genoa and we set sail for Samoa

The best part of the South Pacific was meeting Olivier

Proof positive of the one and only fish I ever harpooned

Akka and Varuna wallow in a dead calm on the Arafura Sea

Tarzoon and his first bird meet on the solar panel

Hauling out Varuna in Sri Lanka

In the midst of a Ceylon tea plantation

Cooling off from the 105° heat of Djibouti

As we enter the Strait of Bab el Mandab, the hourly Red Sea ordeal of changing and reefing sails begins

On our way to the market, some Sudanese fellows invite us into the shade of their tree for a Coke and a brief lesson in Arabic

A close encounter of the nautical kind

The Red Sea bids us an ironically beautiful farewell on my last night in the Gulf of Suez

On our own once more, Tarzoon and I head across the Mediterranean leaving Malta and Olivier behind

Post knockdown, Tarzoon and I take a break from round-the-clock repairs and reorganization in Gibraltar

Minutes from home Varuna bashes into her last gale

Reunited

and Jade. Nina and I would be leaving them alone with my mother, and Jeri and Christian, and they were only sixteen and fifteen years old.

I watched my mother's strength ebb, and on my last evening with her forever, I sat listening, stroking her hair and etching her beautiful face in my memory. Snow whirled around outside the window and the colorful lights and decorations of her final Christmas season twinkled on the streets of the city. I clicked in the cassette of her favorite song, "Memory," which I had first played for her two years earlier in Switzerland. She had insisted that I play it for her every day of that visit. As the music rose to the crescendo, her eyes were pools of tears struggling against sleep.

"Mommy," I said quietly. "It's time to sleep now. I promise I'll call you every other day. And don't forget that I love you, OK?"

"Goodbye, my daughter. Remember, learn as much as you can on your voyage." Her voice was no more than a whisper. "Tania," she said, and I leaned closer, "don't come back. Stay free from those who will hurt you. On the ocean you will always be free. You will see that Nature is the only fair one. Never forget that your mommy loves you more than anything in the world." She could stay awake no longer and I gazed at her for the last time.

Sitting by her bedside, holding her thin hand in mine, I saw returning to my mother's sleeping face the gentleness of simpler times, now long gone by. I remembered the time in Vernon, when we were children, Tony, Nina and I incubated a quail egg, and when the furry brown bird hatched, she always favored my mother, flying to her shoulder and fluttering freely around the house. Cinderella we called her, and for a year, her songs brought a spark of joy to the day. One afternoon, we came home from school and found my mother crying. She sat down with us and said that Cinderella had broken her neck against the window glass and was dead.

"She was too delicate for this world, children. She saw the beautiful trees and the sky and the other little birds and she longed to be with them. Now I know she is happy. She is flying in freedom in heaven. She is where she belongs."

My mother's moments of gentleness were like drops of water to parched throats and, if I tried, I thought that I could remember each one. I remembered how much she used to love to knit and crochet, and the little dolls and doilies she often made for us, and how she painstakingly guided my fingers to create my first scarf. Sometimes she even made our clothes.

When she first returned from the sanitarium, she had pulled out of a bag the sweater that she had started knitting nine years before for my father. "I started this when you were babies. It's about time I finished it, don't you think?" she said, smiling whenever one of us would sit with her and watch her needles click away. She had filled us with hope in those days. I remembered the night she surprised my father with the sweater, made in a large green fisherman knit. He put it on and, it seemed, never took it off. "This is my favorite sweater," he would always say. He still wears it.

When we were at the boarding school in Switzerland, she often wrote us beautiful letters trying to explain her motives, reminding us that she was only acting out of love. One letter I still have, its words thinly veiling the troubled soul that penned them: "Behind the clouds of our sorrow, my daughter, believe that the sun still shines. Soon, the wind will come and whisk away the cloud forever. Tania, who does not walk heavily through dark moments? Who does not weep alone because of an inexpressible sorrow? Nobody knows the trouble your mommy sees. Sometimes, for moments, I feel that I am out of God's presence and everything is in a strange mist. But I must learn to creep along, like a boat in fog. Sometimes, I think that to hear noise would be better than the strange silence that I hear. God is the only friend who will never betray us. He has a plan for us and nothing can stop it. My dear, always be a good team with Nina, Tony and Jade, and remember, no matter what, nobody will take away from you your Mommy's love. I have written this letter with my heart to you, my dear child and friend."

As I lay on a bench in the Tahitian airport, homesickness chewed away at my stomach. I had already been stretching things by leaving *Varuna* alone in a crowded harbor for two weeks, but it seemed just as wrong to be on the other side of the world when so much was still happening at home. Thinking of the million and one questions that I still wanted to ask, I longed to talk more with my mother, tell her again that she had my love. The loudspeaker announced another incoming flight and I went to the bathroom to wash my face. Walking back to my seat, I saw Luc waiting at the arrival gate.

"Hello! Welcome back. How are things at home?" he asked, but I couldn't trust myself to form the answer to even so simple a question without crying and just shrugged my shoulders. I looked at him expectantly, half hoping, but he shook his head. "They're here, and she knows," he said. And, before I could say anything, "I'm so sorry, Tania, but this isn't easy for any of us. Please don't be scared. You'll see, Fabienne is a really nice person and she even feels sorry that you had to meet a creep like me," he said, using his favorite English word that I had taught him. "She really wants to meet you."

As Luc drove me back to the quay, we discovered that I had sent him the wrong date for my arrival and that he had been there waiting for me with friends and flowers a day earlier. He dropped me off at *Varuna* with his dinghy and when my bags were all in the cockpit, he asked, "Are you all right?" He looked at me, waiting for a smile of reassurance. I reluctantly gave it. Promising to come and get me for lunch once I settled in, he motored back to his family.

Unlocking the companionway, I pulled out the slats and stepped down into my dark, damp little home, which hadn't been aired out for two rainy weeks. Completely drained, I threw all the luggage up forward, curled up and went to sleep.

That afternoon, I finally hugged my buddy Dinghy, who had been staying on *Thea*. Luc introduced me to Tristan and Fabienne and we awkwardly sat down at the familiar table for the meal. Suddenly overwhelmed by everything that had happened in the past two weeks, and now seeing the lady and child from the pictures, I excused myself and went out on deck, not wanting to cry in front of them. Fabienne quietly followed and, without saying a word, put her arms around me and let me cry.

Several days later, we moved the boats to Arué, a quieter spot two lagoons up, and moored them close by one another. I had given Luc's office phone number to Jeri so she could leave a message and, every evening, I watched his facial expression as he came home to *Thea*. Every other day, I caught *le truck* to the post office in Papeete, or Luc would take me to his office, and I called my mother. Her voice was too weak to carry over the long-distance static, so these were mostly one-sided conversations where I rambled on about my daily doings, trying to sound happy and full of news I didn't have.

Day in and day out, I moped through the rituals of life in a torpid circle of waiting and despair. Loathing solitude, yet unable to muster the energy to make new friends, I opted instead for spending time with the only person I knew well, Luc, and his family. Fabienne took me under her wing during those joyless days and I accepted her friendship. She was charming and very kind and I liked spending time with her and little Tristan. We went to the market together, prepared meals and, occasionally, she tried to help me forget my problems with stories about her own.

Day in, day out, the bustle of Tahitian life whirled around like a cyclone while I waited quietly in its eye. Finally, Luc came home early one evening, his expression telegraphing the news. The phone call had arrived.

risk trade winds blew over the lagoon of Arué on Tahiti's northern coast, and processions of squalls brought cool waves of relief from the endless days of tropical sun. In the late-afternoon stillness, rhythmic paddling signaled the sunset, as heavily muscled Tahitians and French rowed their canoes up and down the lagoon in front of always another swirling backdrop of color. Along the quay, Tahitian families sat watching, drinking their Hinanos, the local beer, or fishing from the seawall.

As the rainy season wept its last tears over the neighboring islands of Moaréa, Bora-Bora, Raiatea and Huahine, an international parade of cruising sailboats came and went, lingering for a while on its way to other less traveled island destinations, unable to resist the siren song of Tahiti, the Pacific's most fabled waypoint.

Varuna, secured to an abandoned mooring, became a peaceful haven. We had settled in to stay awhile. A new yellow-and-blue wind scoop rigged up on her forward hatch funneled a little of the trade winds down into the cabin like a natural air conditioner, a cheering improvement over the stagnant air that had kept her inhabitants in a perpetual sweat.

A channel separates the islands of Tahiti and Mooréa by only 5 miles, and the lagoon of Cook Bay on Mooréa was only 20 miles away from the busier Arué. For four months, I alternated between the two, depending on what was needed and my mood. When working on the boat, I stayed in Arué, which was convenient to the city of Papeete and its chandlery and markets; when I needed some peace and quiet, I sailed to Mooréa and anchored where the clear waters were turquoise, lapis-lazuli or azure, depending on the depth, and where, 15 feet below *Varuna*'s hull, the sandy bottom seemed close enough to touch.

After a couple of weeks in Arué, *Katapoul*, a boat I knew from Papeete, sailed into the harbor and her skipper, Claude, waved to me. After anchoring, he invited me over for a visit.

One month earlier, when I was leaving for New York, Luc had said that *Varuna* would be looked after, but things had turned out badly. He had detached *Varuna* from *Thea*, and then with some business associates, took off to Mooréa where *Thea* had gone aground on a reef. While they were stuck there, a storm had boiled up a mess in Papeete's harbor, *Varuna*'s anchor dragged and she had ended up knocking against the boat downwind of her.

Claude had come to the rescue, Luc told me later, found a second anchor and secured her. He had also turned over the dinghy that was filling with rain, and retied the radar reflector that had broken a binding and was making a holy racket banging against the mast. Hearing what had happened upon my return from New York, I thanked Claude for taking care of *Varuna* and we chatted for a while, calling across the water. It wasn't until less complicated days that I would discover what good friends he and his girlfriend Margot could be.

Claude was a spry Frenchman, with dry wit and a resemblance to Crocodile Dundee, and he hopped around like a booby, his eyes twinkling, and told me about Margot, who was back in the States visiting her family. *Katapoul*, he said, named from a combination of his brother's nicknames, was 30 feet long. He had built her himself and, as most boats do, the craft with which she was constructed and the care she obviously received revealed much about the warmth and character of her owner.

Over the next few days, we shared our meals, walked around and shopped together. Claude got me laughing again, patiently trying to teach me to windsurf, and after many dunkings and aching arms from pulling up the water-laden sail, I finally gave up and opted for rides on the back of the board as he navigated around the lagoon.

On one of our first days together, Claude and I were walking past the Arué soccer field toward the main road where we were going to hail *le truck* for a ride into town. In the course of conversation, I mentioned to him that my mother had died a week earlier, and he stopped in his tracks.

"My God, Tania," he said. "You're so nonchalant. Your mother just died? You may as well have been telling me that you just bought a new dress."

"We've known that she was dying for the past couple of years," I said, also surprised that I had said it so simply. "Now that it's over, all I really feel is relief. She suffered."

"Still, you're on the other side of the world from your family. This must be very bad for you."

I shrugged and told him that I didn't mean to be nonchalant. So much had happened that, if anything, I just felt numb. Claude didn't push it.

It seemed that as soon as Margot returned to *Katapoul* from the United States, we instantly became best friends. She was a burst of energy, sensitive, intelligent and extremely patient and, best of all, she was twenty. The sailing world is so dominated by men that to find a girl close to my age, and American no less, was a rare treat and we latched on to one another like long-lost sisters. Together, we three worked on our boats and made daily treks into town on *le truck* to the post office, market and finally the *patisserie*, where we sat indulging in cappuccinos and apple tarts. Always joking and betting on our disagreements, we sat back in the shade and watched the splendid parade of people go by.

Margot and Claude were always spiffing up *Katapoul*, oiling, greasing, painting and scrubbing, which gave me incentive to do the same on *Varuna*. Even Lawrence, a quiet boy from a family boat neighboring *Varuna*, offered to help, and together we went about starting *Varuna*'s first major refit project. We hitchhiked to the industrial section of Papeete's waterfront and bought some marine plywood, nuts and bolts. Measuring, sawing and drilling away, we enlarged my little bunk, made an extra cushion out of the ones in the forepeak that I planned to do away with anyway and finally there was a comfortable bed stretching across the width of *Varuna*.

One afternoon, Claude showed me how to tow *Varuna* to the quay with my dinghy. "Imagine that you are truly alone," he said. "And there is no one around to tow you through a narrow pass into a harbor and you have no engine. All you have to do is tie a line with about ten feet of chain between *Varuna* and the dinghy, then row, *hard*. It may take a while, but it's possible to do it yourself. Try it. If you screw up, I'll come to help." Margot stayed in the cockpit while I got in the dinghy and pulled *Varuna* under muscle power a hundred feet across the lagoon. After all my apprehension, the feat was accomplished and I felt extra good about myself and my capabilities.

With Claude's brotherly teasing and dares, Margot and I were coaxed into doing things we would never have ordinarily considered. One day in Mooréa, we climbed *Katapoul*'s mast and together jumped off the top spreader to satisfy Claude's craving for such a picture. We spent a good fifteen minutes contemplating the jump and conjuring up enough scenarios of our splattering all over *Katapoul*'s deck that we froze in terror. Finally, making each other laugh, we counted to three and leapt. Unlike Margot, who kept her legs together, I made the regrettable mistake of going down with mine wide open. The impact with the water made me think that someone had shot me with a cannon on the way down, but after the pain passed, I acknowledged that the experience had actually been quite exciting.

Another day we tried spinnaker flying. Claude anchored the boat from astern, raised the colorful huge triangle of light Dacron, tied lines to the two clews of the sail and between them a board. There Margot and I sat as the sail filled with air and we were lifted and dropped with the wind. Up and down we went, screaming and plopping in and out of the water like tea bags.

Next, Luc found a mechanic who agreed to work on my engine. We brought *Varuna* to shore, unhooked all the connecting fuel and electricity lines and fittings, rigged a block-and-tackle system from the engine to the boom and lifted the disabled red monster onshore and into his waiting van. *Varuna*'s waterline rose a couple of inches with the removal of the weight and, a month later, the engine was replaced in working condition.

The sound of the engine had become so alien that I turned it on and off for all my friends so that they could share my joy. In order to keep it in working condition, something had to be done about the water that leaked past the cockpit cover, which was also the floor of the cockpit, and into the engine compartment. Whenever waves filled the cockpit or, on land, when I took a sunshower or threw buckets of water to wash down my patio, the cockpit drains never worked fast enough to avoid major leaking down into the engine compartment.

Luc tried to help me solve the problem, and we had an aluminum frame welded that fit into another aluminum frame. With the smaller frame bolted onto the cover, the slightly larger one bolted onto the deck, and a gasket in between, an impermeable seal was formed. Then, with the help of a family of missionaries on their own sailboat, *Varuna* was hauled out at a yard in Papeete, where we scraped and sanded her underbody and applied several new coats of antifouling paint to deter the growth of speed-impeding marine life.

One day Claude spied a notice on a bulletin board of a solar panel for sale. A man had salvaged it with several other things from his boat after it had broken up on a Tuamotu reef. Buying it brought an end to all my electricity problems. The engine could fail as many times as it wanted, but there would always be those cells slurping up the sunlight and transforming the rays into electricity that would keep the batteries permanently charged. To protect the batteries, originally lodged in the bilge, from constant submersion, I brought them up to the cabin, wedged the pair beneath the companionway steps and fitted stoppers to secure them in place, in case *Varuna* took a knockdown or a rollover at sea.

I was proud of my home; she had become very pretty and comfortable. The new bed was the epitome of luxury, decorated with sheets and pillows made of colorful Tahitian cotton fabrics. I removed the door to the toilet, which always managed to work its latch open and bang around at sea, and replaced it with a curtain. Claude made a new shelf for *Katapoul* from the wood of the door. Waste not, want not. Everything that was removed from *Varuna* was eventually put to use on another boat.

After I made friends with Claude and Margot, the stone stopped rolling and began to gather moss. I made lots of friends who helped to form beautiful memories of Tahiti. It reached a point where I rarely had a waking moment to myself. But I didn't mind. This was the last time until the end of the trip in New York where I could stay settled for a while without worrying about a departure date.

Through it all—the work, the fun, and, most of all, the friendships with people whom I cared about—thoughts of my mother were never far away. Margot and Claude were always there to listen while I talked their ears off, trying to sort out the past, my mother, my relationships with my father and Luc, and everything that had happened since I'd left New York. They rarely passed judgment, and Claude with his jokes, and Margot, with her serene calmness, always brought me back down to earth whenever I got too worked up. As time began to heal the open wounds, gradually my moments of depression became fewer, and the memories of my mother began to find a quieter corner in my heart.

Every couple of days, I went to the post office and placed collect calls home to the family. My father had come back from the Paris-Dakar race after totaling his car and nearly having his leg amputated from gangrene. After navigating a souped-up Land-Rover across the roadless deserts of Africa, the day before completing the race he and his partner took a detour on a regular road, missed a bridge and crashed the car down an embankment. I suppressed my laughter over this unhappy turn of events, the calamity still a little too fresh in my father's mind for him to appreciate any humor in the situation.

"As soon as this leg heals up," he said, "I'm going to Holland to pick up my new boat. Then, I am going to make the qualifying transatlantic crossing for the BOC."

My father never ceased to amaze me. The BOC was a single-handed around-the-world sailboat race from Newport, Rhode Island, with three stops: one in South Africa, another in Australia and the last one in Brazil. I oohed and ahed for him over the phone, but was unable to understand his thirst for thrills. Aside from a few clumsy words, there was little talk about my mother, who had died while he was gone, and I received some reproofs for staying in Tahiti too long and not writing enough articles. Soon enough, with his leg barely healed, my father hobbled off to Holland and a new adventure.

In the evenings, instead of articles, I religiously wrote long letters and, in return, the "A" box in Papeete's main post office's *poste restante* was always full. Since leaving New York, I had written three articles that were published in *Cruising World*, and readers of the magazine had begun to write letters that were forwarded to me. A few said I was foolhardy and that my father was a raving maniac for putting an inexperienced teenager on a boat and letting her loose on the world. But actually, most of the letters were full of encouragement and support from people who wished they could be out there doing the same thing. Even though at first the negative letters had upset me, the nice letters made me feel good, and I began to correspond with some of the people who had written them. I realized that the commitment was no longer an obligation just to my father and myself, and often later on, when everything got me down, I'd think of them cheering me on. In a way, I was giving a few people the inspiration that if I, a complete ninny, could do this and survive, someday they could live out their dreams, too.

Jeri came to visit for two weeks in March, then my friend Elisabeth. Together, we hiked through overgrown trails and I showed them the giant waterfalls hidden behind massive screens of tropical foliage, and then we bathed in the mountain pools and swam from volcanic black sand beaches. We zoomed around Tahiti on Vespas and then cycled around the neighboring Mooréa as I shared with them the simple pleasures of the life in the islands.

Days in the sun melted one into another—one day, two days, two weeks, two months. The four months that originally seemed so long were finally drawing to an end. I had fallen in love with this land and began to think that I never wanted to leave my friends. Hurricane season had passed and departure day was clawing away at the back of my mind. It was time for Dinghy and me to start thinking of moving on, but there was one last matter to attend to.

Whenever I left Dinghy alone on the boat I always felt guilty at his wide-eyed look of abandonment. When I returned, it always felt wonderful to see him happily pacing the deck, meowing a welcome as he recognized my rhythmic pattern of rowing. As soon as I climbed aboard, he would purr and glue himself to me. On shore at Arué, in a wall-less pirogue shelter, lived a gray tabby kitten who had taken to following me around. I often brought food and played with her, leaving her on the jetty crying as I rowed back to *Varuna*. One day before my departure, I relented, brought her out to *Varuna* and introduced her to my buddy. Dinghy accepted her right away, and from that moment on, Mimine became his little Tahitian *vahine*. Things were falling into place.

A journalist who had interviewed me upon arrival had kindly arranged for Yamaha to give me a 2-horsepower outboard engine for the dinghy in return for a photo session upon departure. A date was set.

On April 28, *Varuna* was filled with French delicacies and everything else that I had finally learned was needed aboard. The engine was working and there were no more reasons to linger. Arué had never seemed so much like home as then. I looked around at all my neighboring boats and the people who had been so nice.

I went to *Thea* for the last time and hugged the family that I had grown to love. I said goodbye to Claude, and then with Margot sailed the 20 miles to Mooréa. Before we left, Claude gave me a drawing of the world in the shape of a melon with a missing slice and insinuations about smelly cat litter, and caricatures of the Australians, Africans, and finally King Kong dressed up like Uncle Sam sitting on top of the Empire State Building.

Margot and I idled around Mooréa for two days, and we cried as she boarded the ferry that was to take her back to Claude. It's hard to say if we would ever have become such good friends had we both been in New York, but now with four months of sharing times in these beautiful islands, working hard on the boats and forging a relationship that had helped me get through a very disjointed time of my life, Margot was one of the closest friends I'd ever had.

For two weeks in Mooréa, I found every excuse in the book to procrastinate—bad weather, broken trailing log, rotten vegetables, needing more books. Any excuse worked. I even managed to get back to Tahiti by ferry one last time to find a piece for the trailing log. Finally, at nine in the morning on Friday, May 9, 1986, the dinghy was deflated, folded up and lashed on deck, and there were no further means of getting to land.

"Never start a voyage on Friday" is an old superstition of the sea, probably because Friday was the day on which Jesus was crucified. On this Friday, I decided to flout supersitition. "If I find one more reason for not leaving," I said to myself, "I may as well stay forever."

If I had stayed and waited for Saturday, I would have heard about the depression that was lurking to the west, and my ear would have started aching that night and I could have gone to a doctor for medication. Would've, could've, should've . . . but didn't.

I pulled up the anchor and motored out of the lagoon and through the barrier reef's passage of Cook Bay. If all went well, the next landfall would be Pago Pago, American Samoa, 1,200 miles to the west-northwest. Agitated and clumsy, I stumbled around the boat, getting ready to raise the sails, and realized that it had been almost five months since I had been at sea.

Keeping an eye on the distance between *Varuna* and the reef as we grew apart, I attached the jib halyard to the corner clew of the genoa and lurched back to the cockpit like a landlubber unaccustomed to the ocean swell. Heading the boat into the wind, I leaned forward under the spray hood, pulled up the mainsail and then the genny, winched them tight, and trimmed the sheets. My arm muscles burned as I rotated the handle to get the sails up as taut as possible. *Varuna* immediately settled in on a beam reach with the wind coming from the north.

My heart began to palpitate as the vision of the jagged peaks of Mont Tohiea, which I had taken for granted while it towered over the anchorages of Opunohu and Cook bays, began to disappear astern. The mood was so deep that I hardly noticed the wind slowly veering west. The fact that we were beating into dying trade winds that should have been coming briskly over our stern quarter, didn't sink in for several hours. All of a sudden, it hit me.

"Wait a second. What's going on?" I said aloud. "Haven't you gods checked the pilot charts lately? On this spot on the ocean, there is a 99 percent chance for wind from behind, and it's supposed to be Force 5. So how come I get the 1 percent chance of wind from the front at Force 2, huh?"

I talked out loud to myself for hours and then, for the first time on the ocean, tried out the new car stereo bought on Canal Street in New York at Christmas. The sound of music was alien and I found myself antsy and uncomfortable, instinctively wanting to identify all *Varuna*'s creaks and groans as she reacquainted herself with the sea. The music didn't suit the moment, so off it went.

Restlessly, I tried to read a book, almost immediately putting it down to go outside and read the skies. The moist and hazy air didn't have much to say, so I crawled back below, chewed on some pumpkin seeds and watched my little buddies, wondering if they felt the same way as I. They were unfazed. Even Mimine didn't seem to be too upset about her new lifestyle.

Slowly, we passed by the small windward island of Maiao, which I had never even heard of until now, being obliged to identify the landmass on the chart. My ear, which had been feeling a little funny that morning, became by evening almost impossible to ignore, thumping away inside my head. At just about the same time, I noticed the barometer's needle slowly plunging. "Oh brother," I muttered, "this figures." We were in for a sloppy ride.

Throughout the night, I changed the genny for my new jib and took reefs in and out of the main as squalls passed overhead. The new jib had reef points, permitting it to be shortened down in nasty weather, until now a totally unexperienced pleasure. Now *Varuna* had a sail that could be used in winds whereas before the sail had to be doused altogether.

On the morning of May 10, we pounded into increasing waves, with both main and jib reefed down, and I spotted the windward island of Raiatea, my last positive navigation verification. I hadn't had the chance to walk the shores of this island, nor its neighbors of Bora-Bora and Huahine. Mooréa and Tahiti had been so fascinating that I was content to drift between just the two. These legendary lands would have to wait for other days.

I didn't dwell on could-have-been's, occupied with a much more immediate problem, the upcoming storm. We were still a little too near land for comfort over leeway, but luckily the wind took its sweet time in losing its head, and gave us enough time to achieve a safety margin with plenty of searoom. Battening everything down in the cockpit, I set the sails and self-steering onto a southerly course drifting away from land and went below to wait it out, securing the companionway slats behind me for safety's sake and to lessen the racket.

Once again, I left *Varuna* and the Monitor to fend for themselves and carry us through the familiar screenplay of a storm. Progress would be killed for an indefinite amount of time, but at least we were now heading out of harm's way. As the storm intensified, burying us underneath the waves, it became damp below and the sloshing bilge odors of fuel and stagnant water began wafting up through the floorboards.

The throbbing ear wouldn't even let me eat in peace; it hurt even when I moved my jaw. The medicated eardrops a doctor in New York had prescribed for my medicine chest proved utterly ineffective, so I numbed myself with aspirin.

I drifted into a fitful sleep around eleven-thirty and awoke with a jolt upon hearing a crashing sound. The smell of sesame oil instantly permeated the cabin. With the bucking movement of the boat, a bottle had jettisoned itself and spilled all over my bunk, making a pungent, greasy mess. In an angry fit, I pulled open the hatch and threw the bottle overboard; it crashed instead against a winch, shattering all over the cockpit.

"I don't believe this!" I screamed, and climbed outside. With the feeble glow of the cabin light illuminating that small patch of life in the middle of the coal darkness, I picked up the shards of glass before one of the cats or I found slivers lodged in our feet. Just before climbing below again, one shaft of light hit the mainsheet that was piled up in the cockpit and I noticed with weary disgust that it was covered with cat poop.

Desperately wanting a cigarette, I suddenly remembered my resolution to stop smoking on this trip and the moment of bravado before departure when I had decided not to bring any. Now, in the first throes of withdrawal, I cursed myself and ate pumpkin seeds until my lips and tongue became raw from the salt.

Sleeping fitfully during the stormy night, I woke up several times from vivid dreams of talking to my friends or begging people for Marlboros. I took more aspirin, cleaned up new things that had spilled or catapulted from their places and went outside to check the weather and the horizon. Spray exploded over *Varuna* and the sea was a witch's caldron, tamped down by pelting rain. Bubble, bubble, toil and trouble.

On May 13, at 5:30 P.M., I was finally able to make a logbook entry that it was over. *"I just cleaned the boat,"* I wrote, *"and things are looking up. The storm dissipated quickly this afternoon. Now you see it, now you don't. And now we're just rolling around in the leftover slop. I'm making a cup of coffee with the espresso maker Claude gave me and will put tons of powdered milk and sugar into it. I need a treat. Varuna is all dried out with fresh sheets. Thank you, God, for making it nice again. I was beginning to wonder. You know, El Nino, nuclear clouds . . ."*

The anxiety over nuclear clouds stemmed from the Chernobyl nuclear power plant disaster that had happened just before my leaving Tahiti. News in the tropics is fairly sketchy, so I didn't really know what to think while sailing alone at sea, looking for mushroom clouds. My imagination worked up a storm, conjuring all sorts of calamities: hurricanes, water spouts, tornadoes, underwater monsters and angry whales. I experienced an almost macabre joy in tantalizing myself with these visions, like reading a juicy horror story in an abandoned house.

The trade winds finally returned erratically from astern, waning and waxing with no respect for my feelings. The skies remained gloomy and we plodded along while I changed sails until my raw hands could no longer take the pain. Squalls attacked us from every which way, unleashing rainstorms, and the trades were often stacked up behind them, bringing huge gusts that raged momentarily and then dwindled to nothing as soon as the sails were reefed down. My ear infection was bad enough without this obnoxious weather pecking away at my spirits. I was just waiting for the cats to pee on my bed, which they did, whereupon I screamed bloody murder, "I hope you guys get reincarnated as *bathroom* attendants at the Grand Central Station *men's room!"*

On the morning of the seventeenth, the steady trades returned from dead astern, beginning slowly and increasing as I poled out the jib and tied the mainsail boom out with the preventer cord. Setting the self-steering, I stood at *Varuna*'s stern, feeling the rushing wind and watching the course, making little tweaks to the left and right until I was satisfied.

In terms of progress, the first four days of this trip were more or less shot, thanks to the storm. The next four days, every mile had been wet and hard won. Now *Varuna* began careening downwind at a fast clip. The taffrail log was broken, and although I didn't know the exact figures on how fast we were going, we were hauling. I screamed to Dinghy and Mimine, "Hey, you guys, come and see how fast we're going! At this rate, we'll be in Pago Pago in seven more days!" Dinghy took a peep out of the companionway just as a wave scuttled playfully into the cockpit, landing a couple of drops on his nose. "Nope, I don't like it. I don't like it at all," he seemed to say and spun 180 degrees back to bed.

"Great!" I shouted. "My luck has changed!" As I followed Dinghy below, *Varuna* took a jerk, I lost my balance and came thudding down on the cockpit seat on top of my bent wrist. A stab of excruciating pain rushed up my arm and I froze. "*No!* It *can't* be." I cried fearfully. "I couldn't have gone and broken a bone out here, could I?"

By evening, the wrist had swollen and turned a delicate shade of blue and I couldn't even hold a toothbrush. To round things off, the earache returned, giving me double reason to raid my aspirin supply. I had a heating balm called Mineral Ice, and an Ace bandage. Gently massaging in the cool gel until the soothing heat penetrated, I made a splint out of a magazine and wrapped the whole thing up.

Fortunately, the wind remained constant for five days until May 22, whereupon it slowly dwindled to a flat calm. The course never had to be readjusted, the wind had remained constant and true, and the original shock to my wrist had time to wear off. I stupidly decided that the Friday thing was just a bunch of malarkey because, thanks to the aspirin, my ear thobbed only slightly and, with the string of fine days, things seemed to be looking up. That was when, while brushing my hair, I saw a brown bug fall onto my lap and several more followed. I had lice.

Between the earache, the nauseousness of having lice living in my hair and the sprained wrist, I'm surprised that I found enough energy to go outside with the sextant to take a sight. My wrist made it twice as difficult because it was impossible to hold myself from falling over on the rolling deck. Rather, I had to rely on leg muscles and a series of orangutan contortions, wedging myself between the spray hood and stanchion, and keeping an eye on the waves to retain balance. Navigation became my sole comfort, I still loved to do all the calculations and plottings.

A friend in Tahiti had shown me an easy way to identify and use the stars for navigation, so I practiced with them on calmer evenings, but they were hard to see and align with the horizon through the sextant. The best time to use the stars is at twilight, just as they appear in the sky and before the sun's light completely abandons your side of the world. But, more often than not, clouds shaded my objectives at just this crucial moment.

On May 24, after a forty-eight-hour flat calm, I doodled in my logbook, an elaborate drawing around a centerpiece of the word, "Shit" and wrote, *"Yesterday, I heated up some salt, put it in a sock and nestled its warmth against my ear. It was a sort of temporary relief and maybe I'll try it again tonight. The ocean is totally flat. There are only teasing gusts of wind, clouds and my books. The spinnaker track slide is stuck halfway up the mast track and I'll have to use the semi-useless old slide because I can't climb the mast steps in my present condition to fetch it down. I think I'm developing a chocolate milk addiction. My ear is still pulsing, my head itches and there are still 300 miles to go. That could mean two more days if we get some robust wind. The barometer has been slowly dropping so, maybe . . . Anything is better than this . . ."*

That evening, at about nine-thirty, the wind of a monstrous squall grabbed the sails that were reefed in preparation, and we took off flying. Thousands of gallons of rain pelted down on deck, and I hung on below as the pots and pans in the lockers clattered their discontent. I tried to have everything battened down and secured in place at sea, but there was always something that went unnoticed and became a lethal weapon. A plastic pitcher was the forgotten object this day and it took a flying leap across the cabin, splattering water everywhere. The cats freaked out and, as I struggled to begin mopping up, out of the corner of my eye I spied Dinghy taking a leak on my fresh pillow.

"This is a *nightmare!*" I thought, and started to cry. My spirit broken, there was nothing to do other than hold on to keep from being thrown around down below.

Five hours later, the squall finally passed, the wind leveled out and I was able to go outside to set the course without getting drenched. When everything was finally back to normal, I crawled down below at around three-thirty in the morning and went to sleep on the acid-smelling bunk.

My navigation had predicted an ETA within twenty-four hours and, waking up at first light on the twenty-sixth, I half expected to see the dark smudge on the misty horizon ahead. The easternmost islands of the American Samoa group, as soon as they were visible, would lead the way to Tutuila Island and Pago Pago. The wind picked up again rambunctiously and I doused the jib, leaving up only the double-reefed mainsail. The day was sunny, we were still barreling downwind and, no matter how uncomfortable things may have been, it was exhilarating to be aboard *Varuna* as she tore along like a wild thing, well above hull speed, ticking off the miles toward her destination.

Sure enough, up popped the island group and 60 miles beyond them my haven. Singing and forgetting my itchy head, aches and pains, I set a course to pass south of the group. Going up forward to take a bucket bath, I tied a rope around my waist for security, while taking in the vision of the lumpy brown silhouettes of Tau, Olosega and Ofu islands as they emerged clearer and closer with every passing mile.

That evening, I heaved to about 15 miles offshore and slept in twenty-minute intervals, planning my first steps on land and thanking the Almighty that this god-forsaken leg was finally behind me. Just before the dawn approached, a rotten egg in the food hammock above my bunk cracked open and the slime dribbled down onto the bed.

The first order of business upon arrival was to gather up every last bit of stinking linen and clothing, pack them into sailbags and catch a bus to a laundromat. Next, I hailed another bus going in the opposite direction and headed for a hospital. People crowded into the small buses like sardines and it took a while to realize that the standard way of getting them to stop was by banging on the roof, which made riding the bus a particularly noisy affair. Unable to bring myself to that level of aggression so quickly, I feebly called out "Stop, please . . ." to no avail, and a sympathetic onlooker pounded away against the ceiling on my behalf.

Things don't change in hospitals, even on the other side of the world. After I signed in, it was about a two-hour wait until a doctor had time to see me. My wrist was sprained, not broken, he said as he wrapped it up properly with a stretch bandage. He prescribed a new batch of eardrops and confirmed the grim fact that the bugs in my hair were definitely lice.

"You have been careless," the doctor said. "Lice are common here, and you can pick them up virtually anywhere somebody else touched his head. Now take this shampoo, wash every day and comb out the nits."

The sailors' shower was a little stall on the quay near where the dinghies were tied. I was incredibly embarrassed about the lice problem and convinced myself that everyone waiting his turn for the shower would be able to smell the medicinal shampoo and then shrink away every time I passed. I scrubbed and disinfected every inch of *Varuna*, and diligently washed and combed my hair every day. But every time I scrutinized it in the mirror, I could still see those miserable little white eggs clinging to the hair.

Pago Pago Harbor is a long inlet that nearly divides in half the island of Tutuila. Because it is surrounded by a cradle of tall mountains, Pago Pago gathers all the passing squalls. I put my blue tarpaulin over the boom for protection and tied it down like a tent to the lifelines. It had started life in Tahiti as a sun awning, but here it could do double duty and protect the companionway and kitty litter from the frequent rainfalls.

At one point, I called home from the direct-dial pushbutton phone next to the shower stall and found out that my best friend, Rebecca, who had surprised me with a pregnancy on my return to New York, had just delivered a baby girl and that I was a godmother. Had it really been five months already? Jeri told me that my father was off sailing alone somewhere in the middle of the Atlantic Ocean with his new boat on the way to Newport for the start of the BOC.

"So, he's really doing it, huh?" I said. Jeri and I joked that we hoped he had one hell of a trip alone across the Atlantic so that in the future he might think twice before urging me to ignore the storm seasons. Tony and Jade were fine, she said, and seemed to be coping all right with the freedom. Nina was doing well in school. Jeri, now that the tax season was over and most of her clients' ledgers were reconciled, was beginning to think about her roof garden and all the flowers and vegetables she could plant. Life was moving along just fine without me. The news about Rebecca's baby gave me pause for thought. It was a benchmark in time such as I had never really experienced before, and hanging up the phone, I felt farther away from home than ever.

The dilapidated colonial town of Pago Pago, with its greasy-spoon restaurants and honky-tonk bars, was a depressing surprise. I had looked forward to a little taste of home out here in the middle of the Pacific, but the incongruousness of the place left me cold. Sodas, hamburgers, fast food, Rambo video posters, pop music, "Dallas" and "Dynasty" on every tube. In contrast to Tahiti's colorful gaiety, the place looked worn around the edges.

A Norwegian boat, *Renica*, arrived in Pago Pago soon after *Varuna*, and I was happy to see Reidar and Magrete and their sons, Bent and Carl-Frederic, again after being anchored near them in Arué for a couple of months in Tahiti. Together with Claude and Margot, we had all shared nice times and again I was welcomed aboard their boat like a daughter. Before journeying on to Vanuatu, 830 miles to the west, as I had planned, they urged me to stop at the neighboring island of Western Samoa for a few days. Having already been once around the Pacific, Magrete and Reidar said it would be crazy to leave the Samoas with only Pago Pago for a memory.

I filled up *Varuna*'s lockers with cookies, muesli, dried fruits, nuts, long-life milk and tofu, and another ton of condiments and food that can only be found in American-stocked supermarkets. Provisioning the boat was always a game of square pegs in round holes, as ten bags of cans, gear, fruits, vegetables, toilet paper and so on had to be squeezed into the lockers under the bunks and the tiny forward cabin that were already stuffed with extra gear and clothes. Always after the boat was provisioned, her white waterline stripe submerged an inch or so with the extra weight.

Next, I traded and photocopied charts from other sailors and revised the South Pacific itinerary. I had wanted to visit New Caledonia to try and revive again the sympathetic French ambiance to which I had become attached in Tahiti. But now, looking at the charts, I saw that there were far too many reefs strewn in the path of that destination and so the plan was dropped in favor of those a little less obstacle-ridden.

At the customs dock, just before I left, one of my new friends, Colleen, came over and said she had left the boat on which she was working as crew and was also going to Apia to search out another position. This was a happy stroke of luck, I thought, and invited her to go along with me. Apia was about 80 miles away, a quick stint for *Varuna*, and for the first time, I would have somebody other than Dinghy aboard to talk to for the day, someone asking now and then if I wanted a cup of coffee or juice.

Colleen was disappointed that not a hint of wind let her experience *Varuna*'s capabilities under sail that day, as it turned out to be a flat-calm trip under power. The two main islands of Western Samoa are some of the largest in the South Pacific and it seemed to take forever to motor alongside the rambling and sometimes mountainous coastline. Finally, by the afternoon of the fourteenth, we motored through the pass of a barrier reef and up to the customs dock of Apia.

We were three boats straddled side by side awaiting Monday morning check-in, when we would be allowed to anchor away from the dock. I was worried about Dinghy and Mimine wandering to land and getting lost. But they stayed on the boats, scaring the britches off the neighbors rafted alongside by jumping down through the hatches and onto their stomachs in the middle of the night.

The Apia countryside was a fairyland of misty, mountainous peaks, speckled with cows. The homes were open-air—concrete foundations with columns holding up roofs shingled with pandanus leaves—and from the road, a traveler could glance like a voyeur right into all these mini-Parthenons of Samoan life. After I had visited a few islands, I discovered that a noticeable common denominator was the ubiquitous pandanus plant, which is an essential ingredient in the lives of the South Pacific islanders. Pliable and durable, it is woven into their baskets, forms their bed mats and the walls of their homes, and shields them from the rain and sun.

The Samoans keep their dead close to home and often, on the front lawns of the houses, there were brightly whitewashed graves decorated with flowers. There are no fences or walls marking boundaries of pastures and property, and the people still proudly rode around on horses bareback, through the flocks of goats and cattle that seemed to belong to everyone.

The Samoans are immense people, not fat but rather healthy, seemingly well fed and well muscled. Because of their Polynesian and Melanesian heritage, a lot of them have fuzzy hair, close to an afro, and many of the men's light brown skin is covered from head to toe with elaborate tattoos of animals and exquisite geometric designs. They wore their beautiful tattoos with such great pride that I began to toy with the thought of having one myself.

The terrain of Apia was flat around the harbor and the sun reflected hotly off the pastel-colored colonial buildings. There was a peaceful, sleepy air about the place, such as I imagined Tom Sawyer's village would have had. There wasn't the inherently fiery Latin personality that I had come across in the French and Spanish countries; rather the islanders seemed more to take after the peaceful, slow-paced Germans and later, the New Zealanders who once colonized the island. The second language is English and almost everyone speaks it with a charming New Zealand lilt mixed with the music of their own accent. To me, Marquesan, Tahitian and Samoan all sound pretty much the same, a sort of phonetically spoken Asian language laced with many twists and rolls of the tongue, and I stuttered along with my usual Please's and Thank You's in Samoan, unable to get much further in the short time I was there.

Aboard *Varuna*, meat and dairy products could last no more than twenty-four hours, but eating out of cans was to be avoided as long as possible. Because of the steamy-hot climate and lack of refrigeration, going to the market for provisions was a daily ritual, until I met *Kreiz*.

The 65-foot French schooner *Kreiz an Ael*, which had arrived in Pago Pago the day before I left, arrived in Apia soon after *Varuna*, and dropped her anchor nearby. Colleen remembered meeting the captain in Tahiti, and before leaving *Varuna*, she introduced me to Fred, who introduced us to his crew—Patrick, a Tahitian boy, and three girls, Estelle, Laurence and Marie—who were all headed for New Caledonia.

I immediately felt like a gawky teenager around these three gorgeous French girls, but they all made me feel right at home and comfortably included me for meals or whenever there was something fun going on. They were a boisterous group and with the exception of Estelle, for whom this trip was a vacation from a dancer's life in France, all had been bitten by wanderlust and were out to see the world.

Kreiz was a commodious beauty; Fred had designed the interior and, once inside, you almost forgot that you were on a boat. There were several sleeping cabins arranged around the main salon, with its dining table, galley and lounge. An immense freezer stored all sorts of goodies like steak, chicken and fish. Being able to store these things and consider them a part of provisioning was completely alien to me. *Varuna* only had an icebox, and providing I could even find ice, things could only be kept one step below warm for not more than a couple of days. After gourmet feasts, I would either cuddle up in Marie and Laurence's cabin with Estelle for discussions on hand creams, foot massages and picture shows, or sit around with Fred in the main salon and discuss engine lubricants and water pumps. There was time for silliness with the girls and a time for seriousness between two captains.

Patrick, the Tahitian, was a shy, handsome boy and he said he wanted to get a new tattoo to add to the one on the back of his shoulder. He and Colleen found a local skin engraver named Sam and we went together to his *fale* to watch Patrick get a new adornment.

A group of huge Samoans gathered around guzzling beer while he lay down on the floor to await his surgery. It took two painstaking afternoons for Sam to create the design that encircled Patrick's thigh. I watched carefully for any aftereffects or signs of excessive pain, but Patrick assured me it wasn't too bad. That afternoon, I decided to have a permanent Samoan anklet tattoo engraved the next day.

When Sam and three of his friends arrived at *Varuna* early the next morning, Colleen ran to purchase a painkiller bottle of rum, I boiled the water and Sam mixed it with the black soot from a kerosene fire to make the dye. Unwrapping a package of sewing needles, he strapped five of them onto a wooden stick with tightly bound string. While preparing, he told us that a real man gets a tattoo with a shark's tooth instead of a needle. The tooth with the dye, which is considerably less pointed than a needle, is tapped into the skin with a mallet. One of his friends wanted to show off his tattoo of a flying fox, and turning around, he revealed the enormous South Pacific bat that covered his entire back.

As I looked at all the pockmarks from the tooth, I began to feel a little queasy; the idea of five needles was bad enough. Colleen arrived back just in time, poured a coffee cup full of rum and, because I'm normally a nondrinker, I inhaled it and surrendered my trust and ankle to Sam's ministrations. For three hours, I lay stunned on my bunk, as he painstakingly designed and then carved away with the sewing needles the most beautiful anklet I could have ever hoped for. Sam assured me that all his designs were one of a kind and that mine was an original. "I can't remember any of them well enough to duplicate anyway," he said.

Patrick was so inspired by my tattoo that he asked Sam for another one, also around the ankle, as soon as mine was finished. But Sam had been slowly draining my bottle of rum and, unfortunately for Patrick, the next creation turned out to be a little erratic. That evening, almost everyone in the anchorage came by to either sneak a peek or to take pictures of my ankle. The next day, when the effects of the rum had worn off, Colleen had a ring tattooed on her finger, and a trend was started.

As a last thank you to each other, I gave Sam, who loved to make music, my guitar. He was so grateful that he turned around and carved for me a pair of oars with *Varuna*'s name on each of them. One was crafted from the wood of a lime tree and the other, mango.

One evening, I returned to *Varuna* from dinner on *Kreiz* to find an anonymous note attached to my lifelines."We just want to tell you that someone wants to spill the beans about your crew from Pago

Pago to Apia. We strongly urge you to go back to Pago Pago and remake the trip alone." No signature.

Feeling as though someone had kicked me in the guts, I read and reread the note, with the hackles rising up and down my spine. As far as I was concerned, taking Colleen was no secret. In Pago Pago, it had never entered my mind that taking someone for 80 miles out of a 30,000-mile voyage could be detrimental to a record, should I ever reach home in time to attain it anyway. That someone would assume I had any intentions of keeping Colleen a secret was an affront to my integrity, and now, to return would go against the grain of what my trip meant to me. I was doing this trip to see the world, not to be in the *Guinness Book of Records.* Even though several other people urged me to retrace my steps alone, I remained adamant. "I didn't bring Colleen on a passage," I insisted, "I only brought her on a one-day trip of 80 lousy miles out of so many. We didn't even sail, we motored."

All these were cavalier thoughts. What my father would say and how disappointed he would be never entered my mind. After all, it was only 80 miles and it wouldn't have killed me to resail it. But in the end, I felt that my honor was at stake, so without regret, I carried on with life and put the whole issue out of mind.

I told Fred that I had been entertaining the notion of going to Wallis Island, a French territory a little to the west of Samoa that boats rarely visited. A friend in Tahiti had told me all about it, insisting that it was a place that shouldn't be missed, even with my hectic schedule. "Please go," he had said, "it's only two days from Pago Pago and on your path." I had promised to meet Magrete and Reidar there and was looking forward to it. I fired up Fred's imagination about Wallis, he described it to Patrick and the girls and everyone was in agreement. "It'll be fun," he said. "We'll sail together and throw dinners to you."

I said good-bye to Colleen and all the other cruising people I had gotten to know in Pago Pago. Taking the route north of Tonga and Fiji, the island groups where almost everyone was heading after Apia, I knew that this was the last common meeting ground. From here on in, I would be taking a sailing route a little less traveled and wouldn't be seeing many familiar boats; the itineraries of the majority were more relaxed than my own, and their courses would take them to islands farther south.

On June 21, at 3:00 P.M., I hauled up *Varuna's* anchor hand over hand and then motored out of Apia Harbor. Behind me, the girls on *Kreiz* huddled on the foredeck, giggling and pressing the button that automatically gathered in their anchor chain. A gentle, fresh wind was blowing from the east. I raised the sails, boomed out the genny, and watched *Varuna* take off down the waves, whispering a phrase I wanted to remember, *"Tofa soy fua. Tofa soy fua. Tofa soy fua . . ."* Thank you in Samoan.

It was a gorgeous 250 miles to Wallis. *Kreiz* was reefed down so that *Varuna* could keep up, and I hoisted as much sail as possible to maintain speed. As a result, we went faster than ever before. My star fixes worked out perfectly when I checked them over the radio with Fred, and I ate like a queen.

With the new solar panel, energy consumption was not the problem it had been on other passages. Thinking up ways to use all my newfound power, I talked with the girls on the VHF when they were bored on their watches and compared notes on the full moon that rose above us. They called to tell me what was on the dinner menu and I called back just to say hello. Every once in a while, they would increase their sail volume and come close to *Varuna* so that we could take pictures of each other.

By late afternoon on June 23, the low, rounded hump of Wallis peeped above a horizon afire in the orange and yellow rays of another setting sun. Even with the security of *Kreiz*, I was nervous about this landfall. Wallis island would be the closest thing to an atoll that I ever had to deal with. The fringing reefs extended well beyond the limits of the coastline and there was only one cut large enough to enter the lagoon. The pilot books bore ill tidings for boats attempting Honi Kulu pass, and had warnings of nasty 5-knot contrary currents and huge waves. The lagoon filled up with the breaking Pacific swells that thundered over the reefs, but the water exited mainly through this one pass. Worried that it would be impossible to enter, we approached, *Kreiz* first and *Varuna* following sheepishly, engines idling.

With a go-ahead signal from Fred ahead, we revved up and forged our way in. Even with *Varuna*'s engine up to full revolutions, the current was so strong that it took nearly twenty minutes to cover the 500-foot-long pass. The evening wind had picked up, too, and I motored against it in the dwindling light to where *Kriez* was anchored, protected from the ocean swell behind a reef. It was too late to navigate our way through the coral heads to a safer anchorage, so we decided to do it early the next morning, when the sun would be at our backs. Otherwise, the glare of the sun in front would obscure proper visibility through the water, and the first hint that a reef was there would come when we heard it crunching against the boat's hull. Early, before the next morning's calm had a chance to be taken over by the trades, we tied *Varuna* behind the larger boat and towed her around the coral heads to an anchorage in the lee of the island.

Ever since we'd met, Fred had been eager to teach me everything he knew about boats, and as Patrick and the girls went to explore the island, we spent the next few days going over *Varuna* with a fine-toothed comb. At twenty-eight, Fred was master of his own magnificent vessel and he hadn't achieved it through sloppy practices. Before attacking *Varuna*, he proudly showed me his engine, his new galley pump, and the master cabin with all his electronics. I commented on his diligence concerning the engine compartment, which was squeaky clean. He said, "When I was taught how to care for a boat, I learned that you should be able to touch any part of the engine with white gloves and they should remain white." I thought about *Varuna*'s little red beast and how rarely I would even lift up the cover, much less bend over to wipe it down.

"Boats are tender," he said. "You have to treat them like vain women who need lots of care." Fred tried pumping *Varuna*'s toilet and shook his head. As we talked about our lives, he dismantled the pump, and painstakingly explained the working of it in detail. In no time, all the gaskets were exchanged for new ones and reassembled again. Up until now, I had never seen the insides of a toilet pump, simply praying that mine would be the special one that never broke.

We hooked up my radio's antenna by running it out the companionway, along the deck grab rail, and taping it up the side of the mast. In the past, I used to go outside with the radio and rotate the small telescopic antenna until I received a faint time tick by which I set my watch. That was the extent of my demands. But the radio was invented for a much grander scheme, and if it has a high enough antenna, it can reach its potential. Suddenly, with Fred's improvements, I could receive all sorts of medium-wave music and news stations in different languages from the surrounding islands. I could hear the BBC, Voice of America, Radio France and Radio Moscow on the shortwave lengths. The world was at my doorstep and I was excited by the new pastime awaiting my next ocean passage.

Then, after Fred put new terminals on the ends of the degenerated circuitry, we gently sponged down my engine with soap and fresh water. We reglued the wooden frame around a cockpit locker and he gave me all sorts of compounds that he had found essential over the years: double-component adhesives and metal pastes.

We bought limes and he showed me how to keep *Varuna*'s teak clean and permanently bright. "These limes are magic," he said, squeezing the juice all over the trim. "Who needs acid cleaners when nature provides the most efficient ways?" The wood gleamed, turning a completely different shade of light brown, breathing free from over a year's worth of grime and oils. We took apart my self-steering gear and replaced all the worn-out pieces, then Fred attacked all the stainless steel on it, and my pulpits, wiping away any rust spots with his own special products.

Fred was fanatic, but his fanaticism was catching. It was fun sprucing up the boats and figuring out ways to fix things with only the materials we had available. And the more time we spent together, the more I recognized how much I already knew. I'd had all sorts of patient teachers over the past year, and each had revealed to me new things about the workings of my own boat. In that time, I had gotten over any embarrassment about admitting ignorance of something and had learned not to hesitate to ask questions, questions and, if I was still too thick to understand, more questions. By no means had I learned everything, but I had come this far with one notable realization: anything can be dealt with by a level head and a little common sense.

The *Kreiz* crew and I had planned on staying for just a few days in Wallis, but we found plenty of good reasons to remain for two weeks. As a vista, the slight, rounded island, unlike those in French Polynesia, was not much to write home about, but the beauty was in what the people did with their land.

It was a minuscule place, about 9 miles long and 5 miles wide, but on this patch they had managed to fit in three magnificent kingdoms. The island was technically under French rule along with Futuna, another territorial island 120 miles to the west, and their connections with the outside world all passed by way of New Caledonia. Strolling down the neat dirt roads lined with flowers and charming thatched homes, it was hard to imagine a place more secluded from the sophistication of its French rule. Beautiful, unmarked and off the beaten track, the kingdoms of Wallis seemed to compete with each other to see which could be the most picturesque. One afternoon, I actually saw a man sweep his lawn.

On Wallis, pigs were the princes. In the place of cats and dogs, piglets, sows and boars roamed around in complete liberty. Perfect little bungalows sat on manicured plots skirted with flower beds. Hibiscus hedges, mutated into myriad strains, colors and sizes, framed every tableau. Fred and I walked around in awe, passing the friendly islanders and saying hello. The fabrics of their *pareus* were exotic and gay; and they draped the beautiful bolts over graves in the cemetery and changed them often.

On shore, where we landed our dinghies, was a house with a family of innumerable children and hordes of pigs. They smiled and generously pointed us to their well water to fill our jerry cans and, politely, we sideskirted their lawn in order not to upset the nap.

The Polynesians have been traveling among these islands for centuries, astounding modern navigators with the prowess of their ancient sailing outriggers. They have created a vast network, connecting the neighboring islands into a sort of brotherhood and, regardless of changes they have endured at the hands of those who have tried to colonize them, fundamentally, they have remained the same.

Patrick, arriving on a sailboat, was welcomed as a long-lost brother by the boys in Wallis, even though he spoke a different language. When I watched them talking, they seemed to understand each other perfectly, as if there were a sort of universal plane on which the different islands could relate to each other. They greeted him like royalty and he basked in his own novelty, Fred looking on with pride, like a father who made these things possible for his son. We would only see Patrick every now and then, when he rowed in with his friends to bring fish they had caught in the lagoon for Dinghy and Mimine.

Magrete, Reidar and their two sons arrived and anchored *Renica* next door to us as a depression disturbed the peaceful skies for several days, postponing our departure. One day, our whole gang was invited to one of the kingdom's annual feasts. Men and women in colorful costumes sang religious songs and danced in front of a veranda where the king and his entourage sat holding court. The dancers had petroleum jelly smeared all over their arms and shoulders, and onlookers stuck paper money on their favorites, in this way making a collection for a new building.

Royal kava, a South Pacific potion made from the root of the kava tree, was served to the king and his family while fifty baskets with roasted pigs lay waiting in the sun. On the way down from climbing a tree to capture the festivities on film, I lost my footing on a stubby outcropping and fell to the ground, landing with my dress over my head. It took a second for the stars to clear before realizing that I was surrounded by a group of giggling children, thrilled by my exotic performance during a familiar ritual that had otherwise been boring for them.

Soon enough, July 4 swung around. Not only was it the day of the anniversary of my country and the Statue of Liberty's birthday gala in New York Harbor, but it was also Fred's birthday. For most of the day, Laurence, Marie, Estelle and I huddled below on *Varuna* with my box of magic markers and colored pencils, making birthday cards and talking about possible presents. I bought a bolt of fabric and used it to wrap up the *Fat Freddy's Cat* cartoon book that I had received in New York and that, by now, I knew by heart. On the card, I drew a picture of *Varuna*, Dinghy and Mimine thanking Fred for everything he had done and for being such a good friend.

That evening, Laurence baked a chocolate layer cake with raspberry filling. Marie set up cameras and took pictures of our group and then we went out on deck to send off a red flare. This was the first time I had ever seen an emergency flare go off. It lit up the whole sky and slowly descended, bathing *Kreiz*'s deck in a rosy glow. The next morning, we realized that we had sent up an SOS a hundred feet from an island littered with people and nobody saw anything. I wondered what would happen in the middle of the ocean.

Soon after, I had a last dinner on *Renica* before they set off for new islands the next day, and that gave the rest of us incentive to pack up and start thinking about moving on as well.

Watching the skies and the barometer on the breezy morning of July 7, we picked up our anchors and said goodbye to each other, promising many letters. *Kreiz* towed *Varuna* out of the lagoon. I stood on the bow, waving and calling goodbye as we threw last jokes back and forth.

Saying goodbye had never become any easier. I thought of the drawing of our two boats that Fred had given me with a caption that described my feelings perfectly: "What a nice meeting. Exactly the thing I hate about our way of traveling. 'Hello' . . . 'Goodbye' . . . 'See you' . . ."

Once were were out beyond the last reef, I cast off and went forward to hoist the mainsail. Taking in two reefs in the gusty wind, booming the main out and tying down the preventer cord, I went back to the cockpit to set the self-steering. Gathering up the jib, I clambered back onto the foredeck and started hanking it onto the forestay. Engrossed in getting *Varuna* under sail, I didn't notice *Kreiz* on a collision course until we were very close, and then stood up in alarm to see if they were going to move. Everybody was occupied in getting his sails up, so I hollered a warning and ran back to disengage the self-steering to round up into the wind before impact.

Too late. The bungie-cord fastening stubbornly refused to undo itself fast enough and, as if in slow motion, I saw Fred turn his head my way, his face register shock and *Kreiz*'s exhaust sputter blue smoke as he slammed her into hard reverse. Surprisingly, the hard jolt I expected never came. *Varuna*'s bow hit *Kreiz* amidships at the same moment that I was finally able to round her up, while *Kreiz* pulled back in full power.

Quickly resetting the self-steering, I looked at *Kreiz*'s hull, expecting to see a gaping hole. There was nothing. Stunned, I looked at *Varuna* and realized that here, on the other hand, something was amiss. The lifelines hung limply down on the deck, and I looked forward to the bow pulpit. Stepping around the spray hood and holding on to the grab rail, I saw the damage. The pulpit had absorbed the entire shock and was smashed backward out of its deck supports and crumpled like an accordion.

All of a sudden *Varuna* was naked and helpless, and I realized how secure those lifelines had made me feel. They had formed the perimeters of my playpen. Whatever happened outside of *Varuna* was all right, just as long as those two long strands of wire on either side held me in. With all my muscle power, I tried to push the pulpit back out and into some sort of shape, but the stainless steel wouldn't budge. I ran back to the cockpit, down into the cabin and heard Fred's voice on the radio.

"Hi, Fred. Wow, that was close. How's *Kreiz*? Does she have any marks?"

"No, she's all right," he said, "but how about *Varuna*?"

"Well, I think I have to go back into Wallis and try to fix her," I answered shakily. "The pulpit is completely smooshed out of shape, so I don't have any lifelines. I don't want to sail like that."

"Wait a minute," he answered. I imagined him sitting at his chart table, talking with the excited girls, trying to think of a solution. His voice came back, "Listen, Tania. I have an idea and everybody here thinks that this is what we should do. Of course we have to help you. We should have been watching out for *Varuna*. Now, what we should do is go to Futuna Island and there we'll do our best to fix the damage. It's only 120 miles away. That's one day's sailing. What do you think?"

"Thanks, Fred. That sounds good to me. Hey, this isn't so bad. We'll all see each other again sooner than we originally thought, right?"

Our moods lifted as we began to joke about a job badly done. If *Varuna* had sunk, we teased each other, then they would have had to rescue me and goodbye would never have to be said. We sailed within sight of each other through the rest of the day and that night on a disagreeable ocean full of squalls and erratic winds.

The next afternoon, a solitary mountain loomed and we motored on the lee side of it until arriving at Sigave, the only anchorage. On Futuna, there was virtually no fringing reef and the only protection for the anchorage was the island itself, as long as the trades blew consistently from the east. A mooring ball lay just offshore, set for the occasional supply ship. As soon as we tied up, a swarm of dugout canoes filled with laughing Polynesians came out to greet us, and when they saw Patrick there was a great round of frivolity and back-slapping.

Fred came to look at *Varuna*'s pulpit, we decided to attack it in the morning, when we felt fresh, and that evening we went ashore to a hut where a lady had agreed to prepare a chicken dinner for us. After the excitement of the day, we all went home to our boats and slept like the dead. When I woke up in the morning, something felt funny.

My eye made the rounds of *Varuna*'s cabin. All my favorite cassettes, which I had listened to over and over again and stored on top of the rest, were gone. Also gone was the tape recorder used to make cassettes for my family and friends at home. I jumped out of the companionway and leapt onto *Kreiz*.

In an early-morning stupor, Marie was poking around looking for her Walkman, and Fred was fumbling for a carton of cigarettes, muttering that he knew that he had placed them "somewhere around here." I told them that some of my belongings were missing, too. As we slowly realized that the boats had been robbed while we were having dinner the night before, the others began running around to assess the damage. Tallying up, they found their waterproof tape deck, more tapes and the Walkman were definitely gone. Marie and Laurence elected to go to the village chief and *gendarmerie*. All we could do was wait to see what transpired.

Futuna was the most untouched place I had ever seen. There was no electricity on the island, apart from privately owned generators, and the younger village people took turns according to gender in showering at a faucet coming out of a cement wall on the beach. Giggling, the girls formed a human wall around the bathers, each in turn. There were two general stores with the inevitable Sao crackers and Laughing Cow cheese with the wedges fitting into the familiar round box. Ever since Tahiti, this had become my standard sea fare, as it was always the cheapest and easiest to prepare.

In the late afternoon, Fred and I set to work fixing the pulpit while the rest went ashore to do some laundry. Fred sized up the problem and formed a plan. He boomed out his spinnaker pole so that it was directly above *Varuna*'s damaged bow, and with a line attached from the pulpit to a block-and-tackle system from *Kreiz*'s spinnaker pole, we winched it back into shape, inch by creaking inch. Fred used gauze and epoxy like a plaster cast to form bases to repair the broken ones and we smeared the gook all around the weakened corners.

Bending stainless steel weakens its properties and I scrutinized the pulpit to discover that there were little faults beginning. It would never again be the same and I would no longer be able to trust my weight against it. This meant that the lifelines encircling the boat couldn't be trusted either. I felt guilty looking at *Varuna*'s bow as if, by no fault of hers, I had marred her beauty and destroyed a certain amount of her integrity. That evening, as everyone came to admire a job well done, Patrick informed us that he had received a message that the captains of the two boats were summoned to the home of the village chief at seven the next morning.

As the rays of an early-morning sun filtered through the foliage and peeked over the mountain, little children, already out and about, followed Fred and me as we followed Patrick's directions and arrived at a small two-story home propped up on pilings. The chief's wife invited us in. Curiously, I peered around the modest quarters of someone so close to royalty; there were only a few wall hangings, a straw mat and, conspicuously laying on a table, two plastic bags. The fat chief suddenly rumbled into the room. Fred and I leapt to attention and introduced ourselves. With all the pomp and circumstance of the Queen of England's changing of the guard, the chief began to talk, waving his arms in the air, as his wife translated the speech into French.

"We are very sorry about what happened," she began. "You see, our children don't understand the word stealing. Here on Futuna everything belongs to everybody. It is such a small place that we can only consider it borrowing. Here are your belongings." Separated into the two bags were the objects borrowed from both boats—mine and Fred's.

Respectfully, we thanked the chief and took our leave, wishing him and his wife well. Even in Tahiti, I had been confronted by this borrowing business. Twice, I had returned to the dockside to find the dinghy missing, and both times, it had been found at the other end of the harbor, tied up where the lendees had left it. This way of life was slightly disruptive, but it served absolutely no purpose to get angry. The people of these islands were just accustomed to sharing everything they had, and couldn't understand anyone who didn't.

That the chief had found our belongings and not the *gendarmerie* demonstrated the clannishness of the islanders when it concerned the colonizers. The French laws were almost rampantly ignored, but not blatantly. These people had survived with their own customs, without the French, for untold hundreds of years, and the way they probably looked at it, the French were just passing through.

Our unexpected two-day stay and our experience with the chief had taught us at least one lesson that flew in the face of the attitudes we had brought from the continents. We had traveled to the other side of the world and had found people who were truly unmaterialistic. To them, our materialism was just a funny game.

On July 10, I said goodbye for the second time to Fred and *Kreiz*'s happy crew, who were eager to pick up mail in Fiji, their next stop. That left me several hours to make my preparations before following. I had mail waiting too, but not in Fiji. Dinghy, Mimine and I were headed for Efate, Vanuatu, 750 miles to the west-southwest. I untied *Varuna* from the mooring at two in the afternoon and sailed away from Futuna, slightly more battle-scarred than would have been ideal, but richer for the experience of the little mountain island in the far reaches of the Pacific.

The first two days were perfect sailing weather—cool, steady trade winds from astern and a drenching sunshine—and I managed to cram in extra hours of sleep between idle musings and raidings of my snack supply. By the second evening, I was ready when the wind veered a bit toward the south and picked up the pace. July 11, 1986, was a day that I will never know; *Varuna* crossed the international date line.

During the night I was reluctant to leave the warmth of my bunk and go out on deck to change the sail arrangement in the worsening conditions. Awaking the next morning to take a sight, I saw that we had drastically overshot the rhumb line and would have to jibe to regain lost ground. Invariably on the ocean, every procrastination led to double the work, but this was one lesson that just never sank completely into my lazy brain.

The spinnaker pole had to come down and *Varuna* had to be jibed over to a port tack, which meant sailing on a more uncomfortable close reach and, in the deteriorating conditions, a reef also had to be taken in on the jib and two in the main. Before 10 A.M. we were pounding headlong into the biggest waves the South Pacific had ever presented to us, and that was how it was to remain until landfall, five days later.

Waves slammed *Varuna*'s bow and rushed into the cockpit, filling it with water from both sides. We were so completely inundated that the drains didn't even have time to empty the cockpit before it was filled again by the next avalanche. It was a consolation to think that my new cockpit seal was keeping the engine drier than it would have been otherwise. Below, Dinghy and Mimine huddled together on the lee side of the bunk and only moved or perked up their ears when they heard me opening a can.

I had to put on foul-weather gear to take sights and because of the pitching, often the positions ended up a bit off. The waves posed as false horizons, and when the sights didn't work out properly, I'd have to go back outside and retake it, wiping off the mirrors when a wave crashed over us, fogging them with salty spray.

Aside from the horribly uncomfortable pitching and yawing, *Varuna*'s extraordinary speed completely thrilled me and I began to feel like a real adventurer. I was keenly aware of everything I did, as if unseen eyes were watching and judging every action. Meticulously, I checked the sails and, for my imaginary audience, became an extension of the boat. Every lurch, every bucking movement, I was with her, horse and rider, all one.

A wave would pick us up and throw us sideways, sending books, radio, cassettes, and hairbrush across the cabin. I was unfazed. It all just seemed part of the consequences of being at sea. Temper tantrums, vindictive cursings of a more then averagely obnoxious wave, the realization that I still had lice, the odor of a cat's refuse wafting from the forecabin, all served to enhance my Oscar-winning role. I felt I could overcome anything. Together, *Varuna* and I forged through those waves as the crowds cheered us on.

On the night of the fifteenth, the sound of lapping water slowly worked its way into a dream I was having. Reaching under my pillow for the flashlight, I pulled myself up to shine it on the floor. The crowds began to jeer as I jumped up in a panic. There was six inches of water above the floorboards, even though I had pumped the bilge several hours earlier. Crash-landing back into reality, I leashed on the safety harness and, flashlight in mouth, ran topsides to pull down the jib. The slamming stopped as *Varuna* spilled the air out of the sails and sat back up straight, gently riding the waves. The mind-numbing din of water rushing past the hull by the thousands of gallons stopped. Pumping the bilge, I searched for the leak's source, and found nothing; everything seemed to be in order.

Shaken up, I hoisted the jib and with trembling hands climbed back down into the cabin to wait. The crowds booed as I lit a cigarette; attempts at quitting had failed. Within fifteen minutes, water refilled the boat and I raced on deck, hauled down the sail and pumped again. *Varuna* bobbed away and the water inflow ceased. Deciding to wait until morning light to figure out the meaning of this new setback, I fitfully lay on the bunk for the next few hours aiming the flashlight at the wet floor.

In the morning, I took off the engine cover, reexamined the sea cocks and closed all the open ones. They seemed in working order. When I opened the port cockpit locker, a flicker of a past memory sparked. I checked the electric bilge pump that had given up long ago and found that its sea cock was open. Vaguely remembering Luc's description of his struggles with a crazy toilet system, I figured out what the problem could have been. When the jib was up, *Varuna* must have been heeling over so far that the entire electrical bilge pump system was beneath the waterline. The anti-return valve must have rusted or broken and water was being siphoned in. In any case, as soon as the sea cock was closed, the problem was solved.

Efate appeared with the sunrise on the seventh day. After our sluggish approach and a coastline search for Port Vila, the harbor's immense bay opened before us as we sailed in and anchored next to the yellow quarantine buoy. Even though this trip had been uncomfortable, *Varuna* had covered an amazing amount of distance—750 miles in seven days—and taking into consideration the size of the waves and the fact that we were heading into the wind, I was proud of her accomplishment. This was to be my first encounter with the Melanesians and my last South Pacific island landfall with *Varuna*, Dinghy and Mimine.

O fficials almost always became a little embarrassed to find themselves alone with me on *Varuna*, and those from Vanuatu customs and immigrations were no exception. I had called the authorities on the VHF and a white launch with black capital letters forming the word POLICE on the side headed out toward us shortly thereafter.

Two ebony-black men in white uniforms and glossy patent leather shoes jumped off their tender and aboard *Varuna* and, realizing I was alone, timidly snuck a peep down into the cabin where Dinghy and Mimine were licking themselves. I smiled and talked with them, recounting my near sinking disaster while filling out all the entry forms for a new port of call. Still not completely sure that I was really by myself, they got back on their tender, shaking their heads, and pushed off.

"Oh, welcome to Vanuatu," they called, speeding away. "Enjoy your stay."

I waved back and looked toward the area where they had directed *Varuna* to anchor. Farther up around the bend of the bay, sailboats swung around their anchor chains and, closer, several more were tied up to the seawall. Turning on the engine, we slowly motored past a shallow reef toward the other boats and, just past the cleared channel, turned on the depthsounder to help find a place to anchor.

The sounder kept pinging 90–100 feet as *Varuna* circled the other boats. "This must be wrong," I said to myself and decided to let the hook go anyway in a clear spot. "All these boats can't be anchored in such deep water. What kind of anchorage would this be?" Putting the engine in neutral, I ran up to the foredeck to pay out *Varuna*'s entire 100 feet of chain, letting it slide through my hands on its descent. At the end of the chain was another 20 feet of rode and I stopped the flow at that point, waiting for the anchor to catch the bottom.

The noise of the engine was muted on *Varuna*'s bow, and the late-afternoon silence was broken by the first sounds of stirring night insects. This place was so quiet. Soft voices wafted over the calm waters and a group of people were sitting on the deck of their boat, watching *Varuna* and smiling. The anchor chain was perpendicular to the water, hanging straight down as we drifted back. It hadn't even touched the ground.

As I heaved it back in, my muscles easily handled the dead weight. It was effortless to do anything physical after being at sea and, wondering if people on the other boat thought I was strong, I went back to the tiller and continued my search for a shallower spot. Farther along, several boats were tied to moorings just off a small island in the harbor and I thought I recognized one of them from Tahiti. Just then somebody got into the dinghy attached to its stern and motored my way. It was Christoph, a roving singlehanded and swinging bachelor I remembered from Papeete. It was great to see a familiar face. I always dreaded the first moments of lonely uncertainty on land, the awkwardness of first meetings, the repetition of life stories and itineraries. Even though I inevitably made friends, in the beginning there always remained the eternal what if. . . . Christoph pulled up alongside, we greeted each other and I invited him aboard.

"Do you have any idea of where I can anchor with a reasonable depth?" I asked.

"You can pick up the mooring next to that black ketch there," he said with his stained-toothed smile, obviously happy to be able to show me the lay of the harbor. I steered *Varuna* up to the floating white ball. Christoph leaned over the side and picked up the ball with the boat hook, tying the attached line down to a cleat on the bow.

Finally, I was able to relax. *Varuna* was secured safely in a snug harbor and there would be no more worries about navigation, course changes, storms and leaks for at least two weeks. Christoph and I sat in the cockpit, looking around, discussing the whereabouts of showers, laundry and a good meal. It was funny how the occupants on two boats could be neighbors in the same place for months, with the only communication being in the form of waves and nods. But, when they meet up again in a new and unfamiliar land, with several extra thousand miles under their keels, all of a sudden the familiar face becomes a best friend. Christoph and I had shared only a nodding acquaintance long ago in a totally different world, but here in Vanuatu we treated each other like cousins.

In between Christoph's boat, *Adonis*, and the neighboring black ketch, there was a small green sailboat that looked as if it had seen better years, as did the black one. I asked Christoph if anybody ever used them.

"And how," he answered. "They both just arrived last night from Fiji. There's a party tonight to celebrate our landfalls. Those two are both singlehanders. Michel is from France and Olivier is Swiss. Wait till you hear their stories."

Interested, I stared at the classic lines of the black ketch. She was small, about 32 feet, obviously made of steel judging by the rust stains that spotted her deck and hull, and she had the look of a warhorse, a boat that had been through many battles and covered many miles.

As Christoph talked about *Akka* and *Penelope*, the two boats anchored near *Varuna*, a bell rang in my head. *Akka?* Swiss? Olivier? It clicked. I remembered Fred telling me stories about a good friend of his named Olivier whom he had known in Colombia and Tahiti. As I looked at the black ketch, everything came together. I had seen *Akka* briefly once before, when Jeri was visiting in Tahiti and we had anchored overnight next to her in Papeete. I remembered a blond man standing on deck looking our way, but had pretended not to notice, while hoping that he would come over to say hello. We had rowed past *Akka* several times and on each pass, I had scrutinized her rugged details, envying the owner's life. Whoever he was, I remembered thinking, he probably wasn't a fanatic for shiny stainless steel or schedules.

Christoph and I caught each other up on our doings since leaving Tahiti four months before. We had traveled completely different routes with one exception. After Tonga and Fiji, it turned out that he had been only the second boat to visit Futuna that year. *Kreiz* and *Varuna* had arrived two days after he left. Small world.

"Well, I have to go ashore to make a phone call," he said when the first excited rush of conversation had ebbed. "The party's on *Akka*. Come over later on."

A few squawking birds skimmed the surface of the water hunting for their evening meals as I climbed down into the cabin to begin cleaning up. Making a landfall always frustrated all attempts to keep order. Binoculars, coffee cup, spilled powdered milk, charts, sunglasses, dividers, hat and sunscreen were all needed at one point or another, and there was never time to arrange them until arrival. I put new sawdust into the cats' litter box and watched Dinghy step in. In Tahiti, I had noticed that he often went into the box, crouched and came out, leaving no messages. I had taken him to a vet and was told to feed him more wet food. But there had been no change and I began to be troubled, not knowing what else to do. After feeding the cats and making a cup of tea, I lay down to take a nap.

A full moon was shining down through the hatch and loud voices and laughter disrupted the stillness of night, waking me up with a start. It was the party, already in full swing on *Akka*. From the port cockpit locker, I pulled out the sun shower, filled it up with the three remaining gallons of water in the jerry cans and lashed the bag to the boom. As the spout gently swung like a pendulum with the movements on *Varuna*, I draped a towel over the lifelines for some privacy, crouched down into the cockpit and took my first freshwater shower in a week.

Christoph's voice called across the water, telling me that I was missing everything. "Let me get dressed first," I called back, assuring him that I was coming.

By the time I finally rowed over and made my appearance in *Akka*'s cabin, which was warmly lit by brass kerosene lamps, one bottle of whiskey had been polished off and, needless to say, things had reached a level of confusion to which I, basically a nondrinker, found it difficult to rally. Nevertheless, I sat in a corner listening, scrutinizing *Akka* and watching these men let themselves completely loose, not wanting to make my presence too obtrusive in a celebration of friends meeting again in yet another land.

Souvenirs of Olivier's travels were arranged all over the boat— South American masks, carpets, pictures and beads studded the walls. Hung between two bronze hatches was a Brazilian ukelele-type of instrument made of a coconut hull, branch neck and a single string, and colorful shells and coral fronds were strewn about everywhere. I studied everything curiously and listened, smiling at little snatches of conversation that stood out like short excerpts from a six-hour comedy.

Didier from *Penelope* showed me his drawing book of sketches and a sculpture he had carved, and insisted on making a portrait of me. Meanwhile, Christoph was off on a tangent about how life is all an illusion and we are just playing out a cassette that somebody else recorded.

Michel, *Penelope*'s captain, had come in late, after trying to sell some shells to a souvenir shop in town to pay for his next meal, to find that his share of whiskey had been inhaled. Before he had a chance to put his hands on another cache, we talked together about a series of French comic books called *Les Passagers du Vent*. When I told him that I too had enjoyed them, he felt it was his duty to recount the lengthy history of the drawings and the individual personalities of those people who were used for models—an opaque monologue that left me puzzling how he would know so much about something so obscure, but Michel turned out to be a man with many answers that didn't always add up.

He told me of his trip, how he had bought *Penelope* for two thousand dollars in the Canary Islands. She was a tiny, ten-year-old day sailer that had been accustomed to playful sailing around protected bays, but Michel saw her as a boat that had enough spunk to take him places. Crossing the Atlantic to Brazil, the Antilles, then to Panama with a mixed crew, *Penelope* had survived being hit by lightning and sinking. Michel made it all the way to Vanuatu, where his last crew member, Didier, was about to catch a plane to continue his art career in New Caledonia. "I can't go to any French territories," Michel said, taking a swig of whiskey, but he didn't mention why.

Throughout the evening, Olivier too had been rambling on about everything and nothing. I vainly tried to follow his train of conversation as it skipped from the stars to desert islands, to the universe, to aliens, to landfalls and missing forks. Although I was unable to grasp his words, I watched his suntanned, handsome face, convincing myself that he was even managing to sound somewhat poetic. Also, he was the only one of the men who wasn't trying to impress me—if anything, he was rather ignoring me—and human nature being what it is, that's probably why I paid closer attention.

Christoph disappeared and then returned, bringing a girl, Lillianne, who lived on the island, and later, as I watched her dance with Olivier, I felt a stab of jealousy. All night, while I sat in my corner on *Akka* talking to Michel, and afterward in Lillianne's jeep, when we drove around the dark streets to a beach, I watched this intriguing brown-eyed, blond man and tried to make sense out of him. "Fred said he really liked Olivier," I told myself. "He was always talking about what a good person he was. I'll just have to wait to judge him properly."

As the light of dawn crept over the party, I slipped away and dinghied back to *Varuna* to get some sleep. At ten that morning, stretched out on my bunk and mulling over the events of the previous evening, I heard a splash in the water nearby. Throwing back the covers, I jumped out into the cockpit to see the subject of my thoughts surfacing next to *Varuna*.

"Good morning," I said. "Would you like some coffee . . . and some aspirin?"

"No, thanks, I'm all right." He smiled, pulling himself into *Varuna*'s cockpit.

"That was quite a party," I said hesitantly. "How does your head feel?"

"Swimming did the job," he said. "I haven't had so much to drink in years, but sometimes it's good to decompress like that after being at sea. Don't you think?"

"Yeah, it was good to talk and laugh."

That morning Olivier and I began to get to know each other, and although he was very quiet and reserved, I gently probed and he opened up. He was thirty-three, he said, and from Neuchâtel, the French-speaking part of Switzerland, near where my mother's apartment had been and the château where we had gone to boarding school. He had a degree in geology, but said he had never worked at it, preferring a life connected to the sea. He had worked as a skipper on charter boats, had navigator positions on racing boats and spent seasons as a sailing and ski instructor.

"Three years ago," he said in French, with the familiar Swiss accent to which I was warmly accustomed from my days in Switzerland, "I was at a crucial moment in my life. I felt I had to do something, but I didn't know what. Most of all, I wanted to have my own boat and see the world."

After skippering a boat from Taiwan to Martinique, he felt his future was a big question mark. One day he saw a message in the classified section of a small newspaper from a man who said that his boat was lying unused in a Spanish marina and had to be moved. He was looking for a qualified person who would like to sail her. Olivier met the man, they came to an agreement and *Akka* came into his life.

Working day and night as a taxi driver for six months, he saved enough to pay the hefty Spanish marina bill and left to see the world, spending time in Brazil, Colombia, Panama and Tahiti. Always on a shoestring budget, he earned money along the way with a variety of interesting and adventuresome schemes—buying rum in Martinique and selling it for good profit in Tahiti, crafting jewelry in South America and taking on a position as a charter boat captain. He was modest about his adventures and slowly, over many days together, told me about all the exotic nooks and crannies to which *Akka* had carried him.

In those early days of Vanuatu, we were to become inseparable, and I tried to forget that my destiny was to follow a route that Olivier might not be able to travel with me. During that month on the island of Efate, we simply tried to make the most of every minute.

Aboard *Akka*'s time-worn 32 feet of steel, one could sense her well-seasoned age of twenty years. She had probably thought retirement was at hand, definitely not a circumnavigation, when Olivier moved aboard. She was pure basics, the only instruments on board being three little cabin lights, his Freiberger sextant, a watch and an antique shortwave radio. For nighttime running lights Olivier used kerosene lamps of green and red glass. Relying almost solely on *Akka*'s sails and antiquated self-steering gear, he had come far, sometimes with crew and sometimes alone. Olivier was as basic as his boat, having no desire to maintain the superfluous, no need to accumulate objects. The few he had were simple and beautiful.

"Until I met you," he said after we had spent two weeks together, "I was planning to go to Australia and Papua New Guinea to search for gold. Now we'll see what happens."

The town of Port Vila stretched along the shoreline for about a mile, with supermarkets, clothing stores, a few restaurants and bars, government offices and souvenir shops on both sides of the main street. Except for when an occasional cruise ship debarked loads of pale Australian tourists, the stores were empty and the deserted streets had the air of a sleepy town at siesta.

It could have been any island in the Caribbean except that the people spoke Bislama, a Melanesian Pidgin, but our communications were in French or English, the official national languages. Olivier and I noticed one word in particular that seemed to be on every sign and in every sentence: *Blong*. We asked Lillianne, who was a translator for the government, what it meant and she said it was a sort of derivation from "belong" and meant pertaining to, of, with. The word struck Olivier and me as comical and, before either of us could become comfortable with endearments, we took to saying "I blong you" to each other for lack of something better.

Vanuatu was my only confrontation with the Melanesians and their culture, and with Lillianne we went to kava ceremonies, and learned about the traditions and unusual customs of the island. On Vanuatu, to please the gods and ensure that their yam harvest would be profitable, men performed Naghol, jumping from bamboo contraptions 250-feet high, their ankles bound by long, flexible vines called *lianes*, calculated to stop their fall inches short of the ground. I could only think that these people must be especially fond of yams.

The kerosene light marking the kava hut after sundown drew us like mosquitoes one evening, as we were curious about this ritual of Pacific Island chiefs, who drank the kava before gatherings to be touched by wisdom. In the shelter of these pandanus-roofed gazebos, one man ground up the root and another pressed the water through the pulp into coconut-shell halves as customers came up for refills. Talking was allowed, but in hushed tones, accentuated by others who would step to the side to hack up and cough out the foul remains. Apparently, the older the root, the more potent the kava.

Lillianne, Christoph, Olivier and I sat down in our turn and forced down a few vile coconut shells full. I couldn't understand the fascination. Around us, grown men were drinking something that tasted like filthy dishwater left to stagnate for a month, coughing it up and sitting down for more. Suddenly, as my tastebuds numbed, the annoying, hacking, spitting noises dulled and a 100-watt light bulb seemed to illuminate the inside of my head. For the next couple of hours, all sorts of incredible thoughts emerged in a nonstop, stream-of-consciousness conversation between Olivier and me, as we became philosophers with the answers to every problem.

During that evening, we found out more about each other than in the two previous weeks combined, and I could understand why the chiefs drank kava before any important discussion. Unfortunately, under its influence the brain is in great shape but disassociates itself from the limbs. When Lillianne signaled to us, I found that I had a bad case of rubber legs, and it was only a very concentrated effort that got me back to the car and the Waterfront Restaurant in time to vomit it all up. For several months after the kava experience, all I had to do was imagine its taste and my bile would rise.

One day, the Waterfront Yacht Club sponsored a 20-mile race

around an offshore island, and we entered *Varuna*. Our main competition was *Adonis*, sailed by Christoph and Lillianne. As we motored toward the starting line, they jeered, "Hey, you'll be lucky if you get back before dark with that little dinghy. We'll have dinner waiting on the fire for you. Don't wake us up."

Throughout the day, Olivier played the captain and Michel and I jumped to his orders. He had raced many boats and, for the first time, I sat back with no worries about where we went, knowing *Varuna* was in capable hands.

On the downwind leg we hoisted the spinnaker that Michel had brought along and, for the first time, *Varuna* felt the edge that a light sail could give. As we sped down on the quarantine buoy, there was a small crowd of people onshore watching the finishing contestants. Proudly, with Michel steering, we rounded the yellow marker, doused the spinnaker and rounded up into the wind, heading for the mooring at a good clip. Olivier and I started coiling the lines, when all of a sudden there was a crunching sound, we lost our balance, lurched forward, and *Varuna*'s mast jerked back as Michel frantically maneuvered the tiller to get us off a reef. Apologizing profusely, he bounced *Varuna* over the coral head gonkers with grinding sounds that made me think that her keel was being ripped out from under her.

Rushing below and pulling up the floorboards to listen for incoming water, I heard nothing. Michel was laughing when I came back out. "If what just happened gave you a hole, then this boat is a piece of junk," he said. "We've hit many reefs inside different lagoons and the most damage was a couple of scratches in the paint job."

"I don't care what you say," I retorted shakily. "We are diving and checking the hull as soon as we tie up."

Later, after finding that the damages were, indeed, only a few faint scratches, we went ashore to watch *Adonis* crawl in, the last straggler. Thoroughly upset over nearly imperiling my boat for an unimportant race, and embarrassed by going aground in front of a crowd, I didn't go to the after-race ceremonies and later found out that *Varuna* had won on corrected time. Instead, I left Olivier and Michel sitting on a bench in front of a spectacular sunset and went alone to the Waterfront Restaurant's bathroom feeling profoundly depressed. Lost in thought, I passed the mirror and was stopped by my own reflection.

"What do you think you're doing?" I asked myself. "Why are you still here? You should have left over two weeks ago. And you haven't even written anything since that miserably short article in Tahiti.

You've been having one continuous ball, hanging out and doing nothing other than enjoying yourself. Daddy didn't give you a boat for a gift; he gave you a job."

I had stayed overtime in certain places before, but always with good reason. Here in Vanuatu, it had already been three weeks instead of the two I had allotted myself, and still I was making no gestures toward leaving. *Varuna* had just hit a reef, it could have been serious and I was feeling guilty about all the time I spent with Olivier, as if I had no responsibilities. Most of all, there was the pressure of the steadily advancing seasons.

Every ocean has a hurricane season during its summer months. In three and a half months, the Indian Ocean's hurricane season would begin and by then I had to be in South Africa or else run the risk of getting tangled in the fury of its off-season. Every extra day spent on land was at least 100 miles lost in making that goal. A clock had begun to tick, getting louder with every passing day.

Looking in the mirror and filled with self-reproach, I made a resolution to write the next morning and to start preparations for leaving. I had a sneaking feeling that it was already too late to get to South Africa in time, but laid that thought to rest and narrowed my worries down to one: just get to Australia first; the rest will come later.

Feeling a little better about my plans, I went back to the boat that night and found Dinghy bleeding from his genitals. "Oh my God," I cried. "No, not Dinghy, please." I tenderly wiped him off and gave him some of his favorite snacks. He lay there limply, quietly meowing his pain. Mimine meowed, too, as she circled his penguin body, nosing him to respond. Feebly, he tried to move about but was too weak.

I scratched his ears in his special place, trying to console him with my voice. He looked so small and helpless. I edged a bowl of water to his lips. He lapped a little and I was swept with hope. All of that sleepless night I spent trying to push away the thought that something could alter the one precious relationship that had sustained me for almost half the world.

First thing the next morning, I bundled him into a large towel, and Olivier brought us to shore in the dinghy where we caught a taxi to the only veterinary clinic on the island. It was actually the department of agriculture, whose job it was to inoculate the vast cattle herds, but they also had a small-animal section. A young Australian man brought Dinghy to a stainless steel table.

"Where does this cat live?" the vet asked as he felt his stomach.

"On a sailboat, with me," I answered. "We've come all the way from New York together."

The doctor's eyebrows rose to his hairline. "What! You brought a foreign animal ashore? He could bring diseases. You're not supposed to do that."

I began to tremble, suddenly struck with a premonition that Dinghy wouldn't be returning home with me. "Look at him. He's bleeding and he never even touched the ground. I carried him the whole way here. What should I have done? Let him suffer and bleed to death on the boat?" I began to sniffle.

"I'm going to have to open him up," he said, softening. "If it's what I think it is, I'm afraid there's nothing I can do. It looks like a cancer in the kidneys."

"Let's go outside and wait," Olivier said, tightening his hand around mine, and ushered me out to a bench. I sat there, dazed to hear the word cancer again after such a short time, and thought about my brave little buddy. All those times that I had gotten mad at him for missing his litter box were for naught. He couldn't help himself. Dinghy was my first pet, my closest companion for half the world. Only he had been there right beside me, living through all the bad times and the good. He alone had tolerated my cursing and screaming, watched me laugh and talk to myself, shared my meals. Whenever life had really gotten me down he had been my only comfort, with his gentle little face rubbing mine before curling up in my arms. My handsome snuggly motorhead was the only one who had shared the memories of those endless days in the sea warp.

The doctor came out and shook his head. I hadn't even had a chance to say goodbye.

I paid the bill and Olivier and I hitchhiked home to a strangely empty boat. Mimine poked her nose at my legs, into all the cabinets, and wandered absently around all the spots where she and Dinghy had liked to sleep together, while I set to getting things ready for departure. As lovely a memory as Vanuatu was for bringing me Olivier, I would also remember that it was here I lost a precious treasure, and I couldn't wait to leave.

Christoph, Michel, Olivier and I exchanged and photocopied charts for our next landfall—Cairns, Australia—and began to provision. Calling home to say goodbye, I talked to my father, who had just finished singlehanding his new boat across the Atlantic but said that he had decided not to enter the BOC around-the-world race after all.

The race would take a year and he said he had second thoughts about leaving Tony and Jade alone for such a long period of time after they had just been through so much with my mother. I was relieved to hear of his change of plans and told him about Dinghy, which, he said in his typically hasty way, was a bad stroke of luck but not the end of the world. And before we hung up, he brought up the inevitable, that I was behind schedule. "You stayed in Tahiti to avoid hurricanes," he said. "But it looks like you'll get them anyway in a different ocean. What made you spend so much time in Vanuatu anyway?"

"Oh well, I made a really good friend here, I wrote an article and won a race," I said, hedging the issue. Knowing how much my father hates to run up a telephone bill, it was easy to put off telling him about Olivier.

Before Mimine became too accustomed to being alone, I decided to get a new kitten. A friend told me about a batch in the country and drove me out there. I chose one at random, thanked the owners and brought the fuzzy tabby ball back to *Akka*. Mimine took him under her wing and he followed her around the boat, clawing his way up the wall hangings, belts, my legs and the table whenever it was mealtime. His clumsy shenanigans inspired the name Tarzoon, in honor of the Belgian cartoon character who was the "Shame of the Jungle."

Michel was the first to depart Efate, planning to stop at an island in the Vanuatu group to the north. Two days later in an early morning calm, *Varuna* and *Akka* motored out of the harbor on Thursday, August 21, 1986, and glided through the passage between the two islands that gave Port Vila Harbor its protection from the sea. While Olivier and I hollered out last goodbyes, I boomed out *Varuna*'s genoa and mainsail in the feeble wind and we drew slowly apart.

Climbing down into *Varuna*'s cabin, I saw poor Tarzoon living out the perils of seasickness. All the milk he had gulped down earlier now lay on my bed. "Bravo, Mr. T," I said, cleaning up the mess. "Are you going to join the ranks of those who bear a complete disregard for my sleeping quarters?" He looked up, and as soon as I had finished and sat down in my corner, he crawled into the crook of my arm. Gently, so as not to disturb him, I picked up the chart.

The genoa slapped around softly as we caught the ocean swell and began bobbing slowly toward Australia, 1,300 miles to the west. I looked out the companionway to the dwindling shape of *Akka*'s sails and at the island in the background, realizing that Vanuatu had been my last South Seas landfall. Behind me were memories to last a lifetime, the richest being of those islands where people I loved had left and entered my life.

For the first time in a while, I remembered Luc, the storms of our brief relationship, and the beauty of a world that I had seen through the eyes of such a dreamer. All the sharper edges were now softening in my memory, and no matter how things had turned out, I couldn't deny that he had taught me much, helping me along in the journey that had finally brought me to Olivier.

As they were becoming accustomed to doing these past four weeks, my thoughts drifted to Olivier. Unlike Luc, he was a man comfortable in his own skin, and with him I felt a certain special calm, without the heady intoxication of grand schemes or the urgency to get somewhere fast.

Unfortunately, my inflexible schedule didn't allow for the luxury of lingering with him and letting our future work itself out with time, and I couldn't help hoping that Olivier would offer to alter his own course and follow mine for a little while longer. Otherwise, we'd have to say goodbye in Australia. If our being together was truly meant to be, I believed that things would turn out for the best and, as he once said, we'd just have to see what happened. "Anyway," I thought, "first I have to get to Australia and that's not going to be an easy task."

Before us lay the Coral Sea, named for the numerous reefs strewn haphazardly below the surface of the water. Between Vanuatu and our next landfall would be my final exam in navigation. For 1,300 miles there would be no way to confirm a position visually. Without a SatNav, *Varuna* had to be navigated by the sun and stars to specific points on the chart, directions altered, then navigated to the next point, all the time sailing around unseen coral heads lying in wait for a boat making a wrong move. Thirty-five miles off the coast of Australia, I had to find a lighthouse propped on top of a reef that would guide us into Grafton passage, through the extremities of the Great Barrier Reef. I was hundreds of miles from nowhere, and there were no second chances; my navigation had to be perfect.

I had about ten days to practice, day in with the sun, and evening out with the stars, calculating optimum angles and times, trying to make myself so comfortable with the sextant that it became second nature. After one squall the first day, the weather was as accommodating as it had ever been, making my last days with the South Pacific a gentle goodbye. On the sixth day, a pod of pilot whales stayed alongside *Varuna* for two hours, a rambunctious one leaping into the air and executing a perfect flip for its solitary audience. Below, Mimine and Tarzoon hopped around, chasing each other's tails.

On the ninth night, my calculations had us passing 15 miles north of Willis Reef on the chart. As the boat lifted with every wave, I cringed, imagining that rushing noise and eventual crash if my navigation were even the slightest bit off. After safely passing this unseen obstacle, we had to hang a quick left in order to dodge another set of lurking reefs indicated on the chart, and then head on the straightest course possible for the lighthouse. I stared endlessly at the horizon and the chart, which was covered in penciled crosses from sun and star sights, and colored scribbles identifying coral heads. The smallest error in mathematics and we'd be history.

First light found me up on deck with the sextant, estimating the night's progress, and the fix told me that the lighthouse should emerge by 11:00 A.M. Hoping that it would be sooner, I nervously sat on the foredeck, scrutinizing the horizon through binoculars. Then I ran back to the Monitor, adjusting it and trying to keep the course as exact as possible. Frustrated, I looked up to black clouds overhead that were beginning to obscure the sun. Untying the bungie cord on the tiller, I took the helm myself for a half hour. Then, antsy because I couldn't see as well from the cockpit as from the foredeck, I gave the steering responsibility back to the Monitor, reclaiming my position on the bow.

The wind began to gust, causing *Varuna* to round up. Concerned over the consequences of even a slight course variation, I reefed the main, keeping a relentless vigil as beneath us the topography of the ocean floor began to slope up toward the continental shelf of Australia, kicking up steeper and steeper waves.

Varuna was picked up by each wave, and I looked down into the troughs as we perched momentarily on the tops of cliffs of water just before surfing down the chutes. I held onto the grab rail and leaned against the mast on the foredeck. It was like being in the first car of a roller coaster. By ten-thirty, the morning sun was shadowed by an enormous gray front with black overtones. There was no lighthouse to be seen and by eleven-thirty, fearing a nervous breakdown, I doused the jib and stopped *Varuna* in order to think. I hate roller coasters.

The most valuable piece of advice I always heard from other, more experienced sailors was: "If you have doubts, seek sea room and wait until you feel right about your landfall. Never make a hasty decision for the sake of an anchorage and a shower." Here, under deteriorating weather conditions, speeding toward the world's largest barrier reef, I was definitely not feeling right.

"Forget it," I said to myself, "I can't handle this yet," and headed under reefed main east back toward the open sea.

The next morning dawned a little cloudy and overcast in spots, but with the security of an entire day's worth of daylight ahead and knowing that I could always turn tail again, I jibed around and resumed the search for the lighthouse. As the sun's fuzzy outline peeked momentarily through the clouds, I hastily grabbed a sight, calculating and crossing it with an RDF bearing received from the coast.

Until 9:00 A.M., squalls and driving rain buried *Varuna* in sea water, obscuring my vision as I tried to scrutinize the horizon. Suddenly, I thought I saw a bird ahead. Keeping my eyes trained on the black speck, I realized that it was motionless and that the vague outline of a lighthouse base was emerging, growing underneath the bird and becoming a mini Eiffel Tower. I gasped, then shouted in elation, then gasped again.

"I found it!" I screamed. This was a moment of triumph and I reached down into the cabin and grabbed little Tarzoon, pointing his head in the direction of the lighthouse. He didn't like the rain, or the noisy squall that had just engulfed us and dug his claws into my arm and jumped back into the safety of the cabin.

The line squalls marched in one after another, intensifying as we sailed close-hauled past the lighthouse at midday, and by the time we reached the pass the wind was raging at 35 knots with gusts up to 45. Swirling currents and steep, confused chop made steering the boat an enormous effort as white water crashed and thundered against and over the exposed reefs on both sides of us. Instead of making progress, we seemed to be pushed sideways toward the reef with the endless squalls punching the lee side of the cockpit under water.

At the tiller, I struggled to keep control of *Varuna*, anticipating the waves and trying to steer her through them from the right angles. With the exhaustion of four days of little or no sleep and changing and reefing sails, every muscle in my body ached and my brain felt ready to burst from the pressure. *Varuna* was no longer able to make headway, but I thought that if I could only get one glimpse of the land that lay 30 miles away through the mist, I could find the energy to carry on. But there was nothing, and the weather was getting worse. In despair, I turned *Varuna* back out to sea again.

Bouncing around for the rest of this day and night, I'd had all I could take—emotionally and physically—and swore by all that was holy that the only way I would leave Australia was on a 747. All I could remember were the head-banging days I had spent paralyzed with fear from storms, howling winds, the lonely and ominous nights, while being tossed around in a 26-foot cork on the world's largest ocean, praying that I would live to see land again. After all, what was I but just another human being on a planet that had too many already? When my emotions plunged into such an abyss, life didn't seem to add up to much anymore and I couldn't see the water for all the waves. On Tuesday, September 2, 1986, all I knew was that I was a very scared nineteen-year-old who wanted to quit the whole shebang.

September 3 dawned a sunny day. *Varuna* had been pacing like a mad dog at a closed gate and we were quite familiar with the area now. The winds were still strong, but at least the squalls had gone elsewhere, and determined to get in, I retraced our steps of a day earlier and found the lighthouse.

What a difference from the day before. The angry, gray, foaming-at-the-mouth waters were transformed into sparkling blue mounds with bubbly crests blowing up into a spray that shimmered like crystals. The sun, I knew, was a major factor in determining my daily mood. It was hard to dwell on black thoughts when the sun beamed warmly down on *Varuna*'s deck, her sails, her wake and my face and everything began to emit a radiant glow. Even Tarzoon and Mimine came out to sit on the drying wood of the cockpit, watching me steer by hand past the lighthouse, playing with the waves and gusts. In the distance, to the right and left, the gentle crests of waves lapped over the reefs. I studied the compass to keep the exact course in the plan of approach that I had had plenty of time to mull over and memorize, and the beauty of the sunny morning erased my fatalistic gloom of the day before.

After the lighthouse and first major outcropping of coral heads, I steered into the well-buoyed system of pathways that run the length of the Barrier Reef, and headed for Cairns. Closing the distance toward the mouth of the Cairns River anchorage, we passed ferryboats bound for the outlying islands along with fishing and pleasure boats as the profile of the hilly green coastline became clear. In a cheery mood, I found myself waving in great excitement to the skippers of other boats. Making a landfall had never been as major an accomplishment.

Six hours after passing Grafton Lighthouse, we motored past the outlying sailboats at anchor and headed toward the docks. Tied alongside an official-looking launch was the familiar rugged shape of *Akka,* and *Varuna's* engine puttered up to her companion.

"Olivier!" I called. His blond head popped instantly out of the companionway and his body followed in the mad rush to get on deck.

"I *blong* you!" he shouted elatedly and signaled for me to pull up against *Akka.* "Perfect timing," he called. " I just arrived and customs, immigrations and quarantine are already here."

Michel's cry over the calm waters the next morning heralded his arrival; Christoph arrived a week later. Together we explored Cairns, which could have come straight from the script of a spaghetti Western. The rambling buildings stretched the length of arid, hot pavements, and inside, fishermen, charter-boat crews, plantation workers and ordinary "blokes and sheilas" gathered in the cool interiors of bars that often had bands playing folk, rock or country music. It was the beginning of summer Down Under and already I could appreciate that people could find solace only in an icy mug of beer. I preferred Coke.

I gave up the idea of abandoning the rest of the trip. When it actually came down to it, I couldn't picture myself quitting the biggest and most important thing I had ever started, emptying out *Varuna,* packing my bags and heading home. She *was* my home.

That resolved, I faced the fact that I was definitely behind schedule. We were already well into the middle of September and there was no way possible to make it to South Africa and the Cape of Good Hope before the December hurricane season. Fears about the weather set me to entertaining thoughts of how the time schedule could be gracefully extended. We still had to cover 450 miles of Barrier Reef up to Thursday Island in the Torres Straits, then sail the 6,500 miles of Indian Ocean to South Africa. Because of the hurricane risk, I would have to forgo Christmas Island, Mauritius, Reunion and Madagascar and sail the entire 6,500 miles nonstop in order to get out of the danger zone as fast as possible.

The idea terrified me. I didn't know if *Varuna* could take the wear and tear of the moody Indian Ocean and I didn't know if enough food and water for the two solitary months could fit aboard. And above all, staring at the endless expanse on my charts, I didn't know if I could handle leaving Olivier so soon after finding him.

Being with him and the two other Frenchmen was a blessing. In the evenings, after working on the boats, we four sat together either on *Akka* or *Adonis*, preparing meals and talking about the future. I wasn't the only one who had decision-making problems in that department, and in the cabins of our boats, we thrashed them out into the wee hours of the mornings, throwing out suggestions and giving each other advice. Cairns was the end of the South Pacific and of an old way of life. For each of us, a new course had to be plotted.

Australia was the last port of call that Michel wanted to risk with *Penelope*. Between Vanuatu and Australia, she had been knocked down by a rogue wave, her cockpit lockers robbed of their covers and inhabitants and her interior swamped. The knockdown had shaken Michel, and he decided that *Penelope* had fulfilled her destiny. Christoph asked him along for adventure *à deux* in Papua New Guinea. But first they had to make some money by picking tomatoes, and they calculated the months needed at labor and the profits they could make from exporting Australian wine to other islands.

As they planned and schemed together, Olivier and I also discussed our own alternatives. He had to get back to Europe and I to America. South Africa was not the only route available. I could also head toward Sri Lanka, up the Red Sea, through the Mediterranean, then across the North Atlantic to New York. This dovetailed with Olivier's plan and was almost 3,000 miles and one month of sea time shorter than taking the southern route around South Africa's Cape of Good Hope. Our timing, as far as the seasons were concerned, would be perfect, even to the point of allowing a month's break in Sri Lanka. Once in the Mediterranean, Olivier could leave *Akka* in Malta, and the Med and Atlantic would be *Varuna*'s last oceans to cross.

The day after these plans were hatched, we rushed to a ship chandlery and bought up all the charts to the Northern Indian Ocean and the Red Sea, as well as a guidebook with all the information on harbors, anchorages, provisioning, visa laws and lists of all the postal general deliveries. I was elated. I didn't have to race up the Barrier Reef alone. Until we reached Malta, which seemed so far away, Olivier and I could rendezvous in different ports, and at sea I would always know that he was living through the same conditions as I somewhere in the general vicinity. Our awareness that we would no longer be alone in every sense of the word unleashed new energy in us.

On September 19, Olivier and I said goodbye to Michel and Christoph, hollering good luck to one another, and motored out the channel for Cairns River. Our little singlehanders group was dissolved.

·   ·   ·

The Barrier Reef is a vast labyrinth of small islands and line reef formations that lie scattered for 1,250 miles along the Australian coastline from Brisbane to Thursday Island. To guide the heavy shipping traffic that arrives and departs from Australia's east coast, a water-highway channel rigged with buoys, cans and lighthouses stretches the length of the reef. We planned to sail by day and anchor at night.

For eighteen days, *Akka* and *Varuna* wove in and out of what looked on paper like an endless latticework of coral heads for almost 400 miles up to Thursday Island and the Torres Straits. Each buoy showed up as the last one disappeared behind, and we followed the dots around headlands while weaving in and out of small islands. Whenever we made landfall, Olivier would anchor first and when *Varuna* arrived, I would tie up alongside, eliminating the tiring morning exercise of lifting anchor.

Olivier was in heaven, gathering up more shells to add to his collection, while I made pizzas, and together we scrutinized the beaches in search of a perfect nautilus shell, without which he refused to leave the continent. The trade winds blew fairly steadily from the southeast except for a few days when we holed up in anchorages to wait out blows or calms. To my eyes, and from any point of view, *Varuna* and *Akka* were the perfect couple floating on the opal lagoons—the dainty little scarred lady next to the rough and rusty adventurer.

Tracing the Queensland coastline, we awoke at six every morning, followed the shipping lanes and pushed onward, passing Aboriginal reserves, frontier towns with hitching posts for horses and campgrounds for bird lovers and animal watchers. We sailed past large sandy hills, dunes and mangrove banks. For a freak oasis in the middle of sand and brush, the steamy rain forest of Cape Tribulation jutted out, propped on a peak. A couple of miles farther north, the beige-and-brown hues of the desert recommenced.

We anchored for two days in the shelter of Lizard Island, and with mask and snorkel and my Tahitian spear gun, I went fishing. Paddling about, I could see bright, sky-blue parrotfish and black-speckled red groupers scurrying away in my path as the mouths of huge clams closed when my shadow covered them. The coral formations were like forests of underwater cactus plants; prickly and smooth, bulbous and scraggly, tubular and lacy, they stood undulating with their arms stretched upward to the surface. The ones on highest ground were a dark brown color from exposure to air at low tide and the lower ones were pastel shades of purple, red, yellow, green and every other color, with schools of tiny fish scurrying about in formation—in and out, in and out.

The tail of a fish fluttered from behind a rock. I took in a deep snorkel breath and jackknifed downward. Passing over, spear gun at the ready, I aimed at my prey, and the elastic shot the spear forward through the water, piercing the flank of the unsuspecting fish. Later on, when we went to ask a neighboring boat if the catch was safe to eat, they said the area was an underwater reserve. The poor fish had thought he was safe from human predators and had gone to sleep under the rock, until I had to come along. I never speared another, and we ignominiously carried on.

With the tedium of the hot days, I sat in *Varuna*'s cockpit religiously crossing off each landmark we passed and in between times, wracked with boredom, plucked each and every hair out of my legs with tweezers. Sometimes, Olivier and I would close the distance between the boats to talk or to show each other the huge legal mackerel we were catching on trolling lines.

On October 6, we arrived at Escape River in one piece, our last anchorage before Thursday Island, and in time for my twentieth birthday the next day. One year earlier, I remembered, I had been in the middle of the South Pacific on my way to my first South Seas landfall, wondering how I would ever get through the next couple of months.

We anchored off a Japanese pearl farm, the first civilization we had seen in over two weeks. Olivier kicked me off *Akka* in order to arrange my gifts. Taking a freshwater sunshower in *Varuna*'s cockpit, I impatiently counted the seconds until I was allowed back on board. *Akka* was spic-and-span, and on her table was a wrapped present with twenty shells surrounding it. Oliver had made a leather folder for carrying my papers and a necklace of pre-Columbian stones.

As testament to an incredible demonstration of willpower, I also had presents that I had brought back from New York to Tahiti. There was a box of candy and some money toward a good restaurant meal from my father. Fritz gave me a silver cat pendant wrapped up in an empty can of 9 Lives cat food and a letter. He wrote: "You know that writing is not my specialty, but this is a historic year. You are 20. I am 40. And my mother is 80. So now, go have a nice party with your cat. Fritz." He meant Dinghy, of course, and I thought about all the other changes that had taken place since I'd last seen my family.

The trip to Thursday Island led through a windless Albany Channel with a current pushing us along at 3 extra knots toward Cape York and the Torres Straits. Here, the Indian and Pacific oceans meet in a passage that is only about 100 miles wide at the most, and almost completely dammed up by reefs, sandbanks and islands. According to the tidal situation, currents up to 6 knots swirl and eddy through small channels. With tidal charts, we had calculated everything just right and used the currents to advantage.

Thursday Island is the administrative and commercial center of the Torres Straits group wedged between Australia and Papua New Guinea. It was a brief sabbatical from the trip, with time to provision and rest up before the voyage to Bali. But there was one last problem to resolve before heading out to sea.

Ever since Samoa, I had tried every different kind of lice shampoo on the market. No matter the strength, none solved the problem, and I was afraid that nothing would help unless I just shaved off all my hair. I had resorted to using the public showers late at night so that no one would smell the medicinal shampoos. Together with Olivier, who had also contacted the buggers in Tonga, before meeting me, we were sick and tired of this degradation, and willing to try anything. In a desperate moment we poured kerosene over our heads, and after our scalps began to burn, we rinsed with generous helpings of Palmolive dishwashing liquid. The clumps of hair that fell out of my head and the subsequent sores were more than worth the price of permanent liberation.

On October 20, we transferred Tarzoon back to *Varuna*, and Mimine stayed to make the trip aboard *Akka*. As we sailed away from the Torres Straits, Booby Light flashed the end of our Australian odyssey, and I regretfully looked back to the land Down Under that we hadn't had the time to explore properly. Ahead was the Arafura Sea, a journey of 1,800 miles across an ocean reputed to be windless and mercilessly hot at this time of the year. As a howling wind pushed us quickly into the Gulf of Carpenteria and *Varuna* slowly began to pull ahead of *Akka*, my thoughts drifted to Olivier and what might be in store for us in Bali.

During the following days, the easterly winds dwindled and slowly veered to the north and northwest, spiraling counterclockwise. I changed the sails accordingly until we began to beat. A depression had formed off Darwin, to the west, and was dishing up a little trouble, but nothing serious. On October 22, the weather conditions had become positively placid, with either a light westerly breeze or none. My endless scanning of the horizon paid off when the yellowish triangle of *Akka*'s sail appeared a few miles astern, and I took down the jib and waited for her to catch up.

Olivier was below, and I motored my way over the calm water, turned off the engine and blasted my horn 15 feet away from his cockpit. He popped out on deck in an instant and, foolishly grinning at each other like Cheshire cats, we waved, happy with the surprise.

"Why don't you come pick me up," he said. "I can leave *Akka* on her own for a couple of hours."

"What if *Akka* starts going faster, or if a squall comes," I protested, immediately apprehensive of the idea.

"Look," he answered in his always confident manner, "*Varuna* doesn't even have a genoa up and she is already going faster than *Akka*. It'll be all right."

"OK. Well, let me get ready and I'll be over," I doused the jib to keep *Varuna* from heeling and turned the engine back on. Olivier, up ahead, was already prepared, standing at the lifelines with one hand keeping balance against a shroud. *Varuna*'s bow pulled up to *Akka* and the waves gently rocked her nearer to the other boat. Timing his move, Olivier gave me directions as I balked at our proximity while struggling to keep Tarzoon from jumping over to the meowing Mimine. Just as Olivier leapt, a little gray ball whizzed across and Tarzoon scratched his way out of my arms and ran to nuzzle his foster mother.

Until sunset, we talked, gave each other bucket baths and played with *Varuna*'s sails to stay close to *Akka*. As the sun disappeared beneath the horizon we welcomed the cool night air and I brought Olivier back home. He put out his kerosene lanterns for me to see him during the night. But, as I slept, we lost sight of each other and at dawn the horizon was empty.

Two days later, on the evening of October 24, I pulled out my logbook and wrote:

"My position for the day was exactly the same as yesterday's. Last night at about 7 o'clock, I saw the lighthouse of the westernmost point of the Gulf of Carpenteria and couldn't pass it on port tack, so I tacked to starboard. During the night we totally regressed back to point A. Started all over again this morning and as soon as it gets dark enough to see the light, I'll know if we made any decent progress. I saw a yellow snake with brown diamonds along its spine swim past, and a turtle.

"There are only 1,200 miles left until Bali. In five days we have only made 300 miles. This is hell. What else can I do besides take out another book and read. During the day, all I do is mop up perspiration and wilt. Night finds me exhausted from the heat. Please, dear God, don't make this too hard a trip and let us get to Bali safe and soon."

Two hours later, I pulled out my logbook and wrote again:

"I saw the light and we were passing it just fine, so I was sitting below reading when I heard a, 'Ho, Ho.' I ran outside and there was Olivier! Right next door and shining a light at us. He said that we were lucky that he woke up just then and looked around or else we would have crashed. Imagine that."

During the rest of the pitch-black night, the wind dwindled practically to zero and we didn't have a hard time staying together, as forward progress waned to a drift over the heaven's reflections on the water. Morning dawned a mirror flat calm, not even a remnant swell. I motored over to *Akka* and Olivier jumped in the water with a line to attach the boats, while Mimine miscalculated her jump and ended up swimming over also.

Only 30 miles away, the Australian desert sweltered, bringing even the ocean up to a lukewarm temperature that only allowed a very temporary relief from the heat. We were stuck in a *pot au feu* and sweat dribbled all over whether we moved or not. A family of mahi mahi swam in *Varuna's* shadow, teasing us and cleverly avoiding baited hooks. Another turtle and snake and thousands of miniature jellyfish swam past, all just indicating that we were not able to even go as fast as they. On a constant shark alert, we dived into the tepid water every fifteen minutes to bring down our body temperatures a couple of degrees. I felt as if I were being fried alive.

For two days, Olivier and I made canned-tuna-and-tomato-paste pizzas and played every form of gin rummy we knew, wishing for all the ice cream we hadn't bought on Thursday Island. During the day, we fished the jellyfish out of the water with my bucket and took pictures with the macro lens. We spent the night sitting in *Varuna's* cockpit while Olivier pointed out all the constellations overhead, showing me which arm of the great Southern Cross pointed vaguely south and what place the stars I knew from my navigation had in other heavenly bodies.

On the second afternoon of these infernal days, an army-green Australian Coast Guard cutter sliced through the water in our direction. Instinctively, as the authorities drew closer, we both wondered if we were doing anything wrong. We stood in the cockpit, and with quivering noses Mimine and Tarzoon gazed up at the towering hulk.

"Hello! Where's your wind?" an Aussie coast guardsman greeted us from the bow.

"Hello," I shouted back in response. "We have no idea, but would you mind asking your weather fax?"

"No problem, mates," he called back, and popped below, coming back a minute later with the sad upshot: "Looks like you've got more of the same until tomorrow night." We winced.

"Could you do with some ice cream?" the man called, surrounded by his cronies, who were all staring down at our little universe of two boats, gently rocking out in the middle of nowhere.

"Absolutely!" I yelled enthusiastically. "Thank you. As much as you can spare!"

"We're slowly baking to death out here," added Olivier. "Thank you." We continued to shout effusive thanksgivings as the pilot maneuvered his bow so that it came directly above *Varuna*'s cockpit and the man launched a green garbage bag our way. Inside there was a block of ice and a half gallon of vanilla ice cream.

"Good luck!" called the Aussies. They revved their engines and pulled away. Like a pair of wild animals, we dived into the cabin, ripped off the cover and began gouging holes in the cold, creamy mixture.

Fortunately, the Coast Guard's weather facsimile was wrong, and that evening, a passing zephyr turned into a legitimate breeze and we got moving again. From then on for twenty days, we managed to stay within sight of each other. *Varuna* sailed much faster than *Akka* in those conditions, and to coordinate our speeds, I kept a reef in the main and used the working jib instead of the genoa to stay alongside *Akka*, who sported her full suit of light-wind sails.

With the heat and meager progress, averaging 50 miles a day, our spirits took a severe beating and lethargy overcame every urge for action. The sight of an enormous manta ray making a leap into the air, the infernal racket of sails slapping against the rattling shrouds, the renewed sputtering of my engine and the loss of water through a leaking jerry can all became just another part of the routine.

Every night Olivier hung out his red and green kerosene lanterns, and I replied with my small white kerosene light. The compensations of having human contact overrode the disadvantage of fatigue from keeping constant vigils, and as we passed the outermost islands of Indonesia, Timor, Roti and Pulau Sawu islands, I scooped up a perfect nautilus shell floating on the water.

Passing the last dent of Australia finally brought us to the doorstep of the Indian Ocean, and we readjusted our lifestyles as the wind picked up from the west, the direction in which we were still headed. Olivier had predicted this. He had an uncanny instinct for reading the weather through cloud formations and ocean characteristics, and I was learning from his knowledge of meteorology. The stringy cirrus clouds racing from the west replacing the puffy cumulus of the day before and the growing swell from the west had foretold the counterclockwise shift.

As *Varuna* began to beat, I reassumed my favorite position standing at the spray hood, and Tarzoon, unaccustomed to the heeling, poised himself to jump up and join me. I heard the familiar scritch of his nails on the fabric, looked around to cuddle my friend and didn't see him. Alarmed, I scanned the empty cockpit. Tarzoon had gone overboard! Looking back to the wake behind *Varuna*, I caught sight of his little head, a picture of terror bobbing up and down in the waves. Screaming with a burst of adrenaline, I leapt to the Monitor, disengaged it, rounded up into the wind and backwinded the sails. Trying to keep my eyes on him, I pushed the tiller over so that *Varuna* would back down on the spot. Tarzoon swam frantically toward the boat and as we drifted closer, I leaned over and scooped him up.

After Tarzoon fell overboard, I realized that I'd probably have a mental breakdown if anything ever happened to him. Torturing myself with the thought that one day, alone at sea, he could very well be lost, I picked up his soaking body and hugged him close, swearing that I would always do my best to protect him.

Like turtles, *Varuna* and *Akka* slowly slammed past Sumba, Sumbawa, Lombok and Nusa Besar islands, and Bali finally became more of a reality. On November 16, after twenty-seven days, *Varuna*'s longest time at sea, we hugged the coast of Nusa Besar with only a channel separating us from Bali's Benoa Harbor. The full moon illuminated white cliffs as the swish of the ocean was broken by the waves thundering against the volcanic walls after their unhindered passage up from southern oceans. *Varuna* and I had crossed the Arafura and Timor seas, and soon we would be acquainting ourselves with our third ocean.

A large fringing reef was a ruff almost encircling the extremities of Benoa Harbor's buoyed entrance channel, and I kept a leery eye on the crashing white water the next morning, as I followed *Akka* through the strong current and messy chop. Halfway through, the engine petered out once again and I found myself in a state of chaos. The main halyard was in total disarray, tangled with all the other paraphernalia—cups, harbor charts, binoculars—and my straw sun-hat kept falling off my head.

As the engine first began to falter, I rushed to raise the mainsail and boom it out to carry us through, while Olivier screamed back at me to get information on the VHF about where we should anchor. He couldn't hear me cursing out the bloody engine over the roar of his own, so as soon as we got into clearer water, I jumped below and hailed the port authorities. Trying to make myself understood to an Indonesian with a minimal knowledge of English, I repeatedly left the transmitter hanging to climb back on deck to see where *Varuna* was headed, as Olivier shouted for me to watch out. Finally I hung up on the amused radio voice, grabbed the tiller and rounded up just before we hit a sandbank.

"Forget it!" I screamed to Olivier. "Nobody understands me. Let's just anchor next to that other sailboat. We can't get into trouble for not understanding."

He anchored and I followed behind, capping off the last harrowing fifteen minutes of the nightmare by running aground in shallow sludge. I pulled open the cover to the sputtering engine, turned it off and sucked on the fuel line to bring back the flow, before realizing that a pipe had burst and my diesel was emptying into the bilge. With burns from the boiling exhaust pipe on my arms, a greasy face and a mouth tasting like a gas station, I sat down in the midst of the bedlam and cried, waiting for the customs man to come and ask for *Playboy* magazines.

Baksheesh was the name of the game in Bali, and it began with our permission to go ashore. A sailing permit was required to stay in Indonesia, and I didn't have one. Until Australia, I hadn't even known that I was going to stop in Bali, much less the exact dates that were required for the permit, so our first bribe was for a hundred dollars each for permission to stay one week. After having spent twenty-seven days at sea, we couldn't wait to get as far away from the boats as possible, and as soon as we handed over our traveler's checks and our legality was established, we hopped on the first bus we could find for the twenty-minute ride to Kuta Beach.

The island roads were bordered for miles on either side by the flat paddy fields, and stunning Balinese women dressed in colorful batiks, with their waists cinched in cummerbunds, walked along the roadside, balancing baskets of rice on their heads. Young couples, doubled up on their bicycles, steered out of the way as our driver zoomed like a madman through their midst. As we neared Kuta Beach, a huge billboard of Colonel Sanders emerged, with *Ayam Goreng*, fried chicken, written beneath his familiar face.

The hive of venders, ethnic eateries and bungalow hotels with elaborately sculpted gardens drew an exotic mélange of visitors from all around the world. We strolled and let our eyes roam over the ornate Asian architecture with its serpentine trimmings, and stone temples with their open roofs, enabling the gods to come and go as they pleased. The Balinese were talented artisans and the streets were jam-packed with Indonesian wares: lacy cotton and rayon clothing, bolts of batik fabrics, jewelry and intricate balsa and wood sculptures of swirling snakes, dragons and mythical monsters. We spent a couple of days there, taking it all in while we bought presents, took hot baths, ate out and rested, with intermittent trips to check on the boats.

On our fourth day, as I was filling out the required autobiography for sending presents overseas to the family, who should enter the post office but Fred from *Kreiz*. He had left the boat in Australia and come to Bali for a simple holiday. It was pure coincidence that our paths had crossed. That night, to make the coincidence one of the more bizarre variety, while we three shared a celebration meal, into the restaurant walked Fred's ex-girlfriend, fresh off a plane from Singapore—another total coincidence. Now we really had to celebrate, so for Olivier's and my remaining two days, the four of us rented a car and drove into the interior through a panoramic landscape of terraced rice farms up to an immense crater lake 7,000 feet above sea level.

On the day before leaving Bali, in the market at Denpasar, we endlessly haggled down the preposterous original prices, and filled up the boats with passion fruits, avocados, grapefruits and pineapples. The next morning we cast off. Six hundred and sixty miles separated *Varuna* from her next destination, the tiny speck of Christmas Island in the middle of the Indian Ocean, the most beautiful trip *Varuna* and I were to share.

The wind was from astern at Force 3, gently prodding us onward at 6 knots toward the asylum of Flying Fish Cove. On the sixth night, December 2, a hump marred the perfect horizon and, after heaving to for the night, *Varuna* glided into the lee of the island to a cleft where we anchored. Six hours later, *Akka*'s black hull emerged around the bend of the cleft and sailed up alongside.

Christmas Islanders, mainly Malaysian and Australian employees of a phosphate mining company, treated our welcome new faces like old friends. Stubby, a man from Borneo, was the proprietor of the island's one free enterprise, a tire repair shop, and taking us under his wing, he showed us to lime trees, fresh fruit and vegetable gardens and his VCR for a James Bond soiree.

Christmas Island had a mind-boggling population of red crabs, and during our visit they were in the process of migrating from the sea, where they laid their eggs, back up into the interior of the island. Everywhere we went, huge congregations of these crabs sashayed back and forth along the streets on tiptoe. The pavements were littered with a red carpet of pungent crushed carcasses that Stubby said played havoc with car tires, thus providing him with plenty of seasonal work. Crackling crab disturbed the quiet hours in between the Muslim prayers that emanated four times a day from a nearby minaret.

From the moment I had stepped ashore, I was given a warning that was to be repeated often during my stay—first from the fellows from customs and immigration, and later from others; "Don't you know that you're very late in the season?" from one person. And from another, "Hurricane season has already begun. It's dangerous here for small boats." These warnings came complete with elaborate descriptions of the enormous swell that bombards the anchorage whenever a hurricane rolls over the island. To say the least, this information did not help to provide an overwhelming sense of security and a nagging worry began munching away at my nerves.

A well-stocked supermarket provided for the residents was at our disposal, at government-subsidized prices, and we stocked up on all the goodies we wouldn't lay eyes on for a while. My engine's burst fuel line was repaired in a workshop and reinstalled. With hurricane season nipping at our heels, Olivier and I said goodbye to Stubby and the other yacht club members whom we had chatted with in the evenings after taking our showers on shore. Giving each other presents to be opened on Christmas, on December 8 we departed for Sri Lanka, 1,800 miles away as the crow flies, through the doldrums and over the equator.

· · ·

Immense waves buried first the boom and, on the next roll, the spinnaker pole as 20- to 30-knot winds pushed us steadily forward for eight days—a far cry from the lax Arafura Sea. The strain on the rigging was relayed to my nerves, and finally, frazzled from the constant watches required to remain together, Olivier and I decided to separate until Sri Lanka. We screamed Merry Christmas and Happy New Year to each other and floundered apart. The next morning, a disagreeable drizzle settled in and I was alone.

For two days *Varuna* slowly eased north toward the equator, as a menacing sky of lumbering black clouds closed in. Passing through the curtain of doldrums, we entered a world of flat calms, squalls, rain and meager advances of only 30 miles a day. I resewed the rapidly disintegrating spray hood, made a splint for a broken mainsail batten, cleaned up, knitted, read a couple of books, and on the third day of a glassy ocean, decided that it was time to try the engine. The starter turned for about thirty seconds, nothing else happened, and a day of mechanics was born.

After a couple of hours of following and tracing all the fuel lines, after twice dismantling the second filter and sucking on the piping, I had an inspiration. When I opened the port cockpit locker, the hunch played out. The needle to the fuel tank gauge was on empty. Six hours later, after ten bloody cuts, many sweated gallons of body fluids, and three more dismantlings of the fuel lines, I discovered that there were two miniature holes in the second fuel filter's casing. All but the two gallons of diesel I had in an emergency jerry-can had siphoned into the bilge. After duct-taping the casing, I was faced with the fact that with only barely enough fuel left for emergencies, *Varuna* was once again engineless.

Every couple of hours, I climbed up several mast steps to see if I could find *Akka*. Sometimes a cloud would get my hopes up until it rose above the horizon and revealed itself, but I continued to search. I missed Olivier and wrote down little prayers in my logbook for him to have a safe trip while, over two weeks, we covered 600 miles, inch by aching inch. My hands developed an elephant's hide pulling the sails up and down to grab every last gasp of breeze.

Books helped me to while away the time, and I read almost one a day. When it was hot and lethargic, I appreciated nothing better than a good spy story that spiralled to an exciting climax. Lusty romances were also a good distraction when conditions outside were meltingly hot and sweaty. I could become the lovely belle Lucinda, who runs off with the Marquis in lavish Nineteenth-century *Gone*

With the Wind settings. I read about oil-rig crises in the North Sea, and followed a juggernaut's progress through a fictional rebel-infested African country. I suffered in prison with Papillon and became an immigrant hobo in Montreal.

As the calm days showed no sign of relenting, the book supply dwindled and I was forced to resort to loftier sagas like *Les Miserables* and hefty volumes of James Michener. But I didn't much care about the sewers of Paris, nor did I really want to hear about a dinosaur during the Far West's evolution. In the boredom of the doldrums, I wanted to read about terrorists blowing up Yankee Stadium. I needed excitement in my life.

The dolphins were great, but they seemed to always come at night. The wind was pathetic and tore my sails more often than it gave any propulsive aid. For one week, three baby dorados used *Varuna's* shadow for shelter, and flip-flop sandals drifted by with families of fish attached. The incongruous sight of floating logs, plastic bags and barrels were the apex of my excitement. Always anticipating a treasure or strange ocean life, I would alter course and drift up to the blobs until it became obvious that each one was just another piece of garbage in the middle of the ocean.

One night, I was awakened by drops of water. Hearing no rain on deck, I reached up to turn on the light and there was a soaking wet Tarzoon shaking himself over me. The little idiot had managed to fall overboard and clamber back up somehow without my noticing.

I thought often about Olivier, wherever he was, and how miserable he must be, certainly making less progress than I with the poky *Akka*. All day long, I played with the sails, coaxing *Varuna* along in vague breezes, and each mile was well earned. During the nights, unable to live with the slatting noise of the limp sails, I took down the slamming offenders and slept. There seemed to be no point in losing sleep for the sake of a couple miles made good. Twice, we were helped along by aggressive fronts with lots of wind. The second one fell on Christmas.

Merry Christmas, Tania, and as a special present, here's a nice gray sky, lots of rain and the gift of sorely needed exercise taking reefs in and out, in and out. I thought about my family back home gathered around another one of Jeri's magnificent trees bedecked in cranberry and popcorn strings with presents heaped around the floor. Tony, Nina and Jade would be gobbling down a traditional meal of turkey, cranberry sauce and the works. I emptied cans of sauerkraut and hotdogs into my pressure cooker and peeled up some potatoes in the cockpit. I thought about Olivier, somewhere behind me, surely giddy after savoring the Johnnie Walker and getting sugar shock from the chocolates I had wrapped for him.

Climbing below, I put the cooker on the stove, filled up the dish at the base of the burner with alcohol and put a match to it to prime and preheat the pressurized kerosene. Dreaming about a white New York Christmas, I waited for the alcohol to burn out and then lit the stove. The blue flame spit out and settled into a methodical hiss, as the cabin filled with the aroma of burning kerosene. When the pressurized steam in the cooker began spinning the escape valve, I waited ten minutes, then removed my meal from the fire. Christmas dinner was ready and I opened my present while it cooled off.

Olivier had made a coral necklace and an earring from a feather he had found on the Barrier Reef. After I gorged myself on a culinary feast, I went to sleep that Christmas night thinking of him and the changes that had swept through my life since the Christmas at home with my mother one year before.

Throughout the passage, whenever a ship rambled across the horizon, if the radio operator was listening and comprehended basics and numbers in English, I'd get a satellite fix. The fixes continued to reconfirm my own navigation, which was indicating appallingly slow progress. I spent hours playing a game of make-believe with myself, trying to picture what Sri Lanka was like and imagining all the news in the mail that I hoped was awaiting my arrival.

New Year's came and went. I almost forgot all about it until I took out the *Nautical Almanac* to calculate a sight. On December 31, 1986, I decided I was better off on *Varuna* in the Indian Ocean than in New York with advertisements, television, radios and people telling me what fun it was supposed to be. I remembered sitting in front of the television at home, struggling to stay awake until the apple floated down in Times Square. Instead, I nodded off to sleep on *Varuna* to be entertained by dreams.

Finally, after three and a half weeks at sea, we inched our way across the equator and back into our native Northern Hemisphere. On Nina's birthday, January 3, a new breeze began to freshen the air and I knew we had finally left the doldrums behind. I began informing Tarzoon of our exact position and ETA every time a fix was plotted and assured him that we would soon arrive.

The northeast monsoon lived up to its description on the pilot charts, and as we crept farther into its neighborhood it began blowing in full force. *Varuna*, reefed down and heeling over 30 degrees as she beat into the 30-knot winds, had little time to adapt to the conditions, and for four days I lived on the walls. I started to see a trickle of ships, and then a steady parade formed. On January 7, we approached a highway on the horizon, my first real encounter with a serious shipping lane.

Twilight descended on an endless stream of lights from the enormous all-business tankers, square car carriers and gargantuan freighters. With only the little red and green masthead light, I felt inconspicuous and could only hope that *Varuna* was being picked up on their radar screens. I radioed a car carrier that was steaming by and the radio operator informed me that, no, *Varuna* did not appear on his screen. We were invisible. He only saw us after I blinked a flashlight in his direction.

Clutching the transmitter and hollering left and right, I must have created an incredible ruckus on the airwaves, making sure that certain ships knew that I was there. Some of them ignored my calls, so I had no idea if they heard me or saw *Varuna*. Paralyzed with fear as they plowed by, at the most desperate moment I even drew Tarzoon close, grabbed my passport and boat papers and prepared to abandon ship.

Dodging in and out of the moving obstacle course, I kept a lookout for the lighthouse on Dondra Head at the southernmost tip of Sri Lanka that would indicate we were only 28 miles away from our destination. Below Dondra Head, there was not a speck of land until the icy wastes of Antarctica. At 3:00 A.M., January 8, the beacon revealed its light, we sprinted as fast as we could across the rest of the shipping lane and set a course for Galle Harbor.

Varuna sped along until hitting the shadow of the landmass that obliterated the wind, and once again, we found ourselves on a flat calm. On tenterhooks, I fidgeted as the sun rose and Sri Lanka emerged from the horizon ahead, shimmering like a jewel in the blue expanse of the Indian Ocean. It had been thirty-one days, my longest trip ever at sea. Waiting for a few gusts to carry us along, I was so ready for land that I thought I could taste it in the heavy morning air. Fishing boats puttered by, reminding me suddenly that I'd better get dressed.

At about midday, after going absolutely nowhere except for the one mile the engine had covered before retiring, I scanned the beckoning shoreline and set a course for more affirmative action. Hailing the next fishing boat that came close, I hoped to stop and bribe them into towing *Varuna* to Galle. As it drew closer, the staccato sound of the green and yellow open boat's engine reverberated through the air. As the first of the three men jumped aboard *Varuna*, I realized that none of us spoke each other's language, and, resorting to sign language, I demonstrated a boat being towed. The men giggled at me as I ran below to pull out forty dollars and a bottle of rum.

"Look," I said, pointing at the loot, waving my arms around exaggeratedly, "me give you this, then you tow me in? OK?"

They haggled among themselves as I tried to fend off the larger boat that was gently rocking against *Varuna*'s hull. "Please," I pleaded, the day was steadily drawing again to a close. They continued to talk, every so often giving me a once-over and readjusting their wraparound skirts that seemed to have wiped up many a bilge.

"OK," the leader said, pointing at my T-shirt. Anxious to make them as happy as possible, I hopped into the cabin, pulled out three T-shirts and distributed them. Finally after several hours of cajoling sign language and half the bottle of rum, they towed me 10 miles toward the coastline until a feeble day breeze picked up. Pointing to the ripples on the water and my sails, they motioned that *Varuna* could now sail herself and they would let me go. I nodded and thanked them as my two crew rejoined their vessel. Grinning and waving, they headed back out to sea.

For three hours, I played with the sails and jiggled the rudder back and forth as we crept by sandy beaches lined with coconut palms. Following the landmarks with the contours on the chart, we were two miles away from the entrance of the harbor when the thunderstorms hit. One after the other they swarmed down, totally obscuring any semblance of wind, so I used the opportunities to scrub the decks and take a shower. All too soon, evening approached and there was no more hope for us to get in before nightfall. It was so close that I could have easily swum to shore had I not seen the enormous dorsal fin of a shark earlier that morning. Resignedly, I went about preparing myself for another night at sea, when a sailboat came out of the harbor and motored up.

"Oh, thank you, God," I said to myself waving and greeting another potential tow. "There's still hope."

"Hi, Tania," one of them called in an Australian accent. "Finally, you've arrived. Everybody is sick with worry."

"What?" I hollered back at them, unaware of anyone that would be waiting and surprised to hear my name. It was practically impossible for *Akka* to go faster than *Varuna* in those pansy winds. "Who's worried?" I asked.

"Your boyfriend. He's been waiting for five days."

"Olivier? You're kidding."

"Here, throw us a line. We'll tow you in." Within half an hour, *Varuna* was tied up and I was in Olivier's arms.

Straightaway, we went ashore to the house of Don Windsor, whom the cruising guides said was the sailor's middleman in Galle. I followed Olivier up the stairs of a veranda, and was greeted by a dark-skinned man dressed in a white robe, who smiled when he saw me.

"Welcome, Tania," said Don Windsor, holding out a telephone receiver. "Your father is on the phone."

he has been described as a drop of milk from the breast of India, and Sinbad of old Arabia called her Serendib. From there evolved the word serendipity, the aptitude for making fortunate discoveries accidentally, and Sri Lanka certainly was a desirable sight for my sore eyes burned by the equatorial sun.

During the twenty-eight days to Bali, six to Christmas Island and thirty-one to Sri Lanka, I had had ample time to picture what this part of the world might be like. My imagination had done somersaults conjuring up elaborate visions inspired by fairy tales that were read to us as children by my mother.

I remembered back to the first time she took us to London when, to keep us quiet, she read from British books of India filled with pictures of exotic Indian rajahs and their princess loves bedecked in jewelry and flowing saris. An elfin sapphire-blue Krishna pranced all over the pages with a swirling octopod Vishnu waving his multiple arms all about. These tales, and later on *The Far Pavilions*, were enough to fire my imagination for this part of the world. Of course, I didn't expect little blue men to be jumping out of every corner but was anxious to see how close these visions would be to the reality of being here.

"Hello, Ding-a-ling!" my father's voice boomed through Don Windsor's telephone that first night. "What in holy hell took you so long? We've been going crazy."

"Daddy? I didn't have any wind or engine, that's all. How did you know I was here?"

"I've been talking to Don Windsor all day. Thank God I had somebody to call. Oh, I'm so relieved. You have no idea what it's like to be waiting like this. . . ." And off he went nonstop, telling me how everyone was wild with worry. As it turned out, Olivier had arrived five fretful days before, mostly because of a firmer grasp of the frustrating weather patterns, and he had steered a course farther east. Most important, his engine had propelled *Akka* out of the doldrums and into the northeast monsoons while *Varuna* had wallowed.

"Well, anyway, here I am, all set to go to Sri Lanka right now and organize a search for you. I can't believe this. Everything's OK? I don't care, I'm coming anyway. Do you need anything?"

"You're coming here?" I asked incredulously, realizing that we hadn't seen each other for over a year and a half. "That's great. Yeah, sure I need stuff."

I eagerly rattled off the top of my head a quick list of boat supplies that I was either without or unable to replace. We arranged to rendezvous two days later at the Galle Face Hotel in Colombo, the capital. Hanging up, I turned to tell Olivier of the latest turn of events. Although it was probably hidden deep in the complexities of my father's brain, I thought I knew the overriding reason he was coming. He wanted to see for himself who this Olivier character was.

The next morning, I went about the business of checking in. Sri Lanka has many complications in store for visitors arriving by cruising boat, and appointing someone to act on behalf of the vessel with immigrations and customs helps to smooth the bureaucratic waters. A man with a business, say a jeweler, and political aspirations and connections, would stand in very comfortable shoes if he were to act as a sailors' agent. Enter Don Windsor, whose house with its large veranda was the first to be seen upon leaving the guarded extremities of the port.

In Don's house the cruising folk gathered, and he opened his arms to them. His showers were our showers; his dinner table was our dinner table; and for a small fee, his servants took our laundry and beat it against the rocks to wash it. A well-educated man, Don seemed to have unturned every stone in Sri Lanka; he could recount extraordinary stories from his country's rich history, as well as arrange welding for an errant piece of a boat's stainless steel. And if you happened to want to buy a little jewelry, well, he just happened to have a few cases to show you. Don whipped out the forms to be filled and took my traveler's checks; soon enough I was legal.

The first day in Sri Lanka was a feast for senses numbed after so long at sea. Olivier and I stood on the corner of the main road, waiting for the bus under the eye of a 15-foot-high orange Buddha. Vintage cars whizzed by, weaving past plodding, wizened brown men leading emaciated cows drawing carts with wooden wheels.

A variety of odors assaulted the nose. No longer did I have to rely on the salt air and occasional redundant meal to tweak my sense of smell. There was no comparison between the smell of land and that of the sea. Sri Lanka had the smell of people, many people, almost 12 million of them, plus their vegetation, their meals in the process of being prepared and their animals.

On the timeless ocean, the days had melted into one another and, if there were no clockworks or responsibilities for navigation, I would surely and happily have lost count of time. The only necessities had been to sleep, prepare food, keep a good course, fix and adjust the odd thing and plot the position once a day. Making a landfall was like shoving an extension cord into a 220-volt socket.

I experienced new languages and accents, arguments, the jigsaw puzzle of lists and trying to plan out one simple day, the apprehensions of planning for the next departure, the organization of the provisioning and the need to grease my jaw muscles in a desperate attempt to catch up on the conversation missed. My eyes had to adjust over and over again, taking in a new world of sights, streets, faces and customs.

My ears were reintroduced to the cacophony of screaming children, reprimanding parents, broken mufflers, outboard engines, braying donkeys, rather than the sound of water, wind and the occasional muttering of my own voice. No longer were there only the familiar things on *Varuna* to touch. On the veranda of 6 Closenburg Road, my hands felt the smooth molded wood of armrests on Don Windsor's chairs. My feet pounded down on the hardened damp dirt roads and hot and sticky asphalt. I could run my fingers through silky hair and rub squeaky skin just washed with fresh water, and I could feel the sensation of wearing clothes and standing up in them with material swaying around my elbows, arms and legs.

A man rolled by on an oversized tricycle, peddling with his right hand the gears that were mounted to one side of the handlebars. Olivier enjoyed watching my pleased reaction. "I love this place," he said. "It's like being in another century." Together we marveled at each new sight until the bus finally arrived, canting over at a 25-degree angle. People rearranged themselves as we slithered aboard into the 5 square inches of extra space between the uniformed children returning from school and sweated out the ride into town. I looked into their faces and they openly smiled back without hesitation. Already, I knew that this would be a special place. A smile is a free pleasure and the people who realized it always made a welcome sight for a tired visitor.

It had been thirty-one days since Olivier and I had seen each other and we had only two days before my father was to arrive to be alone together, gather our wits, clean the boats and do a little sightseeing. *Varuna* looked as if she had taken a turbulent trip to Oz, and Olivier stared at *Akka*'s rust stains with a look of dismay when we returned to scrub down the boats; there wasn't much we could do to the cosmetics in two days. Olivier, being Swiss French, understood only too well that we were facing my father's Swiss-German perfectionism and rued the fact that he hadn't had the chance to overhaul *Akka* in Australia, as he had hoped to do before meeting me.

We bought fruits and vegetables, tied the two boats alongside each other, hung the awnings over the booms for shade in the cockpits and scrubbed to alleviate the salt-stained, travel-weary aura. We did the best we could before visiting the village of Hikkaduwa, a 3-mile-long strip of beach with a pounding surf an hour up the coast from our anchorage that some new friends had recommended.

Driving along the coast, we passed giant coconut palms, strung one to another with sets of lines that climbers used to traverse the treetops and shake down the fruit. All along the seashore were what looked like crucifixes standing sentinel in the surf, where lone fishermen climbed up and cast their lines for hours. We strolled the bazaar of Hikkaduwa and, from a smiling raisin of an old man sitting at an ancient foot-pump sewing machine, I bought a custom-made pair of satin harem pants before heading back to Galle.

That night, the anticipation of seeing my father for the first time since eighteen months earlier in Bermuda kept sleep at bay. My relationship with Oliver aside, so much had happened in that time span that I didn't know what to expect when I saw him. I was sure that he would recognize the many changes in me, and was curious to see if he would be at all different. Eager to catch up on all that was happening on the home front, I couldn't have wished for a better gossip and storyteller to fill me in, and now there was an album full of my own tales to serve up in return.

Meeting my father wasn't the only reason for a visit to the urban alleyways of Colombo; I needed to get some traveler's checks, the baksheesh in Bali and provisioning in Christmas Island having pretty much wiped me out. We awoke early and at 6:00 A.M. met Don Windsor and his son Leonard, who drove us and another sailing couple, Dean and Faye, in his Volkswagen bus on a hair-raising ride to the capital.

Leonard handled that bus as if it were a hot Lamborghini, speeding in and out past the jalopies, buses, bicycles and cow-drawn carts, only once screeching to a halt along with most of the other passing traffic, at an enormous Buddha waypoint. Sri Lanka is considered the cradle of Buddhism, and every 300 feet there was one symbol of worship or another—miniature emerald likenesses, immense sculptures carved out of the sides of cliffs, and Dagobas, the domed prayer sites, some as large as the Egyptian pyramids. Everywhere were pictures, relics and statues of the Enlightened One in postures of meditation, calling to mind the Buddha's years of teaching and his passing to Nirvana.

While Leonard threw a couple of rupees into a collection box, Don jumped out of the car and put his hands together for a moment of contemplation, and we curiously watched the proceedings at a Sri Lankan–style tollbooth of veneration.

In Colombo, after attending to our business, Don Windsor and Leonard, Dean and Faye, and Olivier and I all sat in a state of infectious nervousness waiting at the Galle Face Hotel for my father, who was late. We sat inside on the cool stone terrace overlooking the Indian Ocean, imagining from the ambiance of the manicured garden, the swishing white-pajama-clad waiters and wood-paneled walls that we were characters in an Agatha Christie mystery and that Hercule Poirot himself might just show up any minute.

When my father finally arrived, I didn't even have to see his entrance to know he was there, his energy so charged the room. People turned their heads as he swooped like a dynamo through the lobby and onto the terrace. I had to blink twice to make sure that I knew him. He looked funny, a little chubbier, New York pale and sporting a longish haircut with his jeans and Banana Republic safari vest. I was not the only one surprised.

"My God," he bellowed, simultaneously summoning a waiter over to order a drink, "you look like an Ethiopian refugee. We have to get some meat on those bones. Let's have some lunch right now."

"You feel like the Michelin man," I said, hugging and pinching his waist. "What's this, a coupla spare tires?"

I sneaked a peep at the others; Faye was straightening out her dress, Dean watched our reunion with a pleased grin and Don Windsor was getting up to meet the man that everybody had heard so much about. I knew what they were thinking: "What kind of person would send his daughter off around the world alone so young?" Well, they would soon find out.

"Very funny, Ding-a-ling." He looked over my shoulder at Olivier, who had also gotten up and was standing behind me with a foolish grin.

"Oh yeah. Daddy, Olivier. Olivier, Daddy."

"*Bonjour*, Olivier," my father smiled, extending his hand. The tension could have been cut with a knife as I waited for Olivier to say something smart and witty.

"*Bonjour*, Ernst," he answered. "How was your trip?" Clearly, it was time to introduce Don, Leonard, Dean and Faye, and we sat down for lunch to an excited babble of conversation that could only be conjured up by envisioning six people trying to talk louder than my father.

"Tania, I want you to know that I only brought two pairs of underpants, two pairs of socks, a pair of shorts and a T-shirt with me in order to have enough room for all the things you asked for," he said later, on our way back to the boats. I grabbed his black duffel bag and tore through the sack of Italian nougat bars, Hershey's chocolate, charts, pictures, spare parts and presents.

The next afternoon, he and Olivier hung out on top of my engine compartment and ran around together looking for spare parts, trying to get chummy, while I tried to form on paper the words of my sixth article and squeeze the experiences of almost 5,300 miles, four contries and five months into thirty-five hand-written pages.

A couple of days later, we took a break and my father hired a local driver, Siri, procured by Don Windsor, and set off for three days to see the island and Yala National Park for an elephant safari. At first, my father's philosophy of seeing a little of a lot, instead of a lot of a little, didn't sit well with Olivier, who was inclined toward a more casual pace in getting to know a place.

"But then you will have seen everything at once," insisted my father, incredulous at the notion of dilly-dallying, "and you can leave afterward." I had to try and convince Olivier, who preferred to visit by hitchhiking, buses and trains, that this could be fun also, and so our tour began.

On the eve of the elephant safari, Olivier and I went to sit on the rocks in a nearby marsh to watch the sunset when one of the enormous pachyderms sauntered out of nowhere and relieved himself 25 feet away from us. We were agape. This biological function has got to be the eighth wonder of the world. Besides certain features of noteworthy size, the beast carried at least a ton of water. We counted ourselves lucky to have witnessed this display because the next day's early morning safari only revealed a couple of dozing peacocks, several monkeys, some water buffaloes in a mud bath and the hindquarters of an elephant heading over the horizon.

The route from Yala National Park took us to Nuwara Eliya, a village of houses and buildings topped with red-tiled roofs nestled in a wooded basin at the foot of Sri Lanka's highest peak. Siri drove over the steep winding roads and through the primeval jungles hung with wild orchids, and we climbed steadily into the hill country, around waterfalls, past colonial mansions and thatch-roofed bungalows, over streaming rivers, through the lush green steps of terraced tea plantations.

Occasionally, monkey families preening themselves on the roadside would leap across the thoroughfare and disappear into the forests of rubber trees. The steaming hot coastal climate gradually gave way to more temperate conditions, and finally, as we were drawn into the overwhelming mountain scenery of the interior, we were actually cold.

Our hotel in Nuwara Eliya, with its antiques, wood paneling and hunting trophies adorning the wood-paneled walls, was again a reminder of the British occupation of the island they had called Ceylon, only forty years earlier. We were propped on a hill overlooking a patchwork quilt of greens, field after field of tea bushes outlined by hedges of blooming flowers. We could see the colorful wraps of women with baskets strapped to their backs as they walked up and down the rows, examining and picking the plants.

A mist rolled down from the vista of tropical alps, enshrouding the Tudor and Victorian homes in the village, leftovers from a small British colony that had thrived in the 1800s. By evening, a damp chill permeated the air, seeping into our clothes, and we could vaguely see our breath as we talked.

My father and Olivier seemed to be getting on just fine after dinner. Together, they wiped out an entire night-capping bottle of brandy while talking about the fate of the universe. It usually took a nip or three to lubricate Olivier's vocal cords when he was not completely at ease. Ordinarily, he was a rather silent person and often, I found myself setting the stage with one of his stories so that he could carry on and finish telling them to my father.

Early the next morning, we found Siri trying to start his 1955 relic of an engine in the frosty air, remarkable considering that we were only six degrees of latitude above the equator. Siri reminded me of my mother when on icy mornings in Vernon she would be out with the hair dryer blowing on our Volkswagen's engine to heat it up in order to get us to school on time, while we squealed that we were late.

It was funny how little things could trigger a long-forgotten memory and, at any time of the day or night, something would happen to make me feel that I was back with my family and I'd be swept with a longing to see Tony, Nina, Jade and Jeri. For eighteen months I had been living on daydreams of home and memories that seemed to have had happened to another girl in another lifetime.

A huge pile of mail had been awaiting me at Don Windsor's when I first arrived in Sri Lanka. The dog-eared envelopes and rumpled packages, manhandled around the world, contained the jolting revelation that my brother and sisters were growing up without me, discovering what they wanted out of life, in some cases screwing up, but generally getting on with it. I felt removed whenever I read and reread the letters.

Tony, seventeen, had written that he had his first girlfriend, Maggie, and even went so far as to say that he was in love, which he would never have admitted two years before. Jade, sixteen, had written a list of all the new slang words that were cool at the moment and informed me that my alienation from New York would definitely make me into a social klutz. My father said she was doing well in school and he approved of her friends.

"They're all *normal*," he said, a pointed afterthought.

And Nina, nineteen, it seemed, was her same old radical self, her political views and future aspirations becoming more and more diffused after one and a half years of a Cornell education. It had always been close to impossible to read Nina's handwriting, which now seemed to have gotten worse.

"But it's OK, Tania," she had written, "intellectuals don't write neatly. Look at Einstein." Nina was busy burning her candle at both ends, my father was pleased to inform me, and doing well in school, and he mentioned a vague worry that she might even be expecting too much of herself. I told him to send her on a vacation to me and I would teach her how to calm down.

"That's right," he grinned. "If anyone has perfected the art of taking it easy, it's you."

Tony, he said, had completely stopped his obsessive childish tantrums, which had plagued him long after the troubles with my mother and the divorce. His irrationality had disappeared into thin air after he met Maggie. Jade had even written, "Tania, you won't believe this. Our brother Tony has become *polite*. Tony, Maggie and I were heading uptown on the crowded subway, when all of a sudden two empty seats popped up in front of us. Maggie sat down and Tony turned and asked me if *I wanted the seat*. Yes. You're not seeing things. That was Tony, our brother. Let me tell you, I almost keeled over in shock. . . . "

In yet another attempt to draw out one of his children and instill a zest for life, as my father put it, during the summer of 1985, just after I left New York on *Varuna*, my father, Fritz and Tony had taken a trip to Baffin Island in the Arctic Circle. A helicopter dropped them off on an icy plateau and they were left to fend for themselves for two weeks.

"We wanted to go hiking for several days, but you know Tony," my father said. "He kept whining to us to slow down, his feet hurt, he was freezing, he was tired, why couldn't we stop to rest for a while. Ach! Finally he started to cry that he couldn't go on. I lost my temper and told him that Fritz and I would continue alone without a crybaby and that we would come back in a couple of days." The next day, with the thought of polar bears, he and Fritz got worried, so they turned around and hurried back.

"There was Tony," he continued with pride. "He had set up his tent, a little fire and he was lying down, reading a book, totally calm and happy. So, for the rest of our time, we talked, laughed, caught and smoked many salmon and met some Eskimos."

Immediacy with my family had been impossible until now and my father's presence brought color and animation into personalities that in the year since my mother died had only been words on paper. Throughout our troubled past, we children had only each other for stability in a family that had very little for so long, and now our paths were diverging. I began to worry that by the time I got home, so much would have changed that I wouldn't know them anymore. For the three days that Siri drove us around Sri Lanka, my father and I talked about everything, and I pumped him for description after description, story after story.

. . .

Back in Nuwara Eliya, when Siri's engine finally coughed to a start, we headed for the ancient sixteenth-century capital of Kandy, the home of Buddha's left eyetooth, a symbol of sovereignty preserved in its own temple. It is said that Buddha's tooth was brought to Sri Lanka during the fourth century, hidden in the hair of a princess whose father's throne (he being one of the Kalinga Kings of India), was being threatened by non-Buddhists.

As we strolled past Kandy Lake and into town, I looked into the faces of the thronging people. Although poverty was pervasive in the cities, there was a quiet pride and carriage in the people that I had never found in the metropolis of faces at home, and I wondered what was missing there that these people seemed to have. Not to do any evil, to cultivate good, to purify one's mind, this is the teaching of the Buddha, and it could have been as simple as that.

These people had no conception of the materialism we take for granted back home. For the Sri Lankans, as well as for people in most of the other places I had visited, it was still possible to function without Mr. Coffees, telephone-answering machines, or the 150 different brands of detergent that we have to choose from in a supermarket. They survived with what they had and I felt a parallel between their lives and my life on *Varuna*, even though mine was a matter of choice rather than necessity.

Kandy was a riot of color against the ornate facades of the Eastern-style buildings drenched in sunshine. Most of the men were swathed in somber cloths but the women were wrapped in bright head veils and saris. Many smiles revealed that their owners had red, corroded teeth as a result of their habit of chewing the fruit of the betel palm. On a street corner, Olivier and my father bought a prepared chewing package at a stand and bit into a concoction of lime and betel nuts wrapped in betel leaf. They instantly spit it out, deciding that betel nuts are an acquired taste. I didn't even want a smidgen.

Clashing with the stubby red teeth, splashes of orange identified the small groups of young sandaled monks who seemed to be everywhere. Often, young Sinhalese men join a monastery for several years early in life to absorb the teachings and purity of the Buddhist way of life before heading out into the real world.

Sri Lanka was color, sounds, voices, a curlicue, swirly alphabet and a lovely, round singsong way of talking. I could never tell whether people were saying yes or no, because both were conveyed by a wobbly, slow rotation of the head, making the speakers look like dolls with loose neck springs. Other customs were gentle reminders that Sri Lanka was home to four of the world's great religions—Buddhism, Hinduism, Christianity and Islam—creating important common courtesies: shoes off in temples, and even in temple ruins; modest dress; and as most people use the left hand to clean themselves, it is considered unclean and frowned upon for eating or handing anything to anyone.

It was a great luxury to know that I would be on land for an entire month without lifting the anchor, regardless of my father's repeatedly expressed advice to the contrary during the two weeks he spent with us. I had decided that because I was making the trip, the final decisions would be mine; at least where my health was concerned. I was underfed and very tired, with supposedly only one pleasant trip to look forward to, crossing the Arabian Sea. The Red Sea, the Mediterranean and the Atlantic I didn't even want to think about.

On the third day of our tour with Siri, we headed back from Kandy for a party at Don Windsor's house. All the cruising people had donned their finery and I was introduced to a four-star general, the former prime minister, and deputy thises and thats. I told my stories to a group of journalists at Don's request, while everyone kept coming to wish me a happy birthday, which I couldn't understand at first because my birthday was still ten months away. Finally, when I glanced over at Don and saw him wink, I understood what the occasion for the party was.

He was such a little wheeler-dealer, always thinking up new ideas and schemes to lure in the customers. For sailors, this kind of character was just what we needed. It was always fun to arrive on Don's veranda at the end of a hot day and see what was new.

No matter where a trip started, to arrive in Sri Lanka on a sailboat entailed many miles and days at sea, with the accompanying stories, and we were like a fraternity interested in the circumstances that had led to each of us being there. There was Henry, the seventy-plus-year-old Dutch singlehander with Coke-bottle glasses, who had originally left from Annapolis, Maryland, sailed the world, and now walked around with a gourd of rum hanging permanently from his shoulder, telling his numerous naughty tales to whoever was sitting nearby.

Then, there was the family on *Christina*, who had given up a kiosk in Germany to take off on a circumnavigation and, except for their seven-year-old son, often partook in the annihilation of Henry's rum.

There was the renegade Allistair who fled Australia, with a young daughter and son, in an anarchistic flurry on a small-scale Gloucester fishing sloop, taking with them a monkey and a wild Australian dingo.

My father fit in perfectly, telling all his wild stories of smuggling gold into India and coaxing an ancient station wagon across the Hindu Kush mountain range from Afghanistan to Pakistan. We'd sit around the dinner table gamming and eating dishes of spicy beef, curried vegetables and buffalo yogurt that Don's family served up every night.

Often the conversation focused on the thousand-year religious war still raging between the Sinhalese and Tamils in the north country. The conflict hardly touched us except for the fact that the port and public buildings were all heavily guarded.

More often than not, we entertained each other with horror stories of the Red Sea. Everybody had heard of at least one boat that had been hit by a blind ship, and the hair-raising, blasting headwinds were discussed in minutest detail. We all shared the same reluctance to journey up that infamous stretch but were addicted to talking about it, as though sharing fears and laughing about them helped us enter it with lighter hearts.

The Red Sea is 1,200 miles long, stretching almost exactly from north to south. Mountain ranges on both sides funnel the wind down in tremendous gusts, following the direction of the sea itself and oftentimes making headway close to impossible. Reefs fringe the land, making landfalls and navigation tricky, and at times the wind kicks up dust storms, making celestial navigation unreliable. Everyone had heard from someone else that there were, supposedly, pirates and gunrunners, and the unfriendly countries of Ethiopia, North Yemen and Saudi Arabia limited the available landfalls to Egypt and the Sudan. Also, it was a busy highway for all the shipping circulating between Europe and Asia.

The only alternative to taking an endless pounding, while beating and tacking up the Red Sea shipping lanes, would be to have a good engine and wait for the rare calms. All these facts and stories began building a persistent, nagging dread. Nobody was looking forward to sailing this stretch and advice was passed out a penny to the dozen as we exchanged photocopies of guides and tips for excellent anchorages that somebody had heard about from a friend who had a friend who had a friend. . . .

The minute a new sailboat entered Galle Harbor heading eastabout, the opposite direction from ours, the crews were bombarded with questions about the weather and shipping that they had encountered on their voyage down the Red Sea. Our fears were borne out.

"We had strong winds from behind the whole way," they always said, "and, yes, there were a lot of ships." One 80-foot ketch pulled into Galle missing her mizzenmast, which had been carried away by a tanker. We all shook our heads, and the fact that such a comparatively large boat wasn't seen by the men on the ship's bridge struck a note of communal worry into the hearts of those of us with small boats. But, along with the woes, there were also times to forget what lay ahead and enjoy the present. A camaraderie existed among the sailing people here such as I had never experienced before.

While my father was there to help, we decided to take *Varuna* out of the water at the shipyard in Galle to check the play in the rudder and to add an extra coat of anti-fouling paint. As she was lifted by the crane and water streamed off her hull, I was relieved to see that she had held up very well for more than half a world and still looked almost new. Through no fault of my own, I thought, remembering my lack of sailing expertise in the beginning. With my bungling, she had taken a lot of wear and tear, and most of the damage—as with the pulpit—she had seemingly ignored. *Varuna* had led me by the hand until I had learned how to care for her properly. A real little lady.

Olivier and I spent our last day with my father in Colombo trying to locate some canned food—anything other than sardines—a knife, a rivet gun and a few other inconsequential odds and ends that we could have found on New York's Canal Street in half an hour. The train back to Galle left in the afternoon and Olivier and I had to catch it to get back to the boats.

"Well, Tania," said my father at the train station's entrance as he saw us off, "I hope your trip is good. No, I hope it's excellent. And please try to go as fast as you can or the North Atlantic will be horrible if you wait too long into the season. Anyway, you must be back before November to break the record." We still thought I had a good chance of getting it.

"I know, Daddy. I'll see you again soon and talk to you even sooner."

"Hurry. Remember. This is not a vacation," he continued, and I finished the well-known last line with him, "This is a job."

He said all this kindly and looked at me sadly, trying to keep the optimism in his voice. He had just spent two weeks sleeping on *Varuna*, bumping his head all over the place and experiencing the energy-draining heat. He saw that there were dark circles under my eyes and that I had lost an awful lot of weight. For the first time in a year and a half, I wasn't just a voice over a telephone calling from the next exotic port of call. Nor was I that irresponsible girl he knew when she was sixteen, but a very tired twenty-year-old in the middle of an undertaking more arduous than either of us ever could have anticipated in those early days of excited planning. Then, with a globe, the world really had been in our hands.

Just before we handed over our tickets and passed through the turnstile, Olivier and he shook hands and he hugged me tight. "By the way," he whispered into my ear, "I like Olivier. He is a good friend for you."

It was goodbye again until who knew when. I thought about him hopping on an airplane and going back to the world of air-conditioned movie theaters, bathtubs, telephones, Jeri and my brother and sisters. It would take another nine months of sailing for me to get there too, and as we boarded our train and it began to chug away, the longing for home overcame me in salty tears.

Although he oftentimes infuriated me, I loved being with my father, hearing his stories and grand schemes and was sad to see him go. I remember that with the same verve that he had just brought to Sri Lanka, my father had swept in and out of our lives when we were children in Vernon. Living with my mother in those days had been something close to hell for us, unable as we were to understand her mental condition and torment. Legally helpless, my father had tried to restore the normality in our lives by squeezing in as much love and happiness as we could handle on the weekends he was allowed to be with us.

In the wake of yet another week of upside-down confusion, uncertainty, fights, being late for school every day, and holy-rolling with my mother's religious friends, we craved the weekends, when my father's presence would always bring a burst of excitement and color into our days. He'd regale us with boyhood tales of when he had left Switzerland with twenty dollars in his pocket, hitchhiking through Eastern Europe, the Middle East and ending up in Japan. He told us stories about how he had smuggled gold into India, spied in Red China, performed as a yodeling belly dancer in Beirut, and been put in a Turkish jail for possession of the DDT powder he was carrying to control the flea population living on him. His yarns always went on for days in "to be continued" style.

When he ran out of his own autobiographies, he painted castles in the air with tales of monsters, dragons and fairies, dredged up from the bottomless well of his imagination. One of us was always the hero by turns. In the summer we built a treehouse, went for long excursions in the countryside and up the beginning of the Appalachian Trail.

As the divorce dragged on into winter, we built igloos and snowmen, and then cracked a hole in the ice over our lake, took saunas and ran through the snow to jump in and out of the waterhole. We'd all sit down, and with my father's guidance, try to induce self-hypnosis, but heads or feet always seemed to start itching at just the wrong moment. He organized contests where the first one able to stand on his or her hands unaided for one minute could go to the store and choose the largest salami to be had. Many years later, with gymnastics training, Nina finally did it, but by then, she had become a vegetarian.

My mother was never home on my father's weekends. The courts had made her leave, and God only knows what she did during this time. Knowing what I know now, I believe she probably had checked herself into a hotel and cried over the cards life had dealt her. She'd always make new resolutions, give us little presents she made, come home and then, try as she might to control herself, soon begin acting as irrational as ever.

After a while, rankled by our bubbly joy at the end of his visits, she took to the habit of making us scarce on my father's weekends. Jealous for the same affection, and frightened that she was about to lose us to a judge who was swaying in his favor, she started checking the family into different hotels after school on Fridays, where we stayed until Sunday night. When we finally got back home, we would each find letters under our pillows from my father saying that he had waited, that he loved and missed us and would be back the next weekend. The painful cycle continued until the day my mother picked us up from school with a carful of luggage, and instead of going home, we had found ourselves in the Swiss boarding school.

In Sri Lanka with Olivier, I felt a pang of the same empty feeling that I'd had as a child on those Sunday nights when my father would kiss us goodbye and sadly leave the house in Vernon to head back to New York on the bus.

"You have a really nice father," Olivier said, bringing me back to the present and trying to cheer me up by pointing at the lice nits in the hair of the people who surrounded us on the train. I looked at my blond partner and immediately felt a rush of relief. Having his help and his love through the worst moments and sharing the good times side by side, I no longer could imagine the trip or my life without him.

The month drew to a close, and after he had also hauled *Akka* for some new antifouling, Olivier and I prepared the boats for the 3,100-mile trip across the Arabian Sea and halfway up the Red Sea to Port Sudan. The two harbors of Djibouti and Aden in South Yemen were available near the entrance to the Red Sea, but we were hoping to be able to do the trip nonstop.

We loaded down the boats with leeks, onions, potatoes, carrots, cabbage, water, diesel and the few processed foods that were available and, at 11:00 A.M. on Tuesday, February 10, 1987, both anchors were on deck and no more excuses could be made. We motored out of the harbor. Pulling up the main and jib, I turned off the engine and the habitual gurgling of water rushing past *Varuna*'s hull was drowned out suddenly by the very alien sound of water gushing into the engine compartment.

"Oh God," I moaned. "What now?" We had only just departed. I pulled open the engine cover and saw a pipeline's worth of water rushing out of the stern tube where the propellor shaft passed by way of a stuffing box out through the hull. Furious with myself, I could see immediately what was wrong. The stuffing box should have been lubricated with heavy grease long before in order for the shaft to rotate smoothly within, but I had never gotten around to it. Now, the consequence of my ignorance and procrastination was that the stuffing box had adhered to the shaft and rotated with it when the engine was in gear, which wore away the grip of the flexible tubing that held it in place with a hose clamp. The stuffing box had popped out and the ocean poured in.

With a watchful eye on the ships passing on both sides as *Varuna* crossed the shipping lanes off the southwestern coast of Sri Lanka, I hammered the stuffing box back into the flexible pipe and retightened the hose clamp. The deluge ceased. Then, with a dainty flick of the wrist, I jettisoned my last screwdriver into the murky depths of the bilge. I swear I could have opened a hardware store with all the tools that were providing extra ballast to that hungry bilge after months of playing games with my godforsaken engine: screwdrivers, wrenches, monkey wrenches, Swiss Army knives, vital screws, nuts and bolts and even a pair of scissors.

I continued to follow *Akka* through the shipping lanes, and we discussed my problem over the water. Later in the afternoon, the wind petered out and, with land still hovering on the horizon, we took down the sails and tied the two boats together. Olivier swam over with an extra screwdriver and wrench in his mouth. We tried everything we knew to fix the problem, to no avail. I was horribly pissed at myself. None of this had to happen if only I had properly read the instruction manual and kept the stuffing box greased. Instead, the greasing nipple had rusted and fallen out, and now every time the engine was put into gear, the stuffing box popped out.

We were 15 miles away from Galle and in a dilemma. Should we return, or could I try to sail without an engine the 2,400 miles that were left until Djibouti, where repairs could be made? The latter option would make all our timesaving plans of heading directly to Port Sudan useless. However, if we returned to Galle, the same time would be wasted in a harbor that we already knew. Olivier took *Varuna* in tow for about 20 minutes, and the decision was made for us when *Akka*'s engine overheated. For the Red Sea, I needed the engine, so Djibouti it was.

After two days, Olivier and I were still within sight of each other. There had been intermittent and variable bursts of wind, but only until we got past Sri Lanka's wind shadow. Then, the weather changed dramatically. From bobbing peacefully along on a benign sea, in a matter of minutes *Varuna* began to heel over on a beam reach with a gusty wind, and the volume of noise multiplied tenfold with the sounds of speedy gurgling bubbles passing by her hull. The northeast monsoon piled up behind the island, and then unleashed its fury down through the 40-mile-wide channel between the island and India, whose continental shelf jutted well out into the ocean, building up a confused chop.

After a head-banging night of living on the walls, I awoke early on the third morning to look out of the porthole and check on *Akka*'s proximity. There she was, still about a mile upwind. Olivier and I had an unspoken rule that whoever was upwind had the responsibility of closing in to the other boat. For once, it wasn't me. I popped outside and stood waiting at the spray hood.

The sun was shining down and beginning to heat up the day as the north wind whipped through the rigging on a perpendicular angle to our course, a steady and fast point of sail. The waves were uncommonly steep and the lee rail buried itself underwater as we fell off a wave and created miniature rainbows in the splashing wake. I weighed taking in the third reef, which would let *Varuna* sit up a little straighter, but would also decrease our speed. The jib was already reefed down and there were two in the main. Looking back to *Akka*, I said to myself, "Nah. The two boats seem to be going at about the same speed and besides, we're screaming along."

Satisifed that Olivier was slowly converging on me, I went back down to bed to grab an extra half hour of rest. "He'll wake me up when he arrives," I thought, closing my eyes and reconsidering the decision of taking in the reef. All of a sudden, *Varuna* rose higher than usual on the swell of an extra-large wave, straightened out and then climbed a little higher.

"Oh hell," I remember thinking. The strange sensation of falling slow-motion into limbo was followed by the boat's suddenly lurching over and thudding down on her side, launching paraphernalia across the cabin and throwing me sideways. As I shouted in shock, the crest of the wave crashed over *Varuna*'s frame and plowed down through the companionway onto my bed amid all sorts of clanging, jingle-jangles and the sound of hundreds of gallons of water pouring overboard.

"I was just gonna take in that third bloody reef after all! You couldn't wait two damn minutes, could you?" I spluttered, hyperventilating with anger and frustration, and raced with Tarzoon out to the cockpit to see what happened. *Varuna* had been completely knocked down. The cockpit was still flooded, and my two jerry cans of fresh water, one companionway slat, my favorite hat and funnels, buckets and other gear were bobbing in her wake. I watched as the self-steering straightened itself out and, unbelievably, we continued sailing. By now, Olivier was close by and he sailed downwind of me, hollering over the racket.

"Wow!" he called. "That was incredible. Your mast almost touched the water. I wish I had my camera out. Are you all right?"

"No," I screamed. "Not at all. I've got the biggest goddam mess in the world to clean up and no more water, except for that foul stuff in my tanks."

"Why didn't you take in a reef?"

"Oh, leave me alone," I screamed back. He was right.

"It's not my fault. Scream at the ocean," he answered, smiling, and maneuvered *Akka* to stay close enough for conversation.

"I already did and you're the only one left. I'll catch up to you later on." I waved him off and went to take in that third reef, swearing to leave it there short of a flat calm. Climbing back down into the cabin, I found water lapping all over my bunk with a spilled can of powdered milk adding an interesting hue to the walls and mattress. Most of my belongings that had previously been on the windward shelves now floated in seawater on the lee side. As I began mopping and sponging up the milky mess, I remembered that half of my remaining supply of tools had also been in the cockpit.

It took a better part of the day to calm down and clean up. For several days after the knockdown, whenever I needed little things that had once been in the cockpit, I found that they too now lived in the briny deep.

The next morning, we hit the wind shadow of India and another fat calm, perfect for drying out my mattress on deck. For two days, *Akka* and *Varuna* stayed tied together, drifting along with all the garbage in the Indian Ocean. We were wallowing in the center of converging currents 100 miles off the coast of India and the filth was revolting. Black oils covered the surface and garbage floated every 100 feet. Not only did we stop diving into the water, I didn't even want to wash my hands in it. Rather we pulled the boats together and jumped back and forth. The filth that mired us—sludge, bags, plastics, styrofoam, dishwashing-liquid bottles, flip-flops and wrappers—coated the hulls of the boats with a thick black film. Olivier and I lamented how any sea life could survive such appalling pollution. Indeed, here the ocean seemed completely barren of life and the scene was sad enough to make one cry.

Olivier passed me an extra jerry can with eight gallons of water to replenish my stores and I figured that, with rationing, I could live on one quart of water per day for thirty-two days before having to drink the disgusting water from *Varuna*'s tanks. Finally the wind returned with gusto and we breezed through the shipping lanes at the Eight Degree Channel, the point at 8 degrees latitude where all the shipping passed between the Maldive Islands to the south and the Laccadives to the north. Along with several other giants, we followed the lighthouse beacon on a solitary island and passed onto the Arabian Sea.

During the following week, we took reefs in and out as the northeast wind alternated from heavy gusts to near calms. Night separated itself from day like two completely different worlds. The sun erased my fears of losing *Akka* and, steering side by side, we would have conversations; one day, I even lost my voice from screaming above the roar of the wind. We talked about the meals we were preparing, the positions that we had calculated and the latest antics of the cats; since Australia, Mimine had become a permanent fixture aboard *Akka*.

At night, once the heavy dark shroud was pulled across the heavens, Olivier and I would take three-hour alternate watches, focusing on each other's kerosene lanterns. We set up a Morse Code system with the flashlights for when the changings of the watch occurred and we were too far apart to talk—short, short, short, everything is OK; long, long, long, let's come together; and short, long, short, I blong you.

Sometimes on my watch, the phosphorescence became so thick that it was hard to distinguish Olivier's light from the sparkling crests on the waves. Every night, the dolphins came a-squeaking, torpedoing past *Varuna* like comets of light. I spent many an hour reading for fifteen minutes, then dashing out into the cockpit to pinpoint the feeble glow of *Akka*'s lanterns in the distance. As a rule I kept *Varuna* as upwind as possible so that once the distance between us grew too much, I could speedily bear back down on her. Although there were the obvious disadvantages of lost speed and an additional burden of fatigue, the advantage of occasional contact with Olivier was well worth it to me, although we did feel quite ridiculous to be separately carrying on with life on two boats when we'd much rather be together on one.

Often, it was very romantic and beautiful to bear down on *Akka*'s dark hull in the thick of a velvety night. I would steer up alongside her and listen to the methodical swishing and plunging as she glided like a phantom ship across an ocean sparkling from the bright constellations above and the aqua lightning bugs below. I knew Olivier was curled up on his bunk in a dream world and, fantasizing that I was his guardian angel, I steered alongside, keeping him from harm.

One day, soon after the Laccadive Islands, I made a cabbage salad for my dinner and was attacked by a vicious case of Sinbad's Revenge. Throughout that day and night, I lay curled up in a fetal position, groaning and holding my stomach, which felt as if it were being ripped out. Because of the pain, I couldn't keep a proper watch and the next morning found myself alone. *Akka* had disappeared.

Crushed, I began to cry. The ocean had incredible capabilities of amplifying the emotions and all I could think of were those fourteen days and sleepless nights of course changes and speed adjustments, all lost to a bellyache. I took down the sails to wait, imagining Olivier's dismay when he found out that we had separated. Distraught and with swollen eyes, I changed my mind and decided that he had gone ahead. I hoisted *Varuna*'s sails and then remembered that *Akka* had a tendency to head farther off the wind than *Varuna*, so I headed a few degrees to the south. "But, then again," I thought, "Olivier may have readjusted the self-steering," so I headed more to the north.

I wore a permanent groove on my feet from standing on the mast steps to get a better range of the horizon, and then finally, realizing the futility of it all, I gave up. We were most definitely alone again and I reckoned that we might as well get to Djibouti as fast as possible.

Forced to readjust my life to a new daily pattern, although I sorely missed Olivier and our hollered conversations, songs and jokes, I began to sleep better and was more relaxed. The sea became calm and the wind blew at a gentle Force 2. When my spirits picked up, I decided that it was time to clean house, turned on the cassette player and threw myself into the lockers, closets, shelves, engine, cockpit and even the bilge. Four days of bleached, wrinkled fingers and Motown later, *Varuna* was spick-and-span.

In the midst of the cleaning blitz, a ship appeared on the horizon and I called it on the VHF. It didn't answer, but another one that I couldn't see did. "Well," Sparky told me, "call when you see us and I'll give you a fix." About twenty minutes later, he called again. "Can't you see me?" he asked. "We're about two miles off your stern."

"Nope," I answered. "the ship that was here before has disappeared. There is definitely nothing on my horizon." And then it dawned on me. "Hey, wait a minute. Is the sailboat that you see black with two masts?"

"Yes, I believe it is."

"Oh my God," I realized, "he sees *Akka*."

Listen," I said, recommencing the airwave conversation, "I know who that is. Would you please give me your exact position. I want to try to find him and give him a surprise." Sparky was happy to comply and, giving my profuse thanks, I set out to find my missing half. Plotting and charting the estimated speeds, courses and convergence zones, I doused the jib and headed more south. All night I scanned the horizon from a lofty perch on the mast steps and even frantically sent flashlight signals to a star, but no one appeared. Dawn revealed the looming peaks of Socotra off the coast of Somalia, where many stories of piracy were set by our friends at Don Windsor's. Still I saw nothing—neither a single Jolly Roger nor Olivier.

The next morning we passed the first peaks of Yemen bordering the Gulf of Aden. With the weakening winds befalling us in the narrowing neck of water that stretched between the Arabian peninsula and northeast Africa to the entrance of the Red Sea, the sails began to slam incessantly against the rigging. I prayed that they would make it without needing too much repair as we fought our way up the Red Sea, but looking at the threadbare areas, I could see that this would be asking a lot. The slamming in the lax Arafura Sea and the exasperating doldrums combined had made sure of that. The synthetic fabric was beginning to turn yellow, taking on a glossy, sun-fatigued look about the seams. There was nothing to do about it but pray, and pray I did. As the sails continued to slam, my only consolation was that, even though progress was slow, we were moving, and the bubbles of *Varuna*'s wake kept disappearing steadily behind.

In the meantime, my kerosene and food stores were dwindling. Most of the yummy tins from Christmas Island had already become new fish condos. Tarzoon had mistaken my vegetable bin for the litter box and I had to summon up a great deal of imagination for digestible meals without using too much kerosene for cooking them. Therefore, I didn't eat much except for cookies, crackers and canned soups straight from their coffins. Tarzoon also meowed in distaste and grumpily sniffed his meals of sardines in oil. "Don't worry," I told him. "Djibouti is full of French people. And we know what that means, Mr. T. That means good food." Then I lapsed into daydreams of steaming hot, fluffy baguettes, juicy steaks, runny Brie and cold, fresh, crisp salads.

On the evening of March 6, after twenty-four days of blue, the course had to be altered south toward Djibouti across the shipping lanes that led to Bab el Mandab, the entrance to the long Red Sea corridor. Just off the port of Aden, the lights on the horizon became a continuously moving glow and with an unreliable spark of a masthead light and a kerosene lamp that wouldn't stay lit in the wind, I sat in the cockpit through the long hours of the night, signaling with the flashlight whenever one of those rumbling monsters lumbered too close.

While I flashed, one ship bore down from astern, giving no signs of altering course. I began hopping up and down in agitation. At about 200 feet, it suddenly made a 90-degree turn and I could clearly make out the silhouettes of the crew against the lights as they stood along the bridge deck. As they grazed by, my knees were shaking uncontrollably and I began to wonder, what if they hadn't been watching? What could I have done? *Varuna* was heading downwind and it would have taken at least five minutes to drop the pole and jib and rearrange the sails in order to still have speed to get out of the way. In a brief twenty minutes, a ship could cross my horizon from first sight to last. If they could cross that distance so fast, five minutes and 200 feet would be scarcely enough to change my fate.

Sitting there, after those few anxious minutes, I found myself wondering which prospect had frightened me more: taking a dive into the inky water at night or having to make a major repair or jury rig at sea if we had been hit. With morbid amusement, I realized that it wasn't really the possibility of getting killed that had frightened me. If my time was up, I decided, I'd easily take drowning in the Gulf of Aden in the midst of an adventure over the slow agony of cancer. I remember my mother telling me, when she finally realized she was dying, "Tania, I wish to God I still had enough strength to take a dinghy, head out to sea and never come back." Now I could understand.

Such weighty thoughts were rare, usually triggered by a close encounter with a ship or some other stress-filled moment. Usually, my daydreams were on a much lighter note—how I would decorate if I had a roomier 32-footer; what Olivier's and my children might be like if we ever got married; ideas on saving the world; and incredibly witty remarks for past arguments with my father. Sometimes I tried to write these thoughts down, but they vanished as fast as they had occurred to me at the sight of a piece of loose-leaf paper.

On the afternoon of March 8, after twenty-six days at sea, we followed the lighthouse beacon, then the buoys, past the fringing reef of Djibouti Harbor and I called goodbye to the group of dolphins that had followed us in. In the distance, I could see that *Akka* hadn't yet arrived, but Henry's *Debonaire* from Sri Lanka and the German *Christina* were there. Steering *Varuna* toward them and a clear spot, I dropped the sails and let loose the anchor.

Olivier made landfall the next afternoon, and together we walked the hot and dusty desert streets of our first African city, which was brimful of starving refugees from Ethiopia and Somalia, who came to pick through the garbage of the affluent French army stationed there. The jetty near our anchorage stretched three miles out of the harbor and into a town of contrasts, both Muslim and Christian. A haunting chant to Allah was belted out from every mosque four times a day when almost every man pulled out a straw mat and knelt in the direction of Mecca to the northwest, while little nuns in blue habits went about their shopping.

On one side of a street, there were expensive restaurants and boutiques, and on the other side, entire families lay sleeping on the sidewalk, testament to the almost mind-boggling poverty. Wherever we went, hordes of urchins, lame or blind adults and pitiful pregnant mothers with numerous children hanging onto their skirts followed us imploring, "Baksheesh, madame. Baksheesh, monsieur." I felt helpless in the face of such need, wanting to give every last one of them a little of what I had. In the beginning, I started by giving one-franc pieces or fifty centimes at a time. But we quickly learned that as soon as one person received a coin, the entire street found out and we'd end up being surrounded by a crowd of others who wanted the same. By the time we left, I could only hand out pieces of bread. It was all I could do without emptying my wallet of meager funds onto the streets.

Some people told us that those who were starving to death were isolated to the northern desert province of Eritrea, where freedom fighters had been fighting for independence from Ethiopia since World War II. Word was that the Eritrean frontage for ports on the Red Sea was too valuable to the Ethiopians, and they were dealing with the insurgency by starving the people to death. We did our business in Djibouti sadly, unable to reconcile ourselves to a disaster due purely to politics and greed.

March was the last month of the dependable northeasterly monsoon, which funneled up through Bab el Mandab as southerly winds, and we hoped to use them in getting to Port Sudan, halfway up the Red Sea. If we missed them, the entire 1,200 miles would have to be done beating and tacking into the teeth of ferocious weather. As it stood, we still had a good chance of making 600 easy miles.

I met a Kenyan mechanic named Shabani from a tug in the harbor whose crew was hanging around waiting to be paid by an insurance company for Nixon's old presidential yacht, which they had salvaged off the coast of Somalia. With plenty of time to kill, Shabani was working on *Christina*'s engine. Telling me to bring *Varuna* behind his tug, he agreed to come and fix the stern tube problem. He refit a new greasing nipple and put on a stronger hose clamp. We made several tours of the harbor and it seemed to work, so I cleaned up and we went for lunch aboard his boat while the captain regaled us with wild stories from his salvaging days up and down the sometimes hostile North African coast.

Stomachs filled, we went back to *Varuna*, and I put the two wires together to hotwire the engine—this had become standard procedure since the ignition had failed long ago—and there was a click, spark, and then, nothing. . . .

"Oh no!" Olivier wailed. "That is exactly what happened when my starter broke."

"Oh no!" I moaned in return. In order to remove the starter for repairs, we had to remove the entire engine. Cursing, the three of us launched ourselves into the odious task. By sunset, all the connecting pipes, gears, shafts and electrical wire relays were undone. We lifted up the engine with a block-and-tackle system attached to the boom and removed the starter. Another of the tug's mechanics fixed it, and the next morning, we reinstalled and reattached all the parts to find that from all the jarring and wedging of the previous day, the fuel filter was no longer airtight and had even bigger holes than before.

We tried everything from silicone, tapes, new gaskets and epoxy, all to no avail. Deciding to buy a new one, we stomped around in 115-degree heat and hitchhiked to a number of stores, each one on the opposite side of the city. Handing over my last hundred dollars for the new mount and filter, I almost cried. As we leaned over the engine, our backs cooked under the Middle Eastern sun and the tools became branding irons that had to be handled with rags.

Varuna grew greasier and greasier. Once the new filter was installed, the contact to the starter had no reaction again. Next, we checked all the connecting electrical wires, replaced all the old battery cables with new ones, tested, scraped, loosened and tightened all the contacts. Still there was nothing.

"I think that it's the starter again," I groaned. Olivier exhaustedly nodded in agreement as we felt the month of March slowly slipping through our fingers. It was already the twentieth and only two choices remained: leave without a working engine, or stay for as long as it might take to fix it and run the risk of horrible weather on the nose. The lesser of two evils definitely was to have a working engine for the Red Sea, which was narrow and crawling with shipping and reefs. Again we re-created the block-and-tackle system and manhandled the engine out of the boat. Now all that was left was to find the real problem.

On the day we had spent hitchhiking in search of a new filter, we had been picked up by a charming Mr. Hassein Mohammed Ali, who wanted to do anything he could for us and started by insisting on inviting us to lunch at his house. Fate, deciding not to be exceedingly cruel, also turned Mr. Ali into a mechanic and he offered to help fix the degenerate part.

The problem, he said after another day of sweat, was a worn-out bushing that was making a false contact. We fixed it and reassembled the engine for the second time and, thanks to Mr. Ali, congratulated each other on a dirty job finally well done. The engine purred like a kitten.

Mr. Ali's kindness was not the exception to the rule. Throughout the engine ordeal we discovered how friendly and helpful the Djiboutians could be. While hitchhiking, we never had to wait for more than two cars to pass to catch a ride, and I had received several free parts and pieces, despite my efforts to pay for whatever was needed.

During the engine tribulations, we heard that a singlehander friend, Len, whom we knew from Sri Lanka, was laid up in a hospital with a bacterial infection and we spent some time with him, visiting and bringing chocolates. Len was British, about fifty years old and reminded Olivier of one of his favorite professors from college. He had stopped in Aden, stubbed his foot, and once he was at sea again, the scratch had become infected and a red stripe began shooting up his leg. He had come to Djibouti in a hurry to get some help. Gangrene had set in, and it was touch and go for several days while he was pumped full of penicillin, which saved his leg.

When Len got out of the hospital, we shared meals together and often took strolls into town. One day we stopped at our favorite bistro for a drink and a quick bite to eat, but then changed our minds and headed back out to the boats. After dinner on *Akka*, Olivier and I were sitting out on deck, when we heard a large explosion. Startled, we turned in the direction of the blast and saw billows of gray smoke ascending like a cloud. The next day, the local yacht club where we landed in the dinghies was abuzz with the horrific story. Rumor had it that Palestinians, angry at the French for arresting one of their leaders, had dynamited the bistro, killing eleven people. We rushed to the scene to find the spot where we had enjoyed a drink shortly before the bombing and found it blown to smithereens. We checked Mr. Ali's house, which was just next door, and were relieved to see that the family had been left unscathed.

As soon as Len had recovered enough to depart, we all decided to sail together the 600 miles up to Port Sudan. Supposedly, with the war in Ethiopia, the entire coast was patrolled by unfriendly gunboats and we had started thinking about safety in numbers.

With Olivier's remaining funds, we provisioned sparingly in the exorbitantly expensive French shops, limiting our fare to lots of pasta and rice. Len took on a French crew member. The dinghies were stowed on deck and all spirits were high. For the final formalities,

Olivier and I took *Varuna* under power to the other side of the port to check out. As we tied up along the quay, once again water began rushing in through the stern tube. This was too much.

"Forget it," I said to Olivier. "It'll work in an emergency as long as I keep pumping the bilge. In Port Sudan I'm throwing the whole bloody thing overboard and buying an outboard." We jammed the stuffing box back in, this time with some underwater epoxy and called out to Len, who was waiting. I dropped Olivier back off on *Akka* and on the evening of March 24 sailed out of the harbor with Olivier following and Len behind.

At the port entrance, Len lagged back a little, changing a sail, while *Akka* and *Varuna* picked up speed. Through the night, we tacked toward the notorious straits of Bab el Mandab—translation: "Gates of Hell," "Gates of Tears" or "Gates of Lamentations." We were in for a doozie. My cruising guide warned that the northeast monsoon marched into this narrow neck, funneling its way through the straits and building up quite a momentum. There was no trace of Len behind us, but with his beautiful boat, we figured he'd catch up soon.

Sure enough, like clockwork, as we made our way in, the wind increased and began to howl from astern, eliminating any chance for conversation between the boats. By late afternoon, it was blowing 55 knots and spray was flying over the lumpy water. All of a sudden, I heard, "Pop, *rrrip*, pop," and so began my anticipated trauma with the mainsail.

Catching up with Olivier, who was sitting on *Akka*'s deck, protected by a foul-weather jacket, I found him also sewing up his mainsail. Taking down the jib and tying the main to the boom as we drifted closer, I hollered over the wind as it pushed *Varuna* quickly out of hearing distance, "Look at this mess. What are you going to do?"

"I have to fix my sail," he screamed back, his voice nearly drowned out by the racket of a thousand wailing souls.

"So do I. Let's leave the sails down for the night."

"OK ... *bonne nuit*," he answered.

"Watch out for me. We can't lose each other," I shouted, but we were out of hearing range already and Olivier didn't look up from his mending. The masthead light no longer worked and I had to do something so that all the shipping funneling with the wind in through the straits would be able to see *Varuna*. I unscrewed the fluorescent light from above the bunk, attached one of the old log's trailing lines from it to the battery, and tied the light onto the back-stay.

During the night, every other wave filled the cockpit, my ten-dollar bottle of Djiboutian grenadine syrup dyed the floor red and Olivier and I lost each other. But I didn't worry too much; 80 miles north lay the Hannish Islands, the first stop that Len, Olivier and I had planned. We would see each other the next day and have a happy reunion listening to each other's descriptions of the wrath of Bab el Mandab.

The next morning, I dragged out the storm jib that hadn't seen light since Bermuda and we took off at hull speed. By midafternoon, we zipped past the sinister, dark Hannish Islands as the wind still blew at a good 40 knots. Poring over the charts of the anchorage, I made the decision to forgo the group and carry on to Port Sudan. My nerves couldn't handle making a landfall without a working engine in this horrible wind. "If they stop in the Hannish group," I thought, as we passed the northernmost rock and didn't see Olivier or Len anchored there, "they'll be able to figure out my absence soon enough."

The following morning the wind evaporated and I used the respite to resew the mainsail. The north wind that would fight us all the way up the Red Sea began as a gentle breeze that afternoon. I heard some people from other sailboats talking to each other on the radio, and upon contacting them, found that they were 5 miles away. There was a small island that lay directly in our paths and we set a rendezvous.

They were three boats coming from Aden and sailing in company: *Annatria* with a Swedish and New Zealand couple; *Penny*, with an Austrian family of three; and *Tres Marias* with a Brazilian single-hander who had fallen out of radio contact with the other two boats until I chimed in and reunited them. *Annatria* and *Penny* were at the island first, waiting, when I saw a sail behind me. It was the missing third, *Tres Marias*. I loosened the jib sheet and as the sail flapped freely in the wind waited for Alexio, the first singlehanded Brazilian circumnavigator. He sailed up alongside, I winched back in the sail and we continued on toward the rock, making introductions over the distance. He really could put on a show.

"Sometimes, when I am on the ocean," Alexio said animatedly, with a lot of hand waving, "I get all excited about seeing a floating plastic bag. Now look! Here I am, sailing along and minding my own business when all of a sudden, I see a *girl*, *alone* on her boat, *waiting* for me. What more could I ask?" With the gregariousness typical of many South Americans, he blabbed away about his good fortune in running into me. After more conversation along the same lines on Alexio's part, we caught up to the others. He told them how I had flirted, while I furiously denied any such thing.

Thus I made the acquaintance of Runa and Eileen on *Annatria*, a 26-footer; and Franz, Anna Lisa and Bernard on the 32-foot *Penny*. With big welcoming smiles, they waved greetings to me. While they had drifted, waiting for Alexio and me, *Penny* caught a fish. Franz steered over in my direction wearing a leopard G-string, Anna Lisa smiled from under a hood of long gray hair and Bernard stood on the foredeck to throw me a fresh filet.

Like a group of kindred souls meeting up in an unknown land, the others invited me to join their flotilla and we took off in synchronization, beating into the idyllic wind. I thought about Olivier and Len, somewhere behind, and hoped that they had met up; otherwise, it wouldn't be fair.

A lot of other sailors with whom I had talked often said that they carried firearms aboard in case of life-threatening emergencies. Even my father had a dreadfully lethal Winchester aboard *Pathfinder*. When I left New York, we had seriously discussed my bringing one along in case of a situation where I'd have to defend myself. It was decided that there was a very slight chance that once confronted with a life-threatening situation, I would be able to use a gun to my advantage. It is worse to have a firearm and be scared to use it then to have nothing, and I was pretty sure that I could never shoot another person. Instead, I had left New York with an empty hand grenade and some fake hair for a bearded disguise that I'd bought on 14th Street.

My father and I had assumed that if ever somebody wanted to board, maybe a bearded man would make the predators think twice. If that didn't work, I could pull out the pin, hold up the grenade and say, "If you come on my boat, we all go." If they still ignored the twerp with bold words and decided to come anyway, well, what the heck, I tried.

Thanks to our little nucleus, if there were any shady characters rolling around in the Red Sea, I never had to meet them, although I did wonder about the occasional sinister-looking native dhow that puttered across our horizon. But my cruising guide said that most of them were laden down with sheep being smuggled to other countries.

We formed our own little sailing community at sea, and the VHFs were permanently tuned in to Channel 78. I forgot my pariah engine, whose starter once again refused to work and got to know my new friends through a constant stream of funny chatter that emerged from the little black box over my bed. *Annatria* and *Tres Marias* had SatNavs, which made life easier for the rest of us, although Franz and I would double-check the computer's veracity by taking sun and star sights. Two or three times, while we were bobbing around during the intermittent calms that disrupted the feeble northerly winds, one of the boats would tow *Varuna* while it motored. It was a kind gesture because, with the additional dead weight, speed was greatly diminished, and the others could have very well left me to wait and fend for myself. And so we averaged 40 miles of progress per day, which was typical of sailing north on the Red Sea.

Annatria and *Penny* also had ham radios, which were very useful in this part of the world. All the hams traveling the Red Sea had set up an informational network of news and weather reports that were passed down from those who had weather fax machines, as well as plenty of gossip from the cruising grapevine. Reports of murderous 45-knot winds had us trembling in our boots, and then news of calms had us breathing hopeful sighs of relief. Often, Franz or Runa would tell me about a boat I had met in Sri Lanka or Djibouti that had reached the sailing mecca of Port Suez at the end of the Red Sea and I would feel glad for the owner, knowing that the biggest sailing obstacle had been conquered. I wished I could be up there with them. Sometimes the news wasn't as good as at other times.

One day, our VHF airwaves were buzzing with chat about some horrible news Runa had received on the grapevine. *Debonaire* had gone on a reef outside Port Sudan, he said, and Henry had lost his boat. A pall drew over me. I knew by now that a boat becomes part of the owner's personality and for old Henry, who had lived and traveled with *Debonaire* for many years, it must have been like losing a wife.

On that same day, there was an eclipse of the sun and an empty moon and I discovered that Olivier's passport and boat papers were still in my bag. We had forgotten about them during checkout in Djibouti and he was without all his personal credentials in one of the most paper-happy areas of the world. There was no question about it. I absolutely had to arrive in Port Sudan first. More than ever I hoped he and Len were watching out for each other.

As soon as we passed out of the territorial waters of Ethiopia,

Penny and *Annatria* wanted to cruise up through the Suakin group of reefs and islands to Port Sudan, but Alexio and I decided to beg off. Preferring the safety of deeper sea to day sailing amid a network of reefs, we separated from the other two and began tacking out on a northwesterly course. The last 60 miles to Port Sudan took three sleepless days of pounding and tacking into viciously steep and short waves in strong 35-knot winds.

The wind howled like a hurricane through the rigging; waves crashed over the deck, sloshed down through the Dorade vent and splashed onto my bed. Going out to check on Alexio's whereabouts and survey the surroundings guaranteed me a cold bath, a reminder that we were no longer in tropical latitudes. The chilly north wind and cooler water temperatures had me digging through the piles of summer clothes in search of something warm to wear. *Varuna* plodded onward, burying her nose in every other wave.

Finally, on the night of April 5, we were just off the reefs leading into Port Sudan. We could make it in on one tack, but because it was nighttime, we doused the sails instead, drifting in the light of Sanganeb Reef lighthouse as its welcome beacon swept the water.

In the morning, the wind died down and we sailed carefully toward the harbor, past the spot where Henry's *Debonaire* had sunk. Keeping a very close watch for anything unexpected, we arrived without consequence several hours later and I anchored next to Alexio, behind *Christina* and an abandoned freighter named *Captain Handy*.

The quarantine launch arrived, and after the formalities, I sat down, relieved, and struck up a casual conversation across the water with the people on another sailboat whom I recognized from Djibouti. We shared the usual happy Hellos and How was your trips? and Awfuls.

"Hey, did you hear about Len?" they asked.

"No, what?"

"He's dead," they said.

"What?"

"Just as he was leaving the harbor of Djibouti, the boom jibed, hit him in the head. He was killed instantly."

My knees went weak and I sank onto the seat of the cockpit. When Olivier and I had seen Len lagging behind and though he was changing a sail, it must have been after the accident when his crew member had been turning around to head back to port. I couldn't believe it. I pictured Len, full of plans and ideas and wondered what his last thoughts might have been. One minute you're happy and full of life, and the next . . .

All afternoon and into the evening, I tried to let the news sink in and stop worrying about Olivier. I had assumed that he and Len were together and now my imagination was going off on a series of tangents. What if he couldn't receive the shortwave time-tick station that constantly emits the universal time (reception in the Red Sea was very bad) and he didn't have the correct time for navigation and had foundered on a reef? I worried that he had wandered too close to shore and, without boat papers and passport, had been picked up by the Ethiopian gunboats and now was in some dingy jail. As darkness poured in, I sat numb in the cockpit, thinking about Len and Olivier, and searched the night sky for falling stars.

isery loves company, and no matter how hopeless things seemed, it was funny how nothing helped to alleviate anxieties more than to read about or listen to the woes of others. Oftentimes at sea, whenever the weather had gotten out of hand, I had grabbed a book and tried to gain some consolation from the accounts of other people's hellish difficulties.

On that storm-plagued maiden voyage to Bermuda, it had been Dr. David Lewis's northern transatlantic crossing in a folkboat just as small as *Varuna* that had cheered me up. He had encountered a parade of terrifying gales while keeping a fearful watch for icebergs; and the immensity of the minor depressions that had engulfed *Varuna* dwindled in the face of a trip that had been even worse. In turn, Dr. Lewis had sought consolation by reading the accounts of Hanns Lindemann, another doctor who crossed the Atlantic in a fold-up canoe—both braver, more adventuresome people than I.

Here in Port Sudan, I pulled myself together and moped over to *Christine*'s cockpit to be with Henry, Lauder, Christine and little Sebastian, keeping an ever-anxious eye on the harbor entrance for the familiar black hull. As I listened to the tale of the fall of *Debonaire*, Henry's story helped to take my mind off of Len and Olivier, as his gourd of rum helped him cheerfully keep his mind off his problems. Together, we all commiserated and remembered stories about Len. We shook our heads and, in need of a meal, went to dinner.

Passing camels and donkeys at hitching posts, we made our way up 150 feet of dusty road alongside the harbor. At an open-air restaurant with sizzling grills, tables were crowded with desert men in flowing white robes and turbans, who stopped talking and stared as we entered. Christine and I were the only females, and I looked down self-consciously to see if my clothing was modest enough for the piercing dark eyes.

The Sudan is a country under the strict regime of Islam, where a woman's place is in the house—barefoot and pregnant. When women did leave their homes, we later noticed, every part of the body except a slit for the eyes was wrapped up and veiled over. Hoping that my jeans and sweat jacket were suitable enough, we, too, stole furtive glances. The cheekbones were accentuated in the handsome ebony faces of these men, and we saw that their average height was that of a good-sized basketball player back home.

When it came time to order our dinner, I asked for what I had craved most while at sea—a green salad. When it arrived, I saw that, yes, it was green, but not of the leafy variety. Rather, it was a mushy eggplant concoction that I recognized from meals at Middle-Eastern restaurants on MacDougal Street in New York. Next to a slice of pizza, *falafels*, *shish kebab*, *hummus*, *baba ghanooj* and *tahina* had always been the cheapest foods in my days of street wandering. I remembered downing the ethnic food without ever taking a moment to think that three years later would find me in the countries of their origin.

Surprisingly, here in the Sudan, it all tasted very much the same, but with one additional ingredient: sand. We devoured a meal of green mush, tomato salad and hunks of succulent mutton cooked atop an outdoor coal fire, trying to keep our eyes off the piles of bloody sheep heads that had been thrown over the small stone embankment near our table.

It was all we could do during dinner to avoid the use of our left hands. Every time one of us slipped up, every eye in the place fixed on us and registered looks of disgust. The Sudanese were far more sensitive about this custom than the Sri Lankans, who were more accustomed to Western visitors in their midst. Blushing, we even tried sitting on our left hands, but before long they always seemed to find their way back into use.

On the way back down to the dinghy dock, we passed a herd of dromedary camels that were parked under trees for the night, the long necks of some craning to munch away on the leaves of overhanging branches, the rest lying down in sleep with their legs curled up beneath them. I had read that camels are ornery, and that when one is irritated by its owner or takes an instant dislike to a person, it exhibits its feelings by rudely spitting or taking nips at him. The only way to make amends once you have fallen out of favor is to surrender your clothes or belongings. Only after the camel has emptied its bladder on top of the pile can bygones be bygones. Dissuaded by their loose lips curling back from some well-formed, square teeth, we resisted the urge to reach up and pet them, and found our way back to the boats.

At midnight, I was back in *Varuna*'s cockpit alone. The worry was back and sleep elusive. I prayed for Olivier, and my thoughts drifted to Len, a kind man we might not have known well, but whose dreams for life had mirrored our own and had been cut short before our eyes.

The next morning, Alexio and I were preparing our papers for the long ritual of properly checking in with customs and immigration when the black hull ghosted in past the harbor wall. My whoop of joy startled those on *Christine* and all the neighbors smiled my way. Too many disturbing things had been happening, and finally here was at least one reason to rejoice. Alexio shooed me into his dinghy and I rowed madly across the water toward *Akka*.

"Where were you?" Olivier called as we drew closer. "I waited for three days in the Hannish Islands."

"The wind was really strong and I was too scared to head in between the rocks without an engine. Did you get any of those horrible north winds a few days later?"

"No, it was beautiful and southerly the whole way, till yesterday." All in all, considering all the sad news, this was a reunion of relief, and together with Alexio, we went to check in.

The next day, Alexio returned from wandering about town with news that at 3:00 P.M. the President of the Sudan would be arriving at the local airport. "We must go," he insisted. "The President is said to be a direct descendent of Mohammed. There will be a crowd of thousands." So, we set out on foot to see the grand manifestation of the desert. Along the road were dozens of nomadic tents surrounded by children, women, goats and camels as, in the distance, men in white raced their graceful Arabian horses across the yellow sand flats toward the horizon. Everything seemed to float in an oily mirage created by the heat reflecting off surfaces.

Around the small white airport thronged dark-skinned Sudanese, magnificent light-skinned Bedouins and Arabs. Veiled women bedecked in flowing fabrics of reds, oranges and greens brightened the picture wherever they sat, clustered in isolated groups. As we walked into the midst of a scene from a century past, I stared openly at the people, who showed absolutely no inhibitions about doing just the same.

Different tribes were distinguished by their hairstyles and the shades of earth-colored woolen vests that covered their long white caftans. Some had bushy afros; others had short-cropped hair; still others had beads interwoven with hair strands, or matted dreadlocks hanging down from just above the back of their necks. Blue, green and brown eyes stared our way, and little boys crowded around as if we were the Pied Pipers of Hamlin. I felt a tingling up and down my spine to be in such a different, beautiful world.

Everything about the moment was charmed until Alexio pulled out his newfangled camera. It became immediately clear that these people have a strong aversion to having their pictures taken; they deeply resent the invasion of their privacy, and this fact is common knowledge to most incoming visitors.

"Don't worry," Alexio said, shrugging off our concerns. "I was smart enough to get a permit at the office for tourism. See?" The smiles turned into hostile glares, and some shouts were directed our way as Alexio continued to snap pictures and wave his permit around at the angry men surrounding us. The Arabic language has a harsh sound to a Western ear unaccustomed to its guttural rhythms, and when ripe with emotion, it is positively intimidating.

"Here, Tania. Let me take a picture of you with these people in the background," he said, unfazed.

"Absolutely not," Olivier said, putting his arm around me protectively, and we started to walk away. Alexio followed along, snapping the shutter and waving his permit, with more boys behind him, who came to press against me, while the older men caught up. A little hand pinched me.

"Please stop, Alexio," I pleaded. "Do you really think they care two cents about a piece of paper? If you make them any angrier, they'll chew up that piece of paper, spit it out and you'll be next. Look, all these guys have huge swords."

Heavily engraved metal hilts popped out of three-foot-long leather sheaths strapped down on the backs of the majority of the men. These people weren't complacent townies accustomed to the ways of Westerners. They were nomads who have roamed the Sahara for centuries and were now flocking in caravans to see the descendent of the beloved prophet who had founded their Islamic religion. I admired their air of regal pride and it distressed me to be part of a group who was making them angry. Alexio finally stopped when I found my handbag sliced on the bottom, while the smiling child who did it waited for my belongings to drop out.

"Tania, let's get out of here," Olivier said, and we pushed our way through the mob, with Alexio following close behind in sullen silence. A white Peugeot pulled up as we plodded back toward town, and a dark face peered out of the window at us.

"Hello there. Hop in and I'll give you a ride," said the stranger in perfect English. And so we met Ibrahim, a food distributor for a famine relief agency. In the car, we answered questions, telling him where we came from and what we were doing in the Sudan. It took a while to convince him that we were all sailing singlehanded.

"Yes, we are really alone, each of us," Olivier explained from beside me in the back seat. "Sometimes we meet up with each other. But, essentially, we are always alone, each one to a boat."

Ibrahim took his eyes away from the road, turned his head and stared at me, clearly bewildered; there aren't many Sudanese women who are even allowed to leave their houses alone. Thirsty for more information, he took us to the Red Sea Club, a colonial establishment that still adhered to the old regulations and people could only enter if brought by a member. He bought us Coca-Colas and we told him everything he wanted to know. He was particularly interested in me, and as the afternoon wore on, we learned why. Ibrahim had a wife and several mistresses. It was perfectly normal, he said. If he didn't love his wife so much, he could have wed three more to add to the collection. "The mistresses are to spare her the agony of extra wives," he explained matter-of-factly.

Since Djibouti, I had been having a hard time trying to imagine what living in this kind of society would be like. Depending on who my parents were, I could have been circumcised as a child, and by now my father could have married me off to a man who planned on having backup wives. I had even seen a newspaper from Saudi Arabia that had blackened out the pictures of Western women from the neck down. Ibrahim's notion was that all Western women were promiscuous, that orgies were a way of life for us, and he was incredulous that I could be loyal to only one man. During that afternoon, after I cleared some things up for him, Ibrahim became a good friend, eager to show us the beauty of the only culture he knew.

As in every country under Islamic rule, the vice of alcohol was strictly forbidden, and whenever we went ashore a guard at the harbor gate checked our bags to see if we were sneaking in any contraband. In the Sudan, Ibrahim had confided conspiratorially, there were illegal moonshine stills where they brewed their own firewater from dates, a wicked potion called *aragi*. The day after we met him, he made an appearance at the anchorage.

"Come along now," he said. "I have some surprises for you." We were game, jumped in his Peugeot and drove out into the middle of a desert wasteland, stopping at a slumlike area in front of a shack. Ibrahim got out of the car and made a purchase and we drove to a seawall to talk. To be polite, I took a sip of the pure alcohol, felt a channel burn down my throat and my stomach shrivel up. That was my last sip. Alexio, too, was a nondrinker and even Olivier couldn't handle stuff that hard. Ibrahim, drinking alone, stood like an African prince, gesticulating with his arms as his flowing white robe billowed behind him in the wind.

Arriving at another shack later on, we found what appeared to be a low-end brothel with erotic posters on the wall. Together with a few robed men, we sat in front of a 1950s pickup truck with a television on the hood that was broadcasting *Popeye* in Arabic. Next, Ibrahim, fortified with the spirits, pronounced that he was taking us to the wedding of a friend, and so began an evening of magic and splendor that could have come straight from the pages of the *Arabian Nights*.

The women and children in the wedding garden must have cornered the world market on lace and organdy; yards and yards of it adorned socks, waistbands and hemlines along with acres of satin, sequins and glitter. The children looked like the old-fashioned porcelain dolls that I had always craved as a child, while ravishing, mysterious maidens flitted in and out around the tables. Not only was the apparel exotic, but for once the women were unveiled. Most looked like Hollywood princesses with regal bearing, high cheekbones, sloe eyes and jet-black hair.

As the bride and groom walked into the garden, they were hailed by a bevy of women, who belied their elegance by whooping in high-pitched voices, making a staccato sound with their hands against their mouths like children imitating Indians. The bride was robed in miles of white lace, and even the groom had on makeup—powder and eyeliner. I worried that someone would tell me to put my eyes back into my head, it was all so marvelous.

When the bride and groom sat down, well-wishers flocked

around with advice and congratulations, and eventually, a band began to play. Before we slipped out, I went up to the beautiful bride and wished her a good life. No more than eighteen and overwhelmed by all that was going on, she looked at me with glazed eyes and said thank you.

The splendor of the ceremony contrasted all too dramatically with Port Sudan itself as we drove back through the streets toward the dock. More an expanse of hovels than a city, Port Sudan was baked and blanched by the relentless North African fireball and completely out of touch with modern Western standards. The monetary system was riddled with corruption, and the black-market exchange rate on the street for the Sudanese pound and the U.S. dollar, which everybody wanted, was double that in the banks. International telephone lines were nonexistent, so calling home was impossible. Also, while checking in at the port offices, we saw that even shipping was chaotic. Carriers delivering grain were sometimes laid up in the harbor for months while dockers emptied the holds by the basketful for twenty cents a day. There was a modern vacuum on one of the quays, but it was broken and nobody knew how to fix it.

In town, rickety old cars, buses, Bedouins on camels and carts pulled by braying donkeys kicked up clouds of dust on the dry streets, with groups of men smoking molasses-dipped tobacco in their hookahs on every corner. Astride donkeys and camels, men from different caravan tribes loped into town to provision, just as we were doing, before heading back into the desert.

Blocks and blocks were lined with old men in front of foot-pump sewing machines who created caftans and vests, with scraps of material blowing in the wind. The scent of henna, which is used to dye the hair and skin, overpowered everything, even the market overflowing with spices, oranges, grapefruits, nuts and vegetables. Without enough money to buy the universal Tang, Olivier and I bought two pounds of the cheaper fragrant rose tea.

In the livestock section, beheaded sheep, cows and chickens hung from meat hooks, blood draining from every orifice, while the live ones milled around in panic. The piece of meat you received depended on the time of day you arrived. As orders were placed, first the hordes of flies were waved away from the hanging carcass, then a piece was hacked off with a blunt ax. Observing these conditions, we weren't inclined to feast on rare steaks. Rather, we boiled the meat up thoroughly into soups and stews.

Olivier and I visited the ancient port ruins of Suakin, 30 miles down the coast, to see the remains of a stone-and-mortar desert village, abandoned and fallen to bleached rubble. Caravans used to stop at the busy waypoint of Suakin, bringing their wares to trade with ships bound for India; it was the last point in the Red Sea where seasonal south winds existed so the ships continued no farther, unequipped as they were to beat against the blasting headwinds to the north. Today, with the development of Port Sudan, Suakin was deserted and crumbling, and as we explored its alleyways, we imagined how lively it must have been in the times of the caravan.

The unexpectedly exciting part of the excursion came when we had to take the bus back to Port Sudan. A group of people stood waiting in the main square, and as the transport made itself visible in the horizon, they took their positions like runners at the mark. When the bus came to a stop, bodies flew in through the windows and door, everyone scrambling for a spot. It took Olivier and me several buses to get the hang of things, until, luckily, one stopped right in front of us and we were in, helping the other bodies through the windows when the door jammed up.

In general, the Sudanese were a kind and proud race. Although the country was poverty-stricken and in billions of dollars of international debt, beggars were virtually nonexistent. Instead, people would stop us in the streets just to smile and practice their English, saying, "Strong, strong," when they learned that I sailed alone.

One day in town, Olivier and I were hailed by a shoeshine boy sitting in the shade of a tree and surrounded by cronies who watched him shine the occasional shoe. A few instantly got up and offered me their chairs. In sign language, we talked and laughed with these young guys, and one ran out to buy us some Coca-Cola, while the shoeshine chief pointed at my leather flip-flops, insisting on waxing and polishing the half-inch strap while the others taught us how to say "thank you" and "you're welcome" in Arabic. When we were ready to go, I tried to offer some money to the leader; he furiously refused, shook our hands and waved us on. I couldn't believe it. These people were dirt poor, yet they had bought us drinks, performed a service and, even so, wouldn't accept payment.

"*Shukran*," I thanked him with my new word.

"*Afuan*," he replied in welcome.

Penny and *Annatria* had arrived on our fourth morning, and later on, with Bernard, we set to fixing the engine. Throwing it overboard and replacing it with an outboard was out of the question in Port

Sudan, a city in which it was a challenge to find even a roll of toilet paper. Also, the new starter problem ended up being minor; the only cable that hadn't been changed in Djibouti had a rusty connection and needed cleaning. We made several tours of the harbor to check out the stuffing box and it remained in its place. The epoxy that we had used in Dijibouti had done its job well and *Varuna* once again had a working engine. Then Olivier climbed the mast to check the lights and found several strands on the forestay broken; we replaced the stay with a spare and stowed the frayed one as a reserve. He also fortified *Akka*'s rigging and spreaders to prepare for the ferocious winds, while I borrowed *Penny*'s sewing machine and patched up our sails with old scraps of sailcloth.

By now, we were well into the month of April and the clock was ticking. I was supposed to be back in New York within six months, before the winter season could begin to roil the North Atlantic. Ever since Australia, as a result of the occupational hazards of contrary winds and calms, engine problems and days often lost to my own reluctance to head back out to sea again, I had fallen further and further behind schedule. I had made a commitment to my father to do this trip in a certain amount of time and was determined to see it through as we had planned and get on with my own life. But now, over every move and every decision as Olivier and I prepared for the unpleasant trip up the Red Sea to Egypt, hung the omnipresent worry that time was quickly running out.

After one week in the Sudan, Alexio was finally ready and set out, followed by *Christine* with Henry aboard as part of their crew, and then *Penny* and *Annatria*, leaving *Akka* and *Varuna* as the last stragglers. Just as Olivier and I were finally ready to go also, the fearful winds piped up to a 40-knot sandstorm, screaming like a banshee and covering the town, the boats and rigging in a fine yellow dust. When the winds finally diminished to a more reasonable 15 knots, we motored out of the harbor the 14 miles to the cleaner water of Sanganeb Reeb and anchored to clean the boats and scrub the scummy keels.

The next morning, the wind howled again at 35 knots, dragging the boats and holding us at anchor for six more days. We twiddled our thumbs as the whining wind grated on our nerves, and anticipated a wonderful trip north if this was any indication of weather to come. Beating is already a dirty word in the sailing world, let alone beating into such heavy winds as these, accompanied by steep waves stacked one on top of the other.

On April 30, the wind eased to 20 knots, and we sailed off making

40 miles in the right direction during the first twenty-four-hour period. The second evening's sky was laced with racing mare's tails, and Olivier pointed up drearily and called over that they usually forecast heavy winds. Sure enough, dawn revealed a frothy sea, kicked up by the cantankerous winds we had been dreading.

Maelstrom or none, I put up the tiny storm jib Olivier had given me in Djibouti, and with triple-reefed mainsails, *Varuna* and *Akka* began to beat painfully into the teeth of a monster. Day in and day out for two weeks, always keeping an open eye for the laboring tankers and cargo carriers, we slowly tacked our way up through the beastly chop, inching past Jedda, Saudi Arabia, sometimes with exasperating advances of only 10 miles a day in the right direction. The wind was either strong or very strong and, from time to time, depending on the velocity, I would have to take out the third reef for the second or vice versa, in the process ripping the sail to shreds.

As it stood, the entire main was in such a sorry state that holes were easily made whenever I exerted too much pressure on it with my finger. Holding onto the pitching deck, with scissors, spare cloth and rubber cement underfoot, and thread and needle in my mouth, I spent half my time quilting the main back together, while getting drenched by every other wave. After all the patching, I discovered that sewing only made the situation worse, giving the sail an invitation to tear along the dotted lines. As I continued to patch over the patches, I desperately hoped that my father had received my last letter from the Sudan in time to arrange for a new sail to be waiting in Suez.

Cooking regularly was out of the question; *Varuna* was heeled over so far that more time would have been spent wiping the spilled meals up from the floor than actually eating. When I felt too weak to continue, I'd boil some rice, tuna and tomato paste and share it with Tarzoon. In the early mornings, I'd curl up on my damp bed, aching for some peaceful sleep, as *Varuna* lurched and thumped into brick walls of water. On deck, the spray was blinding as it flew off the crests of steep swells, mixing with the raging winds filled with sand. Sometimes visibility was good and other times, with landbound dust storms, the horizon was a burnt-yellow hue. We tacked east and west, coast to coast, through the north and southbound ships and, every so often, there would be the harrowing near miss. As the smokestacks paraded by, I saw the Russian Hammer and Sickle, the Japanese Rising Sun, and the red, gold and green colors of the African countries that we were passing to port and Arabia to starboard.

Whenever my anxieties and frustrations reached a climax, I

would unleash all my pent-up venom onto the Red Sea. My gratifi-
cation was almost indescribable after I had spit a hysterically vulgar
screaming fit at the bastard. It brooded and growled back while I
stomped around in the cockpit, ranting and cursing at everything I
hated about the trip. From his corner on the bunk below, Tarzoon
watched with philosophical amusement, and finally it got to the
point where I too began to enjoy the outbursts. After I'd lost control,
I would relax completely and cuddle up with my buddy until the
aggravation accumulated all over again when the sea reached a new
threshold of malevolence.

As the crow flies, it was 250 miles from Sanganeb Reef to Ras
Banas, our first planned anchorage in the territorial waters of Egypt.
After two weeks, with our zigzag course of tacking into the wind,
Varuna must have covered 1,000, and finally I awoke one morning to
see the island marking the way to our haven. As we approached the
anchorage, we watched the wind die down to a flat calm, which
ironically was how it was to remain for our two days of rest.

Akka and *Varuna* arrived in company with another familiar boat,
the *Broad* from Sri Lanka, and Olivier and I eagerly tied our two
boats together and jumped into the dinghy to go and say hello. After
the abominations of the trip, it was a godsend to see old friends
again, especially Dean and Faye, who were easygoing and had a
cheerful sense of humor. Dean, an American in his early sixties, and
his Australian ladyfriend, Faye, had just arrived from Jedda, and we
all bewailed our adventures since forsaking the tranquil Indian
Ocean.

Olivier and I remembered Dean telling us about his November
romance with Faye when we had gone with Don Windsor and his son
to meet my father three and a half months before in Sri Lanka. Dean
had sailed the *Broad* to Australia with friends and family, and Brisbane was where he met Faye, who was about the same age as he and
worked as a waitress at a local restaurant. He invited her to sail with
him into the sunset. She gave away her house plants and off they
went to see the world, trailing their dinghy, the *Tender Broad*, behind
them. Adopting us here in Ras Banas, Dean filled up my empty coffee
jar and presented us with a real delicacy of canned smoked oysters,
while Faye baked a cake and some bread, which served our stomachs
well after we had been accustomed to far more basic fare for so long.

We were graciously invited for tea and dinner by some Egyptian
soldiers stationed in simple barracks on the beach. Because we were
forbidden from venturing inland before procuring a visa, they then

insisted on helping us provision, and one man hiked five miles to the nearest village to do the shopping for us. After all we had heard about the legal rigmaroles and difficult attitudes of the Egyptian bureaucracy, the generous soldiers of Ras Banas were a happy find. The negative reports that had filtered down from other boats had probably come from the sort of people who must have had bad experiences wherever they went.

Hurghada, situated at the southern tip of the Gulf of Suez leading to the canal, had become our mecca, and it was also where we all planned to enter Egypt officially. Bidding each other fair winds and goodbye until then, Olivier and I sailed out with the *Broad*, then separated. We pressed north to Ras Toronbi as I prayed to my mainsail, "Please, last until Suez." In the distance, more Egyptian soldiers on camels rode slowly over the sandy plains.

During the nights, when the wind died and we began to motor, the air was always thick with moisture. It collected on the mainsail, dribbled down along the boom's groove and dripped on my head as my hands grasped the tiller and became numb with the engine's vibrations. Tarzoon hated the rumbling monster and hid under a sail on the bow, as far from the noise as possible, leaving me alone and wet in the cockpit.

As the boats hugged the coastline, I stared endlessly at the progression of spooky grayish mountains that walled in the Red Sea; they looked ominous and arid, without a single blade of grass, and made me think that they might have been what inspired the ancient Pharaohs to build the pyramids. Almost every peak resembled a monstrous triangle, and the view was awesome enough to alleviate the tension of the next couple of days while we waited for the antagonistic winds to return. Sleeping in fitfully short intervals, Olivier and I tried to keep watch for each other, but it was impossible to relax with land and its perils so close.

Finally, *Varuna* and *Akka* arrived at the coastal fishing village of Hurghada and anchored close to a nearby mosque wailing its usual litany in yet another Muslim country. That night, the cord on Olivier's dinghy snapped, and the wind carried it off along with my favorite shoes, right back down the Red Sea from whence we came.

I had already been feeling anxious in Port Sudan, but now the shrinking timetable was making the situation serious. To arrive in New York before November 1987, I was going to cross the Atlantic during a high-risk period of storms, and the risk was increasing with every passing day on land. Thanks to our slow crawl up the unaccommodating Red Sea, there was no longer time to allow for snags from here on in, and even the usually calm Olivier was beginning to feel the urgency and worry for me. After allowing ourselves a few days in Hurghada, we fueled up, set out through the reef-speckled entrance to the Strait of Glubal and recommenced tacking up the 200 miles of the narrow bottlenecked Gulf of Suez.

The first day whipped us back with its relentless winds, and before nightfall we had only covered 10 miles to a minimal anchorage behind a reef. The next day we inched another 10 miles up the wind tunnel and crept into the horseshoe shaped sandbanks of Tawila Island, still in the Strait, and took shelter there for a day until the wind died down.

It was at Tawila that we walked along the virgin beaches for the last time, following shell tracks on the sparkling sand. Never again, I thought sadly, would I dinghy up to *Varuna* after a morning of idyllic beauty to see her pivoting slowly at anchor on waters mirroring her elegant shape. From here on in, the Mediterranean ports would have to be pit stops, and besides, the marine life in that sea was reputedly choking from all the pollution. Once we had passed through the Suez Canal, an entire way of life would be overshadowed by the commercialism of Europe. Beyond the canal were the continent of Europe, my final passages and home.

The next morning dawned calm, and we motored out of the anchorage until my engine overheated and a fuel line burst, sending up clouds of black smoke. Olivier came back and towed *Varuna* 5 miles to the next anchorage, where we tried to effect some temporary repairs.

The last two nights, after alternating between motoring and sailing, I pulled ahead of *Akka* in a zombified state, passing the eerie sight of oil rigs propped up like boxes on stilts all over the gulf; the flames from the huge burn-off flares lit up the night in a rosy glow. The lights flickered, reflecting against *Varuna*'s white deck, while I fought to stay awake, keeping an eye on *Akka*'s solitary light behind. Overhead, an unseen Scheherazade pulled black chiffons of cloud across the heavens.

The last day, while I was down below making a cup of coffee, *Varuna*, after tacking normally almost every hour for the previous day and a half, tacked on her own. That had never happened before and I hurried up on deck to see what was the matter. The Monitor was still attached to the tiller and I didn't see anything that could have gone wrong, so, tacking the boat, I reset the self-steering, where-upon we tacked again. Leaning over the aft pulpit on my stomach to scrutinize the self-steering more closely, I saw the problem and it couldn't have been worse.

The most critical part of the mechanical system, the steering paddle, had broken off just above the emergency lanyard intended to keep it attached in the event of such a mishap. Cursing, I threw on the engine and motored back on a reciprocal course, peering at the surface of the water. Losing that piece meant a major setback and an endless wait in Egypt for a spare to arrive, as I didn't have another. The Monitor was my invaluable crew, tirelessly relieving me of the chore of steering the boat, and the thought of going to sea without it was unimaginable. What a relief it was to see the errant part floating on the water several hundred feet back! I scooped it up and my seafaring future was set back in focus.

Akka sailed up alongside and I told Olivier what had happened. Unable to improvise a repair, I told him that I would have to hand-steer the rest of the way. "Listen, Tania," he called back across the water, "we're almost at the last available anchorage. I think I can make it, but do you want to stop for the night?" We hadn't slept for thirty hours; however, if we continued onward, we would arrive around three the next morning.

"No, let's just get this over with."

Resisting the temptation of some rest and a decent meal, we carried on, fueled by the resolution to leave the Red Sea behind as soon as humanly possible. And so, at 3:00 A.M. on June 14, *Varuna*'s engine puttered around the immense tankers awaiting transit in Port Suez and up to the small-boat anchorage. After dropping the hook and making sure everything was secure, I rowed over to *Akka* and melted onto a bunk. Olivier threw a blanket over me and within moments we both drifted into the sleep of the dead. The despised Red Sea was now a memory.

Two oversized boxes from my father were waiting in Suez, stuffed with the new mainsail, a masthead light, an Autohelm elec-tronic steering device, five-minute casseroles, potato and Chinese rice dishes, bags of candies and chocolate, books, letters and a flash-light. What a relief it was to see that my letter from the Sudan had arrived on time! The morning after arriving, I joyfully dug through the bounty of necessities and treats. We hired the agent required in Suez to do the paperwork, and Abdul Manam Asukar was so affable that he straightened out all our canal formalities in record time, ran around getting my Monitor's paddle welded back into place and even insisted on taking our laundry to get cleaned. His wife, Asma, and his daughter, Didi, invited us home for a dinner of Cornish hens and *hummus*, making us feel like welcome family guests, rather than just some more transitting sailors paying for a service.

Several days later, Olivier and I had rehabilitated *Varuna*'s fuel lines and changed *Akka*'s filters. We replenished my depleted tool supply and the boats were ready to make the transit. Dean and Faye had arrived belatedly because of the *Broad*'s ancient engine, which was due for retirement, and together we all went out for a last dinner. They had to get their engine fixed before leaving for Port Said, which probably would take a while, so it seemed we were destined to pass in the night. Anyway, Faye said, she was desperate to see a hairdresser and they wanted to visit Cairo. So, promising to write, we wished each other luck, and after yet another sad goodbye, returned to the boats. Drifting off to sleep that night, I thought I wanted to be just like them at sixty, carefree on the ocean, living as best they could one day at a time.

Unlike the Panama Canal, the 120 miles of the Suez were divided up into two days of motoring on a channel dug through sand dunes that separated Asia from Africa. As we started the next morning, I could see the burnt-out spoils of the Six-Day War between the Israelis and Egyptians littering the banks of the canal. The scars reminded me of a story Asma had recounted about when the enemy had threatened Port Suez. The canal itself was only several hundred feet wide, and from Asma's overlooking windows she had seen the Israelis approach. "I had to hold Didi in my arms," she had said, "to show them I had a baby, so that they wouldn't shoot at our house."

It was hard to imagine that Port Suez was a city fairly recently besieged by a war in which most of the inhabitants had been forced to flee. Port Suez had seemed to be simply a modernized version of Port Sudan. The people had more Arabic ancestry than the Sudanese but didn't like to be called Arabs. "We are descendents of the Pharaohs," some had insisted. Unlike the colorful clothing of the Sudanese, the habitual veils of most of the Egyptian women were black. Most of the men had turned to the Westernized fashions of pants and shirts. We carried on, remorseful that all we were to know of Egypt had come from the perimeters of some of the busiest shipping capitals of the world, Port Said to the north and Port Suez at the southernmost reaches of the canal.

In Port Said, we met a couple on a Swiss boat who were heading in the opposite direction, down the Red Sea and eventually to the Philippines. Morris, the captain, was a bit apprehensive of what lay ahead and, like me two years earlier, not very familiar with the ocean. Olivier and I spent a few days with him and his girlfriend, Ursula, giving them charts, books and advice. Ursula asked for instructions on how to do the calculations for celestial navigation and I felt proud to be able to help. In return, Morris, who was a chef, cooked up gastronomic feasts with dried morel mushrooms and once even a beef Wellington. Thinner than ever, I was glad for the high-calorie repast we shared with our new friends.

Ursula and Morris fell in love with Mimine during our days together and, after mulling over the Mediterranean and Atlantic crossings that lay ahead, and worrying about the cramped quarters on *Varuna*, I reluctantly let them adopt her. They asked for a list of her food preferences, and made a bed for her. I handed over her weekly contraceptive pills with some vitamins and cat treats, knowing she had found a loving new home. On Friday, July 3, we bid Morris, Ursula and Mimine farewell, leaving Port Said for the island country of Malta in the Mediterranean, 1,000 miles to the northwest.

I didn't think we would be flouting superstition too much to leave on this particular Friday—the first Friday departure since that fateful one in Mooréa—because it was also Olivier's birthday. "His anniversary with life can't possibly bring us bad luck," I thought.

Under a blinding sun, we tacked out into strong headwinds and *Varuna* heeled over 20 degrees, the conditions I had anticipated and had hoped would ease up as the day wore on. By nightfall, the wind had dropped off a bit, but was still on the nose, and I was exhausted from tacking and weary from the knowledge that progress had once again been miserable after a day of pounding. We were still smack in the middle of the worldwide shipping lanes bound for the canal.

Traveling up the rush-hour highway of the Red Sea had boosted my confidence as far as shipping was concerned. Naturally, I could remember the occasional heart-fluttering near misses. But *Varuna* had always prevailed, so I figured the radar reflector tied in between her shrouds was alive and well, along with the bright light on the backstay that illuminated the deck and sails. Mistakenly, I thought *Varuna* was visible to everyone.

In the evening, after I had been keeping a constant lookout in the cockpit, my teeth began chattering uncontrollably. A night mist had fallen, enveloping *Varuna* in a damp chill, and I stood at the spray hood, scanning the blurry horizon. There was a lull between ships and those that I could see were not heading my way, so I went below to boil some water for a cup of coffee before making a rendezvous with *Akka.* It was a quarter of nine and Olivier and I had planned to come togoether at the top of the hour.

In the radiating glow of the kerosene light, I poured the alcohol into the dish, and its fire alone heated up the water enough for my coffee. Heaping a couple of spoonfuls of powdered milk and sugar into my favorite blue mug and pouring in the water, I stretched and took a sip. My legs and bottom hurt from sitting scrunched up in the cockpit all day, ready to grab the tiller in the event that a ship needed avoiding, and I daydreamed for a moment about Malta and the exotic ring of the name. . . .

A blaring horn and the rumbling churn of a ship's propellors blasted me out of the reverie and on deck in a flash. Pupils dilating to adjust in the darkness, I looked up and there it was, every sailor's worst nightmare. Twenty feet away, the towering hulk of an immense cargo carrier was barreling down on us.

"Oh my God!" I gasped, frozen in shock. "This is it." The moment had finally arrived. My first reaction was to rush and turn on the engine. But, I didn't have enough time! Should I grab my passport and Tarzoon and jump overboard? Or should I undo the self-steering and luff into the wind? No, undoing the bungie cord would waste at least five precious seconds. In any case, none of these brilliant ideas registered clearly enough as my mind raced from alternative to alternative, all smooshed together in the pandemonium of the moment as I watched the monster close the miserable distance, still honking.

"I'm so sorry, Mr. Tarzoon," I screamed at my buddy as the bow of the ship passed 10 feet in front of us and *Varuna* bounced around in the side wash of thousands of tons worth of displacement. As the midship wall passed, still without contact, and next the looming stern, I chanced the thought that we were saved. My jaw was hanging to my stomach as something snagged the forestay, followed by a resonant twang.

Varuna's mast jerked back and the jib flapped free in the wind. Somebody shined a light down on us and incoherently hollered, as the Arabic letters on the ship's stern diminished with the growing distance, leaving us wallowing and crippled in the darkness.

Running up forward, to my dismay I found that the steel forestay had been sliced and the jib was hanging from its head, saved from a complete loss by the attached halyard and sheets. We had been spared the catastrophe of a dismasting thanks only to another halyard that I had tied down to the anchor roller in the Red Sea for added security in case the forestay broke. With the advantage of hindsight, I realized that even if I hadn't been so stunned, there would have been barely enough time to disengage the tiller, head into the wind and avoid misfortune. Tarzoon and I were lucky to be alive.

I quickly tore down the main and jib to avoid any more strain on the mast and began to figure out a jury rig. Turning on the engine, I saw *Akka*'s kerosene lamp in the distance and motored down to Olivier, who was standing out in the cockpit.

"Olivier, Olivier," I screamed. "I just got hit by a ship." Like a little girl, I was thrilled to have been spared the full potential of the calamity and was now on an adrenaline rush of fright and excitement.

"Are you all right?" was his first worry.

"Yah, yah. But, the forestay is completely broken in half. I think I better go back to Port Said."

"Oh no," he cried. "We can't. We'll be stuck in that god-awful filthy harbor for another week, filling out endless crew lists again. Are you sure it can't be fixed out here?"

"I don't know yet," I said. "But if I can't jury-rig something proper, then I'm going back. I can't fix it myself."

"What do you think," Olivier answered, "that I would watch you fix things from over here? Nothing would give me more pleasure than getting soaking wet and coming over to help fix your forestay in the middle of the ocean on my birthday. Come pick me up."

I motored past *Akka* in the dwindling wind and threw Olivier a line. He jumped, missed and ended up swimming to *Varuna*. Sitting on the rolling deck with my toolbox and Swiss Army knife, we played with the old half-broken forestay that had been replaced in Port Sudan, and used it in place of the totally broken one. We threaded the wire through a hole on the masthead, pulling it through, and then, with an arrangement of wire clamps at the opposite end, we attached it to the turnbuckle on deck. All this was relatively easy now on a calmer sea. Climbing to the top of the mast to thread the new forestay was a little nerve-wracking, as the boat swayed from side to side, but after an hour it was over. Olivier was back on *Akka* and we were on our way again, bundled up in sweaters and socks. I remained wide awake until dawn; even the twinkling lights of far off ships set my heart to racing.

For one week, we made a long tack north until the distant purple mountain ranges of Turkey emerged tantalizingly on the horizon. Then we tacked again, sailing past Rhodes and into the flat, calm wind shadow of Crete, where the winds that raced down from the Aegean Sea and through the isles of Greece were blocked by the landmass.

I nursed *Varuna* along, trying to avoid too much strain on her handicapped rigging. Finally, pooped from endlessly watching out for each other, and with our fuel supplies exhausted, we decided to stop at Loutros, a wise decision for the sake of our relationship. During the last two days, every time we had brought the boats close together, we had been ready to bite each other's head off if one of us so much as overselpt five minutes into the other's watch or drifted the slightest bit off course. Loutros was the last village on the southern coast of Crete where we could reprovision, rest and get our thoughts and emotions back into perspective.

Late in the afternoon of July 15, after a night of intermittent sailing with strong gusts flying down the mountains, we motored into Loutros's beautiful little bay, which looked like an open-air grotto of steep cliffs and light blue and green waters. There was a handful of whitewashed buildings clinging to the side of the harbor, and stepping ashore, we discovered that most of them were rooming houses and the rest, with their checkered tablecloths, were tavernas.

As we drained tall glasses of pistachio milkshakes at the first quayside terrace, we also discovered that the only way to reach Loutros was by ferry. There were no cars, hence no diesel. That we had chosen to make a landfall in a place so impractical struck Olivier and me as particularly comical, and we were forced to reassess our plans. We decided to take the ferry the next day to another village, bring jerry cans, fill them up with diesel and lug them back to the boats.

In the meantime, taking advantage of the situation, we roamed the rocky beach, enjoyed the Greek taverna atmosphere and watched the young vacationers surrounding us, all with the latest hairstyles, fashions and trends. There were the modern Mohican punks, the laid-back bohemians, the rich young American girls wearing two watches each, giggling and flocking around one man, and the regular European families and couples out for a relaxing vacation. It was a happy return to Western civilization, and we found ourselves gaping. It was funny how they all seemed as foreign to us as had the skirted Balinese and the Sri Lankans with their stubby betel-nut-stained teeth only a matter of several seas ago.

After scrubbing the boat hulls, on the morning of July 18 we were off again, bound for Malta 580 miles to the west. Olivier and I separated soon after leaving, and that evening I felt a certain amount of relief at being alone again. I understood Olivier well enough to know that he probably felt it, too. Whenever we sailed together, there was the constant pressure of watches, the constant dread of losing each other, and now that it was over, it was as if a heavy burden had been lifted. I had come to miss those idyllic days alone at sea, and as *Varuna* passed the wind shadow of Crete and we began to beat into a gentle breeze that was to stay with us until, a day away from Malta, my solitude and the sea were reacquainted.

All was well aboard, except for my nagging dread of tankers that made straight nights of sleep a luxury of the past. As *Varuna* plodded west and the days wore on, an alarm clock beeped me awake every half hour for horizon scans. One morning, the diligence paid off. Stepping into the cockpit, I saw a fuel tanker heading toward *Varuna* on a collision course, with its bearing masts perfectly aligned. I turned on the engine and puttered out of harm's way, just in case. When it passed alongside about 200 feet away, I hailed it on the VHF, wanting to hear that they had noticed *Varuna*, and give myself a little morale boost.

"Hello," I said when Sparky answered. "I'm the little sailboat on your starboard beam. Can you see me?"

"Wait a second. Let me go look," was the answer. He hadn't seen me! Well, I sure wouldn't be getting any peace crossing this Mediterranean Sea.

On the morning of July 24, the city carved from the pale yellow rock of Malta rose from the haze on the horizon, and by noon I was motoring past the walls, buildings and fortresses into Valletta Harbour. I could see sailboats tied bow- or stern-to along a quay, and in the middle, *Akka's* white masts and black hull stood out from the other less travel-weary boats. Happily surprised that he had arrived before me, I called out Olivier's name but received no answer. There was some space next to *Akka*, and preparing the fenders and mooring lines, I motored up alongside her, threw the gears into neutral and jumped aboard. As I snugged *Varuna* up, I realized that this was my second to last landfall before home. If all went as planned, the last would be Gibraltar, the gateway into the Atlantic.

Tidying up the sails and rearranging the mess in the cockpit, I chatted with my next-door neighbor and then heard Olivier call from shore. Excitedly standing up, I looked toward the quay and saw a vaguely familiar character standing beside him.

"Hmmm," I wondered, "who's this guy? I know him from some-where." And then, I squealed out loud, "Oh my God, it's Tony!"

"Hey, little sister!" he answered, grinning, and I leapt over all the lifelines, stanchions and docklines separating me from shore and hugged my brother. The insecure, nerdy boy with a Beatles haircut actually had a beard and towered above me.

"God, Tania," he said. "Pops told me you were skinny, but I didn't expect this. He sent me here as a surprise, to fatten you up and bring you a new forestay."

I turned to Olivier and hugged him. Tony had been waiting for two weeks in his hotel room, making daily jaunts down to the harbor to see if we were there. My father had told him to look out for a black ketch also, and that was how he had found Olivier that morning. Olivier had already had his shower and together they had checked Tony out of his room. He was ready to move aboard for his stay.

Next, who strolled by but Alexio, whom we hadn't seen since Port Sudan, with his girlfriend who had come from Brazil to visit. In the time it had taken us to get from Port Sudan to Malta, Alexio had spent several weeks in his birthplace, Russia, and several more weeks cruising the Greek isles. Just then, another sailing friend from Sri Lanka came by to welcome us to Malta. That first night ended up being an excited flurry among old friends and family, with Olivier and me as the bridges. Everyone had sea stories to tell, adventures and woes to recount, and tell we did over dinner. Nothing improves an unhappy turn of events or a soggy storm tale more than the re-telling of it among people meeting again after their paths have di-verged for a few months.

During our four weeks in Malta, one cloud shadowed the royal blue sky and darkened my mood whenever I thought about the im-pending separation from Olivier. With a circumnavigation behind him, he was to refit *Akka* here in Malta and transfer her back to her owner. Yes, we rationalized, it would only be for two months while I finished my trip. He would fly back to Switzerland and then, if all went well, on to the States. But we had been together every step of the way for almost one year, except for the times at sea, and too many things could go wrong in between. It was hard to ignore the fact that ahead lay the most difficult part of the voyage, the ap-proaching winter season on the North Atlantic.

Oftentimes at night, before drifting off to sleep, we talked about the sea, what could happen out there and what we'd do if it did. Len's misfortune had taught me not to take life for granted, and now

I was scared because after so many close calls I no longer felt so lucky, and suddenly I was feeling very mortal. *Varuna* looked less like my first little secure home that I loved and more like a foe waiting to carry me out into a losing battle.

The stress of the past several months, the lack of good food and proper sleep had exacted a heavy physical toll as well. I had already been perpetually tired in the Red Sea and afflicted with severe headaches and dizzy spells; things seemed to deteriorate further here in the Mediterranean. An excruciating European heat wave was killing off many older people in Greece, and articles in the Maltese newspapers said there were so many corpses that they had to be stored in freezers, waiting until burial plots could be found and clergymen had time to perform the ceremonies.

Stricken by fever, deliriums and chills, day after day I lay prone on *Akka*'s bunk, unable to muster enough energy to move, while Tony and Olivier fought off the hordes of flies that crash-landed everywhere. It took a monumental effort to get up and walk the quarter of a mile down the quay to the showers and into town. The heat was claustrophobic and all-encompassing, even affecting Tony, who was the picture of health. Regardless, he got up every morning, hopped on the bicycle Olivier had bought in Egypt and rode into town to buy fresh bread, ham and milk for our breakfast. Finally, worried that this might be something serious, I went to see a doctor who prescribed rest, some strong vitamin supplements and big doses of iron. I was malnourished, he said, anemic and suffering from sheer exhaustion.

In the meanwhile, Tony and Olivier began to work on *Varuna* with a vengeance. They changed the broken forestay for a new one from the States. Tony constructed a box to hold my batteries. Olivier changed the engine oils and fuel filters and installed a new fuse box with breakers for my solar panel, fluorescent light and an Autohelm electronic steering device. I pitched in as soon as I felt better and, in the evenings when the sun's rays moved farther west to bake other lands in intolerable heat, we walked down the long jetty toward a shady bar, crossing a bridge where, underneath in the water, men bathed their stately steeds. The Maltese were avid horse and sulky racers and it wasn't a rare sight to see the teams trotting along the streets.

Tony had turned into quite a conversationalist with plenty of $E = MC^2$ theories on how we could do away with nuclear weapons, and how the little parcels left of Earth's unexploited lands could be saved. He was entering college after the summer vacation to study physics and had a great affection for throwing figures and theories around, seemingly from the top of his head. Olivier and I spent a lot of time arguing the improbable numbers and evaluations with him over many a beer and orange juice.

A local sailmaker made a new spray hood for *Varuna*'s cockpit; the old one had withered and practically disintegrated like powder before my eyes. The weakened spray hood had become more dangerous than none at all because I often relied on it for support while leaning against or on top of fabric that could no longer handle the pressure. With the help of a sewing machine belonging to some friends on another boat, I took the fabric from the old mainsail and measured and sewed up some weather cloths to tie in between the cockpit lifelines for protection from future cold spray and waves. The Monitor was greased and little parts that had shown fatigue were changed for new ones.

After two years of no machines, I had become an expert in the clothes-washing department. I would fill up buckets with soapy water and leave the articles to soak for a day or so, until all the dirt and grease broke loose on its own. Then, all I had to do was stomp my feet in the bucket, using plenty of fresh water for rinsing, and then hang the clothes out on lines rigged in between the shrouds and forestay for that purpose. In the hot sun, it would take a couple of hours for things to dry until enough line space was cleared for the next load.

Depending on the port, the amenities available made the job easier or more difficult. In some places, I could leave the buckets next to the faucet on shore until it was time to stomp and rinse, and in others, jerry cans had to be lugged out to the boat. Here in Malta, with a hose attached on shore leading directly into *Akka*'s cockpit, the procedure was facilitated tenfold. The only better thing would have been a washing machine. I cleaned every last article of Olivier's, Tony's and my clothing, sheets, towels, blankets and fabrics and scrubbed *Varuna* down to perfection. Pretty soon, she was in as tip-top shape as possible.

All too soon, it was time for Tony to return home. His airplane was leaving from Rome, so Olivier and I decided to take the ferry as far as Siracusa on the island of Sicily and see him off. We nearly made the trip with him by lingering on the train too long until it started drawing away. Just in time, Olivier and I leapt off to be reprimanded by a station guard, who softened up when I sadly explained, "*Mi brothero*, say bye-bye for *mucho tiempo*."

Back in Malta, Olivier and I were inseparable, wanting to savor every last minute and make it into a pleasurable memory to be carried through the next couple of months. Doing everything together, we went to the showers every evening, took the bus into town for mail every other day and even managed to get my new taffrail log through customs—a long-drawn-out hassle. My doctor befriended us and invited us for dinner with his family, and took us to see the village nestled in the corner of a little cove where the movie *Popeye* was filmed—a sea shantytown of houses all built a bit off kilter. We took buses to different parts of the island for meals and on other evenings spent time with friends on their boats.

Malta's location out in the middle of the Mediterranean, between Sicily and Africa, meant that the small 95-square-mile island had been virtually defenseless against the conquering civilizations of old. Countless forts, where each ruling empire had tried to ward off the armies of the next—Mesopotamians, Phoenicians, Moors, Greeks, Romans, British and French—were the bastions of the capital city of Valletta, which was all carved from the same golden rock. People who lived there, except for the sun-thirsty tourists, buried themselves in their homes during the heat of the day and, like raccoons, crawled out only at night to sit along the waterfront in clusters. Everything about Malta had a lively Mediterranean ambiance, with grandparents, parents, teenagers and children gaily chattering the evenings away.

Finally, it was time to leave. We had already been stationary for three weeks. *Varuna* was ready, the clock was ticking and I felt strong enough to carry on. Every morning, Olivier and I would look at each other and I would say, "Well, I guess it's time. . . ." And he would answer, "Yes, winter is approaching fast." Tears would flood my eyes and one of us would postpone the inevitable by saying, "Yes, but what's one extra day?" From past experiences, I knew well that the hardest part of leaving was the actual untying of the mooring lines. Once that was done, I was gone and the sea warp would help to heal the open wounds. But the act of untying those lines, or lifting the anchor was like facing a sheer 100-foot wall that had to be climbed and I thought of a million and one reasons not to.

Finally, one day I looked at the North Atlantic pilot charts for October, and that lit a fire under me. Seeing for the first time on paper the ominous weather patterns, instead of just speculating about them, frightened me to the point of leaving almost immediately.

Trying to think of something that we could do simultaneously that would connect us in spirit until New York, Olivier suggested we each read a passage from the Bible at 12:00 Greenwich Mean Time every day. We decided to start the next afternoon with Psalm One.

We packed several boxes of Olivier's belongings that I would take aboard *Varuna* to New York. One box contained his shell collection, cherished mementos from far-flung beaches around the world, and as I held some of the shells in my hand, I remembered Olivier free-diving from *Akka* and emerging with the delicate trophies. We also packed his wet suit and some sweaters on *Varuna*, and he gave me his favorite cassettes.

Looking at the coral fronds that had once decorated *Akka*'s walls and were now hanging from *Varuna*'s portholes, I felt good knowing that a part of him would always be with me, yet achingly sad that all our voyaging together was finished. *Varuna* would now be the tiny carrier that had to deliver this precious cargo and our hopes safely home.

"I promise I'll try not to sink with all this," I choked, trying to make a joke.

"Oh, there's one more thing," he said, handing me two wrapped packages. One was marked, "Happy Birthday," and the other, "For your first rain." It was a private joke we had shared about the joys of the first real rainfall. The skies hadn't wept over the deserts since Sri Lanka, and we had both been looking forward to the moment they would.

The next day, on August 22, Olivier and I were both crying while he untied the lines for me, and after we hugged each other goodbye, I watched through a veil of tears as he and his dinghy shrank away in the distance.

"*Sia chinta camo,*" I called in Indonesian.

"*Isuguru,*" he hollered back in Sri Lankan.

"*Ana ahabek inta,*" I said in Arabic.

Then, "I *blong* you!" he finished, forcing a smile and raising his hand in a last wave. No matter how mutated the forms had ended up, we had tried to memorize the ways of saying I love you in every language we had encountered. They would have to last us for a long time.

The pain was deep as *Varuna*'s engine put more distance between me and the rocky shores of Malta, and I had a very hard time not pushing the tiller over and turning back. What was I doing? I was leaving one of the best things that ever happened to me, and here I was with Tarzoon, alone again. To have had Olivier sailing on the same oceans to the same destinations had given me great courage and strength.

The greatest joys over the past two years had been the simple pleasures of sharing everyday experiences with him. The memories, work, repairs, shopping and even the bureaucratic red tape had been more tolerable because we were together. Olivier was someone with whom I wanted to share the future. He supported my capriciousness with unlimited supplies of patience and love. He had always been there for me, seemingly unaffected by whatever we were going through at any given moment. He was my teacher, my pillar to lean on, and my shoulder to cry on. What had I given him, I wondered, to deserve all this? Olivier and I had lived the same life, together yet on different boats, and this goodbye almost shattered my world.

11

The mental strategy I had adopted for dealing with "those packets of miseries that we call ships," as Kipling once called them, had always depended on percentages. Countless times I had asked myself, "How many chances could possibly exist for *Varuna* to be at any precise time in exactly the same spot as another boat on these thousands of square miles of ocean?"

In the good old days, before the close encounter outside Suez, the notion that those chances were slight had enabled me to sleep many a peaceful night. But now those nights were gone, killed by the memory of the collision that played and replayed in my mind whenever my head hit the pillow. That moment had irrevocably altered the darkness.

In the narrow confines of the Red Sea, all the shipping had been headed in more or less the same directions, either north or south, while sticking to a fairly well-defined perimeter. All I'd had to do was pay attention when crossing that busy highway. The same had applied to all the other shipping routes in the Atlantic, Pacific and Indian oceans. On the pilot charts, in addition to probable weather patterns, there were also lines delineating the most commonly traveled routes of commercial shipping that had forewarned me about congestion.

The Mediterranean had a completely different story from any body of water I had known. Shipping of every variety clogged the 1,000 miles from Malta to the one natural exit at the Strait of Gibraltar at the western frontier. Between that objective and our present position, *Varuna* was smack in the midst of a maritime gridlock of fishing boats, pleasure boats, tankers, navy boats on maneuvers, freighters and cargo carriers that crisscrossed all points of the compass, all with different destinations to the legion of ports in North Africa, Europe and the Middle East.

Notwithstanding the shipping, on the first day out of Malta, and every day thereafter, *Varuna* was dogged by numerous logs, barrels and other hazardous flotsam, highlighted by thousands of plastics in every imaginable form. I had read that the Mediterranean was a sea dying slowly of pollution, but had never dreamed that I would encounter a solid pavement of rubbish.

For the first few days, Tarzoon sat in his corner, watching me alternate between crying, talking into a recorder to Olivier, playing solitaire and changing sails. There were still a little more than 4,000 miles to go until home, and to me, those 4,000 miles seemed more intimidating than the entire voyage thus far. To it all was added a sense of foreboding that nipped at the back of all my thoughts. I couldn't explain it and couldn't shake it. Behind were the landfalls of a lifetime; ahead was that one stop in Gibraltar and the preparation for the longest ocean passage yet, the crossing of the North Atlantic.

Day in and day out, I thought of what was left to be done, the little time there would be to do it, and made list after mental list. Those first few days out of Malta, my worries wore me down to a condition of perpetual tears as I religiously kept watch, snatched a few minutes of sleep here and there, and tried to keep the boat moving as fast as possible.

The outcomes of the games of solitaire began to put a flicker of chance into every move. As the red queens found their places on top of the black kings, we slowly passed through the watery blight that was once called the sea in the middle of the earth, situated as it is between the European olive trees to the north and the North African palm trees to the south.

Concentrating on the cards helped me to keep my mind off how much I missed Olivier, and kept me awake and alert when I thought my eyes would close from the dizziness of hardly any sleep. It became common for me to pop out on deck and see a ship so close that several months earlier it would have been something to write home about. Now, it was such a regular occurrence that I no longer had to steel myself before doing the habitual horizon scan.

The Med was true to its reputation for flaky weather. Every day we alternated between motoring over glassy seas with the sails down, to hoisting some combination of the sails to gain a modicum of quiet mileage in the fitful winds. Passing through the Strait of Sicily and westward to the south of Sardinia, my hands began to wear into raw slabs of meat from all the sail changes and adjustments. The wind was capricious, totally incapable of staying in the same direction or force for more than an hour at a time. It was either forward of the beam or, more often, from astern, always just at the point where a little more variance required changing the spinaker pole tack on the mast to stay on a proper course.

Jibing the boat as she canted downwind was the most complicated maneuver on *Varuna*, because the boom was all lashed down with preventers to keep it from slamming to the other side and the jib was poled out on the opposite side. To alter the arrangement meant uncleating the preventers, retrimming the sails and rerigging the pole. Then, just when I thought that we were in for a night of calm downwind sailing, the wind would veer around 180 degrees to the west, requiring the spinnaker pole to be taken down altogether and preparations made for beating. Just then, the wind would invariably increase to the point where I had to take in reefs. That maneuver accomplished, it would wane. Eventually, the engine and Autohelm would take over the sailing responsibilities, whereupon the wind would return from the east in feeble puffs and the pole would have to be reemployed.

The vicious circle of contrary wind was an indefatigable slave driver that didn't allow much time for eating or sleeping properly. My ocean schedule was thrown completely out of whack, and was now dependent not only on the daily progress of the sun, but also on the moodiness of the wind. It was a small consolation that at least we *had* wind, as irregular as it was, and I prayed that it would stay that way, not looking foward to surprises of a different sort.

Either wind voids or full-throttle tempests had seemed characteristic of the Mediterranean voyages of friends we had met in the Red Sea. Discussed over many a dinner table, storms in the enclosed basin bore reputations as hellions, first for popping up out of nowhere, then for stacking up steep chop with winds capable of raging at hurricane force until, as suddenly as they appeared, they dissipated. Although the sea has a surface of over a million square miles, its greatest depth is only 4,688 feet; the Pacific, in comparison, is almost three times as deep. The Mediterranean swells are much more susceptible to confusion than those in the open ocean, built up as they are by regional winds like the storied mistral, which flows down the Rhone Valley, and the sirocco, which blows up from the deserts of the Sahara.

As *Varuna* plodded over the bumpy swells, persecuted by the wind gusting down the unseen mountain ranges of Europe, I idly compared the conditions to other oceans. The Pacific, I decided, is like blowing over a full bathtub, where the ripples can keep on moving until they disappear, and the Med like blowing into a thimbleful of water.

The occasional foreign weather reports and chatter on the radio in different languages kept me aware that we were creeping by Italy, Tunisia, Sardinia and Algeria, approaching and then passing France, with Morocco and Spain just over the western horizon.

Legs akimbo, I was in my own world, playing countless games of solitaire all day long, every day, believing that the winning or losing of each game dictated my fate—whether I would get home safely or die trying. If the game came to a standstill before all the cards were numerically stacked up on top of the aces according to suit, I was sure we were doomed. That only launched me into dealing the cards with renewed fervor until they had all left my hands and I finally won a game. Then, and only then, was I able to get on with sailing. If a game was in progress, it was of no consequence that we were veering off course; it was of no relevance that the wind had died or picked up, just as long as the cards kept turning. The more fatigued I became, the more I dealt the cards with a vengeance, and once in a while the thought occurred to me that I might be going a bit mad.

One day, just past the Strait of Sicily, a little pitter-pattering noise on deck launched me out the companionway like a jack-in-the-box. Joy of joys, it was drizzling! It was the first heaven-sent water to dampen *Varuna*'s deck since seven months earlier in Sri Lanka. By no means a deluge, it was still a rainfall, and I stood there in the cockpit as happy as if the sky were hailing silver dollars.

Jumping back below, I dug out Olivier's present and unwrapped it. As I had suspected, it was a book. Olivier knew that, after a slow start, I had grown to love reading volumes of James Michener on the ocean, and this one was *Caravan*, a novel about an American embassy official in Afghanistan who had to leave the safe confines of officialdom and join a caravan to the outback. Thanks to Olivier, I was transported to another world for a few days, one similar to the one we had just seen together in the Red Sea.

The wind continued to blow erratically from astern, which the pilot chart said was normal, while predicting a zero percentage chance of serious storms, so I remained unconcerned. For several days, I attended to my duties like a robot between chapters of the book and games of solitaire, as the skies changed above from a semi-cloudy haze to a heavy-looking gray accompanied by gusty winds. By the morning of August 28, as finally a somewhat steady wind began to escalate, I had finished reading *Caravan* and wasn't very worried, especially since we proceeded to make the exhilarating progress of 140 miles during the next twenty-four hours under double-reefed main alone. As the wind jumped way out of the force bracket predicted on the pilot charts and began blowing at about 40 knots, I chalked it off to strong trades, because my pilot books didn't mention these characteristics for Med storms, and the barometer hadn't budged.

It was my habit, albeit a dangerous one, to diagnose present conditions by referring to those of the past. The barometer couldn't be wrong, I reasoned, and in any case, progress was good and Gibraltar only 350 miles away. Tucked into the snug bunk, I tried to rest my weary bones and take my mind off the deteriorating conditions by starting a new book. Within the first few pages, I was lost in the life of that love-torn, secret-tormented milkmaid, Tess.

On the afternoon of August 29, a dark curtain dropped over *Varuna*'s western horizon, the direction in which we were headed. In the past week, we had encountered several other fronts like this, where underneath the ominous cloakings, the wind had either increased or dropped altogether, and now the only course of action was to batten things down and continue. On approach, I could see jagged streaks of lightning bursting from the low-hanging, swirling clouds.

By nightfall, we sailed into its grizzly arms, and the wind increased to a howling velocity. Overcanvased even with three reefs in the main and no jib, *Varuna* began rounding up into the wind and getting slapped broadside by confused waves that filled the cockpit, as streaks of electric light crackled down to the water around us. Too tired to think straight, I couldn't find another ounce of energy to change the sail configuration again, and decided to let *Varuna* lie ahull under bare poles for the duration of whatever was about to happen. Dousing the mainsail and lashing it along the boom—a sloppy, wet ordeal in all this wind—I crawled below for some relief, hoping it wouldn't get much worse. Behind me, I pulled down a large piece of canvas attached to the spray hood to protect the open companionway from spray. A more alert mind would have made the decision to close the companionway altogether with the Plexiglas slats.

As the canvas billowed in through the open companionway, I automatically reached up onto the shelf and pulled out the alarm clock, setting it to the time of the next weather report. Finally we had reached the perimeters of an English broadcast—before it had all been in Italian—and I had to find out what was going on. This weather was a mystery, having no rhyme or reason, and no similarities to weather patterns to which I had grown accustomed in other oceans. Wedging myself in the lee corner of the bunk and snuggling up with Tarzoon underneath a cotton blanket, I melodramatically paralleled the hardships of leaving Olivier and the upcoming trips to those of Thomas Hardy's heroine. Tess was surviving; so could I.

Suddenly, the din of the wind was drowned out by a huge, thundering crash, and my world turned upside down. All hell broke loose as everything on the starboard side of *Varuna* catapulted down on top of me while hundreds of gallons of water engulfed us. *Varuna* lurched and rolled grotesquely sideways and I remember thinking in panic that a ship must have hit us square on this time.

With the first burst of adrenaline, I coughed and spit out the salt water that had rushed up my nose, pulling myself out from under half of *Varuna*'s interior and clambered outside. There was no ship, but the storm still raged, with lightning illuminating the frothy sea. Any lightning storm we had experienced in the past paled in comparison to the fireworks streaking all around *Varuna*. The damage to the boat, revealed by the light of the eerie staccato electricity, almost gave me a stroke.

The spray hood had been completely ripped out of its aluminum supports by the impact of the water and was caught in the lifelines. The deflated dinghy that had been lashed on deck was hanging on for dear life by one line attached to the grab rail. The weather cloths that I had laboriously measured, sewed and two days previously installed with new grommets were completely ripped out and gone. Forty liters of fuel in jerry cans that had been lashed in the cockpit were gone. The solar panel that had faithfully sustained my electricity supply since Tahiti was gone, as well as my foul-weather gear, which had been placed under the protection of the spray hood so I could grab it easily before going out on deck. A sailbag of sand for kitty litter that probably weighed about thirty pounds had been lifted from the cockpit floor and was now lying like a bag of wet concrete halfway overboard. Holding on as the boat rolled around and the wind blasted across the deck, I hastily hauled it in along with the spray hood and the dinghy.

That was outside, but the chaos that greeted me below was even more of a nightmare. Everything from the starboard side of the boat was on the port side, where my bed used to be, spilled, broken and strewn about under water as if we had gone through a blender. Water was sloshing up to one foot above the floorboards, with floating cassettes, papers, cameras, food, water bottles, Tupperware and books. The contents of the toolbox, which had been on the cabin sole underneath the middle section I had added in Tahiti to make a larger bed, was in the icebox and locker above the sink. Judging by the damage, I knew we had come close to having a complete 360-degree rollover until *Varuna*'s ballast had pulled her upright like a weeble wobble before she could make the sidewise somersault.

With one look at all this, and with my heart racing, I tore back outside to pump the bilge with the salvaged handle of a file. Clogged! Oh my God, what to do. The electrical bilge pump had failed eons ago. Through the lightning, I swept the hair out of my face, trying to think straight. We were in the middle of a full-fledged tempest of biblical fury, and *Varuna* was wallowing about, pregnant with sea water and in dire peril. Uncontrollably, my body began to shake itself to pieces.

Suddenly, from nowhere, the twinkling white lights of a ship appeared on the dark horizon. In the throes of panic, I jumped down below, grabbed my emergency-distress beacon and turned it on, praying that the ship was monitoring the frequency and would pick up the position-indicating signal. Turning it on, I knew, meant to anyone who picked up the signal that I had abandoned hope of saving myself and sought rescue.

Seconds passed. I stopped and sat on the starboard bunk, stripped of everything, and tried to calm myself. A pack of cigarettes floated by, and thanks to the cellophane wrapping, the interior was miraculously dry. I lit one with a lighter that had been in the dry hammock above my head and scrummaged for the little airplane-sized bottle of whisky that I had been saving for a special occasion. The burning liquid settled in my stomach and an inner glow began immediately to suffuse me in warmth.

I gazed at the drenched souvenirs on the wall in front of me, the tapa drawing from the Marquesas and the bolts of Balinese fabric. They glared down at me; my photo albums screamed out; my soaking clothes howled; my soggy books yelped and the dripping-wet Tarzoon meowed. Mr. T was the most important. Abandoning *Varuna* would mean leaving everything, and maybe even him, behind. I couldn't do it. We were still floating and I had come too far to fail now.

Five minutes after turning it on, and seeing that the ship had pressed obliviously westward anyway, I turned off the EPIRB and prayed to God that no one had heard it. "As long as I have an ounce of strength left," I thought, "I'll do everything in my power to save *Varuna* and make it to the next port alive." As I started to bail out with a bucket, the fatigue of moments before dissipated and my thoughts became very clear as scenarios ran through my head about what would have happened if someone had come to my assistance. Having summoned help, I would have been obliged to accept it.

For an hour I bailed bucket after bucket of water out into the cockpit. Picking up my soggy floating belongings, when the water was finally beneath the floorboards, I went back out into the exposed cockpit to dismantle the bilge pump. Several hours later it sputtered to life, after I discovered a crease in the hose that had blocked off the suction. Pulling out the kerosene heater that Morris and Ursula had given me in Port Said, I turned it up full blast to start drying things out.

By daybreak, the crisis had passed, things were slightly more ordered, and the activity had helped me to forget the seismic emotions of my fright. My nerves had been as tight as a drum for the six hours since the knockdown, and now as the tension drained with the dawn, every muscle in my body ached. As the wind died, I raised the mainsail only to find that it also had been ripped.

"What else have you got?" I screamed, as I ferreted out my repair kit and started sewing. "Come on! Let me have it now! You'll never have another chance. As soon as I get to land it's bye-bye birdie. *I've HAD it!*"

After I raised the tattered mainsail, we continued making for Gibraltar and I began to jury-rig repairs to the most important items that had taken the brunt of the wave. It was worse than I thought; all the new electrical wiring that Olivier had installed, as well as the old, was shot. The cassette player and masthead light blinked on and off haphazardly until I took a scissors to the wires. The RDF, VHF, shortwave radio and tape recorder were all dead. Inside, the electronic terminals of every last one of them had turned a moldy shade of green. All that was left to me for navigation were my wet HO 249 tables, a soaked *Nautical Almanac*, the sextant and, for entertainment, the half-finished, waterlogged *Tess of the D'Urbervilles*.

At least the navigation situation made me smile. Now, *Varuna* would be just like the convenience-free *Akka*, and, like Olivier, I would be obliged to find land with help only from the sun and stars —no backups from the radio-direction finder or VHF.

While we plodded onward, I brought out books and the mattresses to dry in the sun and unscrewed the RDF terminals, admiring the intricacies of electronics and reflecting on what had happened. My mistake had been running under bare poles.

Had my wits really been about me, I would have put up the jib for some stability, using it to run with the wind. And when the conditions worsened, I would have taken down the jib, replaced it with the trisail and headed *Varuna* into the wind and waves where they would have been deflected on the bow. Fatigue is the sailor's worst enemy. I knew it. But you always think you're doing the right thing until it's too late.

Looking at the charts, I decided to use my last rations of fuel and motor to the southern coast of Spain. The wind had disappeared, I still hadn't gotten any sleep and *Varuna* needed more diesel to make it to Gibraltar. For strength, I cooked up a couple of meals of rice and tomato paste and shared them with Tarzoon on our one remaining dish, making long lists of things that had to be done, and not knowing where and if I would ever be able to find the energy to do any of them.

In between watching out for ships, keeping course and making the few repairs that were possible to effect at sea, I carefully separated Tess's soggy pages one by one, only to find that, she, too, had come to a tragic end.

Almería was the closest town drawn onto my chart of the Mediterranean, so I headed for it in desperation. Three days of coursing adrenaline after the knockdown, an intermittent flash from a lighthouse beamed across the oily-looking calm, darkened here and there by cat's paws of a breeze, and we were drawn toward the vista of Costa del Sol. Within hours, I was trying to use my few words of Pidgin Spanish to figure out where and how to tie up at Almería's marina, negotiate a price with the secretary and ask how to make an international telephone call.

I vainly tried to follow the instructions and make the collect call from the public phone, while the marina handyman kept offering to help, with wandering hands that kept touching my breasts. Unable to cope, I rushed into town to place the call at an international telephone office, thinking I'd have a nervous breakdown if I couldn't talk to my father soon. I wanted to tell him what had happened and ask him to please come to Gibraltar and help me make repairs and bring new equipment. The seasons had no intentions of waiting for me and there was only one week to do all the work myself.

The telephone office was closed for the three-hour siesta usual in southern Europe, so I returned to *Varuna*'s smelly, damp cabin and opened the Bible on my lap. Trying to halt an incurable case of trembling, I read the Thirteenth Psalm at the same moment as Olivier, wherever he was, at 12:00 G.M.T. letting David's lament soothe my racing mind: "How long, O Lord? Wilt thou forget me forever?" Crying over the irony of the psalm and thinking of Olivier, I leaned back and fell asleep.

As the sun was setting that afternoon, I was back at the Offica de Telefono in town placing an order for a collect call to the States, huddled up on a bench, rubbing my arms in the freezing air-conditioned air. An hour and ten cigarettes later, the call still hadn't gone through and I began to crack up. The language barrier, fatigue and the knockdown caught up with me all at once. I tried to hold in the tears but there was no stopping them.

Self-conciously hiding my tear-stained face as a group of younger people came into the office, I heard the familiar sounds of English and new hope made me look up. I asked one of the girls if she could please ask the lady in Spanish why the telephone was taking so long. She looked at me kindly and after getting an answer, said that there was an operators' strike. Christine was her name, and she was like an angel sent down from heaven. After a while, the operator signaled and I leapt into the booth to take the call.

"Oh, Daddy, I'm so scared," I blubbered, telling him what had happened. "You can't possibly imagine how horrible it was. I lost so many important things. I need so much stuff and don't have enough money for it all. I promise I'll pay you back."

"Stay right there in Almería," he said firmly, "and sleep. Only head to Gibraltar when you're good and ready. Don't worry, Schibelpuff, I'll come right away." Hearing his voice and knowing that he was coming to Gibraltar made me think that things could work out after all.

Ever since Australia, thanks to Olivier, I had been able to keep up the hectic schedule that would enable me to arrive in New York early enough to set the record. After the delays in Malta, every passing day counted drastically when it concerned the crossing of the Atlantic, not so much because of the record, but because of the brewing winter. Now, with all the repairs that had to be done in such a short time, I needed help.

When I got back to the boat, my mind was in a tailspin, trying to sort out everything that had happened. I continued to ponder the tantalizing images of quitting and found, now that we were moored safely again, they really weren't as compelling as the image of stepping ashore in New York from the deck of *Varuna*. I was just too close to finishing the biggest thing I had ever started, and giving up the ship now would leave me wondering for the rest of my life if I had made the wrong decision to take the easy way out. I knew I couldn't live with that.

Almería, my first and second-to-last touch with the European mainland, was a place for regaining my resolve. For two days, I rested as Tarzoon jumped ship to kiss the ground and tell his own version to the Spanish cats that roamed the marina. I tried to fatten up with fried calamari and peppers, paella, steaks, salads and fruit ice creams at the lively outdoor terraces of the modern coastal town. When I felt ready again, after replenishing the fuel supply and scooping Tarzoon back on board, I cast off my dock lines and we headed down the coast for Gibraltar.

Varuna's engine faithfully puttered through one day, into the night and into the light of the next, as we skirted the margents of Spain toward the Pillars of Hercules. After thirty-six hours, the famous promontory, looming like a sentinel over the 8-mile-wide avenue of escape to the Atlantic, rose from the tail end of the landscape on the horizon.

Night fell again before *Varuna* could make it in, but the lights of Gibraltar illuminated the port and we motored slowly through a tidal rip that pitched us around a bit and then into the calm waters, that were only disturbed when gusts swept down from the great rock itself. Spying some masts in the distance, I motored to where a bevy of sailboats was anchored at the foot of an airstrip and let go the anchor. The next landfall, I thought as I fell off to sleep late that night, would be New York.

As I checked in at the customs dock the next morning, a little dinghy skittered across the marina, and there was my father rushing up to hug me, so beginning *Varuna*'s brief pit stop in a race against nature's clock. Finally, the ultimate goal was almost close enough to reach out and touch, and after that moment everything began falling into place.

. . .

Only two winds blew consistently through the narrow strait separating Gibraltar, at the southern tip of Spain, from the tip of Morocco in northern Africa—either from the west or from the east—for days at a stretch. The easterly Levanter wind was the messenger that would carry *Varuna* through. If cirrus clouds appeared over the Rock of Gibraltar, they would herald an unknown number of days of the opposing westerly Poniente, and there would be virtually no way for *Varuna* to fight through the straits against the wind and current. Every morning for a week, I would listen for the regular easterly blowing across *Varuna*'s cockpit whispering to me that we still had time.

On the first day, my father helped bring *Varuna* alongside *Lone Rival*, the boat of a family friend named Mark who was also from New York. Together with Mark, and a Canadian named Doug, who had singlehanded a sister ship of *Varuna*'s to Gibraltar, my father had been waiting impatiently with a new VHF, RDF, shortwave radio, tape recorder and all kinds of other gear that he had assembled before jumping on a flight at Kennedy Airport.

After the encounter with the tanker outside the Suez Canal, there was no way that I wanted to cross the Atlantic without the confidence that I could save myself if something as unforeseen as that should happen again, so I had ordered a life raft in Malta, and now it was waiting for me. *Cruising World* had also sent over an ARGOS satellite transmitter that would enable the magazine and my father to follow my daily progress across the Atlantic. That there would be crowds of press and people anticipating my safe arrival only served to heighten the pressure. There would be no room for error now.

With Mark, Doug and my father, I was blessed with a refit crew of willing helpers. We worked from morning to last light every day, buzzing frantically around, repairing, rebuilding, reprovisioning, rewiring and preparing *Varuna* for her next opponent. Standing before the job that had to be done in such a short period of time, I wondered how it could have ever been possible for me to even think about doing it alone.

Doug, who was an electronics technician, took out the old broken VHF and installed the new one with its antenna that my father had brought from New York, while I started reorganizing and hauling everything out from *Varuna*'s interior to dry in the sun. Everything had been soaked in the knockdown, to the point where even the fastened Ziploc bags had water inside. For several days, the cockpit was a bedlam of *Varuna*'s innards—mattresses, tools, spare parts for the Monitor, sailing books, charts, engine pieces, fiberglassing compounds, foods, epoxies, dishes, pots and pans. One by one, I wiped away the salt, sprayed on lubricant and restored the essentials to their places, jettisoning things I had always kept for just in case, and now found to be of no use.

The Teflon bearings of the self-steering gear were worn out from constant use over the past two years, so Mark and my father detached the Monitor from the stern and brought it onto the dock to replace all the weaker points with new parts. Then my father went off to have the bow pulpit welded into a stronger shape; the leftover fragments from my encounter with *Kreiz* in the South Pacific had begun to fall apart.

Gibraltar was well stocked with everything a cruising boat needed for repairs and replacements, and the spray-hood supports were also rewelded. I ordered and installed a new set of weather cloths for the cockpit, had a smaller storm jib made, and continued to sort everything out, in between placing more orders for equipment to meet newly discovered problems and reorganizing the bags of supplies that kept flying into the cockpit.

In order to reduce the weight aboard, I started handing out things I didn't need anymore, like the spare anchor and the dinghy that was beginning to show signs of wear and tear. I bought six sets of long johns and stored them in new Ziploc bags, in the place of summer clothes and souvenirs that were boxed, ready to be taken back home with my father on the airplane. He had brought some extra sweaters and I had Olivier's. The Atlantic was going to be a cold trip, especially for a body so long acclimatized to warm temperatures.

I emptied out Tupperware buckets of grains and beans that hadn't been opened since New York, having discovered long ago that the time it took to cook them in the heat of the cabin had rendered the chore not worth the torture in any of the tropical places we had traveled. I gave Mark the extras and instead filled up the waterproof tubs with electrical equipment, spare parts, nuts and bolts.

While we were tearing *Varuna* apart, Maurice, an Irish bicycle-messenger friend from New York popped by. He had stopped in Gibraltar to make some money to continue his own travels aboard a motorcycle, and it was so good to see a real friend of mine from the old days. He was the first one to bring me news of other friends and to reconnect me with a past I had left behind. I shared my trip with him through photos and stories and, just like the good friends we once were, we sank into the old routine of jokes and gossip and flew around the small enclave of Gibraltar on his motorbike in search of things I needed.

Next, my father bored through the deck with a drill just forward of the mast to install new U-bolts for lashing down the life-raft canister, while I crouched below, gathering up the fiberglass rinds and dust. Then we installed and bolted down the ARGOS onto the wooden platform in the cockpit. We sealed the operation with a polyurethane bedding compound, and I grabbed the caulking gun to smear the sticky white gook around the bottom of the companionway slats that tended to leak salt water down onto the batteries. The welders at the local shipyard added a new handle onto the upper companionway slat so that I could easily close it behind me from the inside, and I fabricated some wood wedges to secure the slats even more tightly in place, in case things got too hairy out there.

We ordered a new smaller solar panel, attached it to a plank and fitted it onto a mount on the aft pulpit in such a way that I could maneuver it to follow the sun's path during the day for maximum efficiency. Then I bought a new breaker panel and on it attached the wires from the Autohelm, solar panel and a new fluorescent light for the backstay. A new storm jib had been created, and with the re-welded pulpit and new weather cloths, *Varuna*'s lifelines and closed-in cockpit felt secure enough to face the worst storm the Atlantic could dish out.

On the fifth day, Maurice and I motorcycled across the border to the neighboring Spanish town of Algeciras to get some foam for mattresses for *Varuna*, and from that night on, sleeping became a new pleasure. The old mattresses had been so saturated with salt water and cat pee that they had shrunk to a quarter of their original thickness and the wooden frame of the bunk always jutted into my back. The salt then drew in all the humidity of the night, turning them into soggy sponges. The new foam was like a new lease on life and I found myself actually eager to try it out at sea.

The British colony on Gibraltar had every amenity and convenience of a bulging-at-the-seams British town, but with a Moroccan and Spanish flavor that added just enough confusion to make it interesting. At the huge Lipton's supermarket emporium, I stocked up on all sorts of canned soups, shepherd's pies, instant noodles, rice dishes, chocolates and dehydrated meats, both the American and English varieties. I bought several boxes of bottled water, and Mark managed to lay his hands on some kerosene, which was hard to come by, for the heater and stove.

Even Tarzoon tried to help by getting out from under my feet sometimes and once fell overboard chasing a fly. Much to the marina's amusement, my seafaring buddy swam calmly up to the self-steering gear on another boat, clambered aboard and shook off the water.

For six days, the Levanter blew while we ran around during daylight hours, and as soon as the sun set, we'd go with Maurice for huge meals at a harbor-side restaurant. Maria, the jolly, fat Spanish proprietress, felt that it was her duty to make me put on several extra pounds. At every meal I received two appetizers, one main course, a salad and two desserts, and she beamed at our table as I devoured every last morsel.

By the end of the sixth day, everything was in order. I checked the engine, liberally sprayed WD-40 over all the connections, and opened the outside lockers to see the jerry cans of alcohol, diesel, kerosene and engine oil, all neatly stowed and battened down in their places. The spray hood was as strong as ever, and the black casings of the new VHF and shortwave radio sparkled out from their mounts on the bulkhead above my bunk.

Proudly, I invited everyone down one by one, insisting that they take off their shoes before stepping in onto my new clean bed. With delight, I would open up the pots-and-pans locker resupplied with new dishes, frying pan and utensils, then the food locker full of colorfully labeled stacked-up cans and buckets full of staples. In the forepeak was an extra water tank with an unscrewable opening large enough to reach into with my arm. I had never used it for water, instead letting it serve as a watertight food locker. Now it was loaded down with perishables: biscuits, cookies, candies, dried fruit and cat treats.

Just for good measure, I opened up the tool and supply locker to take a peak at the organization that had taken place of the previous week's bedlam; everything was neatly greased and bagged. We would be able to be autonomous for anywhere up to two months with all the provisioning. I even had a sailbag full of fresh wood shavings from a nearby woodworking shed for Tarzoon's litterbox. Sitting on the new cushiony bunk, I looked around at the snug cabin. Everything was ready.

On the last night, my father and I went over the charts one more time and I finalized my route. For every month on the North Atlantic pilot charts, the ocean was divided up into a checkerboard of 5-degree squares, and each one had symbols and numbers translated into information on the winds, currents and other prevailing conditions. In the corner of the chart was a graph, also divided into

5-degree squares, containing numbers indicating the average percentage of ship reports where winds of at least Force 8 had been
recorded for the month.

For all the pilot charts I had ever used, I had never crossed a
square with more than 1-percentage factor of Force 8. The few times
that *Varuna* had passed over a 1—once in the Pacific and another
time in the Indian Ocean—my fingernails had been chewed to the
quick in nervous anticipation until we were safely out of the danger
zones.

The October chart for the 3,000-mile North Atlantic crossing was
a scary vision of 1's, 2's, 3's, 4's, and two 5's. Also, there were bold
red lines curving down from the northern seas, indicating that no
matter what route we took, somewhere along the way *Varuna* would
have to pass through the perimeters where average wave heights
exceeded 10 feet.

Unless we ducked the strong current of the eastbound Gulf
Stream by heading in a more southerly route below the Azores, it
would impede progress and we would be faced with fearful storms
kicked up by the underwater river. But then, there was the risk of
heading too far south into the fringe of the horse latitudes, a belt
between the latitudes of 30 and 35 degrees north, characterized by a
dearth of wind altogether.

My fear of the passage increased as I stared at the 3,000-mile
distance and the expected no-win conditions separating me from
home. As the days plodded on toward Old Man Winter, the news
from the November chart held even gloomier tidings. So, choosing
the lesser of two evils, I decided to take the straight path from Gibraltar to New York, passing south of the Azores to avoid the contrary Gulf Stream and the higher risk of storms.

"Yah, but there you will get a lot of calms," my father warned.

"Well, I'd much rather run the risk of a few calms than storms,"
I insisted. The sole advantage of taking the Great Circle route north
of the Azores would be that it was 400 miles shorter, but I didn't
really care about speed.

"Well, you know best," he said.

"Anyway, Daddy," I chimed in, as we folded up the charts that
evening, "you should be concerning yourself about my twenty-first
birthday present that I will have a lot of pleasure opening in the
middle of the ocean."

"Hah!" he laughed, and we headed off with Mark and Doug to
have a last feast at Maria's.

The next morning, I awoke and looked outside the companionway. The sky was bright blue, and puffy clouds streamed across the famed rock towering above the anchorage. The easterly Levanter was still healthy and in full swing, as if it wanted to help me onward. This was the big day. It was now or never.

After wolfing down some breakfast on *Lone Rival*, Mark, Doug and my father were ready to follow me out to the entrance of the strait, catching *Varuna* on video before she turned westward and headed out to sea. Before the pandemonium of casting off the dock-lines, everyone gave me wrapped presents and cards to open on my birthday, and my father slipped me a letter to be opened on the tenth day out.

I climbed back on *Varuna*, shuffled Tarzoon below to the safety of the cabin and undid the mooring lines for the last time. We were off. For better or for worse, my final game of solitaire was almost played out.

eptember 19. It's dusk, our third day out. I've just come back in from battening Varuna down for the night, and finally there's inspiration to write. It feels so nice to put 'Destination: New York' at the top of the page, although I feel lonely after being cut off so abruptly from all the excitement in Gib. The quietude is screaming out at me.

"This passage frightens me more than any other in the entire trip, but Varuna feels good. It's such a pleasure to open her lockers and find them brimming with delicacies, and the ARGOS and life raft give me the security I felt when Olivier and I were sailing together. This is the last crossing and I pray that it will be a safe one.

"Ever since Australia, the journey has seemed long and hard, and the truth is that the ocean can still terrify me. Most of the time, I think about things that a girl my age doesn't think about, and I'm bugged with thoughts of my future. Now that I am on my way home, everything is a big question mark. What will I do? Can I settle back down to do things a girl my age would do? Why are these questions still lurking after so long? Right now, I feel much older than I want to.

"My fix today said that we've made 285 miles since departure. The barometer has begun to fall, so something's brewing. I made a day, date and mileage-by-the-hundreds chart again, and am making a tape for Olivier that I hope we'll listen to together. There are 3,115 miles left to go. I think about Olivier and pray that he is waiting for me. . . ."

Very slowly, the frenetic week at the famous rock was beginning to sort itself out, and I felt a certain relief to be out on a big ocean again, where navigation wouldn't be as crucial anymore, and shipping would no longer be confined to an enclosed body of water. It was taking longer than usual to wind down from the activity on land, and instead I remained idle, dwelling on my questions and feeling them loom larger the more I searched for the answers.

For the first few days, the wind had continued to blow steadily at our back from the east, pushing *Varuna* along at a good clip through the Strait of Gibraltar and the thick of the Europe-Africa, Europe-America shipping routes. It was weary enough duty, and on the second night, when I had grown so tired that the thought of getting crushed by one of the never-ending stream of ships didn't seem to matter anymore, I dozed off in a shallow sleep. Some kind of internal warning signal had awakened me, just in time to run out on deck, grab the tiller and dodge an oncoming freighter.

On the eighteenth, we had finally passed the last outcroppings of Portugal somewhere over our starboard horizon and had forged out into the sanctuary of deeper ocean. Until New York, except for the island groups of the Azores 1,000 miles to our northwest and Bermuda 2,900 miles to the very far west, there was nothing but a vast expanse of gunmetal gray.

This trip, I knew, would bear no resemblance to those already laid under the keel, and my mind kept racing over the knowledge that everything done on *Varuna* was being done for the last time. Foreign landfalls and new people were a thing of the past, and the finality that the name New York conjured up played the largest role in my uneasiness.

Putting the logbook away, I reached for the radio knob to get rid of some static, and tuned in the BBC. The radio was going to become a good friend, and I congratulated myself on buying those extra batteries before leaving Gibraltar to keep it well fed.

Lost in thought, I bent over to rearrange the floorboards that had splintered into five pieces during our Mediterranean fiasco, and then crawled into the forepeak for a snack. Reaching down into the storage tank, I felt around, pulled out a package of gingersnaps and then lurched back to the bunk. Opening up the cellophane, I took out two cookies and put the rest into the overhead hammock, unclosed. If they stayed exposed, then the humidity of the sea air made them chewy, instead of crispy and hard, and I liked my cookies better that way.

After so many passages, I had begun to humor myself with eccentric time-killing techniques that had formed almost instinctively; one of these was the fine art of playing with my food. A simple bite of an apple took on a whole new meaning as the pulp had to be separated from the skin without ever leaving my mouth. The same went for the almonds in chocolate bars; they were never crunched along with the chocolate, but had to be singled out, rolled around and savored. Cans of food lasted forever as I made little designs in the soups, pastes or sauces with my tongue on the spoon and admired them; and that same spoon prolonged cups of coffee, which had to arrive in my mouth spoonful by spoonful. Crawling out on deck with a gingersnap for the evening's entertainment, I stared at the water and watched *Varuna* nod slowly west. As we rocked downwind, I began nibbling away like a gerbil, around and around the cookie, letting the spicy little pieces crumble up in my mouth.

Just then, flying in from the echo chamber of approaching nightfall, a yellow canary landed on the boom's downhaul. I gulped down the few remaining crumbs and called out to it. Responding to the sound of my voice, my new friend assessed the situation and then hopped up onto the boom. I cooed again and then he hopped right onto my head! What an ornithological wonder! He wasn't the least bit afraid of me. I ruminated for a moment on the piles of gooey white poop that always seem to be underneath birds, and shooed him out of my hair. It was too cold to take a bucket bath just because a bird couldn't control its bowel movements. Taking one last scan around, I went below, leaving the feathery hitchhiker to feast on the crumbs in the cockpit. A while later, the sound of a crunching noise pulled my attention out the companionway. Mr. T had a bloody mess of feathers sticking out of his mouth.

"Oh my God!" I screamed. "You murderer!" But it was too late. Except for a couple of feathers blowing away and bloodstains on the deck, there was nothing left. In my eyes, that heartless scoundrel had been soiled and I couldn't bear the thought of touching him for the rest of the day.

Waiting for the wind to sort itself out, I listened to the slamming mainsail and opened up the bag with the letters and birthday presents to look them over, shake and squeeze things. There were only two and a half weeks to go until my twenty-first anniversary with life.

All that day, I had fiddled with the sails, trying to make progress in the wimpy wind. According to my references, this wasn't normal.

We were supposed to be in the belt of the Portuguese trade winds that blow steadily from the north, and they now seemed to be non-existent. Frustrated beyond belief at being entrapped by a calm so early in the trip, my body continued acclimatizing itself, and that night I awoke to see the dark shadow of a boorish squall passing astern.

Unable to relax, I whipped up a midnight snack of Ryvita crackers, Miracle Whip and some dried beef strips that Tony had brought to Malta. Settling down again to munch, I listened to a narrated story on the BBC and waited. Dawn showed up with a gloomy disposition, and the puffy clouds of the day before were replaced by their wicked stepsisters. Soon the wind became confused, making a reappearance from the opposite direction, obliging us to trim in the sails and beat. *Varuna* heeled over on her new point of sail and from then on life carried on aboard sightly tilted.

"September 20. I'm a little confused about the time in America. Europeans with their 'summer hours' have me all mixed up in relation to GMT. They all change at different times. I started knitting a sweater and then pondered my big question of the day: Are there one or two hours' difference in the States?

"The dophins of the Atlantic just arrived in welcome, snorting, whistling, jumping and beating into the waves like us, but they seem to be enjoying it more than Varuna and I. The chill is becoming increasingly uncomfortable and I've started wearing long johns at night. I can hardly wait to be way out in the middle of the ocean and away from these ships; then I can start wishing to see them again. The BBC was talking today about a hurricane that is bringing bad weather to my area. The weather is definitely deteriorating. I sit and wait. . . ."

By the twenty-third, the first storm of the passage glided over our coordinates and *Varuna* began her preliminary gyrations on a cantankerous ocean. I awoke from a dream of New York—where over and over, Jade was calling me a social klutz—stretched my creaking limbs and checked the barometer. It had made a crash landing since the night before, and going outside for the morning horizon scan, I found a parade of wispy mares tails flying in our direction. It was a little worrisome.

September 23 was the day of the equinox, eclipse and the empty moon, all at once, and after seven days of inspecting the *Nautical*

Almanac for endless verifications, I had been expecting this. Judging by past experiences and all Olivier's advice on things celestial, the storm had every chance of getting worse. Eclipse? Equinox? Empty moon? What more could I hope for?

As *Varuna* pounded into the building waves, I knitted and tried to get my mind off the brewing storm by thinking of Olivier and wondering what he might be thinking about at that moment. If all went well, he would be back in Switzerland now, seeing his friends and family for the first time in five years and, if I knew him at all, he would be feeling out of place in the life he had left behind. Perhaps he was already missing the sea and *Akka*, wishing he were here alongside me and *Varuna*. Would I feel that way too?

The thought of impending separation from my boat was sobering and I looked around the secure little home that was protecting Tarzoon and me from the watery elements outside. At that moment, I couldn't have loved her more. Pulling out the tape recorder, I installed a new cassette and began talking to Olivier. Of all people, he would understand exactly how I felt, having gone through it himself by leaving *Akka* in Malta.

Telling him about my feelings and whatever was going on around *Varuna*'s isolated world connected him to me in a way that even the Psalms were unable to do. As I talked, I imagined us sitting together sometime in the future, in a cozy apartment in a faceless city, listening to my voice from a day long gone by.

About an hour after sunset, the remains of the feeble twilight shone through the Plexiglas slats, getting feebler. It was almost night and this was going to be a black one. *La vide lune*, the empty moon, Olivier had called it. I remembered being struck by the poetic translation of the French, and knew that whenever this moment in the month's cycle arrived, the ocean was always at its darkest. The next evening, when the hours of daylight expired, a tiny sliver would light up the skies, growing with every passing night for two weeks, filling up until the moon brimmed over. Then, my luminescent orb of a night light would wane until it emptied itself again, a month from now. Would I be home then, I wondered, looking up to the heavens and wishing to be back at sea?

Staring through the secured slats, I eventually summoned up enough willpower to leave *Varuna*'s cocoon to venture out into the void, whose only substance was the reassuring fiberglass solidity of the cockpit. As I shut the slats behind me, Tarzoon jumped out at the last second to join in the evening stargazing session.

The sky still had intermittent clear patches shining through the clouds, and because the air was so much drier here than in the Med or the Red Sea, the stars seemed frightfully close, like hanging chandeliers. Even though there was no moon, they lit up the ocean along with the phosphorescence that kicked up sparklers on the cresting waves.

The wind had picked up during the day, and by the time it had reached its present force of 30 knots, we were confronted with a minor technical problem. The new triangle of a storm jib was too small for the conditions. It was intended for sailing in stronger winds, which usually churned up the kind of waves where headway would be impossible and I would be forced to take down the sails and lie ahull anyway. The next biggest sail aboard was too big. The sail that would have been perfect for the conditions had gone overboard in the knockdown, and in Gibraltar I hadn't noticed until it was too late to order another. So, *Varuna* staggered into the waves, underdressed, going nowhere.

As soon as the weather straightened out, I planned to remake an old storm jib that had been gathering dust since it had fallen apart in the Red Sea. "Maybe the storm'll get worse and the small sail will come in handy," I thought as Tarzoon and I leapt back down into the neon glow of our cabin, replacing the slats behind us.

"Hallo, it's the 25th, 9:00 P.M., and we've hardly gone anywhere. The storm worsened yesterday and Tarzoon and I scrunched up in a corner while it howled and pounded outside. Since last night, we've been sailing on and off, still with huge waves and a decent amount of wind. Right now, it's beginning to rain. A massive, low-hanging mass of mess is lumbering our way and I've taken down the jib again to avoid a nasty surprise.

"A ship passed right behind us earlier on and I talked with the radio operator. He didn't speak English very well, but I did understand that they left Gibraltar two days ago, while for us it has been nine. He honked his horn three times in salute and asked if I needed anything.

"I just keep looking at the chart and estimating our ETA. At this rate, we've still got 45 days to go. I never realized until Sri Lanka that there are so many ships on the ocean. Here I am, pretty far out, and still seeing a few each day—all going east or west. Sometimes I like to imagine myself driving one of them, zipping across the oceans in one or two weeks. They just keep passing me by, regardless of the weather, while I have to depend on fair winds to push Varuna at a fraction of their speeds.

"I'm fighting off a little personal depression, wiped out two books, and just keep praying for a happy last voyage with Varuna. I finished maneuvering around the neckline and am halfway down the back of the sweater and, as the knitting needles click, I keep dreaming of home."

There was a special feeling about the day as I awoke the next morning, aside from the fact that the weather prognosis was looking up. Even though I had been anticipating it every day so far, it was only after my morning coffee, drowned in powdered milk and sugar, that I was able to pinpoint the source of this new excitement. In the bag with all my birthday presents and letters lived the bulky letter that my father had given me to be opened on the tenth day at sea. The day had arrived. "My dearest Tania, my firstborn," it began, on paper ripped out of a European-style loose-leaf notepad.

"A few times I said to Mutti and Vati that even though I love them, it would be nice to be an orphan, because many desirable things could have been done that I wouldn't do otherwise because I didn't want to hurt them. When I talked to you tonight about the future and your hopes and dreams, and then tears came to your eyes, all those times came back to me. How I wanted to go to Australia to become a sheep farmer. How I wanted to go to the jungles of Brazil. How I cried with all my loves just because things didn't work out the way I thought. This is just to tell you that tonight, more than ever, I can feel how you feel.

"You are now out on the ocean all alone with Tarzoon and *Varuna*. You think of all the people who are dear to you. You try to deal with the present, the past and the future all at once. There are so many ifs and buts and there are no precise answers. I know. But you are not alone with these decisions, uncertainties and desperate searchings. All people have them to a certain degree. Even if it feels as if it will crush you, be grateful. Your sandhills may be other people's mountains.

"In the end, you will be alone to make the decisions. And without any hestitation, Tania, I would now go to sleep on your ship in any situation and only react when you request it. The same goes for your life. But please, my dear firstborn, remember that I am your parent. When I talk, it is not as a co-captain. That doesn't exist. It is only as your Daddy. You and I will both easily remember what has gone on between us in the past. . . . You are very important to me and I care very much.

"All the worries that you have expressed about what is going to happen and how you are going to deal with it are not going to be a problem if you manage to stay true to yourself. This sounds like a ranting TV evangelist, but I can't tell it any better—so be it. I do the best I can. You will be 21 in a few days and a happy birthday to you. Think of where you are right now when you read this and how you will remember it in 10, 20, 50 years. . . . Love, Daddy."

It was rare for my father to reveal the emotions he had expressed in the letter, and the effort that it must have taken for him to write them left me giddy. At that moment, I knew that if someone were to walk up and ask who had been my role model, I would have to say that it was he—even though I would rather have died than admit it before.

During the years after the divorce, as we children grew older and less dependent, my father had slowly become a sort of happy-go-lucky Jesus, hell-bent on creating for us the lusty excitement and dramatics that were his view of life. Always wanting the best for his children, and unable as he was to succumb to the ordinary, the circumnavigation had been his idea of the "all" for me. He had been desperate over my aimlessness in those days, and this had been the only yardstick he could come up with by which I could finally judge myself and change my ways.

In accepting the challenge and leaving New York, I had been searching for the unattainable golden apple of his approval, feeling that it had been lost beyond hope during my teenage years. However, realizing that for my father there would always have to be something more, I now knew that the rest of my life could not be spent doing only what he thought was the best for me. Somewhere along the way, my own dreams had finally been created and it felt all right now that they did not quite mirror his own.

In the end, maybe what I had really been searching for was his love and knew now I needn't have gone around the world to get it. I had been standing on the back of a whale, searching for minnows, and as he said in the letter, I had to be the skipper of my own life now. Unfortunately, I also knew that, like any good father, he would forget he ever wrote that.

I felt lighter as I read and reread the letter, as if the straps on a backbreaking burden had rotted away and the weight was falling off. The need for my father's approval would always lurk in the shadows. But, it just didn't seem to matter in the same way anymore. Life, I thought, wasn't really such a big complicated ordeal after all. As a matter of fact, as a whole, life, and this trip in particular, was pretty damn good. Later on, feeling more like myself, I pulled out the logbook and made the daily entry.

"Afternoon of the 26th. Hallo. The wind died this morning and I refashioned the old storm jib. I had to make holes in the luff and put on grommets and hanks. Then, all three clews, which had been ripped out in the Red Sea, had to be reattached with a hole puncher, hammer and twine. The cockpit is full of little circles of fabric. I hope it'll do. Afterward, it rained for several hours and the knot in my stomach got very tight. So far, this passage is by no means the height of ecstasy. On top of it all, I heard today on the Voice of America that hurricane Emily struck Bermuda, leveling the island, and is headed out to sea. This was all the announcer said: 'For land, she's history, but some shipping lanes still may be affected.' WHAT SHIPPING LANES, FOR CHRIST'S SAKE?

"I don't know what to do. I knit two rows, put it down and agitate. I read three pages, put it down and agitate. I pour myself a glass of medicinal brandy, pour it back in the bottle and agitate. I listen to the BBC, switch to VOA, switch to Radio France, turn off the radio and agitate. The sky is bruised with black and there are curtains of rain. Daddy's so lucky. It took him only eight hours to get home from Gibraltar. It'll take us forever. I want to go home. Click, click click, little red shoes. Nothing."

The next day, the wind changed direction, the barometer climbed back up and, as the Portuguese trades finally arrived, the miles began ticking regularly by on the taffrail log. The chart was already full of holes from the dividers, as if measuring the distance countless times would bring me closer. After finishing off the last of the Miracle Whip, I lay down to take a nap, hoping that the wind would last at least a week, and that I would no longer have to stare at the chart and see only a wide-open space between the X and New York.

I had been reading a book of short detective stories and drifted to sleep imagining myself in the middle of the world's largest cliché: a smoky cabaret with heaps of suave Humphrey Bogarts. Upon awakening, I looked out the companionway and my head crashed against the ceiling in a leap of surprise. There was another sailboat passing a couple of hundred feet astern! That eventuality had never even crossed my mind, because I had been unable to imagine somebody else wanting to travel this ocean in such a horrible season. I ran outside and disengaged the Monitor to head down toward them. After two minutes, it suddenly hit me that this other boat wasn't *Akka* and the occupants might think that I had a couple of loose screws to·go off course just to see them. Self-consciously I reengaged the self-steering gear and headed instead for the VHF.

My reaction reminded me of a funny moment on *Pathfinder* a few years earlier, in the middle of the same ocean, a thousand miles to *Varuna's* south. Fritz, Nina, and I had been sweltering out on deck, poking along in some feeble wind when we finally had our first encounter with another sailing vessel. After two weeks at sea, Fritz had decided that transatlantic voyages were a bit much for a man with his social-butterfly tendencies, and when I had spied a sail on the horizon, he yodeled in excitement.

"*Girls!*" he whooped. "Oh God, make me a happy man and let there be *girls* on that boat!" At the speed of light, he ran down below, brushed his teeth and shaved, ran back up on deck, took a bucket bath, then ran back down below to comb his hair and put on some aftershave and clean clothes. Then, he began pacing the deck.

"Ernst," he blurted, "I know that you are the best navigator since Columbus, *and* the captain, but I also insist that you turn on the motor and get right over there."

"Fritz," my father pronounced, revving up the engine, "you are an animal." Fritz let out a wolf-howl and focused all his attention on the boat in the horizon. We had all been as disappointed as he when we arrived to find four morose-looking men who glumly answered our barrage of questions and requested three liters of gasoline from us.

After the initial surprise and excitement, my present encounter ended up being a French voice on the radio who was staying in a relatively safe part of the ocean, heading from the Azores south to the Canaries. We chatted for a while, and after finding out where I had come from, where I was heading and several *ooh-la-las*, the voice asked me about pirates in the Red Sea. The Gallic baritone then recounted charming anecdotes about boats that had had frightening experiences or dismastings during Atlantic crossings that same year. I told him that my batteries were running low, bid him a *bon voyage* and signed off. By no means a masochist, I didn't feel like hearing any more.

"*Hallo, it's 11:00 Tuesday night, the 29th and we've probably made all of 15 miles today. We're in the Azores high and in the throes of another flat calm. My God. We've barely made 900 miles in two weeks. How long will it take to get to New York? Tarzoon and I are going stir crazy. I'm almost finished with the sweater and don't know what to do with myself. I think about home, family and friends so much.*

"*I stare at the wall for hours and think. Someone once told me that the solitude of the sea must be a very fertile place to find answers. But, for me, answers never seem to come as great revelations, and everytime one is revealed, a new question pops up. Today's is: 'Why the hell have I been given such lousy weather?'* "

The wind eventually returned, still from the north, and we began to skip along, feeling a bit happier with the knowledge that miles were once again being laid behind. I started writing letters to friends I had made along the way and had neglected since Djibouti—Margot and Claude, Fred, Dean and Faye, and Luc. One by one, writing the letters rekindled memories of our times together in different lands and days, and also reassured me, because as each word was committed to paper, I imagined the person reading them. If they read them, it meant that I had arrived to mail them.

When my time wasn't occupied by writing, it was spent anticipating my birthday—which was going to be on the full moon—and listening to the radio. The choice of stations was somewhat limited, as many would broadcast only on certain frequencies at certain times of the day; the reception on one station that had been good in the morning became a symphony of static in the afternoon.

After the frustrations of sorting out the time schedules and being cut off mid-song or mid-sentence, I became a connoisseur of the best talk shows and music programs. Radio France was my favorite. It played lots of music and had funny conversations, bulletins and so on, perfect background for the morning routines. Its antithesis, the BBC, talked about economics, the Persian Gulf crisis, England's industry and other food for thought such as an interview with a goldfish farmer in northern England. Voice of America played baseball and football games, and ran endless anti-everything commercials. Also, Radio France attracted me because it was the only station where I had managed to locate weather reports for my sector of the ocean. We would not pick up the American Coast Guard station's broadcasts until we hit the longitude of 30 degrees, just past the Azores.

The closer we inched toward home, the more aware I became of the news of the world. Although rarely able to find current copies, I had always bought a *Time* or *Newsweek* whenever possible. Even so, my information had been sporadic and I only knew about things I had seen firsthand or had heard about through the grapevine. Until this passage home, I had grown to prefer that perspective. Now I began to crave up-to-the-minute news, and diligently turned the dial and plugged myself into world politics and updates on obscure natural disasters, as well as hearing what was new in music after two and a half years out of the mainstream.

One day, to my surprise, I even heard a hit song by some of my old friends from New York. Before I left, they had been just a bunch of kids playing tuneless tunes in city haunts and wherever the neighbors wouldn't complain. Nobody had ever heard of them then or paid much attention to the inane lyrics of their songs, except those of us who hung out with them. That they had made it big meant that a lot of things had probably changed. To be in the middle of the ocean and hearing the songs of people I once knew triggered memories of the old days, and I felt nostalgic for my teenage years and the carefree life on the streets.

"Hello, it's the 4th of October, only three days away from my birthday. I ended up having to put up the handkerchief jib last night, and haven't really gone anywhere since. There was just too much wind. The waves have gotten bigger and wetter, and I feel very small. The ocean is everywhere; it's coming in through the chain plates, crashing over Varuna in through leaky hatch gaskets and the Dorade vent, overflowing into the cockpit and down to the lockers. Tarzoon and I have the slats closed up tight, making the cabin air quite stale, and we scrunch up together watching Father Time march onward. What a way to grow old.

"I went through the major hassle and acrobatics of cooking a meal of dehydrated Chicken Supreme with rice. I also started crocheting a bag with the leftover wool, which unravels from the little balls that Tarzoon helps to wind. The sweater is finished, and it might even fit Olivier. I've forgotten how big he is. Crash, Bang, splash, boom . . . Goodnight."

The next day, thanks to the waning wind, life got a little bit more civilized and I did my navigation: we had progressed only a pathetic 275 miles since our last fix, three days earlier. With the calm and the sunshine, I resiliconed the chain plates on deck, which had been leaking steadily since the first storm out of Gibraltar. Tarzoon chased the ends of the toilet paper that I was using with some alcohol to remove the old gook. The dolphins came gliding through the transparent water to see what I was doing.

Before the chill of evening set in, I took a bath in the cockpit and washed my hair with dishwashing liquid, the cheapest kind of soap that would lather in salt water. Afterward, feeling my silky hair, I relished the sight of clean long johns that hadn't yet stretched to the point of hanging to my knees. It seemed a proper way to enter into my twenty-second year, smelling like Palmolive.

Sitting on the bunk at nightfall and staring out the companionway at the skies glowing in lunar light, I thought how comical my predicament was. Imagine the utter simplicity of a life whose highlight for the day is marked by a bath—and a saltwater bath, no less. Had I sunk down deeper than deep? No, not at all, I decided. Regardless of the primitiveness of my pleasures, that night I rejoiced, for the morrow would bring the anniversary of my birth. Although on the eve of my birthday, my wish of being halfway across the Atlantic by now still had not been granted, the wind had died, the moon was almost full, and I felt privileged. The majesty of a slumbering ocean, softly lit from horizon to eternal horizon, was all for me alone to behold.

The night was nimble, and waking up the next morning, I forced myself to make a cup of coffee and perform my ablutions before savagely ripping open the presents. There were cards full of jokes and stories from Mark and Doug and strips of candle wax from Maurice. Reading all the notes made me feel as though a party of friends was aboard *Varuna*, and I enjoyed the festivity while it lasted. Olivier's card was a picture of an old man with a striking resemblance to Uncle Sam, pointing his finger at me, saying, "You are 21." Inside, the card said, "I am jealous." Ironically, his present was a sweater made with almost the same stitch as the sweater I had just finished for him. From my father, there was a half-spilled bottle of Lily of the Valley perfume.

"Well," I thought, "I'm twenty-one and don't feel very different, except that I have to cook my own birthday dinner and then, on top of it, do the dishes." Apart from the Barrier Reef birthday gala with

Olivier, this was the second of the last three birthdays that I had spent alone at sea. There was no denying the fact that they had all been unforgettable.

Before the trip, I'd had seventeen birthdays, and could not remember the celebrations of more than two of them. How would I ever be able to forget my nineteenth birthday in the middle of El Pacifico, twentieth on the Australian Barrier Reef off a pearl farm, and twenty-first here in the middle of the mighty Atlantic Ocean. Well, actually, we weren't technically in the middle of the Atlantic yet. That waypoint was still 300 miles distant, and the present absence of wind seemed reluctant to help us make it up.

Three days later, still nothing. Puffy clouds crisscrossed the sky, taking hours to pass from one horizon to the other. At night, they marbleized the black heavens with veins of light and I watched them, waiting for a burst of speed in their lumbering movements that would signify some wind in the neighborhood. In the heat of the afternoon of one of those days, when the bath bucket seemed incredibly heavy, I thought, "Wouldn't it just be easier to lather up and jump in the drink to rinse off?" For the very first time ever alone, I dived overboard while *Varuna* wallowed back and forth.

During the Atlantic calms, which in other oceans had been great annoyances, I began to immerse myself in the solitude, for I knew this was a last chance and it would soon be left behind. Daily duties were done like a spiritual epitaph to a beautiful story. Every night, I made my bed into a real one, with sheets, blankets and a plumped-up pillow to snuggle into. I religiously read every last word in my books, cleaned the dishes pronto, properly folded the sails when they weren't being used, brushed my teeth and hair on cue, kept the cockpit clean and the cabin dusted and marveled for hours at a time on how wonderful nature was to have created such an exquisite creature as Tarzoon. But, as venerable as the calm originally seemed, after six days, it began to get on my nerves.

"Hallo, it is October 12th. GMT-wise it's 12:33 A.M. How's it going? Me? Well, not so hot. For lunch I had canned spare ribs—a foul British invention—and a sweet and sour rice package of Chinese derivation. I just saw the first ship in a while. It came pretty close and I talked with the Russian radio man who spoke a little English. He said that there were no imminent storms and gave me a SatNav position setting us 300 miles east of where I thought we were. Scared that something was dreadfully wrong with my navigation, I asked

him if he was sure; he double-checked, came back and admitted error. Phewee. I'd have jumped overboard. With the past three days' progress, that fix would've put us back 10 days. We've been out here for 26 already and aren't even half-way yet. This will definitely be our longest passage.

"There's a pretty cloudless sky, but I don't care a bit, at this point preferring dark black clouds and lots of wind, just as long as Varuna moves forward. I sit staring at the sea, reading, daydreaming. The freshwater drinking supply is running low and I wouldn't mind a good old-fashioned squall to replenish it. I heard an incredibly loud boom this afternoon, shattering the absolute silence around us. It was an airplane zipping across the sound barrier overhead. Then, a little canary plopped in and Tarzoon wanted to make a lunch of her, so I shooed her off the boat for her own safety."

Going out on deck at about midday, I saw before us our first pod of whales, and in awe, I watched as the leviathans, each seeming to be three times the size of *Varuna*, rolled over in the water ahead of the boat. About 50 feet away a gray lump surfaced and a spout of water spewed out with a great whoosh, then disappeared followed by a V-shaped flipper tail that made another resounding wet splash. It was a little too close for comfort. I held my breath, expecting the moment when one of the swimming blimps would surface again from right below us and topple *Varuna* over. Waiting motionless, I listened for the rumbling bell notes of the whales' songs and sniffed for the ripe air from their blowholes. Recollecting stories of disastrous collisions with the oblivious monsters, I turned on the engine to make our presence known. Totally unconcerned, they continued their migration onward, without so much as a backward glance.

After a little while, kind of hurt that, for them, we had not existed, I looked at the bubbles passing by the hull. Even if only for the small pleasure of seeing a wake, I decided to leave the engine running, whereupon it promptly stopped. The customary grimy, slimy, smelly mechanics of sucking, pulling apart and inspecting ensued, and eventually, the fuel line revealed itself to be clogged.

In tightening the fuel return banjo bolt with my new marvel tool of a socket wrench, I exerted too much pressure and the bolt broke off, leaving the bottom half firmly screwed into the injector. Even if it had been possible to remove it, there weren't any spare bolts available, so that afternoon I reconciled myself to being quite permanently engineless.

With the onset of evening, a steadily escalating breeze began blowing in from the southwest, which could only be the messenger of a depression that was worming its way into the calm high. By morning, I was obliged to replace the reefed working jib with my personally modified storm jib and took three reefs in the main. That accomplished, *Varuna* started climbing the waves that had been part of a serene lake hardly twenty-four hours earlier. The idyllic days of Portuguese trades and Azores high were a thing of the past.

"October 14. The waves are building and, with this wind, it won't be long before the worst hits. Here we go. We're approaching the ominous 5-degree squares on the pilot charts—tons of wind, big waves and high storm frequencies. I've begun to monitor the U.S. Coast Guard's weather station. Hurricane Floyd is off Florida, headed in our general direction, but far away. Maybe it'll converge with a trough north of Bermuda, become an extratropical cyclone and stomp its way elsewhere. This depression's center is several hundred miles northwest of our position, a taste of things to come. My path is blocked by a very nasty little area, and I'm getting cold feet. Thank God we had the prolonged calm and plenty of rest and fortification . . . looks like we're going to need it."

In Malta, Olivier had warned me that progress on the North Atlantic would have to be accomplished mainly by using the depressions to advantage, and he had shown me how to manipulate things to get the most mileage. On a piece of paper, he had drawn the counterclockwise spiral of the average depression as it traveled on its easterly course north of 40 degrees latitude, and showed me how I would have to face it.

"After the barometer starts falling," he had said, "pay attention to the direction of the wind. It will tell you where you are in relation to the center of the depression." If it starts from the southwest, he explained, pointing to the right below the spiral's center on the mock-up chart, that would mean that we were south of the center and should head on a northwest tack. As the center moved eastward, I could expect the wind to begin to veer slowly around to the west. At that point, we would be close to the center.

"Then there will be too much wind to make headway, and you'll have to tack, take down the jib and wait until the eye passes over. When it does," he continued, "the wind will veer to the north and begin to weaken. Then you'll be able to head west on the proper course for New York on a beam reach. The wind will continue to die, all the while veering easterly, until you'll have to put up the spinaker pole." When the wind died, that would mean that the depression had passed and then there would probably be a calm, "unless you get lucky," he had said, "until the next depression, where you'll have to start from the beginning again. Do you understand?"

I had thought that I did, but just for good measure, had folded up the diagram and had brought it along. Now, in the throes of our first depression, I pulled it out and began poring over the meteorology chapter of a book, marveling at how fast a postcard-calm ocean could turn so quickly into a frothing boiling mess.

"October 15. Staring at the chart, the X marking Varuna*'s position is still miserably far from home. We are pitching wildly in the howling winds, slamming and beating, and it is getting difficult even to write."*

The days to follow were a blur of sail changes, veering winds and unprecedented weather systems. Following Olivier's directions sometimes helped me along, and other times nothing in the meteorology chapter or whatever I remembered or had experienced previously could explain the weather or how to better cope with it, other than waiting it out, as it worsened into a full gale.

"October 18. I don't know if I should cry, scream, head back to the Azores or what. We haven't had 24 hours of navigable weather in the last three days. It's been 40–45 knots since 4:00 A.M. and Varuna can't make progress in that kind of velocity. Every tenth wave crashes over us. I slipped and fell this morning and think I sprained my arm; there's a persistent nagging pain. I want to wash my hair, my bed is damp, the sky is villainous, the waves are vicious, and it's howling in the rigging. I can't get up the nerve to go out to the foredeck and tie up the reefed jib and hank on the smaller one. But it must be done."

To leave the relative protection of the cockpit and to go up forward on the lurching foredeck was petrifying, and I abhorred even the preparations for the ordeal. Except for the life harness, I went out naked to preserve my dry clothes. There in the darkness, the silhouettes of gigantic waves bore down on us like freight trains as I struggled to take down a wild piece of fabric with boomerang lines attached. Each time, the fear was more overwhelming and, fighting with the flailing canvas, I wished that it were possible to stay locked up in *Varuna* and get to land without moving a muscle.

"October 19. This weather bears an awful resemblance to my Mediterranean knockdown caper. Black skies, huge waves and tons of wind. But at least everything is battened down this time; the companionway is completely closed and we seem to be keeping up with the waves. Now it's also pouring. When we go this fast, I look at the chart nonstop and calculate. At this rate we could be home in ten days. We have now entered the last square of the 3's. The next two boxes are 5's, then 4, then the last one before New York is a 2. The hard part is next."

Aside from the trips into the cockpit for horizon checks and the sail changes, Tarzoon and I stayed huddled together on the sodden bunk, as I tried to read, crochet or concentrate on the radio to get my mind off the conditions. Determined not to let my physical strength deteriorate to the point it had in the Mediterranean, I forced myself to perform the galley acrobatics of concocting a simple daily meal. I cooked rice, some canned thing or another and vegetables in a pressure cooker and ate it from the same pot.

After we had been engulfed by waves for almost six days, there was hardly anything dry aboard, unless it was lucky enough to be in a sealed Ziploc bag. And because I'd been living so long on the wet bunk, without enough fresh water for a real wash, my skin was sticky from the salt water and my hair matted and itchy. After stripping down and before I pulled on the loathsome foul-weather overalls and jacket to go out on deck for another drenching, I could see the stinging saltwater sores that were beginning to develop on my bottom. There were still almost 1,000 miles to go and I counted the seconds.

I had to add extra days and dates to the bottom of the chart because we had reached the end of my original hopeful calculations and were only two-thirds of the way across. As I stared at the chart, my dividers recalculated the time of arrival over and over again, piercing holes through the paper along the way until it became a mushy pulp that had to be handled with care.

Most of my longest passages had been an average of twenty to thirty days, during which I usually had spent the first ten days agonizing over the departure, and the next ten anticipating landfall. By the twentieth of October, we had been at sea for thirty-four days and could realistically count on at least fifteen more. As the debilitating conditions persisted, everything aboard that was not soaked was dripping with dampness. My morale bottomed out and I grew tired of being the sole person responsible for our progress. There was never anyone who could pop out on deck, just that one time, to relash an errant sail or to look out for ships on my behalf. Sometimes, a crew member conjured up in my dreams would offer to go outside for me but never came back in, and I would have to do the odious chore again.

"October 20. Time is crawling by. I hear things on the radio that stun me. A commentator might say, 'Mr. So and So made a statement on the proposition that was made two weeks ago.' I shake my head and look again at the dates in the Nautical Almanac. *I can remember the proposition being made, but was it really two weeks ago? As far as my time frame goes, it could have been yesterday, or this morning, even five minutes ago."*

VOA and the BBC were running continuous bulletins on the stock-market crash and I listened for updates on the Black Monday debacle as the Dow Jones average slowly began to climb again. Not that I had any stocks or bonds to worry about, but world news had become my fix, my private soap opera, the connection to a home that was getting closer and more real with every passing mile. Wall Street was New York, New York was my singular objective, and I listened more hungrily for news as the weather worsened.

My energies were continually refocused on small calamities aboard—a spilled container of sugar, the solar-panel wiring that corroded through, needing to be respliced and retaped, and the loss of the Swiss Army knife's tweezers. One day something that resembled horrible foot odor permeated the cabin, and after checking my own feet, I was unable to identify its source.

I checked all the lockers, and finally found the culprit behind the sliding panels of the locker next to my bed. A UHT carton of milk that had survived since Malta had exploded, spewing forth a vile lumpy white mixture that covered the bottles of oil and vinegar, wood splints, cans and the rest of its neighbors. As a result, I killed two good hours lugging buckets of water into the cabin, keeping them balanced with *Varuna's* motions, shoving a curious Tarzoon out of the way and scrubbing and drying all the contaminated objects and the locker itself. Two days later, with the first inkling of the malodorous scent, I knew where to look when my last carton of milk expired in yet another glorious ascent to milk heaven.

The next system to hit, a stationary cold front, started as something comparable to steady trade winds from astern on the twenty-second, and by the next morning, we had three reefs in the main and a poled-out storm jib. The puffy clouds stacked up into an ugly black canopy that covered our skies from horizon to horizon.

Unlike the eastbound depressions of days gone by, the wind howled from the southeast, pushing us up and dropping us down the monster waves like a roller coaster gone berserk for thirty-six sleepless hours, whereupon it stopped and poured down rain as we thrashed on beam ends over the bumpy swell. During the four hours of torrential rain that followed, I climbed out into the cockpit and managed to collect several buckets of fresh water as it streamed down the face of the mainsail and channeled along the groove of the boom.

Then, out of nowhere, the wind rushed in from the northeast, picking up at a furious clip until the next day, when the mainsail became too much for the conditions and had to come down. The only foresail that could handle the spasmodic weather was the tiny storm jib, whose miniature size had earlier convinced me that we would never find a use for it. Now it was to be our salvation, as any other piece of canvas aboard would have been too much.

"October 23, and I'm really scared. I can't relax, sleep, eat or think about anything other than staying alive. The waves around us now are the biggest I've ever seen—probably 25 feet high. The weather guys said that we have a cold front passing overhead. My heart is thumping so hard in my chest and I can't stop the tears of fear. Varuna is carried and thrown with each breaking wave, breaking over us, on our sides, in front and behind. The sky is black. There is very little sail up, we're going practically downwind, and we're going fast. I am wedged into my bed with Tarzoon as we listen to the noise and pray. I haven't been able to get a sight, but according to my DR we're about 880 miles from home. It's not like the Med, where after a storm there is a calm. Here it's just one giant, non-stop storm."

The waves steadily grew into the size of alps, and in terror I watched through the Plexiglas slats as they caught up to us from astern, dwarfing *Varuna* and picking her up and throwing her down the slope to wait for the next. The heaving swells crashed everywhere around the boat and hissed and pawed menacingly underneath us as they carried us along on a boiling froth. *Varuna* was continuously swamped, and the type of knockdowns that she had endured near Sri Lanka and in the Mediterranean became an hourly occurrence, except this time we were prepared for the worst, and that made all the difference.

The jerry cans, sails and cat-litter sacks in the cockpit were lashed down, the cubbyholes were stripped bare, and inside everything was securely lodged. As the thundering waterfalls flooded the cockpit, the water slowly funneled out by the way of the drains until it was empty and ready to swallow the next deluge. Unable to take a sight for days, I prayed that I was grossly underestimating our progress and hoped for a wonderful surprise if and when the sun ever shone again.

"October 24. It's the next day, the waves are even bigger and my DR says we're still 780 miles away from the mark. The sun hasn't been out in days. My heart is working overtime and I can't stop the trembling. The looming outlines of the waves are humongous, and we are so small and insignificant. This day feels like it will never end."

Continuing to stare out the hatch, and hypnotized by the towering seas overtaking us, I lived on the edge of existence through that gloomy day and pitch-dark night. For forty-eight hours, I feverishly dealt out game after game of solitaire on the bunk beside me; if anything would get me through this, other than the taffrail log ticking away the miles, it would be my cards of fate.

"It is evening of the 25th, and my prayers are finally being answered. Last night, I reread Psalm 106—'And the waves thereof were still'— and things got less dramatic and began to clear today. This evening, there are no clouds in the sky and I can see the twinkle of stars on the horizon. The wind has veered to the west and is weak right now, but there's another depression coming up. I heard on the news today that this is the 365th day for some girl in a box on top of a pole who is going for the pole-sitting record, and laughed out loud for the first time in weeks. I wondered if she has a television and a telephone to call for take-out Chinese food."

In the aftermath of the storm, there were gentle winds and clear blue skies. I thought about the past three days and how the ocean's fury had brought me closer to the brink of a watery grave than ever before. When the storm had died, the ebb of adrenaline left me bobbing in the wake, feeling strangely empty. The storm had piqued all my senses, and with the calm came an emotional withdrawal.

On the twenty-eighth of October, my calculations established that we had reached the longitude of Bermuda, and so had crossed our outward-bound track of two and a half years before. Crossing that track meant that I was officially finished with the circumnavigation. I felt triumphant and shouted with joy, but then, a sadness began to gnaw away at the excitement. My round-the-world odyssey with *Varuna* was drawing to a close, and that thought began to make these last days at sea all the more sacred. Soon, all the tumultuous emotions, the endearing solitude, the beautiful days and nights at sea, and even the challenges of yet another storm would be no more than memories. This was the beginning of the end of the life I had come to know, and I knew that soon I would leave my ocean friends behind to play the role of an adult in New York City. Every mile *Varuna* laid behind was now over familiar ground, and the tension of homecoming began to build up a flock of butterflies in my stomach. We were really close now.

"October 30. It's 9:00 P.M. and I just saw my first ship in two weeks. I'm dying to talk to them but my electricity is very low. The engine is inoperable, so there is no way to get a charge from the alternator; the new solar panel is too small and the sun is far south and not very strong. I need to conserve power to call when we approach New York. The ARGOS will let everybody know where we are in case I can't use the radio. I hope it's working. I keep catching myself holding lengthy conversations and arguments with no one. We're 450 miles away and I hope I won't go completely nuts before getting home. I forced myself to start Dr. Zhivago *today, the book where Daddy said he found my name just before I was born, and am curiously waiting for a heroine named Tania to pop up from the pages."*

As if trying to prolong my days with *Varuna* and Tarzoon in our own little world, I put off raising the optimum amount of sail. My mind skipped and jumped, not only through the future and what it held in store, but over the days and the cast of characters I had come to know—Stubby, the tire-repair man in Borneo whose business depended on the migration of red crabs; Roberto Vergnes, the eccentric con artist searching for treasure on Cocos Island; Ibrahim in his flowing robes and turban pontificating on the balance between the sexes and swigging from a bottle of desert firewater; Fred showing me how to take care of *Varuna* properly; Kerima de Lescure quietly strumming her guitar and singing her poetry of peace and beauty under the Panamanian palm trees.

The pace and character of their lives had made an irrevocable impact on my own, and as long as I was still at sea, their presence still seemed immediate to me. Once I arrived home, I feared that they would be sealed away into the foggy scrapbook of my brain, and that thought filled my days with a confused melancholy.

"Happy Halloween. Boo. It's the 31st and there's a tropical storm (a.k.a. hurricane) brewing down south, and if it takes the same route as Emily did, then we're right in the path. Yep, we're in the same stomping grounds as a hurricane. A first for Tarzoon, Varuna and me. I desperately need sleep and to conserve electricity, we now live by kerosene light down below."

When we were 310 miles away and only 100 miles from switching to the chart indicating the approaches to New York, I was able to pick up a radio station in New London, Connecticut, and could hear the call toll-free commercials for a set of three LPs with the greatest hits of whomever. It seemed that some regional elections were coming up and all I could hear was Italian names. A weather announcer said that the tropical storm that had worried me a couple of days earlier had headed toward the Gulf of Mexico, staying with the warmer water that those systems crave.

November 1 was my mother's birthday and, as if she were watching over me, we had wind all day that helped guide us in the right direction, across the Gulf Stream coordinates that were broadcast on the weather station. All sorts of eddies, rips, weird waves, birds and jumping fish surrounded us, as sometimes, out of sheer nerves, I even hand-steered, not wanting to let the river set us back one mile. Sandy Hook, the little cove where I had spent my first night out of New York twenty-seven months before, was as far into my future as I could see, and I dreamed about how to sail into it on every tack, with every kind of wind, even rehearsing in my mind where the anchor would be dropped when I arrived.

It took me a week to get through *Dr. Zhivago* and it was only at the very end that I found out that my namesake was a laundry girl. Next I started trying to concentrate on *Dune*. The wind was irregular in strength and direction, but my spirits were high by November 2 because we had made good mileage, using a Gulf Stream eddy to advantage.

As we crossed the westernmost perimeters of the underwater current, the water changed color from a nutrient- and phosphorescence-rich blue to the murky greenish-brown of the eastern coastal waters of the United States. Also, the warm current that flowed up from the Gulf of Mexico gave way to the icy northern November waters, and for the first time, I pulled out of the Ziploc bags the heavy-knit sweaters that Olivier had given me and the sleeping bag I hadn't used since the trip to Bermuda.

Making up for lost time, I started navigating with a passion, using the moon, sun, Venus and Polaris, cherishing the taking of each sight, and promising myself never to forget any of the sailing skills I had learned, especially the navigation. I had always loved joking and complaining about having no SatNav, but toward the end, I realized that taking a sight, plotting it with another sight, and finding a cross in the middle of the watery void on a chart created an addictive feeling of mastery and connection with the Earth and the stars.

White night after white night of anticipation, I probably slept a total of four hours in the final week, and on the evening of November 4, the weather station reported a gale warning and small-craft advisories in effect. The southwesterly winds that had helped us make the last hundred miles at a good clip began gusting, and I fearfully waited for them to veer west and strengthen into something that would oblige us to heave to and wait it out.

"We're 75 miles away and I'm getting so excited that I can't even listen to the radio. It makes me all jumpy. Can you imagine how I feel? It's been 48 days. I'm so close, and I get these feelings, New York feelings. I can almost feel the subway, the East Village, the house. Most of all, I feel Sandy Hook. Ninety-five percent of the time, my mind is locked into that muddy curved sandspit. The chart is full of holes. I spot a few ships. I'm beginning to see planes. I see fishing boats and I can smell land!"

All around us, there were trawlers and fishing boats to be avoided, probably hailing from North Jersey and Long Island harbors. Every plane that thundered overhead across the sky I knew was headed in the direction of Kennedy, LaGuardia or Newark airports. The ocean's salty smell began to resemble that of vegetation and smog, and I inhaled the air as the familiar scents began to re-identify themselves.

At twilight, on our last evening alone, I made my last fix using Polaris and Venus and planned our approach. Then I took down the jib and stopped *Varuna* for several hours to gather my wits, calm down and sort things out neatly. It had been forty-nine days for me, in the immediate ocean sense, but in reality it had been almost two and a half years.

All my worries about how I would fit in and how everything that had changed would affect me seemed to dissipate. I remembered back to the days before leaving New York, when I worried if I would ever adapt to life at sea on my own. Having done it, I realized now how much more is possible. But I could never have known had I not tried.

Now, in the same spot as I had been as an eighteen-year-old, setting off on her maiden voyage, scared and apprehensive of the future, I realized that the future wasn't something to worry about. If living at sea had taught me anything, it had revealed the importance of taking each new dawn in stride and doing the best that I could with whatever was presented.

It wouldn't even matter if I didn't fit in anymore. What is "fitting in" anyway, I thought, being accepted by a peer group? I could no longer play my roles in life to make other people happy. The most disturbing thought at the root of my contemplations was that I could never again be a twenty-one-year-old who was witnessing the fulfillment of a two-and-a-half-year dream.

"But, isn't that what life is all about?" I told myself. "To move forward and keep adding to the memories?" Everyone else would have changed, but perhaps none more than I. There seemed nothing sadder than to think back to a childhood lost, or to remember innocent times when the world was a smaller and simpler place to know. But, I reasoned, come forty, I would again be envying the person I had been at twenty-one. We just can't stop time.

The next morning, I put on my last pair of clean long johns, washed my face with the last drops of the fresh water, bundled up and hoisted the jib. I couldn't stay out there forever. We were going home.

Around 11:00 A.M., still about 30 miles away from the Ambrose Light that indicates the approaches to New York, a powerboat roared in from the clear horizon toward *Varuna*, filled with a crew of people frantically waving and screaming congratulations. I eagerly looked for a familiar face, but I recognized no one, and went below to turn on the VHF. The man who answered said he was from a national news station covering my arrival for the afternoon broadcast and that they had been out searching for *Varuna* since dawn. Other people on board were taking pictures and filming, and I waved for them and talked with the man until they revved up and headed back to the city to make their deadline.

"November 5th, 1:00 P.M. Oh, God. I'm so close. I've got a horrible case of jitters, my heart is drumming and my stomach is one gigantic knot. I haven't slept in a week, and now I'm a new kind of scared. The people who just came were talking about fireboats and helicopters and press boats and TV cameras and press conferences. Oh my, how should I act, what should I say, how will it be? I feel like laughing, crying and turning around and heading out to sea again. The camera crew were all seasick over the windward side of their boat and they still managed to yell questions. I never expected this. Varuna and I continue to plug on through the 30-knot winds toward the hullabaloo. I can't believe it, but I'm just beginning to see the outline of the World Trade Center."

The wind veered to the west and, reefed down to the smallest sails we had, I sat below with a bewildered Tarzoon, crying over what we were leaving behind and savoring our last minutes alone together, as *Varuna* pounded through the chop. Several hours after the first boat, a roaring noise had me running out into the cockpit to see another powerboat muscling through the steepening waves. Automatically waving, I peered at the group hoping, praying to see a familiar face.

First, I saw another group of microphones on extension poles and TV cameras. There was a great commotion aboard, people jumping around, screaming and waving frantically, and then . . . yes, there was my father separating himself from the blur.

"Hello," I screamed, jumping up and down in the cockpit. "Hi, Daddy! It's *over!* I made it!"

"Hey, Ding-a-ling, *you did it!*" he screamed back over the roar of the engines, and jumped around the deck of the boat. "You really *did* it! I am so proud of you!"

Babbling back at the top of my voice how the trip had been, I suddenly saw on the foredeck Olivier's blond head, popping above a yellow foul-weather jacket.

"Oh my God, *Olivier!*" I screamed. "You're here!"

Laughing, he held on to a grabrail as the boat maneuvered closer and shouted back, "I blong you, Tania!"

I blong you.

EPILOGUE

March 9, 1989

More than a year has passed since my arrival home at South Street Seaport on November 6, 1987, where I found out that because of my having a friend aboard *Varuna* for 80 miles in the South Pacific I didn't get the world record. Oh well. I survived my allotted moment in the spotlight, the initial bombardment of cameras, journalists, interviews, television appearances and the like; after two months Olivier and I decided to leave New York for more quiet ways. We moved to a basement apartment in Newport, Rhode Island, where I could write and where we got married in May 1988. Tarzoon is with us, alive and well with a calico New York girlfriend named Suki.

My father is off on his own again, this time in the African Sahara, 200 miles north of Timbuktu, where he is trying to teach agriculture to the handful of inhabitants of a desert village. When I first got back, he thought that it would be a good idea for me to do the Iditarod Trail race to Nome, Alaska, with a sled and pack dogs. I turned the suggestion down.

The final separation from my voyage came during the summer of 1988. In between trying to fill up blank computer screens with words, I paid my father back after selling *Varuna* to her perfect new owner, and she started out her new life by sailing on the Chesapeake Bay. On our last trip together forever, *Varuna* took Tony, Nina, Jade, Olivier and me out to Brenton Reef in Narragansett Bay, where we granted one of my mother's last wishes and gave her ashes to the ocean.

Because we still believe in taking life one step at a time, Olivier's and my plans for the future are open. With both of our energies combined—Olivier's work concerning anything having to do with boats, such as deliveries, general repairs, construction, teaching, and my writing—we hope to find the means to return to the sea. Perhaps some day we will have children who will be able to grow up in the environment of the different world we have come to love. For our future boat, Olivier, who is interested in chartering, wants 60 feet, I want 38, so we'll work out a compromise. As always, in the end what was meant to be will be.

P.S. I now weigh 124 pounds and I'm trying to shed a few.

ACKNOWLEDGMENTS

In the course of the past year, while I was writing my story, the thought that I was actually circumnavigating twice occurred to me on several occasions—once in reality, and the second time as I re-lived the entire range of emotions, beauty and hardships on a chair in front of a word processor. Now, in both respects, the voyage truly is over as I sit down to write my thanks to those who helped.

Olivier comes first, most of all for helping me get around half the world, and then later as the book unfolded, for all the grilled cheese sandwiches, dinners and love. I hope my father already knows how grateful I am for his having had the foresight to see just how feasible the whole idea was from the beginning and for all his help in seeing it to the end. And then there's Jeri, who has been through thick and thin with me and knows it all.

Thanks to *Cruising World* magazine; Hans at Monitor, the people at J. J. Taylor and Bukh; Rau Daschl; the Manhattan Yacht Club; Teddy Charles at Sagman's Marine; the Museum of Yachting; Gilles Huccault, who is responsible for my most beautiful pictures. And particular thanks to Bernadette, who through many a white night and over many teas helped me articulate sentiment after sentiment.

Thanks to all the people who selflessly pitched in and aided me along the way, and there were many; for everybody who thought about and prayed for me or wrote letters of encouragement; and to Mr. Tarzoon, who also did his stint with me through most of both stories. And then, last but not least, a last salute to Ocean U.